SAT*II SUCCESS
U.S. History

PREP

TEST

3rd Edition

Margaret Moran

THOMSON

PETERSON'S

Australia • Canada • Mexico • Singapore • Spain • United Kingdom • United States

About The Thomson Corporation and Peterson's

With revenues of US$7.2 billion, The Thomson Corporation (www.thomson.com) is a leading global provider of integrated information solutions for business, education, and professional customers. Its Learning businesses and brands (www.thomsonlearning.com) serve the needs of individuals, learning institutions, and corporations with products and services for both traditional and distributed learning.

Peterson's, part of The Thomson Corporation, is one of the nation's most respected providers of lifelong learning online resources, software, reference guides, and books. The Education Supersite[SM] at www.petersons.com—the Internet's most heavily traveled education resource—has searchable databases and interactive tools for contacting U.S.-accredited institutions and programs. In addition, Peterson's serves more than 105 million education consumers annually.

For more information, contact Peterson's, 2000 Lenox Drive, Lawrenceville, NJ 08648; 800-338-3282; or find us on the World Wide Web at www.petersons.com/about.

Special thanks to Heidi Sheehan and W. Frances Holder for their editorial assistance.

For more information, contact Peterson's, 2000 Lenox Drive, Lawrenceville, NJ 08648; 800-338-3282; or find us on the World Wide Web at: www.petersons.com/about

ISBN 0-7689-0908-2

Printed in the United States of America

10 9 8 7 6 5 4 3 2 1   04 03 02

CONTENTS

CONTENTS

QUICK REFERENCE GUIDE

For additional review material, be sure to read the
"Answers and Explanations"

FIVE IMPORTANT STRATEGIES

1. Highlight the key words in the question so you will know what you are looking for in the answer choices.
2. With a *not/except* question, ask yourself if an answer choice is true about the subject of the question. If it is true, cross it off and keep checking answers.
3. If you aren't sure about an answer but know something about the question, eliminate what you know is wrong and make an educated guess.
4. To help in making an educated guess, check the time frames of the question immediately above and immediately after the question you are trying to answer. Cross off any answer choices that don't fit within that time frame.
5. All parts of an answer choice must be correct for the answer to be correct.

RED ALERT

TOP 10 STRATEGIES FOR ACING THE TEST

PREPARING FOR THE TEST:

1. Read the *10 Facts About the SAT II: U.S. History Test* on pages 2–5 in this book.
2. Choose your *Practice Plan* from pages 8–10 in this book.
3. Choose a place and time to study every day, and stick to your routine and your plan.
4. Even though they are time-consuming, complete the *Diagnostic* and *Practice Tests* in this book. They will give you just what they promise: practice—practice in reading and following the directions, practice in pacing yourself, and practice in understanding and answering multiple-choice questions.
5. Complete all your assignments for your regular U.S. history course. Ask questions in class and talk about what you are reading and learning. The test is supposed to measure what you know and understand about U.S. history and related social science concepts, methods, and generalizations.

THE NIGHT BEFORE THE TEST:

6. Assemble what you will need for the test: your admission materials, four number 2 pencils, a watch (without an alarm), and a healthy snack for the break if you are taking several tests on one day. Put these items in a place where you will not forget them in the morning.
7. Don't cram. Relax. Go to a movie, visit a friend—but not one who is taking the test with you. Get a good night's sleep.

THE DAY OF THE TEST:

8. Wear comfortable clothes. If you have a lucky color or a lucky piece of clothing or jewelry, wear it—as long as you won't distract anyone else. Take along a lucky charm if you have one.
9. If you do not usually eat a big breakfast, this is not the morning to change your routine, but it is probably a good idea to eat something nutritious if you can.
10. If you feel yourself getting anxious, concentrate on taking a couple of deep breaths. Remember, you don't have to answer all the questions, and you can make EDUCATED GUESSES.

10 FACTS ABOUT THE SAT II: U.S. HISTORY TEST

1. UNLIKE THE SAT I TEST, WHICH ASSESSES CRITICAL READING AND THINKING, THE SAT II SUBJECT TESTS ASSESS SPECIFIC KNOWLEDGE.

The twenty-two Scholastic Assessment Tests, formerly known as the College Board Achievement Tests, assess student knowledge in specific subject areas. The tests are 1 hour each and, except for the Writing Test, use a multiple-choice format to test knowledge of subjects such as biology, mathematics, world history, and modern Hebrew. Some of the world language tests have a listening component. The SAT II: Writing Test has both a 20-minute essay section as well as a 40-minute multiple-choice section.

2. THE SAT II: U.S. HISTORY TEST MEASURES FACTUAL KNOWLEDGE, ANALYTICAL SKILLS, AND THE ABILITY TO EVALUATE DATA.

Study Strategy

Learn strategies for answering the different types of test questions in Chapter 1.

The College Board descriptive information about the SAT II: U.S. History Test states that it assesses a student's knowledge of the nation's political, economic, social, intellectual, and cultural history as well as foreign policy. The literature identifies four purposes for the questions:

- to test recall of basic information, such as facts, terms, concepts, and generalizations,
- to analyze and interpret visuals, such as cartoons, maps, charts, graphs, and photographs,
- to relate ideas to given data,
- to evaluate data.

3. THE SAT II: U.S. HISTORY TEST COVERS U.S. HISTORY FROM THE FIRST AMERICANS TO CURRENT EVENTS.

Study Strategy

See Chapters 2 *through 8 for a brief review of U.S. history.*

Although you will find questions from all time periods of U.S. history, most of them will be taken from the nineteenth and twentieth centuries. The College Board states that about approximately

- 20 percent of the questions are based on history from pre-Columbian times through 1789,
- 40 percent are from 1790 to 1898,
- 40 percent are from 1899 to the present.

The College Board further breaks down the kinds of information that it tests. Because history is a complex entity that mixes many strands, the College Board states that the questions are divided according to the following categories:

- 32–36 percent on political history,
- 18–22 percent on social history,
- 18–20 percent on economic history,
- 13–17 percent on foreign policy,
- 10–12 percent on cultural and intellectual history.

Within these historical periods and categories, the test writers will also ask you about social science concepts, methods, and generalizations.

4. THE SAT II: U.S. HISTORY TEST ASKS ONLY MULTIPLE-CHOICE QUESTIONS.

Study Strategy

See Chapter 1 *for strategies for answering multiple-choice questions.*

The SAT II: U.S. History Test does not contain an essay question. The test is made up of ninety to ninety-five multiple-choice questions arranged in chronologically ordered clusters. That means that you may find a group of seven to twelve questions that progresses from a question on pre-Columbian history through questions on the various eras to the end of the twentieth century. The questions also become more difficult as you progress through the test.

The test uses a variety of types and prompts for its questions. You may find EXCEPT, LEAST, or NOT (reverse true/false) questions, questions based on visuals, and questions based on quotations from documents and people's writings. Most questions simply present a statement for you to complete by choosing one of five possible responses.

5. PACING YOURSELF IS IMPORTANT IN ANSWERING THE SAT II: U.S. HISTORY TEST.

Study Strategy

See Chapter 1 *for more information on pacing.*

You will have 60 minutes to answer ninety to ninety-five questions. That works out to reading and answering one question every 45 seconds. You may not be able to answer all ninety questions, but you will not be penalized for questions that are left unanswered.

6. EDUCATED GUESSING CAN HELP.

Study Strategy

See Scoring High *for more information on how scores are computed.*

While your score will not be affected by unanswered questions, questions that are answered incorrectly will result in a quarter-point deduction for each. In computing your score, the College Board awards a point for each correct answer and deducts a quarter-point for each incorrect answer. The College Board suggests guessing IF you know something about a question and can eliminate a couple of answer choices. Call it "educated guessing."

7. WHETHER AND WHEN YOU SHOULD TAKE THE SAT II: U.S. HISTORY TEST DEPENDS ON THE COLLEGES YOU ARE APPLYING TO.

Not all colleges require SAT II subject tests, so check the catalogues and Web sites of the colleges that you are applying to in order to see which tests, if any, they require. Some colleges may require the SAT II tests for admission, while others may use the tests for placement.

The U.S. History Test is administered six times a year in October, November, December, January, May, and June. To use the test for regular admission, you will need to have taken it by November or January of your senior year. For early admission, you will need to take it earlier. If the college you are going to attend uses the test for placement only, you may be able to wait until May or June.

However, the College Board advises students to take its SAT II tests while the course work is still fresh. Since U.S. history is often a two-year sequence in 10th and 11th grades or a one-year course in 11th grade, it would make the most sense to take the test at the end of junior year.

Even if the schools you are applying to do not require the test, it may be helpful for you to add the score to your other documents. Because courses may vary widely from school to school, the SAT II subject tests provide a degree of comparability among student grades.

8. YOU CAN TAKE THE SAT II: U.S. HISTORY TEST MORE THAN ONCE.

Through the College Board's Score Choice™, you can have your score for the U.S. History Test, or any other SAT II test, reported first to you so you can decide whether to have it sent to your colleges. The College Board points out that this will hold up the reporting process and may mean that your scores reach the colleges after their deadlines. This option is better for juniors who are assessing their strengths and weaknesses than for seniors making final decisions about colleges.

9. ALL THE INFORMATION ABOUT REGISTRATION AND FEES IS AVAILABLE FROM THE COLLEGE BOARD.

To take the SAT I or any SAT II test, you will need to register with the College Board. See your guidance counselor for a copy of the SAT *Registration Bulletin* or write or call:

College Board SAT II Program
PO Box 6200
Princeton, NJ 08541-6200
609-771-7600

Also ask for a copy of *Taking the SAT II: Subject Tests*. The *Bulletin* lists test sites and dates and has information about the process for having your scores reported to colleges. In certain cases, financial help is available for the registration fee. Accommodations can also be made for students with disabilities. Ask your guidance counselor or the College Board if you think that you qualify.

You may take as many as three SAT II subject tests on any one day, but if you are taking the SAT II Writing Test or a Language Test with Listening, either will be the first test that you take on that day.

10. STUDYING FOR THE TEST CAN MAKE A DIFFERENCE.

The first step in studying for the U.S. History Test is to learn the format of the questions and the directions. Then you will not waste time on the day of the test trying to understand what you are supposed to do.

The second step is to review the content of U.S. history. Stop first at page 8 and read the *Practice Plan for Studying for the SAT II: U.S. History Test*.

SCORING HIGH ON THE SAT II: U.S. HISTORY TEST

You have taken hundreds of tests during your time in school. Most of these tests have evaluated your knowledge of a subject or your mastery of a skill. The SAT II: U.S. History Test is no different. The test makers write questions to see how well you remember and understand U.S. history and social science concepts and generalizations. While this examination may seem especially challenging, like other standardized tests, if you have studied and you know some test-taking techniques, you can do well.

USING TIPS IN THIS BOOK TO IMPROVE YOUR SCORE

Study Strategy

Check the Practice Plan *on pages 8–10 for help in setting up a study schedule.*

Throughout this book you will find information that describes and explains the SAT II: U.S. History Test. In this *Red Alert!* section, you will find some basic information as well as tips to help you ace the test. Use this section and the chapters that follow as a study guide to complement your regular U.S. history course work.

Study the strategies and techniques presented in Chapter 1, *Strategies for Multiple-Choice Questions,* and complete the practice sets of questions. By doing these exercises and taking the *Diagnostic Test* and *Practice Tests,* you will improve your test-taking skills. Correct your responses against the answer keys and the *Answers and Explanations,* and you will be able to pinpoint those periods in U.S. history that you need to spend more time reviewing. By reading all the answer explanations, you will also be reinforcing and extending those areas that you already know well.

As you practice taking the tests and checking your responses, always consider what your weak areas are and what you can do to improve. Make a list of the time periods that you need to review, and check them off as you become confident about each one. Strive to answer more multiple-choice questions correctly in the 60 minutes. Work to apply the test-taking strategies suggested in Chapter 1. If you take time to do all the practice tests, you will increase your test-taking skills and your score on the real test day.

SCORING THE TEST

Test-Taking Strategy

To make the most of the test, you will need to pace yourself. See Chapter 1 *for some strategies for pacing.*

The SAT II: U.S. History Test is scored on a scale of 200 to 800. You are thinking that you have to answer all ninety or ninety-five questions correctly to attain a score of 800. Well, you don't. Based on a recent release of the scaled scoring chart from the College Board, students who answered some combination of correct and incorrect answers and left blank some number of questions that resulted in raw scores of 90 to 81 received "perfect" scores of 800. Your response to that fact may be "What?"

And students who answered some combination of correct and incorrect answers and left blank some number of questions that resulted in raw scores of −21 and −22 achieved scores of 230. "WHAT?"

The College Board has devised a scoring system that converts raw scores to scaled scores. According to the College Board, the purpose is "to ensure that a score earned on any one edition of a particular Subject Test is comparable to the same scaled score on any other edition of the same test." This is one element of the comparability that helps colleges in evaluating students' Subject Test scores. The scaled scores assign a value to each raw score. For example, for a recent SAT II: U.S. History Test, the middle range of scores looked like this:

50	620
49–48	610
47–46	600
45	590
44–43	580

You receive 1 point for every correct answer, a quarter-point deduction for every incorrect answer, and no penalty for questions left blank. In figuring out your own score, give yourself 1 point for each correct answer, and multiply the total number of incorrect answers by 0.25. The scale may change from year to year, but you can figure out generally what your converted score will be by establishing 81 to 90 as 800 (or 83 to 95) and then deducting 10 points for every 2 points that your raw score decreases, for example:

80–79	790
78–77	780
76–75	770
74–73	760
72–71	750

What does this mean to you? Well, for one thing, knowing that you can answer some combination of questions correctly and incorrectly and leave some blank and still get a score in the 500s and 600s should take some of the anxiety out of your test-taking.

EDUCATED GUESSING: A HELPFUL TECHNIQUE

You may be concerned about guessing when you are not sure of the answer or when time is running out. We have more to say about pacing in Chapter 1, but even the College Board recommends guessing IF you know something about the question and can eliminate one or more of the answer choices. Call it "educated guessing." Here are some suggestions for making an educated guess:

- Ignore answers that are obviously wrong.
- Discard choices in which part of the response is incorrect. Remember that a partially correct answer is a partially incorrect answer—and a quarter-point deduction.
- Reread the remaining answers to see which seems more correct.
- Choose the answer that you feel is right. Trust yourself. Your subconscious usually will guide you to the correct choice. Do not argue with yourself. This works IF you know something about the question content to begin with.

You may still be concerned about the quarter-point deduction, known as the "guessing penalty," but we are not talking about guessing but about making an "educated guess." If you use our suggestions, your chances of increasing your score are very good. You will have to answer four questions incorrectly to loose a single point, yet one correct educated guess will increase your score by 1 point. IF you know something about the question and can eliminate one or more answer choices, why not act on what you know and fill in the oval for your best answer choice?

SOME REMINDERS ABOUT THE SAT: II U.S. HISTORY TEST

Study Strategy

See Chapter 1 *for strategies.*

Study Strategy

See Chapter 1 *for more on pacing.*

Here are three important ideas to remember about taking the test:

1. It is important to spend time practicing the kinds of questions that you will find on the test.

2. You can leave some questions unanswered and still do well. Even though you will be practicing how to pace yourself as you use this book, you may not be able to complete all ninety or ninety-five questions on the day of the test. If you come across a really difficult question, you can skip it and still feel that you are not doomed to receive a low score.

3. There is a guessing penalty. If you do not know anything about a question or the choices, do not take a chance. However, if you know something about the question and can eliminate one or more of the answer choices, then it is probably worth your while to choose one of the other answers. Use EDUCATED GUESSING. Even the College Board advises this strategy.

PRACTICE PLAN FOR STUDYING FOR THE SAT II: U.S. HISTORY TEST

The following plan is worked out for nine weeks. The best study plan is one that continues through a full semester. Then you have time to think about ideas and to talk with your teacher and other students about what you are learning, and you will not feel rushed. Staying relaxed about the test is important. A full-semester study plan also means that you can apply what you are learning here to class work and apply your class work—everything that you are reading—to test preparation. The plan is worked out so that you should spend between 2 and 3 hours on each lesson.

Week 1

First: Take the Diagnostic Test, pp. 13–31, and complete the self-scoring process.
List the areas that you had difficulty with: pacing, question types, or content.

Then: Reread pp. 2–7 about the basic facts of the test and its scoring.

Week 2

Lesson 1
- Read *Top 10 Strategies for Acing the Test,* p. 1.
- Reread *Scoring High on the SAT II: U.S. History Test,* pp. 5–7.
- Read Chapter 1, *Strategies for Multiple-Choice Questions,* pp. 49–69.
- Do one set of practice questions at the end of the chapter, and review the explanation of the answers.

Lesson 2
- Review the list you made after the *Diagnostic Test* to see what you need to learn/review about early U.S. history in order to do well.
- Read Chapter 2, *Reviewing the Colonial Period to 1789,* and find out more about any of the people, terms, and concepts that are unfamiliar to you.

Week 3

Lesson 1
- Reread *Top 10 Strategies for Acing the Test,* p. 1.
- Reread *Scoring High on the SAT II: U.S. History Test,* pp. 5–7.
- Review Chapter 1, *Strategies for Multiple-Choice Questions,* pp. 49–69.
- Do one set of practice questions at the end of the chapter, and review the answers.

Lesson 2
- Review the list you made after the *Diagnostic Test* to see what you need to learn/review about the new nation.
- Read Chapter 3, *Reviewing the New Nation to Mid-Century,* and find out more about any of the people, terms, and concepts that are unfamiliar to you.

Week 4

Lesson 1
- Review Chapter 1, *Strategies for Multiple-Choice Questions,* pp. 49–69, and do another set of practice questions at the end of the chapter.
- Review the answers for these practice questions.
- Review the content from Chapters 2 and 3 that showed up as gaps in your knowledge when you took the *Diagnostic Test.*

Lesson 2
- Take *Practice Test 1* and complete the self-scoring process.
- Compare the score to your score on the *Diagnostic Test.* Which question types continue to be a concern?
- Reread Chapter 1, *Strategies for Multiple-Choice Questions,* as needed.

Week 5

Lesson 1 • Read Chapter 4, *Reviewing the Events Leading to the Civil War and Its Aftermath,* and find out more about any people, terms, or concepts that are unfamiliar to you.

Lesson 2 • Read Chapter 5, *Reviewing Becoming an Urban and Industrial World Power,* and find out more about any people, terms, or concepts that are unfamiliar to you.

Week 6

Lesson 1 • Review the content in Chapters 2 through 5 that showed up as gaps in your knowledge when you took the *Diagnostic Test* and *Practice Test 1.*
  • If you still feel unsure of some question types, review Chapter 1.

Lesson 2 • Take *Practice Test 2* and complete the self-scoring process.
  • Compare the score to your score on the *Diagnostic Test.* Which question types and historical eras continue to be a concern?

Week 7

Lesson 1 • Read Chapter 6, *Reviewing the Nation's Goals and Ideals, 1898– 1929,* and find out more about any people, terms, or concepts that are unfamiliar to you.

Lesson 2 • Read Chapter 7 *Reviewing the Great Depression, World War II, and the Post-War Nation,* and find out more about any people, terms, or concepts that are unfamiliar to you.

Week 8

Lesson 1 • Read Chapter 8, *Reviewing the Kennedy Through Bush Administrations,* and find out more about any people, terms, or concepts that are unfamiliar to you.

Lesson 2 • Review the content in Chapters 2 through 8 that showed up as gaps in your knowledge when you took the *Diagnostic Test* and *Practice Tests 1* and *2.*

Week 9

Lesson 1 • Take *Practice Test 3* and complete the self-scoring process. Check your results against the other two tests.

Lesson 2 • If you are still unsure about some content and test-taking strategies, review those chapters and the practice activities.
  • Reread *Scoring High on the SAT II: U.S. History Test,* pp. 5–7, and *Top 10 Strategies for Acing the Test,* p.1.

THE PANIC PLAN

Eighteen weeks, nine weeks, how about two weeks? If you are the kind of person who puts everything off until the last possible minute, here is a two-week panic plan. Its objectives are to make you familiar with the test format and directions and to help you get as many right answers as possible.

Week 1

- Read *Top 10 Strategies for Acing the Test*, p. 1, and *Scoring High on the SAT II: U.S. History Test*, pp. 5–7.
- Take the *Diagnostic Test*. Read the directions carefully and use a timer.
- Complete the self-scoring process. You can learn a lot about the types of questions in the multiple-choice section by working through the answers.
- Read Chapter 1, *Strategies for Multiple-Choice Questions*, paying particular attention to the types of questions that you had difficulty with on the *Diagnostic Test*.
- Read Chapter 2, *Reviewing the Colonial Period to 1789*, pp. 70–103.
- Read Chapter 3, *Reviewing the New Nation to Mid-Century*, pp. 104–133.
- Take *Practice Test 1*.
- Complete the self-scoring process, and see where you may still have problems with question types. Reread those sections of Chapter 1 and complete at least one set of practice questions.
- Read all the answer explanations including those you identified correctly.

Week 2

- Reread *Top 10 Strategies for Acing the Test*, p. 1, and *Scoring High on the SAT II: U.S. History Test*, pp. 5–7.
- Complete *Practice Test 2* and score it. Read all the answer explanations including those you identified correctly. Where are you still having problems with content? With question types?
- Read Chapters 4 through 8.
- Reread Chapter 1, *Strategies for Multiple-Choice Questions*, as needed.
- Take *Practice Test 3* and score it. Read all the answer explanations including those you identified correctly. Still having content problems? Review those areas in Chapters 2 through 8.
- Work at least two practice sets of multiple-choice questions in Chapter 1.

WHY TAKE THE DIAGNOSTIC TEST?

What do you know about the format and questions on the SAT II: U.S. History Test? If you knew all you needed to know, you probably would not be reading this book. Taking a practice test is one way to learn about the test and what it will be like taking it on the real test day. You will need to pace yourself so you can answer as many questions as possible in the 60 minutes. Taking the *Diagnostic Test* will help you learn how much time you can spend on each item.

Practice may not make perfect, but you can improve your score with practice. The more you learn about your strengths and weaknesses in test-taking abilities and in analytical skills and the more you work on strengthening them, the better your score.

How should you take this test? Just as though it were the real test, so that means setting aside 1 hour of uninterrupted quiet time to take the test, plus the time to score your answers.

- Make a photocopy of an answer sheet at the back of this book.
- Assemble four number 2 pencils along with the answer sheet.
- Get a timer or a stopwatch to time the test.
- When you have completed the test, check how many questions you were able to answer. This information will help you in pacing yourself for the *Practice Tests* and for the real test.
- Then check the multiple-choice questions against *Quick-Score Answers,* p. 32.
- Read the explanation for each answer, even if your answer was correct. You might learn something you didn't know about that period in U.S. history.
- By reading the answers, you may also be able to pick up a pattern about which eras in American history you need to spend more time reviewing. Knowing your weak areas is the only way to strengthen them.
- Turn to the *Practice Plan* and design your study plan from now until test day.

DIAGNOSTIC TEST

While you have taken many standardized tests and know to blacken completely the ovals on the answer sheets and to erase completely any errors, you need to indicate on the answer key which test you are taking. The instructions on the answer sheet will tell you to fill out the top portion of the answer sheet exactly as shown.

1. Print *U.S. History* on the line to the right under the words *Subject Test (print)*.

2. In the shaded box labeled *Test Code* fill in four ovals:

    —Fill in oval 2 in the row labeled V.
    —Fill in oval 5 in the row labeled W.
    —Fill in oval 5 in the row labeled X.
    —Fill in oval C in the row labeled Y.
    —Leave the ovals in row Q blank.

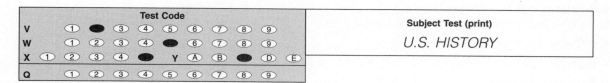

There are two additional questions that you will be asked to answer: How many semesters of U.S. history have you taken? Have you taken courses in government, economics, geography, psychology, sociology, and/or anthropology? The College Board is collecting statistical information. If you choose to answer, you will use the key that is provided and blacken the appropriate ovals in row Q. You may also choose not to answer, and that will not affect your grade.

When everyone has completed filling in this portion of the answer sheet, the supervisor will tell you to turn the page and begin. The answer sheet has 100 numbered ovals on the sheet, but there are only 90 (or 95) multiple-choice questions on the test, so be sure to use only ovals 1 to 90 (or 95) to record your answers.

GO ON TO THE NEXT PAGE ➤

DIAGNOSTIC TEST—*Continued*

Directions: Each of the questions or incomplete statements below has five suggested answers or completions. Choose the response that is best and then fill in the corresponding oval on the answer sheet.

1. By the time the Europeans arrived, the Native Americans of the Northeast Woodlands lived primarily by
   (A) fishing
   (B) farming
   (C) hunting and gathering
   (D) trade
   (E) raiding

2. Great Britain's policy of governing its colonies to build up its own gold reserves and expand trade is known as
   (A) nationalism
   (B) favorable balance of trade
   (C) mercantilism
   (D) Navigation Acts
   (E) enumerated goods

3. "On almost all questions, great and small, which have come up since the first session of Congress, _____ and _____ have been found among those who want to limit federal power. In respect to foreign policy, the views of these gentlemen are, in my judgement, equally unsound and dangerous. They have a womanish attachment to France and a womanish resentment against Great Britain."

   The above statement was probably written by
   (A) Thomas Jefferson
   (B) James Madison
   (C) Alexander Hamilton
   (D) Alexis de Tocqueville
   (E) Edmund Burke

4. The two men whose names are omitted in the quotation above are most probably
   I. Thomas Jefferson
   II. James Madison
   III. Alexander Hamilton
   IV. Alexis de Tocqueville
   V. George Washington
   (A) I and II only
   (B) II and III only
   (C) I and III only
   (D) III and IV only
   (E) II and V only

5. The issue of protective tariffs led to fierce debate in Andrew Jackson's administration over
   (A) internal improvements
   (B) Indian removal
   (C) states' rights
   (D) popular sovereignty
   (E) specie circular

6. All of the following were true of U.S. foreign policy during the second half of the nineteenth century EXCEPT
   (A) the United States purchased Alaska from Canada
   (B) business interests influenced U.S. annexation of Hawaii
   (C) the Open Door policy in China brought the United States little gain
   (D) the Spanish American War resulted in U.S. acquisition of an empire
   (E) in an effort to improve relations with Latin American nations, the United States invited them to an Inter-American conference in Washington in 1889

DIAGNOSTIC TEST—*Continued*

7. The major problem with enforcing the Sherman Antitrust Act was

(A) few cases were brought to court under the act

(B) the law did not define the terms *trust, conspiracy,* and *monopoly,* so it was difficult to prove illegal activity

(C) the administrations of Harrison, Cleveland, and McKinley did not actively prosecute companies and individuals under the law

(D) there was little political support for the law

(E) the law was used against labor unions rather than corporations

8. "The next great economic disturbance in which phases of ultra-radicalism appeared was the coal strike of 1919. As always, the ultra-radical element took advantage of an industrial disturbance. . . . Evidence obtained at the time of this strike showed active participation therein of the Communist Party of America."

The writer of the above would most likely agree with which of the following statements?

(A) All union members are ultra-radicals.

(B) Immigration should be severely limited.

(C) The Communist Party works with unions during strikes to negotiate better contracts for workers.

(D) The Communist Party should be banned.

(E) Without Communist influence, workers would not strike.

9. All of the following were part of Eisenhower's foreign policy EXCEPT

(A) breaking off diplomatic relations with Cuba

(B) supporting a revolt by the Shah of Iran against Communist-leaning politicians

(C) providing economic support to the South Vietnamese under Diem

(D) sending troops into Hungary to aid the freedom fighters

(E) supporting nuclear disarmament

10. All of the following are characteristics of the 1960s EXCEPT

(A) failure to make progress in eliminating racial inequalities

(B) conservative backlash against civil rights and antiwar demonstrations

(C) "war on poverty"

(D) inability to balance the cost of social programs and the war in Vietnam

(E) deepening government commitment to an unpopular war in Vietnam

GO ON TO THE NEXT PAGE

DIAGNOSTIC TEST—*Continued*

11. Which of the following statements is consistent with the data in the graph below?

   (A) The number of minority students enrolled in higher education is estimated to grow between 2000 and 2005.

   (B) Americans' recognition of the need for a college degree in order to advance in the workplace is evident in the projected increase in college enrollment between 2000 and 2005.

   (C) Part-time enrollment for men and women shows an increase between 2000 and 2005.

   (D) More men than women are enrolled as full-time students.

   (E) The number of college students aged 18 to 25 is greater than the number of college students aged 25 to 30.

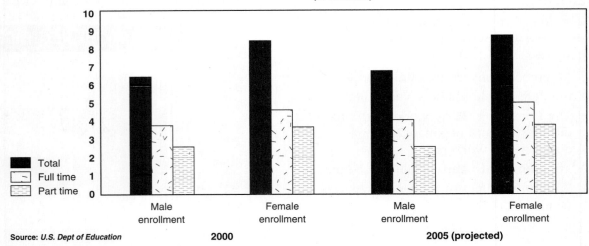

COLLEGE ENROLLMENT
(in millions)

Source: *U.S. Dept of Education*

16

DIAGNOSTIC TEST—*Continued*

12. Which of the following statements about the economic development of the thirteen British colonies is INCORRECT?

(A) Large Southern plantations were the exception rather than the rule.

(B) Slavery failed to develop in New England because of the environment.

(C) The Middle Colonies developed an economy based on subsistence farming.

(D) Southern farming for the most part was at the subsistence level.

(E) New England developed a mixed economy of farming, manufacturing, fishing, shipbuilding, and trade.

13. All of the following were weaknesses of the Articles of Confederation EXCEPT

(A) nine of the thirteen states had to approve all laws

(B) a national court system ruled on the constitutionality of laws

(C) Congress worked in committees without a chief executive

(D) all states were required to approve amendments

(E) Congress could raise money by borrowing or by asking the states for money

14. *Marbury* v. *Madison* established

(A) the principle of one man, one vote

(B) the principle of judicial review

(C) the principle of implied powers in the Constitution

(D) Congress's right to regulate interstate commerce

(E) the principle of separate but equal

15. James Madison vetoed a bill to continue work on the National Road at federal expense because

(A) Southerners wanted the road to go south rather than west

(B) Westerners were against the use of federal money for internal improvements

(C) Madison believed that using federal money for internal improvements was beyond the scope of what the U.S. Constitution authorized

(D) New Englanders supported the bill and Madison, as a Southerner, opposed it

(E) canal owners lobbied Madison to veto the bill in exchange for their support

16. Which of the following best describes the purpose of the Freedmen's Bureau?

(A) To oversee the distribution of land and supplies to former slaves

(B) To help freed slaves adjust to their new lives

(C) To sign up former slaves to run for office

(D) To feed, clothe, and educate former slaves

(E) To assist former slaves in finding work and to negotiate fair work terms for them

GO ON TO THE NEXT PAGE

DIAGNOSTIC TEST—*Continued*

17. Which of the following statements about the labor market in the second half of the nineteenth century is NOT true?

(A) Union strikes and boycotts were considered "conspiracies in restraint of trade."

(B) The national labor market was highly competitive because of the movement of people from farms to cities and the influx of immigrants.

(C) The AFL effectively recruited and organized immigrants.

(D) A series of economic depressions drove wages down.

(E) Installment of new machines sometimes resulted in technological unemployment.

18. The Zimmerman Note

(A) requested U.S. neutrality in World War I

(B) offered Canada an alliance

(C) announced that all vessels near Great Britain, France, and Italy would be sunk without warning by U-boats

(D) promised Mexico that in exchange for an alliance, it would return Texas, New Mexico, and Arizona at the end of the war

(E) revoked the Sussex Pledge

19. Which statement best describes why Prohibition failed?

(A) Racketeers took control of the illegal manufacture and sale of alcohol.

(B) It was easy for people to set up stills and make alcohol for their own use.

(C) The long unpoliced borders and coastlines made smuggling alcohol into the country relatively easy.

(D) Many Americans did not take the law seriously.

(E) Communities continued to observe local option laws.

20. Roosevelt's stated purpose in proposing the alleged "court packing" bill was to

(A) avoid Supreme Court rulings against the National Labor Relations Act and the Social Security Act

(B) remove judges who were still living in the "horse-and-buggy era"

(C) increase the efficiency of the federal judicial system

(D) establish a "Roosevelt court"

(E) preserve the constitutional system of checks and balances

21. The ruling in *Miranda* v. *Arizona* established

(A) the right to privacy

(B) the right to be represented by counsel

(C) the principle of clear and present danger

(D) the rights of a suspect under questioning

(E) that the defendant had been rightfully convicted for failure to relocate

22. The Truman Doctrine was issued in support of "free peoples who are resisting attempted subjugation by armed minorities or by outside pressure" in

(A) Turkey and Greece

(B) Poland and Hungary

(C) Albania and Yugoslavia

(D) East Germany

(E) Cyprus

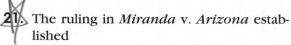

23. The only Native Americans who were able to unite and become strong enough to resist the English colonists successfully were the

(A) Powhatan Confederacy

(B) Seminoles

(C) Iroquois League

(D) Pequots

(E) Wampanoag

DIAGNOSTIC TEST—*Continued*

24. A major characteristic of colonial British society on the eve of the revolution was the

(A) lack of free Africans in the colonies

(B) ability of indentured servants to move into the middle class after they served their term of indenture

(C) relatively low position of women

(D) value placed on education

(E) lack of diversity among the population

25. The major achievement of the government under the Articles of Confederaion was

(A) the defeat of the Whiskey Rebellion

(B) levying of the nation's first protective tariff

(C) establishment of the procedure for settling the Northwest Territory

(D) the negotiation of the treaty with Spain giving the United States the right of deposit at New Orleans

(E) removal of the Native American threat in the Ohio Valley

26. Which of the following contradicts Thomas Jefferson's position as an advocate of states' rights and strict construction?

(A) He opposed Hamilton's financial program during Washington's administration.

(B) As president, he reduced taxes.

(C) He maintained U.S. neutrality with Europe.

(D) He authorized the Louisiana Purchase.

(E) He employed *laissez-faire* policy toward the economy during his administration.

27. The painters and novelists of the new nation took inspiration for their works from all of the following EXCEPT

(A) European Romantics

(B) Native Americans

(C) factory life

(D) nature

(E) colonial life

28. The major difference between the Knights of Labor and the AFL was that the Knights of Labor

(A) did not accept African Americans, women, and immigrants as members

(B) was organized by industrial unions, and the AFL was organized by craft unions

(C) were radical labor unionists

(D) advocated arbitration rather than strikes

(E) campaigned for shorter workdays and higher wages

29. The National Origins Act of 1924 can best be described as

(A) a necessary stopgap measure after World War I to control limitless immigration

(B) an effort to remedy the Gentlemen's Agreement of 1907 between Theodore Roosevelt and Japan

(C) having been passed in response to Sacco and Vanzetti

(D) discriminatory against all those who did not come from Northern or Western Europe

(E) an effort to equalize the flow of immigrants from all countries

GO ON TO THE NEXT PAGE ➡

DIAGNOSTIC TEST—*Continued*

30. Which of the following agencies benefitted African Americans LEAST during the New Deal?

(A) AAA

(B) SSA

(C) NYA

(D) CCC

(E) NRA

31. Which of the following did <u>not</u> contribute to the growth of suburbia after World War II?

(A) The availability of low-cost housing

(B) The development of a national highway system

(C) Low-interest loans to veterans

(D) A boom in the construction of schools, factories, offices, and government buildings

(E) The railway system

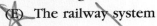

32. According to the two pie graphs below, the fastest growing source of government revenue between 1972 and 1982 was

(A) Personal Income Taxes

(B) Social Insurance Contributions

(C) Corporate Income Taxes

(D) Excise and Customs Duties

(E) Estate and Gift Taxes

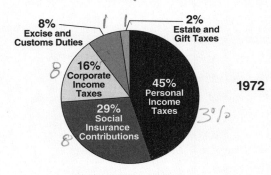

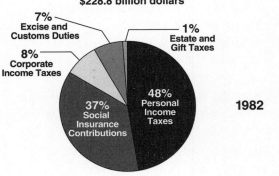

Department of Commerce

33. Social Insurance Contributions (FICA) include

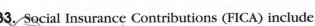

(A) Old Age, Survivors, and Disability Insurance; Medicare; Unemployment Insurance

(B) Old Age, Survivors, and Disability Insurance and Medicare

(C) Old Age, Survivors, and Disability Insurance; Medicare; and Medicaid

(D) Worker's Compensation

(E) Unemployment Insurance

34. The Stamp Act was significant because
    - (A) it was the first tax levied on goods imported from Great Britain
    - (B) it was to be strictly enforced by the British
    - (C) it was the first tax placed on goods made and sold in the colonies, and therefore, not part of mercantile policy
    - (D) if enforced, it would drain colonial merchants of gold and silver
    - (E) it was the first instance of taxation without representation

35. *Common Sense* would most likely have been bought and read by
    - (A) Patriots
    - (B) secessionists
    - (C) Unionists
    - (D) Loyalists
    - (E) abolitionists

36. All of the following were part of U.S. foreign policy under Washington EXCEPT
    - (A) Pinckney's Treaty
    - (B) Jay's Treaty
    - (C) Proclamation of Neutrality
    - (D) Treaty of Greenville
    - (E) XYZ Affair

37. Which of the following was an example of sectional interests intervening in national politics?
    - (A) Hartford Convention
    - (B) New England Confederation
    - (C) Albany Congress
    - (D) Annapolis Convention
    - (E) Niagara Movement

38. "The autumn of 1854 witnessed the erection of the first log-huts . . . by a few families of New England settlers. During the year 1855 its population increased rapidly, chiefly by the arrival of emigrants from the Northern States. Its log-hut existence gave way to a more advanced stage, . . . and the growing prosperity . . . early began to excite the jealousy of the abettors of slavery. Viewed as the stronghold of the Free-state party, it was made the point of attack . . ."

    The description above was most likely written about
    - (A) the settling of Missouri
    - (B) the settling on the frontier of Irish laborers who had left New England mill towns
    - (C) the fight over the admission of Kansas as a free or slave state
    - (D) a settlement of New Englanders in the South
    - (E) a settlement of Republicans in the South

39. Which of the following Union strategies did the most damage to the South's economy during the Civil War?
    - (A) Capture of Richmond
    - (B) Accepting of escaped slaves into the Union lines
    - (C) Control of the Mississippi River
    - (D) Blockade of Southern ports
    - (E) Destruction of Southern railroads

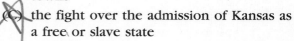

GO ON TO THE NEXT PAGE

DIAGNOSTIC TEST—*Continued*

40. " . . . [C]onsider all surplus revenues which come to him simply as trust funds, which he is called upon to administer . . . in manner which, in his judgment, is best calculated to produce the most beneficial results for the community."

The above reflects the philosophy of

(A) Andrew Carnegie

(B) Theodore Roosevelt

(C) William Jennings Bryan

(D) Frederick Douglass

(E) Jane Addams

41. Between 1860 and 1920, the largest number of immigrants from one country to come to the United States was

(A) Russian

(B) Austro-Hungarian

(C) German

(D) Canadian

(E) Mexican

42. Which of the following presidents is correctly paired with the domestic policy enacted during his term in office?

(A) John F. Kennedy: "war on poverty"

(B) Lyndon B. Johnson: Medicare

(C) Ronald Reagan: establishment of the Peace Corps

(D) Jimmy Carter: integration of Little Rock High School

(E) Dwight Eisenhower: Camp David Accords

43. The most significant difference between Spanish and French colonial policies in the Americas was that the French

(A) did not establish an extensive system of colonial settlements

(B) were on friendly terms with the English colonists

(C) were not interested in converting Native Americans to Catholicism

(D) system of colonial government was more democratic than the Spanish system

(E) established a successful fur trade with Native Americans

44. In the English colonies in the 1600s, the role of Africans shifted from that of indentured servant to slave for life because

(A) European indentured servants were no longer interested in coming to the colonies

(B) agricultural colonies like Maryland were looking for a cheap, plentiful labor supply

(C) Africans found it difficult to cope with European ways

(D) New England merchants found that they could profitably transport Africans on the Africa-to-Caribbean leg of the trans-Atlantic trade

(E) the English believed that they were superior to the Africans

DIAGNOSTIC TEST—*Continued*

Question 45 refers to the cartoon below.

45. What action of Andrew Jackson is the subject of the cartoon?

(A) Jackson's support for the annexation of Texas

(B) Jackson's support of Indian removal

(C) His issuance of the "Proclamation to the People of South Carolina"

(D) His veto of the charter of the Second Bank

(E) His veto of the Maysville Road bill

46. Labor did not think of itself as a powerful force in the U.S. economy in the 1830s and 1840s because

(A) immigrants were willing to work for low wages

(B) the Panic of 1837 caused many people to lose their jobs

(C) only Massachusetts recognized the legality of labor unions

(D) Americans were used to working on their own as farmers or skilled craft workers

(E) women who made up a significant part of the work force of early factories were reluctant to join unions

47. "No race can prosper until it learns that there is as much dignity in tilling a field as in writing a poem. It is at the bottom of life we must begin, and not at the top."

The above statement reflects the philosophy of which of the following African Americans?

(A) Paul Laurence Dunbar

(B) W.E.B. Du Bois

(C) Langston Hughes

(D) Booker T. Washington

(E) Ralph Ellison

48. All of the following are examples of reforms supported by progressives EXCEPT

(A) adoption of the Australian ballot

(B) welfare reform

(C) use of the initiative, referendum, and recall

(D) direct election of U.S. senators

(E) women's suffrage

GO ON TO THE NEXT PAGE

49. Which of the following novelists of the early twentieth century wrote about the hypocrisy and materialism of small-town life?

(A) Sinclair Lewis

(B) Ernest Hemingway

(C) Edith Wharton

(D) Gertrude Stein

(E) Langston Hughes

50. Which of the following applied pressure to Franklin Roosevelt to ensure that defense industries did not discriminate against African American workers in hiring and employment practices?

(A) Martin Luther King

(B) Marcus Garvey

(C) Ralph Abernathy

(D) A. Philip Randolph

(E) Mary McCleod Bethune

51. U.S. immigration policies in the 1950s reflected all of the following EXCEPT

(A) the desire to help displaced persons and children orphaned by World War II

(B) fear of immigrants who might subvert the U.S. government

(C) the goal of equalizing immigration between Asian nations and European nations

(D) the desire to provide a haven for those fleeing Communist governments

(E) the need to hurry development of the U.S. missile program by admitting a limited number of scientists and technicians

52. César Chávez used which of the following tactics in the National Farm Workers of Association strike against grape owners in California?

(A) Sit-down strike

(B) Injunction

(C) *Huelga*

(D) National consumer boycott of grapes

(E) Jurisdictional strike

53. All of the following were goals of James I's charter to the Virginia Company EXCEPT to

(A) bring Christianity and civilization to the native people

(B) build a commonwealth based on God's word

(C) explore for precious metals

(D) trade with the native people

(E) find a Northwest Passage

54. The Maryland Toleration Act of 1649 was significant because it

(A) made it easier to fulfill the terms of indenture

(B) granted religious freedom to Christian sects

(C) provided for gradual emancipation of slaves in Maryland

(D) was the earliest colonial statute related to religious freedom

(E) allowed any male to hold office

DIAGNOSTIC TEST—*Continued*

Questions 55 and 56 refer to the following map.

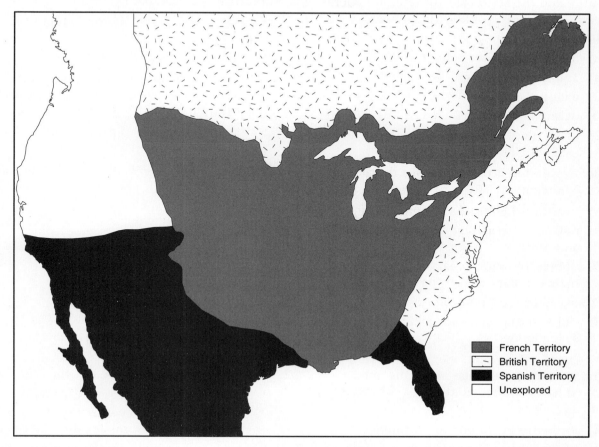

French Territory
British Territory
Spanish Territory
Unexplored

55. The map above shows North America in which of the following years?

(A) 1754
(B) 1763
(C) 1776
(D) 1789
(E) 1803

56. Ten years later, the above map would look different because the

(A) British would have lost its territory along the Atlantic in the Revolutionary War
(B) Russians would have claimed the northern California coast.
(C) Northwest Territory would have been carved out of the Great Lakes area
(D) United States would have taken control of the center of the continent after the Louisiana Purchase
(E) French would have lost their territory after the French and Indian War

GO ON TO THE NEXT PAGE ➤

57. Belief in the divinity and unity of people and nature and the supremacy of intuition over reason as a source of knowledge were characteristics of

    (A) the Hudson River School
    (B) Transcendentalism
    (C) nationalism
    (D) deism
    (E) the Harlem Renaissance

58. The decision in *Scott* v. *Sanford* did all of the following EXCEPT

    (A) overturn the Missouri Compromise
    (B) outlaw the teaching of slaves to read and write
    (C) uphold the right of slaver owners to their property in new territories
    (D) overturn the Compromise of 1850
    (E) call into question the validity of popular sovereignty

59. The primary reason that Mexicans immigrated to the United States between 1910 and 1920 was

    (A) for better economic opportunities
    (B) to participate in the *bracero* program that provided workers for the United States defense industry
    (C) to flee the Mexican Revolution
    (D) to be able to practice their religion as Roman Catholics without government interference
    (E) the U.S.'s proposal to impose quotas on Mexican immigration

60. The primary reason that the TVA was controversial was that it

    (A) used government money to build factories
    (B) moved farmers off their lands
    (C) served as a yardstick to measure the fairness of electricity rates charged by private utilities
    (D) diverted the river through a series of twenty dams
    (E) aided large farmers at the expense of small farmers

61. Which of the following laws of the New Deal was declared unconstitutional?

    (A) Civilian Conservation Corps
    (B) Works Progress Administration
    (C) Federal Housing Authority
    (D) National Industrial Recovery Act
    (E) National Youth Administration

62. The General Court banished Roger Williams primarily because he

    (A) believed that the colonists should pay the Native Americans for their lands
    (B) preached separation of church and state
    (C) believed in the right of women to vote
    (D) challenged the rights of leaders to force people to attend religious services
    (E) was a secret Pilgrim

63. The greatest disparity in wealth in the British colonies was found among people in

    (A) the Piedmont
    (B) New England towns
    (C) cities in all the colonies
    (D) the cities of the Middle Colonies
    (E) the backcountry of all the colonies

DIAGNOSTIC TEST—*Continued*

64. "This kingdom . . . has always bound the colonies by her laws, her regulations . . . in every thing except that of taking their money out of their pockets without their consent. Here I would draw the line."

The above statement was most likely spoken by

(A) Benjamin Franklin

(B) Edmund Andros

(C) Patrick Henry

(D) William Pitt

(E) Alexis de Tocqueville

65. Which statement best describes the significance of the War of 1812?

(A) Neither the United States nor Great Britain lost any territory; they agreed to return to their prewar boundaries.

(B) The two nations eventually agreed on a boundary between the United States and Canada.

(C) Any movement toward secession among New Englanders ended with the end of the war.

(D) The United States emerged as a power in its own right having fought the most powerful nation in the world to a draw.

(E) The possibility of U.S. entanglement in European wars increased after the war.

66. A major document of the women's rights movement was

(A) Declaration of Sentiments and Resolutions

(B) *The Feminine Mystique*

(C) "Ain't I a Woman"

(D) *Liberator*

(E) *A Century of Dishonor*

67. The most significant fact about free African Americans in the North before the Civil War was

(A) custom rather than law kept whites and blacks separated

(B) African Americans could not attend public schools

(C) African Americans faced competition in the job market from European immigrants with fewer skills

(D) in most Northern states, African Americans could not vote, serve on juries, or testify against a white person

(E) free African Americans were free and not free

68. The most significant effect of "dollar diplomacy" was

(A) the Panama Canal

(B) intervention in domestic elections in Nicaragua

(C) suspicion and mistrust of the United States

(D) large profits for U.S. banks from Latin American investments

(E) the reduction of U.S. protective tariffs

69. All of the following contributed to the period of intolerance after World War I EXCEPT

(A) fear of the Bolsehviks

(B) the Sacco-Vanzetti case

(C) anti-immigration laws

(D) anti-Semitism and Catholic-baiting

(E) the power of organized labor

GO ON TO THE NEXT PAGE

DIAGNOSTIC TEST—*Continued*

70. Which of the following is the correct chronological order in which the events occurred?

   I. Gulf of Tonkin Resolution
   II. invasion of Cambodia
   III. Tet offensive
   IV. commitment of U.S. ground troops to the war in Vietnam

   (A) I, II, III, IV
   (B) I, IV, III, II
   (C) IV, I, II, III
   (D) IV, I, III, II
   (E) III, IV, I, II

71. The end of Communist governments in Eastern Europe in the late 1980s proved the wisdom of the

   (A) domino theory
   (B) Eisenhower Doctrine
   (C) Truman Doctrine
   (D) policy of containment
   (E) Marshall Plan

72. The case against John Peter Zenger is considered a landmark in the development of which freedom?

   (A) Speech
   (B) Religion
   (C) The press
   (D) Right to bear arms
   (E) Right to assemble

73. A broad discussion of the significance of the Stamp Act, Declaratory Act, and the Townshend Acts would necessarily mention which of the following?

   (A) Power of the purse
   (B) Virtual representation
   (C) Balance of trade
   (D) Mercantilism
   (E) New England Confederation

74. Which of the following events is an example of the economic problems facing the government under the Articles of Confederation?

   (A) Whiskey Rebellion
   (B) Stono Uprising
   (C) Kentucky and Virginia Resolutions
   (D) Shays's Rebellion
   (E) Tariff of Abominations

75. Which of the following was not one of Lincoln's beliefs about reconstructing the South?

   (A) Reconstruction was part of his responsibility as commander in chief; it was not Congress's responsibility.
   (B) Congress did not have the authority to abolish slavery; a Constitutional amendment was needed to end slavery.
   (C) Lincoln wanted a generous practical policy of reconstruction in order to "bind up the nation's wounds" with "malice toward none, with charity for all."
   (D) Lincoln believed that the rebellion had been caused by individuals; the Southern states had never left the Union.
   (E) The right of African Americans to vote should be guaranteed in each new Southern state constitution.

76. African Americans were disenfranchised in Southern states by all of the following practices EXCEPT

   (A) poll tax
   (B) literacy test
   (C) property test
   (D) white primary elections
   (E) separate but equal ruling in *Plessy* v. *Ferguson*

DIAGNOSTIC TEST—*Continued*

77. "You come to us and tell us that the great cities are in favor of the gold standard. We reply that the great cities rest upon our broad and fertile plains. Burn down your cities and leave our farms, and your cities will spring up again as if by magic; but destroy our farms, and the grass will grow in the streets of every city in the country."

The above reflects the philosophy in the election of 1896 of a

(A) Silver Democrat
(B) Republican
(C) Gold Democrat
(D) Wall Street banker
(E) Greenback Party member

78. The U.S. Senate did not ratify the Treaty of Versailles principally because

(A) Wilson agreed to the end of the Ottoman Empire in the Middle East
(B) Wilson waffled but then agreed to require Germany to repay the Allies for their costs in fighting the war
(C) Wilson insisted that the League of Nations be part of the peace treaty
(D) Wilson would not agree to the division of Austria-Hungary
(E) of Wilson's intemperate remarks about the "narrow, selfish, provincial purposes" of his critics in Congress

79. "If you are scared to go to the brink, you are lost" reflects the foreign policy of

(A) President Dwight Eisenhower
(B) President John F. Kennedy
(C) John Foster Dulles, Secretary of State
(D) Madeline K. Albright, Secretary of State
(E) Neville Chamberlain, British Prime Minister

80. In the coalition Franklin Roosevelt put together, which of the following groups was new to the Democratic Party?

(A) Northern political machines
(B) Southern whites
(C) African Americans
(D) Southern political machines
(E) first- and second-generation immigrants

81. Executive Order 9981 guaranteeing equal opportunity in the military was issued by

(A) General Douglas MacArthur
(B) Franklin Roosevelt
(C) Harry Truman
(D) Dwight Eisenhower
(E) Lyndon Johnson

82. President Nixon resigned rather than face Articles of Impeachment accusing him of

(A) income tax evasion
(B) using income tax records against political enemies
(C) ordering a cover up of the break-in and attempt to wiretap Democratic National Party headquarters
(D) obstruction of justice, abuse of power, and refusal to supply subpoenaed information
(E) the use of campaign funds to buy the silence of the Watergate burglars

GO ON TO THE NEXT PAGE ➤

**EXPORTS TO AND IMPORTS FROM
ENGLAND BY THE 13 COLONIES, 1700–1775**
(in pounds sterling)

Year	Exports	Imports
1700	395,021	344,341
1710	249,814	293,659
1720	468,188	319,702
1730	572,585	536,860
1740	718,416	813,382
1750	814,768	1,313,083
1760	761,099	2,611,764
1770	1,015,535	1,925,571
1775	1,920,950	196,162

Source: *Historical Abstract of the United States*

83. Which statement best supports the data in the above table?

    (A) The colonies generally bought more from England than they exported to it between 1700 and 1775.

    (B) Mercantilism sought to create a closed system in which the empire would provide for all its own needs.

    (C) The end of the French and Indian War created a demand in England for raw materials and a market for manufactured goods.

    (D) According to mercantilism, the colonies should never compete with England.

    (E) There was a steady increase in both exports and imports from 1700 until 1775.

84. In order to gain passage of the Assumption Bill, Alexander Hamilton agreed to

    (A) withdraw his tariff bill

    (B) specify that speculators would be paid the full value of their bonds

    (C) hold the bill authorizing the First Bank until Washington's second term

    (D) support building the new capital city on Southern land

    (E) support Madison's version of the bill

85. The Grange movement did all of the following EXCEPT

    (A) successfully lobby for passage of laws in several states that set maximum railroad passenger and freight rates

    (B) win *Munn* v. *Illinois*

    (C) support *laissez-faire* capitalism

    (D) organize businesses such as mills, banks, and grain elevators

    (E) admit women on an equal basis with men

86. The Census Bureau's report in 1890 that the frontier was "closed" resulted in

    (A) the opening of Oklahoma to white settlement

    (B) concern that there would be nowhere for the "social discontent" to go

    (C) speculation in the remaining open land

    (D) a shift in power from rural areas to cities

    (E) forced removal of Mexican Americans from their lands in New Mexico and Arizona

DIAGNOSTIC TEST—*Continued*

87. The election of 1928 is significant because

(A) it demonstrated the anti-Catholic prejudice that had been underground up to that time

(B) Hoover broke the Democratic Party hold on the "solid South"

(C) Smith transformed the Democratic Party from a rural, small-town party to an urban party

(D) it showed a shift in the rural/urban alignment of the parties

(E) the election repudiated the policies of Harding's return to normalcy

88. The counterculture of the 1960s was characterized by all of the following EXCEPT

(A) antiwar protests

(B) a sexual revolution

(C) the reemergence of the women's movement

(D) materialism

(E) distrust of authority

89. During the Nixon administration, state governments would most likely have favored which of the following forms of federal aid?

(A) revenue sharing

(B) grants in aid

(C) block grants

(D) categorical grants

(E) supply-side economics

90. The trend in the 1990s was

(A) rising employment and decreasing inflation

(B) an expanding federal deficit

(C) declining unemployment and rising inflation

(D) rising unemployment and rising inflation

(E) a favorable balance of trade

S T O P

If you finish before the hour is up, you may review your work on this test only. You may not turn to any other test in this book.

ANSWERS AND EXPLANATIONS

EXPLANATION OF ANSWERS

Test-Taking Strategy

If you don't know the answer immediately, try educated guessing.

1. **The correct answer is (B).** While Native Americans of the Northeast Woodlands supplemented their diets by hunting and gathering and some also fished, almost all of the nations were farmers, choice (B), which answers the key word in the question stem *primarily*. Fishing, choice (A), was the major occupation of the peoples of the Northwest Coast. Most Native American groups hunted and gathered food, choice (C), and conducted some trade, choice (D). Some peoples of the Southwest, such as the Apache, were greatly feared raiders, choice (E).

2. **The correct answer is (C).** Mercantilism contributes to a sense of nationalism, choice (A), and can be a result of a strong sense of national identity, but it is an economic policy. A favorable balance of trade, choice (B), for the home country is a desired result of mercantilism. The Navigation Acts, choice (D), and enumerated goods, choice (E), were two ways Great Britain tried to enforce mercantilist policies on its American colonies.

3. **The correct answer is (C).** The policies of the two men whose names are omitted—determination to limit federal power, support of France, and dislike of Great Britain—fit the description of Republicans. Thomas Jefferson, choice (A), and James Madison, choice (B), were Republicans, so you can eliminate both those choices. Choice (D), Alexis de Tocqueville, was French, so it is unlikely that he would write so harsh a description of men who supported France against Great Britain, and he would have had little interest in internal U.S. politics. Edmund Burke, the Anglo-Irish statesman, might have had an interest in whether U.S. officials supported France against Great Britain but, like de Tocqueville, would have had little

interest in internal U.S. politics, so you could eliminate choice (E). Alexander Hamilton, choice (C), was a staunch supporter of federal power, hence a leader of the Federalist Party, and an opponent of Jefferson and Madison, and, thus, the correct answer.

4. **The correct answer is (A).** In the passage written by Alexander Hamilton and quoted in question 3, the two men whose names are omitted are Thomas Jefferson and James Madison, choice (A). Madison and Hamilton, choice (B), were political opponents, belonging to the Republican and Federalists Parties respectively. The same is true of choice (C), and choices (D) and (E) make no sense.

5. **The correct answer is (C).** Choices (A), (B), (D), and (E) have nothing to do with protective tariffs. Choices (A) and (B) were issues during Jackson's administrations but do not involve the protective tariff (except indirectly as a source of revenue for government activities). Because the South did not want a high tariff for fear of damaging its profitable trade in cotton, Southerners in Congress opposed the tariff with the argument that states could nullify any federal law that they found to be unjust and unconstitutional.

6. **The correct answer is (A).** Choice (A) is correct because the United States bought Alaska from Russia, not Canada, in 1867 at the insistence of U.S. Secretary of State William Seward. Choices (B), (C), (D), and (E) are all true of U.S. foreign policy in the last half of the nineteenth century and, thus, incorrect answers to this EXCEPT question.

7. **The correct answer is (B).** Choices (A), (B), (C), and (E) are all true with regard to enforcing the Sherman Antitrust Act, but the major problem with the act was its vagueness. The key terms, *trust, conspiracy,* and *monopoly* were not defined. Choice (D) is illogical; if there had not been political support for the bill, it would not have been enacted into law.

8. **The correct answer is (D).** The quotation is from a report issued by U.S. Attorney General A. Mitchell Palmer in 1920. This type of question asks you to look for consistency between the data and the possible responses. Choice (A) is not supported in the reading because nothing is said to imply that the writer thinks those striking were ultra-radicals. The quotation says, "As always, the ultra-radical element took advantage of an industrial disturbance." This implies that the ultra-radicals came from outside the strike. No mention is made that the strikers or the ultra-radicals were immigrants, so choice (B) is illogical. There is no support in the reading for choice (C); the reading says that the Communist Party participated, but the term *ultra-radical* implies that their presence was not a peaceful attempt to negotiate with owners. The reading does not support choice (E) because the reading states that the ultra-radicals took advantage of a strike that was already in progress. That leaves choice (D) as consistent with the writer's opinion as expressed in the quotation.

Test-Taking Strategy

For a not/except *question, ask yourself if the answer is true. If it is, cross it off and go to the next answer.*

Test-Taking Strategy

The key words here are major problem.

9. **The correct answer is (D).** Any intervention by the United States in Hungary was considered dangerous and impractical.

10. **The correct answer is (A).** Although some may disagree with the extent of desegregation efforts in the 1960s, progress was made, so choice (A) is correct. With this progress came a backlash, choice (B), a certain amount of it from blue-collar, white ethnic workers. Choices (C), (D), and (E) resulted in high inflation, increased taxes, and a legacy of mistrust of government on the part of many citizens.

11. **The correct answer is (B).** Choice (A) is incorrect because there is no mention of minority students in the data. Choice (E) is also incorrect for the same reason; the age of college students is not indicated on the graph. The bar graph contradicts choice (C); part-time enrollment is shown as holding steady between 2000 and 2005 at 2.6 million for men and 3.7 million for women. The graph also contradicts choice (D), because more women than men are enrolled as full-time students. That leaves choice (B), which is supported by the general increase in student enrollment and is a logical extension of the data and interpretation of what you know from outside information.

12. **The correct answer is (C).** Choices (A) and (D) say the same thing in different ways and are both true about the economy of the Southern Colonies. Choices (B) and (E) are both true about the New England Colonies. Choice (C) is not true about the Middle Colonies. Known as the "Breadbasket," they developed cash crops in wheat, corn, and rye. Delaware and Maryland developed economies based on tobacco agriculture.

13. **The correct answer is (B).** Under the Articles, there was no national court system. Because there was no chief executive, choice (C), there was no unifying force for government policies. Because all thirteen states, rather than a majority, were required to ratify amendments, it was unlikely that small states and large states or Northern states and Southern states would agree on issues, choice (D). Although nine of the thirteen might agree on laws, it was difficult to get the representatives of any nine states to appear for sessions, choice (A). Congress was hampered in its duties because it could not levy taxes; it could only request money from the states or borrow it, which required approval, choice (E).

14. **The correct answer is (B).** If you did not know the answer immediately, you could eliminate two answers, choices (A) and (E). Madison served as both secretary of state and president before cases began to go to the Supreme Court about the rights of African Americans, the most logical topic for a "separate but equal" court case, choice (E), and before Jacksonian democracy enlarged the franchise. Choice (A) was established by a series of cases in the latter half of the twentieth century, among them *Wesbery* v. *Sanders. McCulloch* v. *Maryland* established the principle of implied powers, choice (C), and *Gibbons* v. *Ogden* established Congress's right to regulate interstate commerce, choice (D).

Test-Taking Strategy

When a question asks you to interpret data, make sure that you base your response on the data. Don't jump to unwarranted conclusions.

Test-Taking Strategy

This is similar to the not/except questions. If the answer is correct about the content of the question, cross it off and go to the next answer.

---

15. **The correct answer is (C).** Choice (B) is true of Westerners in the 1820s but in 1816, they still supported using federal money for internal improvements. While it is true that New Englanders in the 1816 supported internal improvements, choice (D), Madison did not oppose the bill simply because he was a Southerner. Choices (A) and (E) are simply incorrect.

16. **The correct answer is (B).** Choices (A), (B), (D), and (E) are all true, but choice (B) contains all the elements of the other three answers and, thus, is the best description of the purpose of the Freedmen's Bureau. Choice (C) is incorrect.

17. **The correct answer is (C).** The AFL was a craft union, and most immigrants were unskilled or semiskilled labor rather than craft workers. AFL's refusal to recruit unskilled and semiskilled workers led in 1935 to the establishment of the Congress of Industrial Organizations, made up of industrial unions rather than craft unions. Although choice (E) is true, it often meant that when one job was mechanized, another job opened up.

18. **The correct answer is (D).** Wilson tried to use the note to secure broad authority from Congress to protect U.S. ships engaged in peaceful pursuits. Wilson planned to arm merchant ships so they could fight off German U-boats. Regardless of the outrage over the note, the isolationists in Congress blocked the vote. Choice (C) was a provision of the Sussex Pledge, choice (E). Choices (A) and (B) are incorrect.

19. **The correct answer is (D).** Choices (A), (B), (C), and (D) are all reasons why Prohibition failed, but choice (D) is the most important reason why "the noble experiment" failed. Tired of the self-sacrifice and idealism required by World War I, Americans simply refused to obey the law. Choice (E) is incorrect; a constitutional amendment takes precedence over any local law.

20. **The correct answer is (C).** In offering his proposal, which included the request to appoint lower-level federal judges as well as to enlarge the Supreme Court, Roosevelt used choice (C) as his reason. His unstated purposes were choices (A) and (B). These, in turn, would have created choice (D). As Supreme Court justices retired between 1937 and 1940, the new Court upheld New Deal measures, including the National Labor Relations Act and the Social Security Act. Choice (E) was the reason people gave in opposing Roosevelt's proposal.

21. **The correct answer is (D).** *Roe* v. *Wade* established choice (A). *Gideon* v. *Wainwright* established choice (B). Choice (C) was the principle in *Schenck* v. *United States*. *Korematsu* v. *United States* is the case referred to in choice (E).

Test-Taking Strategy

The key words are purpose *and* best describes.

Test-Taking Strategy

Tackle this question the same way you would a not/except *question. If the answer is true for the content of the question, cross it off, and go on to the next answer.*

Test-Taking Strategy

The key phrase is best describes.

Test-Taking Strategy

The key word is stated.

Test-Taking Strategy

Be sure all parts of an answer are correct. A partially correct answer is a partially incorrect answer— and a quarter-point deduction.

22. **The correct answer is (A).** Choices (B), (C), and (D) were already in Communist hands by the end of World War II. Greece was fighting a Communist takeover when the British announced they could no longer provide aid to Greece or Turkey. A judgement was made that if Greece fell, Turkey would also. The Russians would then be able to control sea traffic from the Black Sea into the Mediterranean. Truman announced immediate aid to both Greece and Turkey, choice (A), to strengthen their governments and fight off the Communists. Choice (E) is irrelevant. It did not become an independent nation until 1960 when the British turned over the government.

23. **The correct answer is (C).** Made up of five, and after 1722 six, nations (Mohawk, Oneida, Onondaga, Cayuga, Seneca, and, later, Tuscarora), the Iroquois were members of the Iroquoian linguistic group and were able to unite because of a common language, common traditions, and a common enemy. They were able to play one European enemy against another—the French against the British—to get weapons and to maintain their lands for more than 150 years. The Powhatan Confederacy, choice (A), was also a political union of some 30 groups under the leadership of Powhatan, but English weapons proved too powerful, and after Powhatan's death, the confederacy was not able to resist the encroaching English settlers. *Seminole,* choice (B), was the name given to the coalition that developed in Florida of Creeks escaping from British settlers in Georgia, fugitive slaves escaping from Southern slave owners, and native Appalachee. The coalition fought two Seminole wars, one against Andrew Jackson from 1817 to 1818, and the second from 1835 to 1842 that resulted in their forced removal to Indian Territory. Both the Pequots, choice (D), and the Wampanoag, choice (E), had been decisively defeated by English colonists in New England by 1675 and lost their lands, the latter in a bloody war known as Metacom's War.

Test-Taking Strategy

Absolute statements are usually incorrect.

24. **The correct answer is (B).** Perhaps the defining characteristics of the colonies was social mobility. Choice (A) is an example of an absolute statement; it is not reasonable to expect that there were no free blacks in any of the colonies, so choice (A) should be eliminated. Choice (C) is the opposite of the situation. Women were highly regarded for their contributions to the welfare and economic life of the colonies. Choice (D) is incorrect; even as late as the mid-1800s, there was no general belief in the need for universal education. Choice (E) is incorrect; by 1775, slightly less than half of the colonial population was English. The Middle Colonies had the greatest diversity.

Test-Taking Strategy

Chronology can help you eliminate some answers in this question.

25. **The correct answer is (C).** The Whiskey Rebellion, choice (A), did not occur until Washington's first term in office (Shays's Rebellion occurred under the government of the Articles). Pinckney's Treaty, choice (D), and the Treaty of Greenville, choice (E), also did not occur until Washington's administration. Choice (B) is incorrect because the central government under the Articles did not have the power to levy taxes.

26. **The correct answer is (D).** Choices (A), (B), (C), and (E) are consistent with a strict constructionist view of the Constitution and a philosophy of limited federal power. Buying new territory stretched Jefferson's idea of the constitutional power of the presidency.

27. **The correct answer is (C).** The factory system did not exist in the United States until the nineteenth century. Influenced by the themes of European Romanticism, choice (A), the artists and writers of the early republic set out to establish a national identity through their works. For example, James Fenimore Cooper in his novels and George Caleb Bingham and George Catlin in their paintings used Native Americans, frontier life, and nature as themes, choices (B) and (D). Writers like Washington Irving and Nathaniel Hawthorne drew on the colonial past for themes, choice (E).

Test-Taking Strategy

The key word is major.

28. **The correct answer is (B).** While choice (D) is true—the Knights did advocate arbitration over strikes—this is not the major difference between the two organizations. How they were organized was the basic or fundamental difference. Choice (A) is untrue; the Knights of Labor did accept African Americans, women, and immigrants as members. The AFL did not. Neither union was radical, making choice (C) incorrect. Both organizations worked for choice (E).

29. **The correct answer is (D).** The key words are *best be described.* Although nativists might agree with choice (A) and the Sacco and Vanzetti case, choice (C), probably added to interest in passing laws about immigration, the best—most inclusive—answer is choice (D). The law did more than close down the Gentlemen's Agreement that allowed some Japanese immigrants into the country, and it favored immigrants from Western and Northern Europe, making choice (B) incomplete and choice (E) incorrect.

Test-Taking Strategy

The key words are benefited *and* least.

30. **The correct answer is (B).** Nearly 60 percent of African Americans were tenant farmers and domestics. However, the Social Security Act excluded them, so the greatest inequality resulted from the SSA. AAA, choice (A), did not apply to tenant farmers. Choices (C) and (D) provided jobs, but African Americans were discriminated against in the kinds of jobs they were assigned and in the amount they were paid. NRA codes, choice (E), provided for lower wages for workers in the South, many of whom were African American.

31. **The correct answer is (E).** Railroads lost business to long-distance trucks and to passenger cars. Even though commuter trains, mainly in the Northeast, still carried people to work from the suburbs, the railroads operated at a great loss. By the 1960s, many had filed for bankruptcy. Choice (C), in combination with choice (A), allowed many to buy homes in subdivisions, such as Levittown.

32. **The correct answer is (B).**

33. **The correct answer is (B).** Unemployment insurance and worker's compensation are not included in FICA, so choices (A), (D), and (E) are incorrect. Medicaid, choice (C), is a joint federal-state program and not part of FICA.

34. **The correct answer is (E).** Both choices (C) and (E) are true, but choice (E) relates the Stamp Act to the larger picture of the steps leading to the Revolution. Choice (A) refers to the Townshend Acts. Choice (B) relates to the Sugar Act. Choice (D) was true of the Currency Act.

35. **The correct answer is (A).** *Common Sense,* written by Tom Paine, called upon colonists to declare independence from Great Britain and would most likely have won an audience among Patriots, choice (A), not Loyalists, choice (D). If you did not know this, chronology would have helped you eliminate choices (B), (C), and (E). Question 35 comes after a question on the colonial period and before one about foreign policy under George Washington; therefore, terms that refer to the immediate pre-Civil War and Civil War periods would be out of time sequence and incorrect.

36. **The correct answer is (E).** The XYZ Affair occurred during John Adams's administration when he sent John Marshall, Elbridge Gerry, and Charles Pinckney to France to negotiate disputes following Jay's Treaty. Three French agents demanded money loans and bribes before France would negotiate. Choice (A) opened the Mississippi to U.S. citizens and gave them the right of deposit at New Orleans. Choice (B) ended British occupation in the Old Northwest and arranged for payment of prewar debts. Washington issued choice (C) to keep the nation out of the European wars. Choice (D) ended the Native American wars in the Old Northwest and forced Native American nations to give up most of their land in the region.

37. **The correct answer is (A).** The Hartford Convention was called by New England Federalists who opposed the War of 1812 because it hurt trade. Choice (B) was an attempt at a colonial alliance to settle boundary disputes and for mutual defense, but it was marred by rivalries among the New England colonies. Choice (C) was called by seven colonies to seek the support of the Iroquois Confederacy but ended with a plan for colonial unity that was rejected by the colonial governments. Choice (D) was called to redress weaknesses in the Articles of Confederation and ended in the call for a convention to organize a new government. Choice (E) is the name of a group organized in 1905 and dedicated to improving the rights of African Americans.

38. **The correct answer is (C).** There are several clues in the reading: the years *1854* and *1855, New England, emigrants from Northern States, abettors of slavery,* and *Free-state party.* They all point to Kansas and the fight between the proslavery and antislavery forces who moved into Kansas to settle it before the territory was ready to request statehood. It might help you to know for other questions that the Emigrant Aid Society, an abolitionist organization in the

ANSWERS AND EXPLANATIONS

North, subsidized antislavery settlers. The town being described is Lawrence, Kansas, which was burned by proslavery forces. John Brown and his supporters retaliated by killing five proslavery men at Pottawatamie Creek.

Test-Taking Strategy

The key words are most damage.

39. The correct answer is (D). By the end of the war, only about 200 ships a year were able to run the blockade, whereas some 6,000 entered and left Southern ports before the war. The blockade cut off the sale of cotton to Great Britain and France and kept the Confederacy from resupplying. Choices (B), (C), and (E) did damage the economy but far less than choice (D), so choice (D) is the best answer. The capture of Richmond, choice (A), did not occur until the end of the war.

40. The correct answer is (A). This is from an article by Carnegie and states what has become known as the Gospel of Wealth. It is not consistent with the thinking of any of the other choices: Theodore Roosevelt, choice (B), who believed in "muscular Christianity"; Bryan, choice (C), who championed the cause of small farmers and silver miners; Douglass, choice (D), who worked for abolition; and Addams, choice (E), who worked for the betterment of poor urban immigrants.

41. The correct answer is (C). Choice (E) may confuse you, but large numbers of Mexican immigrants are a twentieth-century phenomenon, beginning during the Mexican Revolution of 1910–1920. Of the total 5.6 million Mexican immigrants between 1820 and 1997, more than 3.4 million immigrated between 1981 and 1997. Austro-Hungarians, choice (B), were the third-largest group, with Russians, choice (A), fourth, and Canadians, choice (D), eighth.

42. The correct answer is (B). Choice (E) can be eliminated immediately because the question asks about domestic policy, and the Camp David Accords dealt with Israel and Egypt. Choice (A) is incorrect because the "war on poverty" was Lyndon Johnson's major domestic program. Choice (C), the Peace Corps, is incorrect for two reasons; it was established during Kennedy's administration as part of his foreign, not domestic, policy. The integration of Little Rock High School occurred during Eisenhower's administration, not Carter's, so choice (D) is incorrect.

Test-Taking Strategy

The key words are most significant.

43. The correct answer is (A). Choices (B), (C), and (D) are incorrect. The French and Indian War indicates that the information in choice (B) is incorrect. The French Catholic missionaries, many of whom lost their lives, went among the Native Americans in an attempt to convert them. Choice (D) is incorrect because the French system of government was very similar to that of the Spanish colonies; neither was democratic. While choice (E) is true, it is not the major difference between the French and Spanish colonies in the Americas. The most significant difference is that the Spanish set up a vast colonial network of settlements divided into viceroyalties that stretched from deep into South America to as far north as California, whereas the

Peterson's ■ *SAT II Success: U.S. History*

39

www.petersons.com

French had a line of settlements strung from Canada and the Great Lakes to the Gulf of Mexico.

44. **The correct answer is (B).** Choice (D) is also based on economics but was a secondary effect of the Southern Colonies' need for cheap and plentiful labor. Choice (A) is incorrect; colonists found that enslaved Africans had several advantages over indentured servants. Africans could not escape by blending into the population, were not free when their term of indenture was over, and were well suited to the hot climate of the South. There also seemed to be an endless supply of Africans. Choice (E) is a rationalization that the English used to justify their enslavement of Africans. Choice (C) is an example of something a slave owner might say to justify slavery.

Test-Taking Strategy

Always look for visual clues to the meaning of cartoons and photographs.

45. **The correct answer is (D).** Opponents of Andrew Jackson referred to him as King Andrew, and this cartoon shows him dressed as a king, trampling on the Constitution and holding a paper marked "veto." The last two are clues that indicate that the cartoonist is taking issue with Jackson's veto of the charter for the Second Bank. Choice (A) is incorrect because the annexation of Texas did not come to a vote during Jackson's time in office. Choice (B) is incorrect because, although Jackson opposed the decision of the Supreme Court, no veto was involved. Jackson's actions in both choices (C) and (E) supported the Constitution, so they are incorrect.

46. **The correct answer is (D).** Choices (A), (B), and (C) were weaknesses of labor unions in this period but not the reason why labor was unaware of its power. Only later did workers discover that by banding together, they could force employers to improve working conditions, shorten working hours, and raise pay—all basic demands of later unions. Choice (E) is incorrect; the efforts of the women in the Lowell factories to unionize in the 1840s illustrates the opposite.

47. **The correct answer is (D).** The statement was written by Booker T. Washington as part of the *Atlanta Compromise.* The clue is the phrase "as much dignity in tilling a field." This should signal that Washington was the author because of his espousal of vocational education and labor versus the arts and sciences. Dunbar, choice (A), was a poet and writer who often wrote about African American rural life. Du Bois, choice (B), had views directly opposed to those of Washington. Hughes, choice (C), was a poet and writer who used the rhythm of African American music in his works. Ellison, choice (E), won the National Book Award for his novel *Invisible Man.*

48. **The correct answer is (B).** The question is about a group that worked for change sometime between the late nineteenth and early twentieth centuries. You can tell this because of the time frame for the question before it and the one after it, and because the amendment for the direct election of senators was ratified in 1913 and for women's suffrage in 1920. Since this is an *except* question, you are

looking for the choice that is not true. Choice (B) is the answer because there was no welfare program to reform in that period.

49. **The correct answer is (A).** Lewis's best-known works are *Babbit* and *Main Street.* Hemingway, choice (B), was a member of the "lost generation." Wharton, choice (C), wrote about New York society around the turn of the twentieth century. Stein, choice (D), was a writer of experimental prose and an expatriate. Hughes, choice (E), was a writer and poet of the Harlem Renaissance.

50. **The correct answer is (D).** To head off a march through Washington, D.C., by an estimated 50,000 African Americans, Roosevelt met with A. Philip Randolph, the head of the Brotherhood of Sleeping Car Porters, and agreed to establish the Fair Employment Practices Commission to ensure that African Americans were not discriminated against in defense industries. King, choice (A), was the head of the Southern Christian Leadership Conference in the 1950s and 1960s. Abernathy, choice (C), took King's place after his assassination. Garvey, choice (B), founded the Universal Negro Improvement Association and a "back-to-Africa" movement. Bethune, choice (E), headed the National Youth Administration under Roosevelt and was a member of his informal "Black Cabinet."

51. **The correct answer is (C).** Although the Walter-McCarran Immigration and Nationality Act removed the ban on immigrants from Asia, it continued the quota, or national preference system, which discriminated against non-Northern and non-Western Europeans.

52. **The correct answer is (D).** Choice (A) was usually used in factories. Choice (B) is used against strikers. Choice (C) is the Spanish word for strike. Choice (E) is a disagreement between unions over which union should represent workers in a company or in an industry.

53. **The correct answer is (B).** King James's charter included all the elements except choice (B). Although it was a commercial charter, it did include the stipulation to bring Christianity and civilization to the native peoples, choice (A), because religion was very much a part of seventeenth-century life. However, the concept of building a commonwealth based on the Bible, choice (B), was the founding principle of the Massachusetts Bay Colony. The first colonists in Jamestown spent so much time looking for precious metals, choice (C), that the colony almost died out—"the starving time"—and had it not been for help from the Powhatan Confederacy, it would have collapsed. It was many years before Europeans gave up the idea of finding a way through the North American continent rather than around it to reach Asia, choice (E).

54. **The correct answer is (D).** Choices (B) and (D) are both true, but choice (D) puts the Maryland Toleration Act in the larger context of colonial history and is, therefore, a better choice. Choices (A) and (C) are distracters because although it seems to make sense that toleration could apply to either indenture or emancipation, think about

Test-Taking Strategy

Knowing the time frame of the question will help you eliminate three of the answer choices.

Test-Taking Strategy

For not/except *questions, ask yourself if the answer is true. If it is, cross it off and go on.*

Test-Taking Strategy

The key word is significant.

this time in colonial history. Indenture for Africans was just beginning to be transformed into servitude for life, so choice (C) is illogical, and Maryland needed more workers, not fewer, so making it easier to end a term of indenture is also illogical. Choice (E) is incorrect.

55. **The correct answer is (A).** After the French and Indian War in 1763, choice (B), the French had no presence in North America until 1800. Much of the area held by France in 1754 was a Spanish possession between 1762 and 1800, when it was returned to France. Choices (C), (D), and (E) are incorrect because the United States of America replaced the British colonies along the Eastern seaboard after 1776.

56. **The correct answer is (E).** To answer this question correctly, you would have had to answer the previous question correctly. Then you would know that in 1764, the map would have looked different because the French lost their territory as a result of the French and Indian War, choice (E). For choice (A) to be correct, the year would have to be 1781 or later. For choice (C) to be correct, the year would have to be 1787 or later. For choice (D) to be correct, the year would have to be 1803 or later. Choice (B) is incorrect information.

57. **The correct answer is (B).** The Hudson River School, choice (A), was a style of mostly landscape painting that was influenced by romanticism. Nationalism, choice (C), influenced the choice of subjects of the arts and literature in the United States of the early to mid-nineteenth century. Deism, choice (D), is a belief in a Supreme Being. A religion of nature and a religious movement of the seventeenth and eighteenth centuries, it influenced some of the founders of the new nation, such as Thomas Jefferson. Choice (E) was a literary and artistic movement among African Americans in the 1920s.

58. **The correct answer is (B).** The Dred Scott decision stated that Congress did not have the power to determine whether a state could be slave or free, thus overturning choices (A) and (D) and upholding choice (C). It also called into question popular sovereignty, choice (E). Choice (B) is the answer and is also untrue because slaves codes had already forbidden the teaching of reading and writing to slaves.

59. **The correct answer is (C).** Choices (A), (C), and (D) are true, but choice (D) is an effect of choice (C), and choice (A) had been true for a long time before 1910. Choice (B) refers to a program in World War II to bring Mexicans to the United States for jobs as farm workers, not in defense plants. Choice (E) is incorrect.

60. **The correct answer is (C).** Choice (A) is incorrect. Farmers were moved off land, but it was marginally productive, so choice (B) was not controversial, nor was choice (D). The TVA did benefit large farmers, choice (E), to a greater degree than small farmers, many of whom were African American, but that did not cause much controversy. The use of TVA rates to measure the fairness of utility prices

nationwide was controversial because private utility owners claimed that the TVA was tax-supported and paid no corporate income tax, so it could afford to charge less.

61. **The correct answer is (D).** The NIRA was declared unconstitutional because the Supreme Court found that the Constitution gave the federal government the power to regulate interstate commerce but not all aspects of business. One provision of the law especially odious to employers was Section 7A, which gave employees the right to bargain collectively with their employers. Choice (A) provided work for youths between the ages of 18 and 25. They received food, clothing, shelter, and wages in exchange for outdoor work, such as building fire trails and planting trees. The WPA, choice (B), cooperated with local and state governments to provide workers for useful public works projects, such as building schools and roads. The three levels of government shared the cost and the administration of the program. The FHA, choice (C), still exists and helps people borrow money to buy homes. The NYA, choice (E), distributed money to needy students in exchange for performing work around their schools. The focus on the work programs was providing workers for "socially useful work" rather than "make-work" jobs. These programs kept young people from being unemployed and helped many of them continue their education.

Test-Taking Strategy

The key word is primarily.

62. **The correct answer is (B).** Choices (A), (B), (C), and (D) are all true of Williams' beliefs, but choice (B) challenged the basis upon which the commonwealth rested. While his other teachings may have offended the Puritan leaders, it was choice (B) that was the most dangerous to their authority. Choice (E) is incorrect.

63. **The correct answer is (C).** Don't be fooled by this question. It is not asking you for the greatest disparity between areas but within a single area. The population of choices (A), (B), and (E) were fairly homogeneous—poor white farmers. Colonial cities had economically diverse populations that ranged from wealthy merchants to homeless beggars. Choice (D) is contained in choice (C), so choice (C) is the better response.

Test-Taking Strategy

Always read the question carefully. Highlight important words.

64. **The correct answer is (D).** One clue is the use of the third person (*their*) in referring to the colonies. That eliminates choices (A) and (C); logic says that Franklin and Henry would have spoken in the first person. Choice (B) can be eliminated because Andros was removed after he antagonized the colonists of New England. Choice (E) was French, so he would not be speaking of "this kingdom." William Pitt the Elder spoke these words in defense of the colonies' rights.

65. **The correct answer is (D).** The key word is *significance.* Choice (E) is incorrect and the direct opposite of what occurred, so it can be eliminated immediately. Choices (A), (B), (C), and (D) are all true, but which is the most significant? Which had the greatest impact on the future of the nation? Choices (A) and (B) are linked and resulted in the creation of an undefended border between the

two nations. Choice (C) meant that the nation would not have to expend any resources in its early years trying to remain united, which is important. Choice (D), however, established the new United States as a power and ended any idea of reunion or domination by Great Britain. This is most significant for the long-term future of the nation.

Test-Taking Strategy

Check the time frame of the question and the answers. Knowing that this question is about the early to mid-nineteenth century will help you eliminate choices (B) and (D).

66. **The correct answer is (A).** This document asked that all rights of U.S. citizens be extended to women, including the right to vote. It resulted from the first women's rights conference at Seneca Falls, New York, in 1848. Choice (B) is the title of Betty Friedan's book of the 1960s that reignited the women's movement. Choice (C) is a famous speech by Sojourner Truth, a former slave, an abolitionist, and a women's rights activist. Choice (D) was the name of Frederick Douglass's newspaper, and choice (E) is the title of Helen Hunt Jackson's book, published in the late nineteenth century, about the abuses of U.S. Indian policy.

67. **The correct answer is (E).** All five choices are correct, but choice (E) is the most inclusive and, therefore, matches the key words.

Test-Taking Strategy

The key words are most significant.

68. **The correct answer is (C).** The legacy of William Howard Taft's "dollar diplomacy" was mistrust and suspicion of the U.S.'s motives toward Latin American nations. Choice (A) occurred before Taft's administration. The United States intervened in Nicaragua several times, including once during Taft's administration, but choice (B) is not broad enough to be significant. Choices (D) and (E) are incorrect.

69. **The correct answer is (C).** This is a cause-and-effect question. Choices (A), (B), (D), and (E) all contributed to the intolerance of the period while choice (C) was a result of it. Choices (A) and (E) were related in many Americans' minds. These people feared that the Bolshevik Revolution of 1917, which toppled the czar in Russia, would inspire the radicals in the United States to overthrow the government. A series of mail bombs thought to have been sent by radicals fueled suspicions. At the same time, labor unions organized a series of strikes in 1919 that resulted in violence. Choice (B) was used as an excuse to push through laws in 1921 and 1924 restricting immigration. Jews and Catholics were seen as clannish and divided in their loyalties, and their customs and traditions were unfamiliar and, therefore, seen as odd and potentially menacing, choice (D). Racism is another element of intolerance that could have been included in the list.

70. **The correct answer is (B).** The Gulf of Tonkin Resolution (I), which gave the president the authority to use "all necessary measures to repel any armed attack or to prevent further aggression," was passed in 1964. In 1965, President Johnson made the decision to commit ground troops to the war (IV). The Tet offensive (III) occurred in 1968, and in 1970, President Nixon sent troops into Cambodia (II).

71. **The correct answer is (D).** Containment theory, first used by Truman, stated that the United States should take an aggressive posture toward the Soviet Union, short of instigating a third world war. In time, the Soviet Union would become less belligerent or would change. The end of communism in Eastern Europe—and the Soviet Union—seems to have proven this theory. Choice (A) refers to the idea that if one country in Asia fell to communism, they all would. Choice (B) promised military and economic aid to nations in the Middle East and potential U.S. intervention against Communist aggression. Choice (C) provided aid to Turkey and Greece after World War II to fight off Communist takeovers. Choice (E) provided materials and financial aid to seventeen European countries to rebuild after World War II.

72. **The correct answer is (C).** Zenger published articles in his newspaper accusing the colonial governor of New York of election fraud, misappropriating public funds, and bribery. According to British libel law, it did not matter if the accusations were true. Zenger was indicted on the charge of seditious libel, but his lawyer argued that truth did matter and won Zenger's acquittal. Although British libel laws did not change, this case emboldened colonial newspapers to express opinions that were unpopular with the government and laid the foundation for freedom of press, as guaranteed in the U.S. Constitution.

73. **The correct answer is (B).** The debate over the Stamp Act in the colonies, the passage of the Declaratory Act stating that Parliament had the power and right to make laws for the colonies, and the passage of the Townshend Acts all revolved around the principle of virtual representation. Did Parliament have the right, based on virtual representation, to levy taxes on the colonists? Or did the principle of direct representation govern the situation and only the colonists could tax themselves? By passing the Townshend Acts, Parliament tried to negate the power of the purse, choice (A). Choices (C) and (D) are incorrect, and mercantilism, choice (D), would have been an indirect factor behind the debate because it underlay why Parliament wanted to control its colonies.

74. **The correct answer is (D).** Shays's Rebellion protested the high taxes after the Revolutionary War and the practice of confiscation and sale of farms to pay creditors. Choice (A) occurred on the frontier at the beginning of Washington's administration to protest a tax on whiskey. Choice (B) was an uprising by slaves in South Carolina in 1737. Choice (C) was written to protest the Alien and Sedition Acts and asserted the right of states to nullify federal laws. Choice (E) was the name given by Southerners to the high protective tariff of 1828.

75. **The correct answer is (E).** Suffrage for African Americans was never part of Lincoln's official plan for Reconstruction. Lincoln believed choice (D), while on the one hand, Charles Sumner

Test-Taking Strategy

The key words here are under the Articles of Confederation. *Knowing that, you could eliminate all the choices but (D).*

espoused the theory of state suicide, and on the other, Thaddeus Stevens advocated the theory of conquered provinces.

76. **The correct answer is (E).** Choice (E) relates to public accommodations. According to choice (A), African Americans had to pay a tax to vote; many did not have the money. Because African Americans' access to education was limited, choice (B) was discriminatory. Few owned property, making choice (C) discriminatory as well. Because the Fifteenth Amendment did not cover primary elections, African Americans were not always allowed to vote in them.

77. **The correct answer is (A).** The clues are *gold standard* as well as the high regard the speaker has for farms and the disdain for cities. The quotation is from William Jennings Bryan's speech at the 1896 Democratic convention. Choices (B), (C), and (D) would not have spoken against gold. Greenback Party members, choice (E), wanted paper money backed by neither gold nor silver.

78. **The correct answer is (C).** In order to win concessions from the Allies at the peace conference that would benefit American interests, Wilson agreed to choices (A) and (B). He also agreed to the division of Austria-Hungary, so choice (D) is incorrect. Wilson made his remarks, choice (E), after thirty-nine senators and senators-elect came out against the League of Nations; his remarks undoubtedly did not help, but they did not cause the rejection of the Treaty.

79. **The correct answer is (C).** John Foster Dulles is known for his "brinkmanship" foreign policy, his threat of "massive retaliation" against communism, and his articulation of the domino theory. If one nation in a region fell to communism, all would. Eisenhower, choice (A), under whom Dulles served, was more cautious. Albright, choice (D), as Secretary of State under Bill Clinton, is in the wrong time frame. Chamberlain, choice (E), also in the wrong time frame, was the opposite of Dulles and is known for his appeasement policy toward Hitler. Choice (B) is incorrect.

80. **The correct answer is (C).** From Reconstruction until Roosevelt, African Americans had traditionally voted the Republican ticket, the party of Lincoln. Southern small farmers, choice (B), had voted for Hoover in 1928 but returned to the Democratic Party under Roosevelt. Since the late 1800s, immigrants, choice (E), had traditionally voted for Democrats who ran the Northern big city political machines, choice (A).

81. **The correct answer is (C).** Truman signed the Executive Order in 1948, but by 1950, only the Air Force was desegregating its forces to any extent. It was not until the Korean War that the military began actively integrating its units.

82. **The correct answer is (D).** Choices (A), (B), (C), and (E) are all true of Nixon's actions in office. However, choice (A) had already been settled, and Nixon had agreed to pay back taxes. Choice (D) covers the information in choices (B), (C), and (E) and is, therefore, the most complete choice.

83. The correct answer is (A). While in any given year the colonies may have exported more to England than they imported from it, the data supports the generalization that the colonists bought more from England than they exported to it (5 out of 9 years and more than 2 million pounds sterling). Choices (B) and (D) are true statements about the mercantilist system, but they are irrelevant to the data on the table. Choice (C) is not borne out by the data on the table; in 1770, after the French and Indian War, exports were up, but imports decreased. Choice (E) is an incorrect reading of the data on the table.

84. The correct answer is (D). The Assumption Bill was part of Hamilton's plan to put the new nation on a strong financial basis. Madison was the primary adversary of assuming all state debts related to the war and of repaying the war bonds at full value because speculators had bought them at deep discounts from the original bondholders, so choice (E) is illogical. Choices (B) and (C) are not true, and Congress declined to consider Hamilton's tariff plan, choice (A).

85. The correct answer is (C). *Laissez-faire* capitalism opposes government intervention in economic affairs and was the opposite of what the Grange advocated. Choice (B) was an important victory because the Supreme Court ruled that public utilities like railroads and grain elevators had to submit to public regulation for the public good. The Grange recognized the importance of women, choice (E), to farm life and welcomed them into the movement.

86. The correct answer is (B). Oklahoma was opened to settlement in 1889, so choice (A) is incorrect. The shift, choice (D), had occurred as a result of the transfer in the U.S.'s economic base from farming to industry. Choices (C) and (E) are incorrect.

87. The correct answer is (D). Choices (B), (C), and (D) are all true, but choice (D) is the most inclusive of the three answers, so it is the best choice. Anti-Catholic prejudice had been apparent since the mid-1800s with nativist activities aimed at Catholic immigrants, so choice (A) is incorrect. Choice (E) is also incorrect.

88. The correct answer is (D). Hippies dropped out and started communes. Although this was not a major movement, it was emblematic of a rejection of the values of the previous generation that saw a dramatic rise in the standard of living. Dropping out went hand in hand with a distrust of authority, choice (E). Choice (C) may have confused you with the word *reemergence,* but after World War II, women retreated to the home, and the ideal family included father the breadwinner and mother the homemaker. Betty Friedan's *The Feminine Mystique,* published in 1963, challenged this ideal.

89. The correct answer is (A). Revenue sharing, begun in 1972 and ended in 1987, was a program of federal aid that gave states, and their cities, counties, and townships, a share of federal tax collections. The money returned to the states was huge, and there were few restrictions on how the states and their localities could spend it.

Choice (B) is the umbrella term for the various kinds of state and local aid that the federal government provides, so it is an illogical answer. With choice (D), there are a number of restrictions attached to how states and localities may spend the money. Choice (C) has fewer restrictions than choice (D) on how federal money aid may be spent but more than choice (A). Choice (E) is an economic policy.

90. **The correct answer is (A).** The trend since the early 1990s was one of rising employment and decreasing inflation until both were fairly steady. Since the late 1990s, the federal deficit has been shrinking, so choice (B) is incorrect. While choice (C) historically has been true, it was not true in the 1990s, so it is incorrect. Choices (D) and (E) are incorrect.

Chapter 1

STRATEGIES FOR MULTIPLE-CHOICE QUESTIONS

Study Strategy

Check the Practice Plan for Studying for the SAT II: U.S. History Test, *pp. 8–10.*

This chapter provides some basic information about the SAT II: U.S. History Test as well as strategies for answering the different types of questions. During your time in school, you have answered hundreds, probably thousands, of multiple-choice items. This SAT II Test is not that different, and like other tests, if you have studied and know some test-taking techniques, you can do well.

PRACTICE PLAN

Use the *Diagnostic Test* as a tool to improve your objective test-taking skills. Use the techniques explained in this chapter to practice answering the questions. Then correct your responses with the *Quick-Score Answers* provided for the test. If you do not understand why an answer is correct, refer to the explanations given after the *Quick-Score Answers.* It is generally a good idea to read the answer explanations to all the questions anyway, because you may find ideas or tips that will help you better analyze the answer choices to questions on the next *Practice Test* you take and on the real test. The answer explanations often have additional information about the topic that could come in handy in answering a future question.

After you have finished reviewing all the answers, ask yourself what your weak areas are and what you can do to improve, not just in test-taking techniques but in your knowledge of particular historical eras. Are there some periods that you need to spend time brushing up on? Review the strategies in this chapter and then study Chapters 2 through 9, which offer a brief review of U.S. history. Then try taking *Practice Test 1.*

BASIC INFORMATION ABOUT THE TEST

FAST FACTS

Test-Taking Strategy

Be sure to take a watch with you on test day so you can pace yourself. Don't use the alarm.

1. The SAT II: U.S. History Test consists of ninety to ninety-five multiple-choice questions. There are five possible answer choices for each question.
2. You will have 60 minutes to answer the questions.
3. You will receive 1 point for each correct answer. Points are not deducted for questions that you leave blank. If you answer

incorrectly, a quarter of a point is subtracted. This is the guessing penalty.

4. Topics in political, economic, social, intellectual, and cultural history as well as foreign policy are used as the basis for questions. Although the test covers U.S. history from the First Americans to the present, there are fewer questions on the early period:

- 20 percent from the First Americans through 1789,
- 40 percent from 1790 to 1898, and
- 40 percent from 1899 to the present.

Don't expect much on the most recent ten years though. This is not a current events test.

5. The College Board breaks down its content coverage into the following categories:

- 32–36 percent on political history,
- 18–22 percent on social history,
- 18–20 percent on economic history,
- 13–17 percent on foreign policy,
- 10–12 percent on cultural and intellectual history.

Within these historical periods and categories, the test writers will also ask you about social science concepts, methods, and generalizations. Because history in reality does not break down into neat categories, you will find that any given question may straddle several categories.

6. There are four question types: visuals (cartoons, maps, charts, graphs, and photographs), short quotations, and either statements to complete or questions to answer. The majority of items will be of the basic statement or question type. The graphics questions are straightforward, read-and-interpret questions. Occasionally, you may find an additional question related to the visual that asks for an answer requiring knowledge other than what is shown on the graphic.

7. According to the College Board, the SAT II: U.S. History Test assesses four types of knowledge and abilities:

- recall of basic information, such as facts, terms, concepts, and generalizations;
- analysis and interpretation of visuals, such as cartoons, maps, charts, graphs, and photographs;
- relating of ideas to given data; and
- evaluation of data based on "internal evidence . . . or external criteria."

Test-Taking Strategy

Working out a plan to pace yourself is important.

8. The questions in the beginning of the test tend to be easier, and questions become more difficult as you progress through the test.

9. The questions are not randomly ordered. They are clustered in groups of perhaps ten questions that move from the earliest period through the twentieth century. That is, in every block of ten or so questions you will notice a progression from the Pre-Columbian or colonial periods to the mid- to late twentieth century, and then in the next block, the questions will jump back to the early period.

10. You can answer some combination of answers correctly and leave some questions blank and still get a good score.

It is important to remember these last three facts. They mean (1) that you should try to answer as many of the questions at the beginning of the test as possible, (2) that you can use chronological order to help you answer questions, and (3) that you do not have to answer all the questions.

EDUCATED GUESSING

One technique that is especially helpful is "educated guessing." Use this strategy when you do not know the correct answer immediately, but you do know something about the content of the question and can eliminate at least one answer choice.

- First, ignore answers that are absolutely wrong.
- Eliminate choices in which part of the answer is incorrect.
- Discard choices that are illogical or unrelated to the subject.
- Check the time period of the question and of the answer choices. Discard any answers that don't fit.
- Check the key words in the question again.
- Reread remaining answers to discover which seems most correct.
- Choose the answer that feels right. Trust yourself. Your subconscious usually will guide you to the correct choice. Do not argue with yourself.

You are probably thinking about the quarter-point deduction for an incorrect answer, and you are wondering if taking a chance is worth the possible point loss. Recognize that if you use this strategy, your chances of scoring higher are excellent. You are not guessing, but making an "educated guess." You will have to answer four questions wrong to lose a single point. If you have an idea about which choice is correct, act on it. Even the College Board suggests that you guess as long as you can eliminate some answer choices as wrong.

PACING

Test-Taking Strategy

In skipping questions, be sure to skip their answer ovals on the answer sheet.

Answering ninety to ninety-five questions in 60 minutes may seem like running a marathon. It is important to remember that you may not be able to answer all the questions, even with educated guessing. But you should pace yourself so you can read all the questions, answer the easier ones, and leave the harder ones to return to.

Because the questions at the beginning of the test tend to be easier, you might plan to spend more time on those questions and less time on the final questions. For example, rather than allotting yourself 45 seconds to read and answer each question, think about dividing your 60 minutes into 15-minute or 20-minute segments. Then divide up the questions so that you tackle more in the first 15 or 20 minutes when you are fresh than in the last 15 or 20 minutes when you are tired and the questions are more difficult. Or if you start slowly, surge in the middle, and lag at the end, you might try to pace yourself to answer more questions in the middle of the test. One of the benefits of taking the *Diagnostic* and *Practice Tests* in this book is that you can devise a pacing schedule that fits how you work.

In developing your plan, however, understand that when we say you may be working on fifteen questions in the final 15 minutes, we do not necessarily mean that you are doing the last fifteen questions on the test in those final 15 minutes. We mean that you are working on the last fifteen questions that are the most difficult for you. You should skip truly difficult questions on your first pass through of the test rather than spend time trying to figure them out. Even the College Board suggests this.

Here are some other suggestions to help you pace yourself:

Test-Taking Strategy

Don't make marks on the answer sheet except to fill in answer ovals. Stray marks confuse the machine that scores the tests.

- Don't spend too much time on a difficult question.

- If you read a question and the content and none of the answer choices seem familiar, skip the question. Put an "X" next to it in the test booklet, and be sure you skip the answer oval.

- If you read a question and don't know the answer immediately, but at least one of the answer choices seems wrong, try the steps listed above on page 51 for making an educated guess. If you can't immediately eliminate any other answer choices, don't spend any more time on it. Put a check (✔) next to it and move on, skipping the answer oval for the question.

- When you have read through the entire test and answered what you can immediately or with a few seconds' thought, go back first to the questions marked with a check and try those again. If you still have time, try the questions you marked with an X.

One word of advice: Don't worry if a question at the beginning of the test seems difficult to you. Although we say those questions tend to be easier, all things are relative. What may be a snap question for some students because the subject was a favorite of their teacher's may be a blank to other students because their class never got past World War II.

ANALYZING QUESTIONS

The SAT II: U.S. History Test assesses your understanding of content and your ability to manipulate content. That means how well you interpret data, draw conclusions, evaluate accuracy, assess the consistency among positions, and so on—the kinds of skills that you have learned and use in social studies classes.

As you've just read, the test assesses four types of knowledge and abilities and uses four question types to do this. The following examples illustrate how the test writers mix and match question types and content to assess what you know and can do.

RECALL QUESTIONS

Some questions simply ask for straight recall of information. They want to know what facts, terms, concepts, and generalizations you are able to recall. These questions may be in the form of a straightforward question or sentence completion, such as the following:

Which of the following was true of the Emancipation Proclamation of 1863?

(A) It immediately freed slaves in Southern states or parts of Southern states under Union occupation.

(B) It freed slaves in Southern states still at war with the Union on January 1, 1864.

(C) It freed slaves only in the border states.

(D) It guaranteed freedom for slaves who escaped behind the Union lines.

(E) It freed all enslaved blacks when the war ended.

The correct answer is (B). This question asks you to look for what is true in the following list. The Emancipation Proclamation did not affect slaves in Southern states or parts of Southern states occupied by the Union, choice (A). Choice (C) is wrong because it was very important that the border states stay in the Union; freeing their slaves might have driven them out. The Confiscation Act freed slaves who escaped behind the Union lines, so choice (D) is wrong. The Thirteenth Amendment ended slavery, so choice (E) is incorrect. The Emancipation Proclamation did decree that slaves in states still at war with the Union on January 1, 1864 would be free. It was a proclamation without any force, but it did help to sway the British away from supporting the South.

A recall question may also use a qualifier such as NOT, LEAST, or EXCEPT, such as the following:

All of the following spurred European interest in exploration EXCEPT

(A) the rise of nation-states

(B) the Renaissance

(C) development of a market for luxury goods from Asia

(D) technological advances, such as the printing press and the astrolabe

(E) development of African slavery as a business

Test-Taking Strategy

If you did not immediately know the answer to either question, it is possible that you could make an educated guess by eliminating answer choices.

Both of these questions ask you to recall certain information that you have learned. The second question has a twist. It wants the wrong answer, that is, it wants you to select the choice that was not responsible for driving European interest in world exploration. To answer questions like this that ask you to find the answer choice that does not belong, ask yourself if the answer choice is correct in relation to the content. If it is, cross it off, and try the next response. Keep going until you find a response that is not true in relation to the content of the question. Similar questions may use key words such as NOT and LEAST.

The correct answer is choice (E). If you were not sure whether the other choices were correct, you could at least determine that choice (E) is incorrect because the trans-Atlantic slave trade was a result of explorations, not a motivating factor.

Recall questions can also be based on visuals.

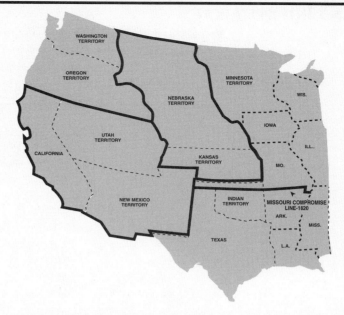

The Compromise of 1850 affected which of the following?

(A) California

(B) California and the Utah and New Mexico Territories

(C) Kansas and Nebraska Territories

(D) Minnesota Territory

(E) Oregon and Washington Territories

Test-Taking Strategy

Knowing at least the area of the Louisiana Territory would have helped you eliminate at least two choices in this question if you needed to make an educated guess.

The correct answer is choice (B). The Compromise of 1850 affected all the territory received from Mexico at the end of the Mexican War. Choice (A) is only partially correct. Choice (C) and much of choice (D) were part of the Louisiana Territory. Washington Territory was created from part of the Oregon Territory, choice (E), after the Treaty of 1846 fixed the border with Canada.

ANALYSIS AND INTERPRETATION

Visuals can also be the basis of questions that ask you to analyze and interpret data. The visuals may be cartoons, maps, charts, graphs, or photographs. The following question asks you to analyze data and then recall information in order to answer it.

**Sales of U.S. Passenger
Cars, 1915 and 1955**
(in millions)

1915	10
1920	18
1925	38
1930	27
1935	32
1940	38
1945	1
1950	60
1955	78

Based on the data in this table, one might conclude that the number of cars sold in 1930 was a consequence of

(A) the mobilization of the automobile industry to fight World War II

(B) a decrease in the price of steel

(C) the dumping of Japanese cars in the U.S. market

(D) the worsening economic depression in the United States

(E) a federally regulated effort to help the auto industry

The correct answer is choice (D). First, you need to read the data and decide what it shows—a downturn in car sales. Then you need to look for an answer choice that gives a negative cause. If you did not immediately connect 1930 with the depression, choice (D), you could try educated guessing and eliminate choices. Choice (E) could be eliminated, because it never happened and because it would have, or should have, had a positive effect on car sales by lowering the cost. The same two reasons eliminate choice (B). Choices (A) and (C) are negative causes, but the United States did not enter World War II until 1941 and dumping is a later twentieth century international market phenomenon. Thinking about time period would have helped you eliminate both of these answer choices.

Some questions may ask you not only to analyze information but also to make inferences about it. Questions based on quotations are often used to test this kind of ability.

"The autumn of 1854 witnessed the erection of the first log-huts . . . by a few families of New England settlers. During the year 1855 its population increased rapidly, chiefly by the arrival of emigrants from the Northern States. Its log-hut existence gave way to a more advanced stage, . . . and the growing prosperity . . . early began to excite the jealousy of the abettors of slavery. Viewed as the stronghold of the Free-state party, it was made the point of attack . . ."

The description above was most probably written about

(A) the settling of Missouri

(B) the settling on the frontier of Irish laborers who had left New England mill towns

(C) the fight over the admission of Kansas as free or slave state

(D) a settlement of New Englanders in the South

(E) a settlement of Republicans in the South

Test-Taking Strategy

Be sure to highlight the key words in the questions in some way—underline, circle, bracket. Be sure you understand what the question is asking you.

This question from the *Diagnostic Test* is a good example of how you can use key words as guides in analyzing and interpreting material. There are several clues in the reading to help you determine that the correct answer is (C) if you did not know the answer immediately: the years *1854* and *1855, New England, emigrants from Northern States, abettors of slavery, and Free-state party.* They all point to Kansas and the fight between the proslavery and antislavery forces who moved into Kansas to settle it before the territory was ready to request statehood.

RELATING IDEAS TO GIVEN DATA

According to the College Board, these questions ask you to relate "hypotheses, concepts, principles, or generalizations to given data." You may be given a specific piece of information and asked for the concept or principle it describes or vice versa. For example, you might be asked the following:

Which of the following was Theodore Roosevelt's most significant use of his "big stick" policy?

(A) The United States established a protectorate in Cuba after the Spanish-American War.

(B) The United States sent marines to occupy Veracruz and prevent President Huerta from receiving weapons from Germany.

(C) Roosevelt legitimized the "big stick" policy by issuing the Good Neighbor Policy toward Latin America.

(D) The United States supported Panamanian rebels in their revolt against Colombia.

(E) The United States intervened in the internal affairs of the Dominican Republic when that nation could not repay its foreign debts.

The question stem provides the concept, Roosevelt's "big stick" policy, and the answer choices provide what may be examples for you to choose an answer from. Choices (A), (D), and (E) state correct information about Roosevelt and his foreign policy, but choice (D) is the best answer. Choice (A) refers to the Platt Amendment, choice (D) to the establishment of Panama, and choice (E) to a situation that caused Roosevelt to use the Roosevelt Corollary to the Monroe Doctrine for the first time. Of the three, the most significant effect in the long-term history of the United States and the world was the assigning to the United States of the right to build a canal across the isthmus of Panama, so choice (D) is the best answer. Choice (B) is an action of the President Wilson. Choice (C) is only partially correct. Theodore Roosevelt legitimized the "big stick" policy through the Roosevelt Corollary, while it was Franklin Roosevelt who adopted the Good Neighbor Policy toward Latin America.

The question could be reversed so that the specific is presented in the question stem and the answer choices provide concepts, principles, or generalizations.

Theodore Roosevelt's support of the Panamanian rebels in their revolt against Colombia is an example of his use of

(A) the Good Neighbor Policy

(B) the Roosevelt Corollary

(C) Alliance for Progress

(D) his policy of the "big stick"

(E) Pan-Americanism

You already know that the correct answer is choice (D). Choice (A) is a policy of Franklin Roosevelt; choice (B) is the way Theodore

Roosevelt legitimized his "big stick" foreign policy; choice (C) refers to Latin American policy under John F. Kennedy; and Pan-American-ism was a policy of Secretary of State James G. Blaine under President Benjamin Henry Harrison that resulted in the first Inter-American Conference in 1889.

EVALUATION OF DATA

There are not many of this type of question on the test. The question presents data and asks you to evaluate their validity for a specific purpose. The answer choices ask you to use either internal evidence, such as accuracy and logical consistency, to assess the information or external criteria, such as accepted historical scholarship.

In doing research for a book about working conditions in the textile mills in Lowell, Massachusetts, which of the following would be most useful?

(A) A diary of a Lowell factory "girl"
(B) Newspaper accounts of the activities of the Lowell Female Labor Reform Movement
(C) U.S. Census data from 1830 and 1840 for Lowell
(D) Account books from the Lowell textile mills
(E) A tour of one of the reconstructed mills

This question asks you to think like a historian and decide what kinds of primary and secondary resource material you would need for your research. Primary research is always preferable to secondary sources, so although a tour of the mill would be interesting, it would not tell you in the words of a Lowell "girl" what it was like to work there. Choice (A) would give you the words of only one worker, while choice (B) would give you the response of many women to the poor working conditions. Choice (B) is the best answer. Choice (C) would not address working conditions nor would choice (D).

A question that requires you to consider the consistency of information might read like the following:

Any discussion of the events that led to the Civil War would have to include the

(A) Wilmot Proviso, the Missouri Compromise, and the Tariff of Abominations

(B) Wilmot Proviso, the Compromise of 1850, and the National Road

(C) Compromise of 1850, the Missouri Compromise, and Fort Laramie Treaty

(D) Missouri Compromise, the Virginia Resolves, and the Ordinance of Nullification

(E) Kentucky and Virginia Resolutions, the Tariff of Abominations, and the Ordinance of Nullification

Test-Taking Strategy

All parts of an answer must be correct. If part of an answer is incorrect, the whole answer is incorrect—and a quarter-point deduction.

All the elements in choice (A) are events that added to the growing animosity between North and South and led to the Civil War. In choice (B), while the controversy over the National Road was an example of sectional conflict, it was not a causal factor of the Civil War. In choice (C), the Fort Laramie Treaty, which promised the Native Americans $50,000 a year for 50 years in exchange for safe passage for settlers, is incorrect. In choice (D), the Virginia Resolves were passed before the Revolutionary War to protest Great Britain's policy of taxation without representation. In choice (E), the Kentucky and Virginia Resolutions are incorrect; they were passed to protest the Alien and Sedition Acts of 1798.

In the end, knowing the type of question you are being asked is less important than paying attention to what the question is asking you. Circle, underline, or bracket the key words in the question. Use them to guide you to the correct answer.

ATTACKING THE QUESTIONS: PRACTICAL ADVICE

When you take the SAT II: U.S. History Test, you will want to have every advantage possible. Of course, the ideal is to know the correct answer as soon as you read the question and the answer choices, but that does not always happen. Here are some methods to help you score well.

1. Read the question carefully. Circle, underline, or bracket key words and phrases. You will find words in the question prompts such as: *significant; direct result of, consequence of; true, correct; most characteristic of, best known for, best describes; primarily, primary reason, primary purpose; most influential; most accurately characterizes*. These are qualifiers or descriptors that clue you to what you should be looking for in the answer choices.

A word like *significant* means you should be looking for why something is important in the larger context of U.S. history. Words like *best describes* or *most characteristic of* are asking you to analyze the information and come up with an opinion based on facts. In both instances, one or more of the answer choices may be correct; you need to look for the one that is most inclusive, giving the broadest view of the subject.

2. Knowing that the questions are in chronological order can help you to eliminate answers that do not make sense for the period. For example, identifying the Wilmot Proviso as having happened in the first half of the nineteenth century can help you eliminate any answers that refer to any other period.

3. Most of the questions are straightforward, but you may find some that use qualifiers such as *not/except, inconsistent,* or *incorrect.* For these questions, read each answer and ask yourself if it is true about the subject of the question. If it is, cross it out, and go to the next answer. You are looking for the choice that is **not** true.

4. Be sure to use educated guessing if you know something about the content of the question and can eliminate one or more answer choices.

PRACTICING

Study Strategy

Check the Practice Plan for Studying for the SAT II: U.S. History Test, *pp. 8-10.*

Study Strategy

Read all the explanations. The reasoning involved and the additional historical information may help you with questions on the real test.

Read and answer *Practice Set 1* on the next page. Jot down your answers to the questions in the margin or on a separate sheet of paper. If you do not understand a question, you may check the explanation immediately. You may refer to the answers question by question, or you may wish to score the entire set at one time. Either is acceptable.

Follow the same procedure with *Practice Sets 2* and *3*. You might want to complete *Practice Set 2* and correct the answers before you try *Practice Set 3*. That way, you will have another chance to work on any specific areas of weakness.

Practice Set 1

1. The significance of the Massachusetts Bay Company was its

   (A) charter as a joint-stock company
   (B) establishment of a flourishing colony
   (C) transformation from a trading company into a commonwealth
   (D) limitation on the number of men who could serve in the General Court
   (E) merger with Plymouth Colony in 1691

2. The Virginia Resolves are significant because

   (A) they were passed to protest the Stamp Act
   (B) they were based on the argument that the colonies could not be taxed by Parliament because they had no representation in Parliament
   (C) they laid the groundwork for Virginia's claim to western lands
   (D) in passing them, the Virginia legislature seceded from the Union
   (E) in passing them, Virginia agreed to Congressional Reconstruction

3. Elizabeth Cady Stanton is most closely associated with which area of social reform in the nineteenth century?

   (A) abolition
   (B) the temperance movement
   (C) universal education
   (D) women's rights
   (E) prison reform

4. The direct cause of Congress's vote to impeach Andrew Johnson was

   (A) his opposition to Congressional Reconstruction
   (B) his opposition to the Fifteenth Amendment
   (C) corruption during his administration
   (D) his violation of the Tenure of Office Act
   (E) his veto of the Civil Rights Act of 1866

5. "I had opportunity to observe closely the operation of two powerful forces that were at work on the Negro's status—the exodus and the war. Negroes migrating to the North in great numbers, and I observed the anomaly of a premium being put on this element of the population that had generally been regarded as a burden and a handicap to the South."

   The above was most probably written about

   (A) contraband going behind the Union lines in the Civil War
   (B) movement of blacks to Northern cities during the Vietnam War
   (C) exodusters
   (D) migration of African Americans in the 1890s
   (E) Great Migration of 1915–1930

Explanation of Answers for Practice Set 1

QUICK-SCORE ANSWERS	
1. C	4. D
2. B	5. E
3. D	

1. **The correct answer is (C).** The key word here is *significance*. When you see this word, ask yourself what the significance is of this event or person to the development of U.S. history. Massachusetts is not particularly significant in terms of choices (A) and (B) because the Virginia Company was also a joint-stock company, and for the most part, all the English colonies flourished except for Plymouth, which did merge with Massachusetts Bay, choice (E). But keep looking because although important, choice (E) is not particularly significant in a larger sense. That leaves choices (C) and (D). Considering the development of the colonies, would limiting participation in government be significant, or its opposite, insignificant? The transformation of Massachusetts Bay from a trading company into a commonwealth made it the first self-governing political unit in what would be the United States.

2. **The correct answer is (B).** The key word here is *significant*. Choice (A) is true, but the meaning of the Virginia Resolves in the larger context of U.S. history is choice (B). They established the argument of "no taxation without representation" that became a rallying cry for the Revolution. Choices (C), (D), and (E) are incorrect. You could have eliminated choices (D) and (E) by checking for the time frame of the question. It comes after a question about exploration and before one on the mid-nineteenth century.

3. **The correct answer is (D).** The key words here are *most closely*. Stanton was involved in the abolition movement, choice (A), but she is best known for organizing the Seneca Falls women's rights conference in 1848 and her work for women's suffrage. The woman most closely associated with temperance, choice (B), is Frances Willard, who served from 1879 to 1898 as the president of the Women's Christian Temperance Association. Horace Mann is considered a pioneer in the fight for universal education, choice (C). Dorothea Dix is known for her work on prison and asylum reform, choice (E).

Test-Taking Strategy

Read the question stem carefully. Circle the key words so you know clearly what you are looking for.

4. **The correct answer is (D).** The key words are *direct cause.* His enemies in Congress hated Johnson for choices (A) and (E), but his impeachment hearings directly resulted from choice (D), his firing of Edwin Stanton, his secretary of state. Choice (B) is incorrect because it was the Fourteenth Amendment that he opposed; the Fifteenth Amendment was not ratified until after his administration. Choice (C) was not an issue in his administration, but in that of his successor, Ullysses S. Grant.

5. **The correct answer is (E).** The word *war* is one clue, as is the phrase "the anomaly of a premium." The word *war* will help you eliminate choice (D). Although the United States did fight the Spanish-American War in the 1890s, the war lasted only three months, not long enough to create an economy that would need additional workers. The time frame of the questions in this group will help you eliminate choice (A). Question 4 is about Andrew Johnson's impeachment, so an answer about the Civil War for question 5 cannot be correct. (Contraband was the name given to slaves who escaped behind the Union lines.) You might think exodusters, choice (C), is correct, because the quotation uses the word *exodus,* but the exodusters moved west, not north, shortly after the Civil War. The phrase about a premium on African Americans indicates that they were in demand; this would equate with the need for workers in the North as the nation geared up for World War I, choice (E). No similar movement occurred during the Vietnam War because so many African Americans already lived in the North, choice (B). Don't be confused by the Great Migration that brought some 20,000 Puritans to Massachusetts Bay.

Practice Set 2

1. The British reaction to the Boston Tea Party involved all of the following EXCEPT

   (A) passage of the Massachusetts Bay Regulating Act
   (B) Edmund Burke's warning against blaming all Americans for the acts of some
   (C) the Boston Massacre
   (D) passage of the Boston Port Act
   (E) suspension of the Massachusetts legislature

2. Andrew Jackson's intention in issuing the Specie Circular was to

   (A) halt land speculation and inflation
   (B) destroy the Second Bank of the United States
   (C) shift the blame for the Panic of 1837 to Nicholas Biddle
   (D) ensure that the federal government withdrew its deposits from state banks
   (E) remove government controls over speculation and inflation

3. *Plessy* v. *Ferguson* established

   (A) the scope of presidential war powers
   (B) the principle of judicial review
   (C) the principle of implied powers in the Constitution
   (D) Congress's right to regulate interstate commerce
   (E) the principle of separate but equal

4. The major difference between Booker T. Washington's views and W.E.B. Du Bois's views was Du Bois's

   (A) emphasis on vocational training for African Americans
   (B) emphasis on a liberal arts education for African Americans
   (C) emphasis on the right of African Americans to demand whatever education they needed to gain full equality
   (D) support for the Niagara Movement
   (E) emphasis on continuing protests against injustice and appeals to black pride

5. Roosevelt's policy of "pump priming" during the depression meant

   (A) raising tariffs to protect American manufacturers and farmers
   (B) increasing the supply of goods and lowering taxes
   (C) increasing federal spending to stimulate the economy
   (D) stagflation
   (E) an increase in wages annually if the general level of prices in the economy rose above a certain level

Explanation of Answers for Practice Set 2

QUICK-SCORE ANSWERS	
1. C	4. C
2. A	5. C
3. E	

Review Strategy

This is a not/except *question. Ask yourself if each answer is a correct response to the question. If it is, cross it out and go on to the next answer.*

1. **The correct answer is (C).** If you did not remember that the Boston Massacre preceded the Tea Party, you could try eliminating answers. The British reacted to the Tea Party by passing the Coercive Acts, which the colonists called the Intolerable Acts. Choice (A), also known as the Massachusetts Government Act, and choices (D) and (E) are elements of those laws. The Boston Tea Party caused even some of the colonists' supporters in Parliament to speak out against the colonists, but in so doing, Edmund Burke also warned his fellow Englishmen about the dangers ahead if they pursued war with the colonies, choice (B).

2. **The correct answer is (A).** All these answers have some information that is relevant to Andrew Jackson's terms in office, so you need to read each one carefully. Jackson did set out to destroy the Second Bank, choice (B), of which Nicholas Biddle was president, first by vetoing the renewal of its charter and then by removing federal deposits from it. There was a Panic of 1837, but Martin Van Buren was president by then, choice (C). Jackson had the federal government withdraw its money not from state banks but from the national bank, choice (D); he then had the money deposited in state banks, known as "pet banks." Jackson's intent in destroying the Second Bank was to make the federal government less powerful. He unwittingly accomplished choice (E) and set the groundwork for the Panic of 1837. His intention, however, had been to halt land speculation and inflation, choice (A), by requiring that public land be paid for in gold or silver.

3. **The correct answer is (E).** You may think that choice (A) refers to the Presidential War Powers Act of 1973, but this is law, not a Supreme Court decision. *Marbury* v. *Madison* established choice (B). *McCulloch* v. *Maryland* established choice (C). Congress's right to regulate interstate commerce was set forth in *Gibbons* v. *Ogden*.

4. **The correct answer is (C).** The question asks for the *major* difference between Washington and Du Bois, so you need to look for the most inclusive correct answer. Choice (A) is incorrect because that was Washington's position. Choices (B), (C), (D), and (E) are all things that Du Bois supported in contrast to Washington, but choices (B) and (E) are elements of choice (C), so choice (C) is the best choice.

5. **The correct answer is (C).** The objective of deficit spending is to create jobs. With greater employment, workers will have more money to spend. This stimulates demand, thus increasing production that creates even more jobs. It was the theory behind Roosevelt's economic policy of "priming the pump." Many Democratic presidents since Roosevelt have followed it. Choice (B) is the definition of supply-side economics, the theory behind Ronald Reagan's economic policy; it states that by giving people more money, they will increase their savings and their purchasing power, thereby generating more economic activity. Stagflation, choice (D), is a condition of the economy in which inflation combines with low economic activity; it was the prevailing economic condition of the 1970s. Choice (E) is the definition of cost-of-living adjustment, which is also found in some government programs, such as Social Security. Choice (A) is a definition of the policy known as protectionism.

Practice Set 3

1. The Virginia and Kentucky Resolutions rest on the argument that the judge of the constitutionality of a law passed by Congress is

   (A) the Supreme Court
   (B) Congress
   (C) state legislatures
   (D) popular sovereignty
   (E) presidential veto

2. The "Solid South" came apart in the election of

   (A) 1912
   (B) 1920
   (C) 1928
   (D) 1932
   (E) 1936

Questions 3–5 refer to the following map.

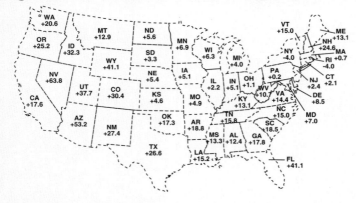

3. According to the map, which two Northeast states were the only states to lose population between 1970 and 1980?

   (A) New York and Pennsylvania
   (B) Massachusetts and Rhode Island
   (C) New York and Rhode Island
   (D) Pennsylvania and Rhode Island
   (E) Massachusetts and Pennsylvania

4. Which region of the 48 contiguous states had the greatest percentage increase in population between 1970 and 1980?

   (A) New England
   (B) Mid-Atlantic
   (C) Midwest
   (D) Southeast
   (E) Southwest

5. Which of the following states experienced the greatest percentage increase in population between 1970 and 1980?

   (A) New Hampshire
   (B) Florida
   (C) Nevada
   (D) Arizona
   (E) Texas

Explanation of Answers for Practice Set 3

QUICK-SCORE ANSWERS	
1. C	4. E
2. C	5. C
3. C	

Test-Taking Strategy

Thinking about the time frame of a question can help you sort through the answer choices when you are not sure of the correct answer.

1. **The correct answer is (C).** Logic tips the scale toward choice (C) as the answer because these are state resolutions. Because the question is about the period of the early republic and these are Southern states, they would be trying to further states' rights and not the power of the president or of the Supreme Court. Therefore, logic indicates that choices (A) and (E) are incorrect. Popular sovereignty, choice (D), is a later development of the nineteenth century to solve the slavery question. Choice (B) does not make sense.

2. **The correct answer is (C).** The "Solid South" is a term used to refer to Southern politics after Reconstruction. In an effort to rid themselves of the Republican governments that were imposed during Radical Reconstruction, most Southern men joined the Democratic Party. In 1928, Herbert Hoover was able to break this Democratic hold over the South in his defeat of Al Smith. Although Smith lost the rural and small-town Southern vote, he attracted to the Democratic Party city dwellers, Catholics, immigrants, and the working class.

3. **The correct answer is (C).** Questions 3, 4, and 5 are straightforward questions that ask you to read the map and choose the correct answer based on what you see.

4. **The correct answer is (E).**

5. **The correct answer is (C).**

Chapter 2

REVIEWING THE COLONIAL PERIOD TO 1789

The following review of Native American peoples, European exploration and colonization, the expansion of the thirteen original English colonies, the movement toward independence, and the beginning of the new nation highlights key events and people. According to the College Board, approximately 20 percent of the SAT II: U.S. History Test is drawn from this period.

SECTION 1. DISCOVERY, SETTLEMENT, AND EXPANSION TO 1754

Review Strategy

See page 80 for the origins of slavery in the Americas.

The study of U.S. history is the study of the intertwining of many different strands of historical development. A point at which to begin is Europe in the sixteenth century. The rise of nation-states, religious upheavals, and economic developments led Europeans to seek riches, territories, and dominion outside Europe to bolster their power on the continent. In studying U.S. history, it is important to understand how and why these events interacted to create European colonies in the Americas. It is also possible to see in this early period the foundations of later developments in U.S. history: not only political developments, such as the beginnings of representative government, but also social and cultural developments such as the subjugation of Native Americans and the institutionalization of slavery.

FAST FACTS

The First Americans

- Experts estimate that when Columbus reached the Americas, some 1 to 2 million Native Americans lived north of Mexico in eight major culture areas in what is now the United States and Canada: Subarctic, Northwest Coast, California, Great Basin and Plateau, Plains, Southwest, Northeast Woodlands, and Southeast. Another 20 million lived in Mexico, and 30 million lived in South America. The First Americans probably came across a **land bridge** now covered by the Bering Strait some 15,000 to 30,000 years ago.
- Some 12,000 years ago, as the Ice Age animals began to disappear, people turned to hunting smaller game, fishing, and gathering

NATIVE AMERICANS OF THE UNITED STATES

CULTURE REGION	GENERAL GEOGRAPHICAL AREA	GENERAL CULTURAL CHARACTERISTICS	REPRESENTATIVE PEOPLES
Subarctic	Interior of present Alaska and Canada	Fishing and hunting	Tanama, Ingalik, Ahtena
Northwest Coast	Coastal plain from present California-Oregon border to about the current Canada-Alaska border	Fishing and hunting sea animals; some hunting of small game on land and food gathering; potlatch ceremony to display wealth	Tlingit, Chinook, Tillamook
California	Present state of California	Food gathering, especially acorns, and hunting and fishing; arts and crafts such as baskets	Pomo, Chumash, Yana
Great Basin and Plateau	Intermountain Basins and Plateaus in present states of Washington, Oregon, Idaho, Nevada, Utah, Colorado, Wyoming, Montana	**Basin culture:** Nomadic hunters and gathers moving in small bands of extended families; influence of Plains' peoples seen in adoption of the horse and buffalo hunting **Plateau culture:** Originally nomadic fishers and small game hunters and gatherers; influence of Plains' peoples seen as groups begin hunting buffalo on horseback	Shoshone, Nez Perce, Cheyenne
Plains	Center of the United States	Originally farmers and hunters; by 1700 almost every Plains nation has horses; begin to hunt buffalo on horseback; develop culture traits that Americans come to think of as "Indian," such as tipis	Kiowa, Pawnee, Sioux
Southwest	Present Southwestern United States and parts of Southeastern California, Western Texas, Southern Nevada, Utah, and Colorado	Early sedentary farming cultures: Mogollon, Hohokam, Anasazi (cliff dwellers); later peoples called *Pueblos* by the Spanish because they live in small villages; weavers, basket makers, and potters	Apache, Pima, Zuni

NATIVE AMERICANS OF THE UNITED STATES

CULTURE REGION	GENERAL GEOGRAPHICAL AREA	GENERAL CULTURAL CHARACTERISTICS	REPRESENTATIVE PEOPLES
Northeast Woodlands	From the Mississippi east to the Atlantic Ocean and as far south as South Carolina, Tennessee, and Arkansas	Early peoples known as Mound Builders: Adena, Hopewell; sedentary farmers who build large ceremonial mounds; evidence of a class system and some hierarchical government; trading network; arts and crafts for trade Also hunters and farmers; villages, some fortified; governed by village councils	Iroquois, Shawnee, Sauk
Southeast	Below the Northeast Woodlands to the Gulf of Mexico and into East Texas	Mound-building culture, Mississippian, also in Northeastern Woodlands; lasts into the 1600s among Cherokee, Natchez, and a few other peoples; well-developed hierarchical organization with priests as the head of government, warrior class, traders, farmers, artisans, and slaves	Creek, Choctaw, Yamasee

plants. About 5,000 years ago, some peoples began to domesticate plants. With a stable food supply, groups established permanent settlements, and the population increased. Specialization in arts and crafts resulted, and hierarchical organizations grew up, often combining religious and secular power and a social structure. In some areas, monumental buildings were erected. The Native Americans who met the Europeans in the 1400s and 1500s had a wide range of cultures, dependent for the most part on the **environment.**

- There was a great diversity among Native Americans. Not only did they provide for their food in different ways, but their **artifacts,** those things they made for their own use and for trade, were vastly different depending on where they lived. For example, Plains Native Americans who moved in pursuit of food carried their goods in leather bags, while sedentary farmers like the Pueblo peoples wove baskets and made pottery. It is generally thought that there were 200 different languages spoken by Native Americans north of Mexico.

European Voyages of Exploration

- Several factors spurred European interest in exploration. (1) The Crusades of the eleventh and twelfth centuries had interested Europeans in trade with Asia for luxury goods, such as spices,

KEY EXPLORERS AND THEIR ACHIEVEMENTS

DATE	EXPLORER	COUNTRY	ACHIEVEMENT
1487–1488	Diaz	Portugal	Sails around southern tip of Africa
1492–1504	Columbus	Spain	First European to explore the Western Hemisphere; explores the West Indies and the Caribbean
1497–1498	da Gama	Portugal	Sails around Africa to India
1497–1501(?)	Cabot	England	Explores Newfoundland and Nova Scotia
1499	Vespucci	Spain	Explores coast of South America
1500	Cabral	Portugal	Explores Brazil
1508–1509 1513	Ponce de Leon	Spain	Explores Puerto Rico Explores Florida
1516–1520	de Soto	Spain	Explores Central America
1519	Magellan	Spain	Circumnavigates the globe
1519	Cortés	Spain	Explores Mexico; conquers the Aztecs
1524	Verrazano	France	Explores northeastern coast of North America
1531	Pizarro	Spain	Explores Peru; conquers the Incas
1534–1542	Cartier	France	Explores St. Lawrence River
1539–1542	de Soto	Spain	Explores lower Mississippi River
1540–1542	Coronado	Spain	Explores southwestern U.S.
1542–1543	Cabrillo	Spain	Explores western coast of North America
1603–1615	Champlain	France	Explores St. Lawrence River valley Founds Quebec
1609	Hudson	Netherlands	Explores east coast of North America, including Hudson River
1610–1611	Hudson	England	Explores Hudson Bay
1673	Marquette/Joliet	France	Explores Mississippi River
1679–1682	La Salle	France	Explores Great Lakes region; reaches mouth of the Mississippi River

sugar, and silk. (2) European merchants, especially in trading cities such as Genoa and Venice, and the Hanseatic League, a confederation of cities on the North and Baltic Seas, wanted new trade routes to Asia to cut out Middle Eastern middlemen. (3) Technological advances, such as the astrolabe and compass, made it possible for sailors to try new and dangerous water routes. (4) The rise of **nation-states** encouraged economic development and also rivalry among European nations for new territories and new wealth. (5) The **Renaissance** engendered a sense of curiosity and adventure among Europeans.

First Spanish Settlements

- Spanish settlement in the Americas began in the Caribbean, moved north into what is now the United States, and moved west and south into Central and South America. Between 1492 and 1800, Spain had conquered and colonized large sections of Central and South America and set up settlements in what are today California, New Mexico, Arizona, Texas, Mississippi, Louisiana, and Florida.

- The oldest permanent European settlement in the United States is **St. Augustine, Florida.** Settlements often began as a mission or a mission and **presidio**, a fort, with towns being established at a later stage of development. New Spain was divided into **viceroyalties** and governed by **viceroys** appointed by the monarch.

Test-Taking Strategy

Items 4 and 5 illustrate the Columbian Exchange.

- Long-term Spanish influences include (1) the use of Spanish as the dominant language in Central and South America; (2) the introduction of Roman Catholicism to Native Americans; (3) the subjugation and killing of Native Americans and taking of their lands and wealth; (4) introduction of European crops, livestock, iron products, and firearms into native cultures; and (5) the introduction of Native American crops into Europe.

French Policy

- The French did not begin attempts at colonization until the early 1600s. In 1608, **Samuel de Champlain** founded Quebec in what is today Canada, but its northern climate attracted few colonists. By 1680, the French had established a line of settlements from Canada and the Great Lakes to the Gulf of Mexico.

- Unlike the Spanish, the French had not found gold but had found an abundant source of furs for export. Only some 10,000 settlers had come to New France by 1680 because (1) the mainland settlements were not so rich as the sugar island colonies of the French, (2) most French monarchs were more interested in securing their power in Europe than in establishing American colonies, and (3) **Huguenots,** religious dissidents, were not allowed to emigrate.

Test-Taking Strategy

Keep in mind the last sentence and be sure to identify those later consequences.

- Government was by a council appointed by the king, similar to the government of New Spain. In 1608, the French, under Champlain, had joined the Algonquins and Hurons in a fight against the **Iroquois.** The hatred of the French that this battle aroused among the Iroquois had significant consequences for later British colonists.

Contact Between Native Americans and Europeans

- The Spanish, French, and English handled their relations with Native Americans differently. With the establishment of the **encomienda system,** the Spanish in the Caribbean used the native peoples for forced labor. Many Native Americans died from smallpox and other European diseases and from brutal treatment. **Bartolomé de Las Casas,** a former conquistador turned priest, protested to the pope and the Spanish king. In time, the encomienda system was ended, and enslaved Africans replaced the already dwindling native populations on the Spanish sugar plantations of the Caribbean. On the mainland in New Spain, the Spanish, supported by their military, set up **missions** and forced Native Americans to (1) give up their cultures, (2) wear European-style clothing, (3) learn Spanish, (4) convert to Christianity, and (5) labor for the priests.

- Because they had little military support, the French did not establish missions. Unarmed French missionaries went among Native Americans to preach and convert them and were often tortured and killed for their efforts. The English treatment of Native Americans varied from colony to colony but often began with good relations, for example, the **Pilgrims** and **Wampanoags** and **William Penn** and the **Delaware,** or **Lenni Lenape**. As more settlers moved to the colonies and encroached on Native American lands, fighting erupted between colonists and Native Americans, with the Native Americans always losing.

Jamestown: The First English Colony

- The first permanent English settlement was **Jamestown,** founded in 1607 by **Captain John Smith.** The **Virginia Company** had received a **charter** from James I granting it the right to settle the area from the **lost colony of Roanoke,** off the coast of what is today North Carolina, to the Potomac River. The charter also granted the colonists the same rights as English citizens.

Review Strategy

See page 80 for the origins of slavery in the Americas.

- In order for the colonists to survive the first years, known as "the starving time," Smith established work rules and traded for food with nearby Native Americans, most notably **Powhatan,** the leader of the **Powhatan Confederacy,** whose daughter, **Pocohantas,** in time married **John Rolfe.** It was Rolfe who was responsible for establishing **tobacco** as a major **cash crop** for the Virginians. In 1619, the first Africans were brought to the colony, as were the first white women.

THE THIRTEEN ENGLISH COLONIES

NEW ENGLAND COLONIES

Colony	Date	Founded by	Reasons	Importance
Plymouth	1620	Pilgrims	Religious freedom	**Mayflower Compact**
Massachusetts Bay	1630	Puritans, Massachusetts Bay Company	Religious freedom; build **"a City on a Hill"**	Representative government through election to **General Court**
Plymouth and Massachusetts Bay joined	1691			
New Hampshire and Maine	1622	John Mason, Sir Ferdinando Gorges	Profit from trade and fishing	Colonists from Massachusetts move into area; by 1650s under Massachusetts' control
New Hampshire	1679	Royal charter from Charles II		
Connecticut	1636	Thomas Hooker	Expansion of trade, religious, and political freedoms; limited government	**Fundamental Orders of Connecticut:** (1) any man owning property could vote; (2) limited power of governor
	1662	Receives charter from king and becomes separate royal colony		
Rhode Island	1636	Roger Williams buys land from Narragansetts	Religious **toleration**	Separates church and state unlike Massachusetts Bay Colony

MIDDLE COLONIES

Colony	Date	Founded by	Reasons	Importance
New Netherlands	1624	Dutch under Peter Minuit	Trade, religious freedom	Diverse population
New York	1664	Royal charter from Charles II to his brother, James, Duke of York	Takes valuable trade and land from rival	
Delaware	1638	Swedish settlers	Trade	
	1664	Seized by English	Take land from rival	

76

MIDDLE COLONIES				
Colony	**Date**	**Founded by**	**Reasons**	**Importance**
Delaware	1682	Land grant to William Penn, proprietary colony	Known as Lower Counties	Provides Pennsylvania with coastline
New Jersey	1664	Lord Berkeley, Sir George Carteret, **proprietary colony**	Division of New York because too large to govern; trade and religious and political freedoms	Few colonists; remains mostly Native American lands
New Jersey	1702	Becomes royal colony		Protection of religious freedom and right of assembly to vote on local matters
Pennsylvania	1682	William Penn, proprietary colony	Religious and political freedoms	**Quakers' "Holy Experiment;"** attracts diverse population; pays Lenni-Lenape for their land
SOUTHERN COLONIES				
Jamestown	1607	Virginia Company	Trade, farming	Establishes self-government under the **House of Burgesses**
Virginia	1624	Becomes royal colony under James I		Continues House of Burgesses
Maryland	1632	Land grant from Charles I to Lord Baltimore; on his death to his son, Cecil, Lord Baltimore; first proprietary colony	Religious and political freedoms	Roman Catholics; elected assembly; **Act of Toleration** providing religious freedom to all Christians
The Carolinas	1663	Land grant from Charles II to eight proprietors	Trade, farming, religious freedom	Rice and indigo cultivation; need for large numbers of laborers leads to African enslavement
North Carolina	1712			
South Carolina	1729	Proprietors sold their rights to the king; became royal colonies		Establishes representative assemblies

SOUTHERN COLONIES				
Colony	Date	Founded by	Reasons	Importance
Georgia	1732	James Oglethorpe, proprietary colony	Haven for debtors; buffer against Spanish Florida	Originally southern part of South Carolina; initially only small farms and no slavery; grows slowly, and Oglethorpe allows slavery and plantations

Test-Taking Strategy

Remember the significance of the House of Burgesses.

- The political significance of the Virginia Colony is in its establishment of the **House of Burgesses** in 1619. This was the first **representative government** in an English colony. Male colonists elected burgesses, or representatives, to consult with the governor's council in making laws for the colony. Prior to 1670, colonists did not have to own property in order to vote. In that year, the franchise was limited to free, male property owners. In 1624, James I withdrew the charter from the **Virginia Company** and made Virginia a **royal colony** but allowed the House of Burgesses to continue.

Plymouth Colony

Test-Taking Strategy

Why are the Mayflower Compact and the Plymouth Colony significant?

- The **Pilgrims,** persecuted for their refusal to conform to the **Church of England,** received a charter from the **London Company** for land south of the Hudson River, but their ship was blown off course to the area that is today Cape Cod. Before landing in 1620, they wrote and signed the **Mayflower Compact,** the first document in the English colonies establishing **self-government.**
- Like the colonists at Jamestown, the Pilgrims relied initially on help from the local Native Americans. In time, the colonists became farmers and timber exporters, but few new colonists joined them, and in 1691, Plymouth Colony joined with the Massachusetts Bay Colony.

Massachusetts Bay Colony

- **Massachusetts Bay Colony** was founded in 1629 by the **Puritans** under a charter from King Charles I. They, too, were seeking religious freedom, but, unlike the Pilgrims, they did not wish to separate from the Church of England. The Puritans wanted to "purify" the church of practices that they believed were too close to those of the Roman Catholic Church. With their charter, they set up the Massachusetts Bay Company and used it to establish a colony that would be a **commonwealth** based on the Bible.

Test-Taking Strategy

What is the similarity between Jamestown and Massachusetts Bay?

- In the beginning, laws were passed by the **General Court,** which was made up of freemen, those few male colonists who owned stock in the Massachusetts Bay Company. The other colonists rebelled, and in 1631, the leaders admitted to the General Court any Puritan man in good standing. As the colony continued to grow, the number became unwieldy, and the law was changed so that freemen in each town in the colony elected two representatives to the General Court. Like Jamestown, Massachusetts Bay had established a **representative form of government**—though limited in scope.

Colonial Government

Test-Taking Strategy

Be sure you know what the phrase power of the purse *means. You'll find it again in the events leading up to the Revolution.*

- Except for Pennsylvania, which had a **unicameral legislature**, the colonies had **bicameral legislatures** modeled on the upper and lower houses of Parliament. The upper chambers were made up of the governor, his advisers, and councillors appointed at the suggestion of the governor by the monarch or proprietor, depending on the type of colony. In Rhode Island and Connecticut, the upper house was elected by the colonists, and in Massachusetts, the upper house was elected by the lower house. The lower houses were elected by the colonists, supposedly every two years, but some governors, such as Berkeley in Virginia, refused to call elections for years. This is why the **power of the purse** had become important. The legislatures had developed the right to levy taxes and pay the salaries of governors. By threatening to withhold his salary, the legislature could pass laws over a governor's objections.

- Voting requirements changed as the colonies grew. Originally, only Puritans could vote in Massachusetts Bay, and in royal colonies, only **Anglicans.** Catholics, Jews, Baptists, and Quakers were restricted from voting in certain colonies, and no colony allowed women, Native Americans, or slaves to vote. In all colonies, white males had to own land in order to vote. Over time, this changed so that men could own property other than land or could pay a tax to be eligible to vote.

English Events, Colonial Effects

- In 1686, following his accession to the throne as James II, the former Duke of York combined New York, New Jersey, and the New England colonies into the **Dominion of New England** with the intention of ending the region's illegal trading activities. Appointing **Sir Edmund Andros** as governor, James abolished the colonial legislatures and allowed Andros to govern with unlimited powers.

Test-Taking Strategy

Think about why the English Bill of Rights was significant to the colonists.

- In 1688, the English, angered by James's policies and his conversion to Catholicism, deposed him in the **Glorious Revolution.** William and Mary of Orange were installed as monarchs. Andros was removed from office, and the charters were returned to the colonies along with their representative governments. An additional event of significance to the colonists was the drafting of an **English Bill of Rights** guaranteeing certain rights to every citizen, including the right to representative government.

The Origins of Slavery in the Americas

- The origins of **slavery** in the Americas began with the Spanish on their sugar islands in the Caribbean. To replace Native Americans, the Spanish and later the English began to import Africans as slaves. In 1619, the first Africans to arrive in the colonies came off a Dutch ship at Jamestown and were treated as **indentured servants.** As it became more difficult to find the large number of workers needed for tobacco agriculture, the policy changed.

- In a court case in Jamestown in 1640, the indenture of an African was changed to servitude for life, *durante vita*. In 1663, Maryland passed its first slave law. The plan for government for the Carolinas recognized Africans as slaves, and, therefore, as property. Slavery was legalized in Georgia when the colonists came to realize that they would make money only through plantation agriculture. New York and New Jersey began as a single Dutch colony, and Africans were recognized as indentured servants. After the English seized and divided the colony, slavery was legalized. However, the Northern colonies did not farm **labor-intensive crops,** such as tobacco, rice, and indigo, so there was little need for slaves. In the North, most slaves were household help.

- Estimates vary, but it is generally agreed that some 20 million Africans survived the **Middle Passage** of the **triangular trade route** between Europe, Africa, and the colonies. They came from the **West Coast of Africa,** and most were sold into the Caribbean or South America. After being captured by fellow Africans and force-marched to the sea in chains for sale to Europeans, Africans were kept in **slave factories** until ships were available. These factories had holding pens for the Africans as well as offices, warehouses for trade goods, and living quarters for the European traders. The Africans were then marched on board ship in chains and kept below decks where an average of 13 to 20 percent of the human cargo died during a voyage. On arrival in the colonies, the Africans were sold without regard to keeping families together.

- The English institutionalized slavery because (1) they needed labor and (2) they viewed Africans with their foreign languages and ways as less than human. The English had found neither Native Americans—who died from disease or who, as runaways, melted back into the forests—nor white indentured servants—who worked only

Test-Taking Strategy

Be sure you understand who indentured servants were, why they were not a satisfactory workforce, and what part they played in Bacon's Rebellion.

for a specified time or who, as runaways, could melt into the general population—a satisfactory workforce.

KEY PEOPLE

Review Strategy

See if you can relate these people to their correct context in the "Fast Facts" section.

- **Nathaniel Bacon, Bacon's Rebellion, Sir William Berkeley, Virginia**
- **William Bradford,** *History of Plimouth Plantation*
- **Iroquois League, Five Nations,** later **Six Nations**
- **Anne Hutchinson, Rhode Island**
- **King Philip's War or Metacom's War, New England**
- **Pequot War, southern New England**
- **John Winthrop, Massachusetts Bay**

KEY TERMS/IDEAS

Review Strategy

See if you can relate these terms and ideas to their correct context in the "Fast Facts" section.

- **Chesapeake country, Chesapeake Bay**
- **Columbian Exchange** of items and ideas among different cultures
- **covenant,** Massachusetts Bay Colony, congregations, saints or true believers
- **Great Migration, England to Massachusetts Bay Colony, 1620–1640**
- **joint-stock company, Virginia Company and Massachusetts Bay Company**
- **New England Confederation; colonies of Connecticut, New Haven, Plymouth, and Massachusetts Bay; first attempt at union**
- **royal colony, proprietary colony**
- **Salem witch trials, 1692, Cotton Mather**
- **Treaty of Tordesillas, line of demarcation, Spain and Portugal in the Americas**

SECTION 2. COLONIAL SOCIETY AROUND 1750

By 1760, some 2 million people lived in the English colonies, with about half the population in the five Southern Colonies. The original colonists had settled along the coast, but, by the 1700s, settlers were moving inland to the **frontier,** or **backcountry.** In the Northern colonies, this meant the forests of Northern New England, New York, and Central Pennsylvania. In the Southern Colonies, settlers were leaving the **Tidewater,** that part of the Atlantic Coastal Plain between New Jersey and Georgia, for the **Piedmont,** an area that gradually slopes into the Appalachian Mountains. By the time of the American Revolution, colonists had settled the Piedmont and were moving across the Appalachians.

FAST FACTS

Social Classes

- With the exception of slaves and free blacks, colonists had an opportunity for **social mobility.**

SOCIAL STRUCTURE OF THE THIRTEEN ENGLISH COLONIES	
Gentry/Upper Class	Plantation owners (Southern Colonies), merchants, high government officials, clergy
Middle Class	Owners of small farms, skilled craftworkers, shopkeepers, and professionals, such as doctors and teachers
Lower Class	Tenant farmers, hired farmhands, servants, unskilled workers, indentured servants, free blacks
Slaves	

Rural and Urban Life

- Most of the early colonists lived in villages or small towns and went out each day to farm their lands, especially in New England. Later, as the pattern of settlement grew and people moved to the frontier and the backcountry, a trading town would grow up here and there at an intersection of roads or waterways, but most people lived on their farms, far from one another and from town. Social life meant trips to town for shopping, to church, and to an occasional house-raising or barn dance. On plantations, white women managed the house while their husbands or fathers managed the business of the plantation. A white overseer managed day-to-day operations in the fields where enslaved Africans—men, women, and children—supplied the unpaid labor. Some Africans were trained as skilled workers and as house servants.
- Philadelphia was the largest city in the 1750s, with a population of 20,000. New York and Boston ranked second and third. Charles Town, South Carolina, and Baltimore, Maryland, were the only large cities in the Southern Colonies. Although many immigrants stayed in the cities because they offered more opportunities, the cities were as foul and disease-ridden as they were in Europe. Over time, dirt streets were paved with brick or cobblestones, streetlights were installed, laws were passed to keep streets clean and to keep the peace, and parks and libraries were built.

ECONOMIC DEVELOPMENT IN THE THIRTEEN ENGLISH COLONIES

Colonies	Environment	Economy	Results
New England	Forested, rocky soil with long, cold winters and short growing seasons	Subsistence farming; manufacturing, shipbuilding, fishing; trade	Family-farmed land with an occasional hired hand or **indentured servant;** little use for slavery; trade with England and the West Indies, including **triangular trade** for slaves
Middle	Fertile soil; temperate climate with longer growing season	Major **cash crops:** wheat, corn, rye; **"breadbasket colonies";** later trade and manufacturing centers	Some large estates; family farms large enough to hire farm workers or keep indentured servants; little slavery except for tobacco plantations in Delaware
Southern	Fertile soil; mild winters with a long growing season; abundant waterways for irrigation and transportation	Small farms for vegetables, grain; labor-intensive tobacco, rice, indigo agriculture on plantations; little manufacturing or Southern-owned shipping; few large cities	Most farms were small and worked by farm families at a **subsistence level;** almost self-sufficient plantations with hundreds of slaves were the exception; few free blacks in towns and cities

Colonial Families

- Colonial families of ten or twelve children were not unusual. Most women married in their early 20s and many died in their childbearing years, having had five or six children. In the rural areas, women took care of the children and the household chores: weaving cloth; sewing clothes; making soap, candles, and bread; cooking, cleaning, and washing; tending a small vegetable and herb garden; and doctoring the sick, often with medicines of their own making. On farms at planting and harvesting times, women and girls worked in the fields.

- Men worked in the fields, tended to the farm animals, and were responsible for selling or trading any **surplus.** Boys worked alongside their fathers as soon as they were big enough. In cities, work was still assigned by gender, but women and girls sometimes helped out in their fathers' or husbands' shops, and widows often took over their husbands' work.

- Women could learn trades and skills, such as printing and silversmithing, but any money a woman earned working outside the home belonged to her husband or, if she was unmarried, to her father. Women could not vote, and married women could not own property. Single women, although not married women, could enter into business, sign contracts, and sue in court. Women had little opportunity for education, in part because there was little schooling available in the early colonies, and later because education was limited to boys. Note, however, that because of their importance to the colonies' development, women in the colonies had more rights, higher **status,** and greater economic independence than women in England.

The First Great Awakening

- By the early 1700s, the influence of Puritanism on the **Congregational Church** and on New England in general was vastly reduced. A general lessening of interest in religion seemed to be spreading throughout the colonies, and in the 1730s and 1740s, an era of **religious revivalism** called the **First Great Awakening** engulfed the colonies. Spurred by charismatic preachers, such as Englishmen **John Wesley** and **George Whitefield** and **Jonathan Edwards** of Massachusetts, thousands repented of their sins and joined Protestant churches, many of them new.

Test-Taking Strategy

The last cause listed here had a significant effect on colonists' view of their relationship with Great Britain.

- The preachers taught that a person did not have to belong to an **established church** (Puritanism and Anglicanism) to be saved. A person had only to repent of his/her sins, believe in Jesus Christ as savior, and experience the Holy Spirit. The Great Awakening created (1) divisions among congregations and thus the rise of new congregations and sects, (2) a fear of education on the part of some while motivating others to found schools, and (3) a new sense of independence by encouraging people to actively choose their church.

New Immigrants

- The majority of original colonists was English, but by 1775, just under 50 percent of the colonists were English. While New England remained mostly English, the Middle and Southern Colonies gained diverse populations of Protestant Scotch Irish, Scots, and Welsh; Irish Catholics; French Huguenots; **Sephardic Jews;** and German Protestants joined the Dutch, Swedes, and Finns already living in the Middle Colonies to make up about a third of the total colonial population. Africans made up the remaining 20 percent. New immigrants were motivated by the same **push/pull factors** as the original colonists: (1) to escape religious persecution, which often also meant (2) escaping curtailed civil rights, and (3) for economic gain.

The Growth of Slavery

- One reason that colonists used Africans as slaves was that the supply seemed limitless. In Virginia in the 1660s, there were only 300 Africans, but by 1756, there were 120,000 in a population of

293,000. About 3,000 were free blacks. In the forty years between 1714 and 1754, the number of Africans in the colonies rose from 59,000 to almost 300,000. **Natural increase** accounted for some of this, but most slaves were newly arrived Africans.

- New England and the Middle Colonies had few slaves in proportion to the overall slave population in the colonies. The climate and terrain were unsuited to plantation-style agriculture. In the early days of Massachusetts Bay, Puritans had banned slavery. However, in 1698, the **Royal African Company** authorized New England merchants to buy and sell Africans in the trans-Atlantic slave trade.

- Slaves had no legal rights: (1) slave marriages were not recognized, (2) slaves could not own property (they *were* property), (3) they had little legal protection against a cruel owner, (4) they could be sold away from their families, and (5) it was illegal to teach a slave to read and write.

Free Blacks

- Free blacks were few in number, although it was easier to be freed in New England and the Middle Colonies because there was less economic incentive to keep a slave. Blacks were free (1) if they were the descendants of the early indentured servants, (2) if their mothers were white, (3) if their owners freed them, or (4) if they bought their freedom with savings that their owners allowed them to keep from outside jobs they did.

KEY PEOPLE

- **Anne Bradstreet, poet, Massachusetts Bay Colony**
- **Phillis Wheatley, poet, former slave**
- **John Peter Zenger, trial for seditious libel, freedom of the press**

KEY TERMS/IDEAS

Review Strategy

See if you can relate these terms and ideas to their correct context in the "Fast Facts" section.

- **Massachusetts General School Act of 1647**
- **Sinners in the Hands of an Angry God,** Jonathan Edwards

SECTION 3. THE MOVE TO INDEPENDENCE, 1754–1776

The world view of colonists in 1754 on the brink of the American Revolution was being shaped by a number of factors: (1) the experience of self-government, (2) the thinking of the Enlightenment, (3) belief in religious toleration and freedom to choose one's own religion, and (4) social mobility, except for enslaved Africans. The catalyst for revolution would turn out to be the actions of a British government determined to subordinate its colonies to the service of mercantilism.

FAST FACTS

Mercantilism

- Under the policy of **mercantilism,** European colonies existed for the purpose of building up **specie,** or gold supplies, and expanding trade for the home countries. To achieve these goals, nations had to build a **favorable balance of trade** by **exporting** more than they **imported.** England, later Great Britain, saw its colonies: (1) as sources of raw materials; (2) as markets for English goods; (3) as bases for the Royal Navy because a strong navy was needed to protect English interests much as the **Spanish Armada** had protected Spanish interests; and (4) as a way to develop a commercial navy.

- To enforce mercantilism, the English Parliament passed a series of **Navigation Acts** between 1651 and 1673. Among the laws were: (1) only English or colonial ships could transport goods to or from the English colonies (which greatly benefited New England shipbuilders), (2) certain goods such as tobacco, sugar, and cotton—**enumerated goods**—could be sold only to England, and (3) all goods bound for the colonies had to be shipped through England where they were unloaded, an **import duty** paid on them, and then reloaded for shipment to the colonies. This increased the price of foreign goods in order to protect English manufacturers.

- Colonists found it easy to evade the Navigation Acts by smuggling. In 1673, England passed a law appointing **customs officials** to collect **customs duties** on goods brought into the colony, but they often remained in England and hired deputies who did little to collect taxes and could be bribed to ignore smuggling. It was also difficult to police the long coastline. As a result, the British government adopted a policy of **salutary neglect** or noninterference until 1764.

- Throughout the late 1690s and into the mid-1700s, the British government continued to pass laws aimed at controlling trade to and from the colonies.

MERCANTILE LAWS	
Woolen Act, 1699	Colonists could not export raw wool, yarn, or wool cloth to other colonies or to other countries, thus slowing colonial manufacturing but protecting English trade.
Hat Act, 1732	Colonial hatmakers could not sell their beaver hats outside the colonies.
Molasses Act, 1733	A tax was placed on sugar, rum, and molasses bought from the French West Indies rather than from the British West Indies.
Iron Act, 1750	Colonists were forbidden to build mills for smelting iron.

French and Indian War

- Mercantilism heightened the rivalries among European nations, especially between France and England. The immediate causes for conflict in North America were (1) conflicting claims to land, (2) fur trade with Native Americans, and (3) the arming of Native Americans for raids. The **Iroquois,** who traded with the British, were moving into areas where Native American allies of the French lived and trapped, while British colonists were moving across the Appalachians into territory the French claimed, especially the Ohio Valley, where the French had built a series of forts.

ANGLO-FRENCH WARS		
War in Europe	**War in North America**	**Result**
War of League of Augsburg	King William's War, 1689–1697	French loss of Nova Scotia, Newfoundland, and Hudson Bay to Great Britain
War of Spanish Succession	Queen Anne's War, 1702–1713	
War of Austrian Succession	King George's War, 1742–1748	Loss of remaining French territory in North America to British: Canada and all land east of the Mississippi River
Seven Years' War	French and Indian War, 1754–1763	

- The **Treaty of Paris, 1763,** officially ended the French and Indian War: (1) France ceded the Louisiana Territory to Spain to repay its debts, (2) France gave Canada and its land east of the Mississippi River to Great Britain, (3) Spain, as an ally of France, turned over Florida to Great Britain. Only Great Britain and Spain retained land in North America.

Test-Taking Strategy

The New England Confederation and the proposed Albany Plan of Union got colonists thinking about united action and are, therefore, significant.

- As the first conflicts in the French and Indian War were occurring, representatives from seven British colonies met at Albany, New York, in 1754 to ask the **Iroquois** for help. The Iroquois initially remained neutral, but as the war progressed and they saw the French losing, the Iroquois agreed to work with the British. At this Albany Congress, Ben Franklin suggested the **Albany Plan of Union,** based on the **Iroquois League of Six Nations.** The plan called for a Grand Council of representatives chosen by the legislatures of each colony and a president-general named by the British Crown in order to make laws, raise taxes, and prepare for the defense of the colonies when the colonies needed to act together. The colonial legislatures rejected the idea because they did not want to give up power, even to their own representatives. Like the **New England Confederation,** however, the Albany Plan was a step toward uniting the colonies.

Test-Taking Strategy

If you were writing the test questions, what would you ask about the consequences of the French and Indian War?

- The colonists experienced some unintended benefits from the French and Indian War: (1) colonial militias gained experience and skill in warfare, (2) the colonists saw that the British could be defeated, (3) militias had to accept blacks because there was a shortage of able-bodied men willing to fight, (4) colonists no longer feared Native Americans without the French to arm them, and (5) colonists learned more about people in other colonies, lessening their suspicions of them and at the same time learning the benefits of cooperation.

Steps to the Revolutionary War

Test-Taking Strategy

Connect this decision to keep a standing army with the Quartering Act.

- In answer to **Pontiac's War** against forts on the frontier, the British government issued the **Proclamation of 1763** forbidding colonial settlement from west of the Appalachian Mountains to the Mississippi until treaties could be signed. Colonial trappers, traders, settlers, and **land speculators** protested the proclamation as unnecessary British intervention and ignored it. As a result of Pontiac's War, the British government decided that a British army should be sent to the colonies to protect its interests.

- The French and Indian War had cost Great Britain a great deal of money, and with the end of the war had come the responsibilities and costs of managing a new empire not only in North America but also in India. The British government pointed out that the colonists had gained much from the war: (1) the end of threats from the French and Native Americans and (2) the continued protection of the British army and navy. The British government expected the

BRITISH LEGISLATIVE ACTIONS LEADING TO THE REVOLUTION

LAW	PROVISIONS	CONSEQUENCES
Sugar Act, 1764	Reduced tax on molasses brought into colonies from British and non-British ports; meant to strengthen the Molasses Act, 1733	Colonists had been smuggling molasses from French colonies and not paying the tax. Strict enforcement meant paying the tax or not having molasses.
Currency Act, 1764	Forbid the colonies from issuing their own paper money; taxes to be paid in gold or silver coin, **specie,** rather than paper money	Because the **balance of trade** had shifted to Great Britain around 1750, colonial merchants had been sending large amounts of currency to Great Britain to pay their taxes, already making it difficult for merchants to do business.
Quartering Act, 1765	Passed as a way to save money on keeping the British army sent after the Proclamation of 1763; colonists to provide barracks and supplies for the soldiers	Colonists feared this was the beginning of a permanent British army that they would have to support.
Stamp Act, 1765	Provided that colonists must buy a special stamp to place on almost every kind of document: wills, marriage licenses, playing cards, newspapers, etc. (The English had been paying this tax since 1694.)	It was the first tax placed on goods made and sold in the colonies and, as such, did not support **mercantilism.**
Townshend Acts, 1767	Placed **import duties** on such goods as glass, paint, paper, and tea; created more **admiralty courts;** suspended the New York legislature because it had refused to obey the Quartering Act	This was the first tax levied on goods imported from Great Britain. Revenue raised by the tax was to be used to pay salaries of royal governors and judges in the colonies, thus negating the **power of the purse.**
Tea Act, 1773	Continued tax on tea imposed by the Townshend Act; gave **monopoly** on selling tea in the colonies to the British East India Company; allowed company to choose merchants to sell its tea in the colonies	Tea merchants not chosen to sell the company's tea feared they would lose their businesses. There was also concern that in time the sale of other goods could be controlled in the same way.

BRITISH LEGISLATIVE ACTIONS LEADING TO THE REVOLUTION

LAW	PROVISIONS	CONSEQUENCES
Intolerable Acts, 1774 (also known as **Coercive Acts**)	Aimed specifically at Massachusetts as a result of the **Boston Tea Party:** • **Boston Port Act:** closed the port until the colonists paid for the tea • **Quartering Act:** required colonists to house troops sent to Massachusetts to enforce the Intolerable Acts • **Administration of Justice Act:** allowed a soldier or official accused of a crime to be tried outside the colony if the governor believed the person could not receive a fair trial in the colony • **Massachusetts Bay Regulating Act:** revoked the colony's charter	The acts, which took away rights that colonists believed were theirs as British subjects, angered not only colonists in Massachusetts but throughout the colonies.
Quebec Act, 1774	Extended the province of Quebec south to the Ohio River valley and west to the Mississippi River; British officials would govern it directly, but colonists could keep their laws; Roman Catholics could continue to practice their religion	Although the act was not meant to punish the English colonists, they viewed it as such because it negated the claims of Massachusetts, Connecticut, and Virginia to parts of the new province and allowed Roman Catholicism.

colonists to pay for these benefits. Not surprisingly, the colonists disagreed. The war was over, and they expected things to return to what they had been before—with one difference: the colonists saw a divergence between their interests and those of Great Britain.

Test-Taking Strategy

Compare British policy before and after Grenville became prime minister.

• British policy toward the colonies changed significantly with the selection of **George Grenville** as Prime Minister in 1763: (1) the **Navigation Acts** were to be strictly enforced, (2) customs officials could no longer remain in England and send deputies to collect taxes, (3) **writs of assistance** were to be issued to allow officials to search for smuggled goods and collect unpaid taxes, (4) British warships were to patrol the coastline, and (5) smugglers were no longer to be tried in front of friendly juries of their peers but in front of **admiralty courts.** This violated one of the basic rights of the English people guaranteed in the **Magna Carta.**

• At the passage of the **Stamp Act, Patrick Henry** raised the cry of **taxation without representation** in his **Virginia Resolves,** which the House of Burgesses passed. According to his argument, each colonial charter guaranteed its citizens the same rights as people living in England. In England, the right to tax the people rested with the House of Commons, but the colonists had no representatives in the House, and, therefore, the House could not levy taxes on them. Only their own colonial legislatures could tax them, and their legislatures had not passed the Stamp Act. This is the theory of **direct representation.**

- Representatives from nine legislatures met in New York for the **Stamp Act Congress.** In a petition to **George III,** they (1) declared their loyalty and (2) agreed with the government's right to regulate trade but (3) argued that the Sugar and Stamp Acts were taxation without representation. Colonial merchants and planters signed **nonimportation agreements,** and colonists organized **boycotts** of British goods in which the **Daughters of Liberty** took part. **Sons of Liberty** attacked merchants willing to use the stamps as well as the tax collectors. In time, the boycotts caused rising unemployment and hurt British merchants who lobbied Parliament to repeal the Stamp Act, which was done in 1766.

Test-Taking Strategy

The conflict between these two theories was the basis of the conflict with George III and Parliament.

- Although Parliament repealed the Stamp Act, it also passed the **Declaratory Act** in 1766. The act stated that Parliament had the power and right to make laws for the colonies "in all cases whatsoever." Thus, the basic question of whether Parliament, having no representatives from the colonies within its body, had the right to make laws taxing the colonies was answered to the satisfaction of Parliament and the monarch. Parliament based its position on the theory of **virtual representation.** The House of Commons was sworn to represent every person in England and the empire—whether or not he or she could vote. The colonists, however, were used to **direct** or **actual representation;** they had been electing representatives to their assemblies since the earliest days of the colonies.

- Colonial resistance to the Townshend Acts took the form of writings, boycotts, and protests. **John Dickinson** wrote *Letters from a Pennsylvania Farmer,* promoting unity of action among the colonists. The Massachusetts legislature drafted the **Massachusetts Circular Letter,** urging the other colonies to resist. Virginia, Maryland, and Georgia endorsed the letter, and Parliament retaliated by forbidding their legislatures and that of Massachusetts to convene. The House of Burgesses adopted a resolution that only colonial legislatures could tax the colonists. Mob violence broke out. In order to (1) ease tensions, (2) aid British merchants who were losing money again, and (3) end the drain on government revenues because of the costs of enforcement, Parliament, under the direction of the new prime minister, **Lord Frederick North,** repealed the tax provisions of the Townshend Acts—except for a small tax on tea as a symbol of the government's right to tax.

- The Townshend Acts were not repealed soon enough to prevent the **Boston Massacre,** in which five colonists were killed and six wounded after a detachment of British soldiers opened fire on a mob that was throwing rock-filled snowballs at them. One of the dead was **Crispus Attucks,** once a slave and now a free sailor and member of the Sons of Liberty.

KEY PEOPLE

Review Strategy

See if you can relate these people to their correct context in the "Fast Facts" section.

- **Samuel Adams, Committees of Correspondence**
- **William Pitt (the Elder), Prime Minister of England, French and Indian War**

SECTION 4. THE AMERICAN REVOLUTION, 1775–1783

Although colonists in growing numbers had opposed the various taxation policies of Great Britain over the years, the number had always been relatively small and, to a certain extent, limited to the merchants and upper class. However, as the taxation policies became broader in scope and more widely enforced, the discontent spread among the colonists until mob violence erupted when new laws were passed. Tax collectors were tarred and feathered, shops of suspected British sympathizers ransacked, British revenue ships set afire, people who bought British goods intimidated, and British soldiers harassed.

The Intolerable Acts added new reasons to the arguments of those calling for independence. Britain had expected that the other colonies would see the rightness of laws meant to punish Massachusetts for its lawlessness, but a number of colonists felt otherwise. That the new royal governor of Massachusetts, **General Thomas Gage,** began enforcing the Intolerable Acts did not help the cause of **Loyalists,** or **Tories.**

FAST FACTS

Steps to Independence

- The **First Continental Congress,** proposed by the House of Burgesses, met in Philadelphia in fall 1774. Fifty-six male delegates assembled, representing all the colonies except Georgia, whose royal governor would not allow anyone to attend. **Patrick Henry** said, "Virginian, Pennsylvanian, New Yorkers, and New Englanders are no more. I am not a Virginian but an American." Still, there was no majority favoring independence within the Congress or among the colonists. About a third of the colonists, calling themselves **Patriots,** wanted independence from Great Britain, while another third wanted to remain loyal to Great Britain and work out their differences, and a third was indifferent. The First Continental Congress passed the **Suffolk Resolves** and the **Declaration of Rights and Grievances** and called for another meeting in 1775.

- Even before the First Continental Congress met, fighting had broken out between colonists and the British army around Boston. Learning of arms caches at Concord and several other villages near Boston, General Gage sent soldiers on the night of April 18, 1775, to surprise the colonists. An efficient network of spies dispatched **Paul Revere, Dr. Samuel Prescott,** and **William Dawes** to alert the towns. Reaching **Lexington** on the morning of April 19, the British were met by armed **minutemen.** In the confusion, someone fired a shot ("the shot heard 'round the world"), and the British soldiers opened fire. Eight colonists were killed and ten wounded. The British went on to **Concord,** where they exchanged fire with more minutemen and then marched back to Boston with angry colonists shooting into the columns of retreating **Redcoats.** After Lexington and Concord, the Massachusetts militia, with reinforcements from other colonies, effectively hemmed the British in Boston until March 1776, when **General William Howe** and his army sailed for Canada, which allowed the **Continental Army** to enter Boston.

- The **Second Continental Congress** met in spring 1775. Between 1775 and 1781, it was to transform itself from an advisory body to the governing body of the new nation. Its original charge was to attempt to make peace with Great Britain while insisting on the rights of the colonists. The Second Continental Congress accomplished the following:

  - Passed the **Olive Branch Petition**

  - Passed the **Declaration of the Causes and Necessity of Taking Up Arms**

  - Established an army from the militia around Boston and placed **George Washington** in command

  - Established a navy

  - Authorized private ships, **privateers,** to attack British shipping

  - Sent representatives to France, Spain, and the Netherlands asking for military and economic support in the event of war against Great Britain

  - Authorized and signed the **Declaration of Independence**

  - Adopted the **Articles of Confederation**

  - Acted as the national government to (1) prosecute the war, (2) conduct diplomatic relations with foreign governments, and (3) oversee ratification of the Articles of Confederation.

- In response to the Second Continental Congress's actions, George III issued the ***Proclamation of Rebellion*** asking his "loyal subjects to oppose rebellion." He also ordered a naval blockade of the colonies and hired 10,000 German **(Hessian) mercenaries** to fight in the colonies.

- In April 1776, North Carolina instructed its delegates to the Second Continental Congress to support independence. A month later, Virginia followed suit. On June 7, **Richard Henry Lee** of Virginia introduced a resolution declaring "these United Colonies are, and of right, ought to be, free and independent states." While debate continued on **Lee's Resolution,** a committee composed of **John Adams, Roger Sherman, Benjamin Franklin, Robert Livingston,** and **Thomas Jefferson** began work on a declaration of independence, with Jefferson writing the first draft. Adams and Franklin contributed revisions, and the document was presented to Congress on June 28. Lee's Resolution was passed on July 2, and the Declaration adopted on July 4. All references to the monarch's part in the slave trade were removed so that the colonists would not lose the support of powerful and influential slave traders and slave owners.

The Declaration of Independence

Test-Taking Strategy

The Enlightenment and especially the writings of John Locke were significant influences on the leaders of the revolution.

- The **Declaration of Independence** has four major sections: (1) the **Preamble,** which describes why the colonists are seeking their independence; (2) the Declaration of Rights; (3) the List of Grievances; and (4) the formal Declaration of Independence. Jefferson drew on **Enlightenment** philosophers, such as **John Locke** in his appeal to **self-evidence** and the **natural order (natural law).** Jefferson invoked Locke's idea of a **social contract** between the ruled **(consent of the governed)** and their ruler. If the ruler abuses the contract **(absolute despotism),** then the ruled have the right to overthrow him or her. Although George III is listed as the cause of the separation, Parliament was as much to blame, even though some members, like William Pitt, had supported the colonists. The signers formally declared their separation in the last section and asserted their rights "to levy war, conclude peace, contract alliances, establish commerce," and all other acts of an independent nation.

- The Congress had three purposes in adopting the Declaration of Independence: (1) certain generally accepted rules for conducting war would go into effect, (2) borrowing money to finance the war and governmental functions would be easier as a national entity, and (3) the Declaration was seen as a way to unite the colonists. However, colonists who remained loyal to Great Britain would be considered traitors.

Waging War

- The new nation faced a number of disadvantages in its war with Great Britain: (1) difficulty in recruiting soldiers; (2) resistance to recruiting blacks for the army (although some 5,000 fought for the

Patriots); (3) shortages of supplies for the military; (4) lack of a large, well equipped navy; (5) few Native American allies (most of the Iroquois League fought with the British in an effort to keep the Americans from their lands); (6) lack of European allies until late in the war; (6) lack of unity (Loyalists and those indifferent to the cause); and (7) a weak central government, for example, lacking the power to levy taxes.

- As early as 1776, **France** had been secretly sending arms, supplies, and money to the new United States. In 1778, France recognized the colonies as a separate nation and agreed to enter the war as an ally. France lent the new nation money and sent a large contingent of well-trained and well-equipped soldiers to reinforce the Continental Army as well as a fleet that effectively hindered British troop movements. Spain and the Netherlands joined the war against Great Britain. Russia, Prussia, Denmark, Sweden, and Portugal formed the **League of Armed Neutrality** against the British navy.

- Historians estimate that from 20 to 30 percent of the colonists remained **Loyalists.** Although Loyalists lived in all states, the largest numbers lived in New York, Georgia, and South Carolina. Many were officeholders, wealthy landowners and merchants, and professionals—people who had financial ties to Great Britain. At the end of the war, some 80,000 fled, about half to Canada. Their property was confiscated by the states and sold.

- Although the fighting ended in 1781, the **Peace of Paris (Treaty of Paris)** was not ratified until 1783. **Benjamin Franklin, John Jay, John Adams,** and **Henry Laurens** negotiated the following concessions: (1) independence, (2) the territory between the Appalachians and the Mississippi River from the Great Lakes to Florida (the latter returned to Spain), (3) fishing rights in the Gulf of St. Lawrence and off Newfoundland, (4) payment by both countries of debts owed prior to the war, (5) agreement by Congress to ask states to allow Loyalists to sue for the value of their confiscated property; and (6) agreement by Great Britain to remove its troops from U.S. soil.

Government Under the Articles of Confederation

Test-Taking Strategy

The weaknesses of the Articles were important, but the most significant act of the new government was its establishment of a policy for settling new lands and creating new states.

- From 1781 until 1789 when the U.S. Constitution was ratified, the new nation was governed under the **Articles of Confederation.** Because the former colonies were fighting against strong external control of their affairs, their leaders shaped a document that allowed each state a great deal of freedom at the cost of a **weak central government.** State governments were similar to their colonial governments and divided power among a governor, legislature, and judiciary, with most power reserved to the legislature. Although each state constitution included a bill of rights, political power rested with the wealthy. Voting was restricted to propertied white men, and although slavery was prohibited in Northern states, the Southern economy continued to depend on it.

- Under the Articles of Confederation, the new nation accomplished the following: (1) signed the Peace of Paris ending the Revolutionary War, (2) established a policy for settling new lands and creating new states (**Land Ordinance of 1785, Northwest Ordinance of 1787**), and (3) established the departments of Foreign Affairs, War, Marine, and Treasury.

ARTICLES OF CONFEDERATION	
WEAKNESSES	**CONSEQUENCES**
No chief executive; the Congress worked through committees	No coordination of committees and no uniform domestic or foreign policy
Required nine of thirteen states to approve laws (each state had one vote)	Rarely delegates from all thirteen states in Congress at once; often voted as blocs of smaller states (5) versus larger states (8)
Required all states to approve amendments	Never get agreement of all thirteen states, so Articles never amended
No power to levy or collect taxes; Congress could raise money only by borrowing or asking states for money	No reason for states to agree to requests; Congress always in need of money to fight the war
No power to regulate **interstate commerce**	Led to disputes between states and inability to regulate trade with foreign nations to protect American business
No power to enforce treaties	No power to force British to abide by the Peace/Treaty of Paris of 1783
No power to enforce its own laws	Only advise and request states to abide by national laws
No national court system; state courts interpreted national laws	Difficult to get states to abide by state court decisions

KEY PEOPLE

Review Strategy

See if you can relate these people to their correct context in the "Fast Facts" section.

- **Edmund Burke, Irish-born British politician**
- **Thomas Paine,** *Common Sense, The Crisis*

SECTION 5. DRAFTING THE CONSTITUTION

The weaknesses of the Articles were soon apparent. Although the new government could, among other powers, establish post offices, borrow and coin money, declare war, ask states for recruits to build an army, and build and equip a navy, these powers meant little in reality. Each member of Congress was paid by his (no women allowed) state and voted according to his state legislature's instructions. Most importantly to the new nation ravaged by recent war, the Confederation Congress did not have the power to deal with the **economic depression** that hit the nation after the war or the nation's growing sectional differences. Faced with mounting economic problems, including an **unfavorable balance of trade,** the states met several times to discuss solutions.

FAST FACTS

Working Out Compromises

- In 1786, at the **Annapolis Conference,** delegates recommended a convention to make changes in the Articles. Meeting in Philadelphia, the fifty-five delegates soon saw that a new document was needed. Competing interests put forth different plans, and the major areas of compromise were as follows:

	VIRGINIA PLAN	NEW JERSEY PLAN	FINAL U.S. CONSTITUTION
Representation	Based on wealth or population	Equal representation for each state	**Senate:** two representatives per state **House:** based on population
Executive	National executive chosen by Congress	Executive Committee chosen by Congress	**President** chosen by **electors,** in turn elected by the people
Judicial	National judiciary chosen by Congress	National judiciary appointed by Executive Committee	**Supreme Court** appointed by the president with Senate confirmation; lower courts established by Congress
Legislative	Two houses: upper elected by the people with lower elected by the upper house	One house: appointed by state legislators	Two houses: upper chosen by state legislatures (changed to direct election by Seventeenth Amendment); lower elected by the people

- Other compromises included in the **U.S. Constitution** are: (1) the **Three-Fifths Compromise** for counting slaves in determining taxes and representation for the House, (2) prohibition on importation of slaves after 1808, (3) the right of Congress to regulate **interstate commerce** and foreign trade but not levy export taxes, and (4) a four-year term for the president.

Ratification of the Constitution

- Advocates and opponents soon squared off over **ratification. Federalists** favored ratification because they claimed that without a strong federal government, the nation would be unable to protect itself from external enemies or solve internal problems. Initially, they argued against a **Bill of Rights** as unnecessary but agreed to its addition to gain support. **Anti-Federalists,** mainly farmers and others from the inland areas, claimed (1) that the Constitution was extralegal because the convention had not been authorized to create a new document, (2) that it took important rights away from the states, and (3) that the Constitution needed a Bill of Rights to guarantee individual liberties.

- By June 1788, nine states had ratified the Constitution, but without Virginia and New York, the union would have little chance of survival. In Virginia, **Patrick Henry** led the fight against ratification. Only promises that Virginian George Washington would be the first president and that a Bill of Rights would be added convinced Virginians to vote "yes." The fight in New York enlisted **Alexander Hamilton, James Madison,** and **John Jay** to write a series of essays called *The Federalist* in defense of the Constitution. Once New York ratified, and the new government took office in March 1789, Rhode Island and North Carolina became the last of the original states to ratify.

KEY TERMS/IDEAS

Test-Taking Strategy

See if you can relate these terms and ideas to their correct context in the "Fast Facts" section.

- **Great Compromise, Roger Sherman; New Jersey Plan, William Patterson; Virginia Plan, Edmund Randolph**
- **right of deposit, New Orleans, Spanish interference with trade**
- **sectionalism: social, cultural, economic, and political**
- **Shays's Rebellion, poor economic conditions in new nation**
- **Virginia Bill of Rights, U.S. Bill of Rights**

SECTION 6. THE U.S. CONSTITUTION

You may be asked questions about what led to the passage of certain amendments, the consequences of certain amendments, or the significance of certain Supreme Court decisions. This section will give you the basic facts about the Constitution so that you have a context for understanding the significance of later events related to the Constitution.

FAST FACTS

Test-Taking Strategy

Pay particular attention to amendments related to large themes in U.S. history, such as the Civil War (Thirteenth, Fourteenth, and Fifteenth Amendments).

- The U.S. Constitution consists of a **Preamble, seven Articles,** and **twenty-six Amendments.**

- The Constitution sets out the structure and powers of government but does not try to provide for every possibility. Knowing that they would not be able to provide solutions to all the circumstances that the nation would face in the future, the Framers developed the amendment process to allow later generations to change the government as situations arose.

- The **amendment process** and the **system of checks and balances** enables the government to be both flexible and stable.

- The U.S. Constitution is based on six principles of government:

    - **Popular sovereignty:** The people are the only source of governmental power.

    - **Federalism:** Government power is divided between a national government and state governments.

    - **Separation of powers:** Executive, legislative, and judicial powers are divided among three separate and co-equal branches of government.

    - **Checks and balances:** The three branches of government have some overlapping powers that allow each to check, that is, restrain or balance, the power of the other two.

    - **Judicial review:** The courts have the power to declare unconstitutional actions of the legislative and executive branches of government.

    - **Limited government:** The Constitution lists the powers granted to the federal government, reserved to the states, or shared concurrently.

- The first ten amendments to the Constitution are known as the **Bill of Rights** and were added to satisfy the **Anti-Federalists,** who opposed ratification because the proposed Constitution did not spell out the rights of the people.

- The **Thirteenth, Fourteenth,** and **Fifteenth Amendments** were passed after the Civil War to ensure the rights of newly freed slaves. These amendments figure prominently in the history of

PROVISIONS OF THE UNITED STATES CONSTITUTION

ARTICLES

Article I	Establishes the Legislative Branch Make up of the House of Representatives and the Senate, elections and meetings, organization and rules, passing of laws, powers of Congress, powers denied to the federal government, powers denied to the states; Three-Fifths Compromise for apportionment was repealed by the Fifteenth Amendment; **"necessary and proper clause;" "commerce clause"**
Article II	Establishes the Executive Branch Term, election, qualifications of the president and vice president; powers of the president; duties of the president; impeachment
Article III	Establishes the Judicial Branch Federal courts, jurisdiction of federal courts; defines treason
Article IV	Relations among the states Honoring official acts of other states; mutual duties of states; new states and territories; federal protection for states
Article V	The amendment process
Article VI	Public debts, supremacy of national law, oaths of office; **"supremacy clause"**
Article VII	Ratification process

AMENDMENTS

First Amendment	Freedoms of religion, speech, press, assembly, and petition
Second Amendment	Right to bear arms
Third Amendment	Restrictions on quartering of troops
Fourth Amendment	Protection against unlawful search and seizure
Fifth Amendment	Rights of the accused in criminal proceedings, due process
Sixth Amendment	Right to a speedy, fair trial
Seventh Amendment	Rights involved in a civil suit
Eighth Amendment	Punishment for crimes **(cruel and unusual punishment)**
Ninth Amendment	Powers reserved to the people **(nonenumerated rights)**
Tenth Amendment	Powers reserved to the states
Eleventh Amendment	Suits against states by a resident or by another state must be heard in state courts, not federal courts: repealed part of Article III

PROVISIONS OF THE UNITED STATES CONSTITUTION

AMENDMENTS	
Twelfth Amendment	Election of president and vice president
Thirteenth Amendment	Ratified as a result of the Civil War; abolishes slavery
Fourteenth Amendment	Ratified after the Civil War; defines the rights of citizens; replaces part of Article I by requiring that African Americans be fully counted in determining apportionment; sets out punishment for leaders of the Confederacy; promises payment for federal debt as a result of the Civil War but not for debts of the Confederacy. This amendment's **"equal protection under the law"** provision figures prominently in later civil rights decisions by the Supreme Court.
Fifteenth Amendment	Ratified after the Civil War; grants the right to vote regardless of race, color, or previous servitude. Southern states defied the amendment until the 1960s when Congress passed various voting rights acts.
Sixteenth Amendment	Grants federal government the ability to tax income
Seventeenth Amendment	Provides for direct election of senators; replaces Article I, Section 3, paragraphs 2 and 3
Eighteenth Amendment **Twenty-First Amendment**	Prohibits manufacture, sale, or transportation of alcohol Repealed Eighteenth Amendment
Nineteenth Amendment	Grants women the right to vote
Twentieth Amendment	Modified sections of Article I and the Twelfth Amendment relating to when the terms of office begin for members of Congress and the president and vice president; known as the **"Lame Duck" Amendment** because it shortened the time that a defeated legislator/ official served between the election and the new term of office
Twenty-Second Amendment	Limits presidential term to two terms if elected on his/her own and to one term if serving out the term of a predecessor for more than two years
Twenty-Third Amendment	Provides three presidential electors for the District of Columbia
Twenty-Fourth Amendment	Abolishes the poll tax for federal elections; part of the civil rights legislation of the 1960s
Twenty-Fifth Amendment	Provides for presidential disability and succession if the president is unable to perform his or her duties
Twenty-Sixth Amendment	Expands the right to vote to include 18-year-old citizens
Twenty-Seventh Amendment	Limits the ability of Congress to raise its own salary

Reconstruction. Beginning in the 1960s, the Supreme Court used the Fourteenth Amendment as the basis for many **civil rights** decisions.

- The Constitution can be changed formally by the amendment process, but it can also be changed informally through (1) legislation, (2) executive action (Executive Orders), (3) party practices (as one example, the Constitution does not mention political conventions to nominate presidential and vice-presidential candidates, but parties hold conventions every four years), (4) custom (secretaries of the Executive Departments make up the president's Cabinet), and (5) court decisions.

- The Supreme Court is the major shaper of judicial change. Since John Marshall's tenure as chief justice, the tension between **strict constructionist** and **loose constructionist** views has existed on the Court and between its supporters and opponents.

KEY PEOPLE

- **Anti-Federalists:** opposed ratification of the Constitution on a number of issues, centered on (1) the increased powers of the central government over those listed in the Articles of Confederation and (2) the lack of a listing of the rights of individuals; Thomas Jefferson, Patrick Henry, John Hancock, and Samuel Adams, among others

- **Federalists:** supported ratification, basing their arguments on (1) the weaknesses of the Articles of Confederation and (2) the need for a strong government to guide the new nation; James Madison, John Adams, and Alexander Hamilton as chief advocates

Review Strategy

As you read Chapters 3 through 8, look for landmark Supreme Court cases and other cases that have shaped national policies.

- **John Marshall:** Chief Justice of the Supreme Court from 1801–1835; known as the Great Chief Justice; would be called a judicial activist today. Under the Constitution, the powers of the Supreme Court were not spelled out. Marshall established the status and independence of the Supreme Court and led the Court in many rulings that set the basic principles of constitutional law for the United States.

- **Thurgood Marshall:** argued ***Brown* v. *Board of Education of Topeka, Kansas*** (1954) that overturned the decision in ***Plessy* v. *Ferguson*** (1896); became the first African American Supreme Court Justice; liberal and judicial activist

- **Warren Court:** named after Chief Justice Earl Warren (1953–1969); judicial activist. The Warren Court wrote many landmark decisions in civil rights and individual rights, including ***Brown* v. *Board of Education of Topeka, Kansas*** and ***Miranda* v. *Arizona*.**

KEY TERMS/IDEAS DEFINED

- **elastic clause:** Article I, Section 8; also known as the **"necessary and proper clause"**; grants Congress the right to make all laws "necessary and proper" in order to carry out the federal government's duties; this is an expressed power and the constitutional basis for implied powers

- **supremacy clause:** part of Article VI; the Constitution, laws passed by Congress, and treaties of the United States have superior authority over laws of state and local governments
- **concurrent powers:** powers, such as the right to tax and to establish and maintain courts, that are shared by the federal and state governments but exercised separately and simultaneously
- **denied powers:** powers denied to all government; Article I, Sections 9 and 10
- **enumerated powers:** powers stated directly in the Constitution as belonging to the federal government; Article I, Section 8; Article II, Section 2; Article III; Sixteenth Amendment
- **expressed powers:** also called **enumerated powers**
- **implied powers:** based on the "necessary and proper" or elastic clause; powers required by the federal government to carry out its duties as stated in the Constitution; not listed, but based in expressed powers, such as the power to collect taxes implies the power to establish the Internal Revenue Service
- **inherent powers:** belong to the federal government by virtue of being the federal government
- **reserved powers:** powers that belong to the states; Tenth Amendment
- **judicial activism:** theory that the Supreme Court, through its decisions, should shape national social and political policies
- **judicial restraint:** theory that the Supreme Court, through its decisions, should avoid an active role in shaping national social and political policies
- **loose constructionist:** one who argues that the Constitution needs to respond to changing times; the **Warren Court,** for example
- **strict constructionist:** one who argues that the judiciary's decisions need to be based on the Framers' intent; Justice Clarence Thomas, for example

Chapter 3

REVIEWING THE NEW NATION TO MID-CENTURY

Red Alert!

See 10 Facts About the SAT II: U.S. History Test *for basic information about the test format, pp. 2–5.*

As you review the information on the concepts, trends, events, and people who were important in the nation's history between 1790 and 1898, remember that the College Board asks questions about political, economic, and cultural and intellectual history and foreign policy. As you review your course materials and read this book, look for trends, cause-and-effect relationships, differences and similarities, and the significance of events and actions on the development of the nation. Be prepared to analyze events and people's motives and to evaluate outcomes. The who, when, and why is only part of what you need to learn.

SECTION 1. THE NEW NATION, 1789–1800

Once nine states had ratified the Constitution, the members of the **electoral college** assembled in their states in February 1789 and voted for president and vice president. **George Washington** was unanimously chosen President, and **John Adams,** who received the next highest number of votes, was elected vice president. They took their oaths of office on April 30 and thus, began the new nation.

FAST FACTS

The Presidency of George Washington

- The new government had to deal with (1) the national debt, (2) foreign affairs, and (3) its own frontier. However, it had to deal with these in the context of realizing the promises of the new Constitution for the new nation. The government under Washington had to determine how to establish and maintain a balance between the powers of the federal government and the rights of the people and the states.

- The **Washington presidency** is as important for the **precedents** it set as for the business of the nation that it conducted. Washington established, among other precedents, (1) that the president was to be addressed as "Mr. President"; (2) that a president should serve only two terms (Franklin Roosevelt in 1940 was the first president to seek a third term, and the Twenty-Second Amendment turned Washington's precedent into law); (3) that the president should be advised by able and experienced leaders; (4) that the president can grant or withhold diplomatic recognition to foreign governments; (5) that federal troops can be used to enforce the law by virtue of the president's power as commander in chief; (6) that the president is, in essence, the leader of his political party; (7) that the president should deliver the State of the Union speech before a joint session of Congress; (8) that Senate approval of presidential appointments refers only to confirmation, not removal from office; (9) that the Senate's role of "advise and consent" means ratifying or rejecting treaties, not negotiating them; and (10) that, although Congress's role was to make laws, the president should take an active role in shaping and urging the passage of laws he deems worthwhile and necessary.

- According to the Constitution, the heads of the **Executive Departments** are to report to the president, but it does not state the number of departments and what they should be. In 1789, Congress created the **Departments of Treasury, State,** and **War** (in 1949, the Departments of War, Navy, and the U.S. Air Force were combined into the Department of Defense). Washington selected experienced leaders to fill these posts: as Secretary of State, **Thomas Jefferson,** who had written the Declaration of Independence and been minister to France under the Articles of Confederation; as Secretary of War, **General Henry Knox,** who had held the post under the Articles of Confederation; and as Secretary of the Treasury, **Alexander Hamilton,** who had written part of *The Federalist*. Along with the Attorney General, these men became known as the **Cabinet.** By the middle of his first term, Washington was consulting them almost weekly, a custom that has continued.

Test-Taking Strategy

The impact of the Judiciary Act of 1789 has had great significance on U.S. history. Why?

- The **Judiciary Act of 1789** filled in another piece of the new government by establishing the **federal court system**. The Act created (1) the positions of Chief Justice and five Associate Justices for a national Supreme Court and (2) thirteen district courts and three circuit courts. (The number of Associate Justices and lower courts has increased with the increase in the size of the nation.) (3) The Judiciary Act also gave the Supreme Court the power enabling the Court to declare void any state laws and any decisions of state courts that the Court held to violate the U.S. Constitution or federal laws and treaties made under the Constitution.

- Washington chose three Southerners and three Northerners for the Supreme Court positions, naming **John Jay** of New York, a co-author of *The Federalist,* as the first **Chief Justice.**

- The first Congress established the position of **Attorney General** to advise the president and the government on legal matters. (The Department of Justice was not established as a separate Executive Department until 1870.) **Edmund Randolph,** a lawyer who had drafted the **Virginia Plan** during the Constitutional Convention, was named to the post.

Review Strategy

See Chapter 2 *for a listing of the first ten Amendments.*

- The **Anti-Federalists** urged passage of the promised **Bill of Rights.** In September 1789, the first Congress passed and sent to the states for ratification twelve proposed amendments to the Constitution. Ten were ratified by 1791 and added to the Constitution as the first ten amendments.

Hamilton's Financial Program for the New Nation

- A major problem facing the new government was debt from the war—$50 million owed to foreign countries and to U.S. citizens. The states owed about $25 million. The Constitution gave the new nation the power to levy taxes and create a money system. It was up to Hamilton to make these powers a reality. Hamilton proposed a four-part plan: (1) repayment of the entire war debt owed by the national government and by the states, (2) establishment of a **national bank,** (3) adoption of a **protective tariff,** and (4) adoption of an **excise tax on whiskey.** Hamilton set out his plan in a two-part report: ***Report on the Public Credit*** and ***Report on Manufactures.***

Review Strategy

Note the sectional rivalries that are beginning to take shape in the new nation.

- As the first step, Hamilton planned to sell government **bonds** that had a 20-year payback period to repay both federal and state debts. The money from the new bonds would be used to buy back at face value the bonds issued during the war. These bonds were now valued at little more than the paper they were printed on, but Hamilton's plan had two goals: (1) to establish the new nation as a good credit risk by paying off its debts, especially to France and the Netherlands, and (2) to encourage support for the nation through the self-interest of the bondholders, mostly wealthy people.

- Opposition came from those states, mainly in the South, whose debts were small or who had repaid their creditors. Opponents, led by **James Madison,** also argued that it was **speculators,** many of them New England merchants, who would profit from repayment. Hamilton argued that the nation must establish itself as creditworthy. To appease the Southerners in Congress, Hamilton agreed to support the proposal to have the new nation's capital built in Southern territory. The compromise resulted in the building of **Washington, D.C.,** on land along the Potomac River that was donated by Virginia and Maryland, and passage of the **Assumption Bill,** assuming all debts**.**

- The second part of Hamilton's program called for creation of the Bank of the United States, a **national bank** with branches in major cities. The bank would serve as the depository of government tax revenues. Operating capital for the bank would come from those reserves as well as from the sale of shares in the bank. The bank would also issue **currency** for the nation that would, in time, replace local and state bank notes, thus stabilizing the value of the nation's money system. This would benefit the nation as a whole and business in particular.

Review Strategy

See Chapter 2 *for a discussion of the Constitution's powers.*

- Opposition was strong, not only in Congress, where Madison again led the fight, but within the Cabinet, where Jefferson was a powerful opponent. The arguments were that (1) the sale of shares in the bank at $400 a share meant that only the wealthy could afford to invest; (2) government money would be deposited only in branches of the national bank, thus depriving private banks of business; and (3) the Constitution gave the federal government no power to create a banking system. The last argument was based on the **enumerated powers** in the Constitution.

- Hamilton countered by arguing that the **"elastic and proper clause"** of the Constitution gave the government the power "to make all laws which shall be necessary and proper for carrying into execution the foregoing powers," among which were the powers to tax and to borrow money. Hamilton persuaded Washington of the legitimacy of his argument based on the **implied powers** of the Constitution, and the Bank of the United States, the **First Bank,** was chartered in 1791 for 20 years.

- The next step in Hamilton's fiscal program was to increase the modest **tariff** that was levied by Congress in 1789. Congress saw the tariff as a way to generate a little revenue for the government, whereas Hamilton saw the tariff as a way not only (1) to raise revenue for the government but also (2) to protect the nation's emerging industries by raising the price of foreign goods. Hamilton, an advocate of a strong central government that favored wealthy businesspeople, had a vision of the United States as an industrial power. He realized that the nation would have to manufacture much of what it needed if it were not to remain dependent on other nations. Hamilton's vision clashed with those in Congress who saw the nation as one of small farms, and his tariff was never acted on.

Test-Taking Strategy

The unintended result of the Whiskey Rebellion was its long-term significance.

- In 1791, Congress did pass Hamilton's excise tax on whiskey. The tax fell hardest on frontier farmers whose major crop was corn. Because of the difficulty of transporting corn to market, Western farmers turned their corn into whiskey, which they then sold for cash. The frontiersmen refused to pay the new excise tax, and in 1794, federal marshals attempted to enforce the law in Pennsylvania but were forced to flee. Hamilton convinced Washington to send militia from neighboring states, and the **Whiskey Rebellion** fizzled out at the sight of 15,000 troops. The unintended result was the shift in loyalty of frontiersmen from the Federalists to the Democratic-Republicans.

The Rise of Political Parties

- Another unintended result of Hamilton's fiscal program was the rise of the **political party system** by 1794. Those who sided with Hamilton believed in a broad interpretation of the Constitution (**loose constructionists**) that allowed for expansion of the federal government. Hamilton distrusted the ability of ordinary people to manage government and attracted to the **Federalists** wealthy merchants, manufacturers, lawyers, and church leaders from New England and New York who believed that the federal government should help underwrite the nation's industrial development. (The party slowly died as a result of its opposition to the **War of 1812.**)

- The **Democratic-Republicans** who did not support expansion of governmental powers beyond what the Constitution stated (**strict constructionists**) opposed the Federalists. Jefferson became leader of the Democratic-Republicans, or simply **Republicans** (in the mid-1820s, they became known as Democrats). Jefferson and the Republicans believed in (1) limited federal power, (2) strong state governments, and (3) guarantees of individual rights. To them, the best society was one based on small farms. The Republicans' strength lay in the South and on the frontier.

New States

- Washington's administration also dealt with the addition of new states: Kentucky, Tennessee, Ohio, and Vermont. The Mississippi River became the nation's Western boundary. The new nation alternated between fighting the Native Americans on its Western frontier and making treaties with them. The British in the Upper Midwest and the Spanish to the south armed Native Americans in an attempt to keep the new nation from expanding.

Foreign Policy Under Washington

- To keep the new nation out of the European conflict that developed after the **French Revolution,** Washington, in 1793, issued the **Neutrality Proclamation.** He was concerned that the nation was (1) still too weak to defend itself and (2) too dependent on British trade to enter the war on the side of the French against the British. Jefferson and the Democratic-Republicans favored honoring the U.S. treaty with the French and entering the war. Congress agreed with Washington and passed the **Neutrality Act,** which made the proclamation into law.

- A number of problems with Great Britain remained for Washington's administration to resolve: (1) the British were still occupying some of their forts and trading posts in the area between the Ohio and Mississippi Rivers; (2) the British were apparently arming Native Americans for raids against Americans; (3) the United States was now refusing to repay Loyalists for property lost in the American Revolution; (4) the British, at war with the French, were capturing U.S. ships that traded with French colonies in the Caribbean; and (5) the British were **impressing** U.S. sailors suspected of deserting the British navy.

- **Jay's Treaty** solved the most important issues. The British agreed (1) to leave the frontier in 1796 and (2) to grant the United States trading rights with British islands in the Caribbean. (A joint committee was to work out the other issues, but the capture of U.S. ships and impressment were not resolved.) The treaty was ratified despite opposition from Republicans who wanted to honor the alliance of 1778 with the French and who saw the treaty as an attempt by the Federalists to increase trade with Great Britain.

Review Strategy

See Chapter 2 *for a listing of the amendments to the Constitution, especially the Twelfth Amendment.*

- Opposition to Jay's Treaty figured in the election of 1796, the first presidential election in which members of opposing parties competed. Because the person with the highest number of votes would become president and the person with the next highest number would be named vice president, **John Adams,** a Federalist, became president, and Thomas Jefferson, a Republican, was chosen as vice president.

The Adams Presidency

- As President, Adams was faced with increasing hostilities from the French who were seizing U.S. ships in the Caribbean in retaliation for Jay's Treaty. Adams sent **Charles Pinckney, Elbridge Gerry,** and **John Marshall** to France to negotiate a solution. **Charles Talleyrand,** the French foreign minister, sent three agents to the Americans to demand money, which they refused to pay. The Americans referred to the agents only as X, Y, and Z. News of the **XYZ Affair** angered Americans who claimed "Millions for defense but not one cent for tribute." Talleyrand claimed the situation was all a mistake, and Adams sent a new delegation. The sea war continued until 1800, when the French agreed that the **alliance of 1778,** which had made allies of France and the new United States, was null and void. The Republicans' support for the French severely damaged the party.

- Party rivalry led to passage of the Alien, Naturalization, and Sedition Acts. The **Alien Act** gave the president the power to expel any alien believed to be dangerous to the nation. The **Naturalization Act** extended from five to fourteen years the time an alien had to live in the United States before being eligible for citizenship. The **Sedition Act** made it a crime to oppose the laws or make false or critical statements about the government or any official. The first two laws were aimed at French immigrants, many of whom supported the Republicans. The last law affected a number of Republicans, including several members of Congress.

Review Strategy

As you study the nation to 1860, keep track of the arguments for nullification. This issue had a significant impact on U.S. politics and policies.

- The laws backfired and increased support for the Republicans, who protested the Sedition Act on the grounds that it violated the **First Amendment**'s guarantees of freedom of speech and freedom of the press. Believing that the states had the right to declare laws of the federal government unconstitutional, Jefferson urged the states to **nullify** the Alien and Sedition Acts. Jefferson wrote the **Virginia Resolution,** and James Madison wrote the **Kentucky Resolution,** which declared the laws unconstitutional.

KEY PEOPLE

- Citizen Edmond Genet
- Pinckney's Treaty, right of deposit at New Orleans, 31st parallel as boundary between Georgia and Spanish Florida

KEY TERMS/IDEAS

- Battle of Fallen Timbers, General Anthony Wayne, Blue Jacket, Northwest Territory, Treaty of Greenville
- Washington's Farewell Address: warnings against political parties, sectionalism, and foreign alliances

SECTION 2. THE AGE OF JEFFERSON, 1800–1816

Jefferson called the election of 1800 the **"Revolution of 1800"** because it quietly handed the reins of government from the Federalists to the Republicans. The election also demonstrated the need for a better way to elect the president and vice president. It took seven days and thirty-six ballots in the House of Representatives to break the tie and select Jefferson as president and **Aaron Burr** as vice president. As a result, the **Twelfth Amendment** was ratified in 1804 to change the process so that candidates were clearly listed as being nominated either for president or for vice president.

FAST FACTS

The Jefferson Presidency

- In seeking the presidency, Jefferson sought to increase the power base of the Republican party by attracting New England merchants. Once in office, Jefferson had the Naturalization Act and the excise tax on whiskey repealed, and the Alien and Sedition Acts were allowed to expire. He chose to allow the First Bank to continue undisturbed, but he sought to reduce the size of the government and of the federal budget and to pay down the debt. Jefferson believed in a **laissez-faire** philosophy of government in which the government's role would be limited.

Marbury v. _Madison_ (1803; principle of judicial review)

Case: With less than three months left in his term, President John Adams, in January 1801, appointed a number of Federalists as justices to lesser federal courts for terms of five years each. The Senate confirmed the appointments, and Adams signed their commissions in the last hours of his term, the so-called midnight judges. Several of these commissions were not delivered, and the newly elected President Thomas Jefferson, an Anti-Federalist, had Secretary of State James Madison withhold them. William Marbury asked the Supreme Court to issue a writ of mandamus to force Madison to give him his commission. Marbury based his suit on a section of the Judiciary Act of 1789 that created the federal court system.

Decision: The Supreme Court ruled that the section of the Judiciary Act that Marbury cited conflicted with the Constitution and was, as a result, unconstitutional. Marshall based the Court's opinion on the premise that the Constitution is the supreme law of the land, the so-called Supremacy Clause of Article VI. As a result, all other laws are subordinate to it. Judges take an oath to uphold the Constitution and, therefore, cannot enforce any act ruled in conflict with the Constitution.

Significance: In this decision, John Marshall led the Court in establishing its power to review laws and declare them unconstitutional, if necessary.

Test-Taking Strategy

The constitutional factors involved in the purchase of Louisiana are important.

• Jefferson's strict constructionist views were put to the test over the **Louisiana Purchase.** In 1800, Spain had signed over Louisiana to France. By 1802, the French, intent on creating an empire in North America, were no longer allowing Western farmers to use the port of New Orleans. Jefferson sent **James Monroe** and **Robert Livingston** to France to offer to buy New Orleans and West Florida for $10 million. The French countered with an offer of $15 million for all of Louisiana. Concerned that the Constitution did not authorize the president to purchase land, Jefferson believed an amendment was needed. Livingston then warned that **Napoleon** might reconsider if kept waiting. With misgivings, Jefferson asked the Senate to ratify the **treaty of cession** which authorized the purchase. On the other side of the debate, Federalists protested that the treaty violated the Constitution. Jefferson finally based the purchase on the **implied powers** of the Constitution that required the president to protect the nation. The Louisiana Purchase (1) almost doubled the size of the U.S., (2) gave the United States control of the Mississippi River and New Orleans, and (3) removed the French threat from the frontier.

THE CAUSES OF THE WAR OF 1812

• In the early 1800s, a Shawnee holy man named **the Prophet** and his brother, the chief **Tecumseh,** tried to unite Native Americans from the Great Lakes to the Gulf of Mexico to block any more U.S. settlers from entering their lands. Tecumseh and the Prophet built a village along **Tippecanoe Creek** in Indiana Territory, where many Native Americans came to hear the Prophet. In 1811,

General William Henry Harrison, governor of the Indiana Territory, led a force of some 1,000 against Tippecanoe. The Prophet staged a surprise attack, and each side suffered heavy losses, but Harrison burned the village and claimed victory. His soldiers also claimed to have found British weapons in the village.

- When Napoleon came to power after the French Revolution, war dragged on in Europe between France and its enemies for a number of years. The new nation was caught between the warring factions who would not honor its **neutrality**. Both sides continued to capture U.S. ships for trading with the other side. In 1807, after the **HMS *Leopard*** fired on, boarded, and seized four crewmen from the **USS *Chesapeake,*** Jefferson ordered an **embargo** on trade with all foreign nations. Jefferson hoped that France and Great Britain would be forced to respect U.S. rights in exchange for U.S. goods. However, the embargo had little effect on those nations but caused a **depression** in the United States that affected not only merchants, ship owners, sailors, and manufacturers, but also farmers, who lost their foreign markets. The **Embargo Act** became a major issue in the election of 1808, but the Republicans were able to elect **James Madison,** Jefferson's choice, as president. At the end of Jefferson's second term, Congress, with Jefferson's approval, repealed the Act.

- In 1810, Madison signed **Macon's Bill No. 2** which stated that if either France or Great Britain would agree to respect U.S. rights as a neutral nation, the United States would cut off trade with the other country. Napoleon agreed, and Madison cut off trade with Great Britain in 1811, only to find that the French continued to seize U.S. merchant ships. The British began to **blockade** some U.S. ports and continued to impress U.S. sailors. Then, on June 16, 1812, the British decided to suspend attacks on U.S. ships because it needed U.S. foodstuffs, and its merchants needed markets and trade goods. However, not knowing this, the United States declared war on Great Britain on June 18.

Review Strategy

Note the sectionalism that divided support for the War of 1812.

- The **War of 1812** had a number of causes, many of them championed by the **War Hawks** in Congress, young men from the West and the South. The causes were (1) impressment of sailors, (2) attacks on U.S. merchant ships, (3) arming of Native Americans on the frontier by the British, (4) the desire to expand U.S. territory to include British Canada and Spanish Florida (Spain was an ally of Great Britain), and (5) a strong sense of **nationalism**. New Englanders did not share the enthusiasm for this war and referred to it as **"Mr. Madison's War."**

Fighting the War of 1812

- The Americans began the war thinking they could easily invade and capture **Canada** because the population was sparse, and most settlers were French, not British. However, the U.S. army was small—less than 7,000—and ill prepared. When Madison asked for state militia, some New England governors refused to send troops. Lacking a commanding general and an overall strategy, the Americans, at first, lost Detroit and Fort Dearborn and were turned back in an attack across the Niagara River in New York State. The Americans were able to take **Lake Erie** and then won the **Battle of the Thames,** holding the British off along the Western end of the Canadian front. But in the East, the Americans failed in several attempts to invade Canada.

- After the British defeated Napoleon in 1814, they turned their full attention to the war with the United States and planned a three-pronged attack: (1) invasion from Canada, (2) an attack on Washington, D.C., and (3) an attack on New Orleans. The British sent some 14,000 troops from Montreal to invade New York State. Meeting the Americans near Plattsburg on **Lake Champlain,** the British were driven back and did not invade the United States from Canada again. The British captured and burned Washington, but they were stopped at Fort McHenry. **General Andrew Jackson** soundly defeated the British at the **Battle of New Orleans**—two weeks after the war ended.

Dissension on the Home Front

- In December 1814, a group of disgruntled Federalists from New England met secretly at what became known as the **Hartford Convention** to discuss their dissatisfaction with government policies. The group wrote seven constitutional amendments that were meant to redress these grievances by increasing the political power of the region. One of the reasons that the New England governors had not sent militia for the invasion of Canada was because they feared the potential power of any new territories created from an annexed Canada.

- A committee of delegates arrived in Washington to present their demands to Madison as the end of the war was announced. Although the Hartford Convention had discussed secession and the members had rejected it, opponents of the Federalists were able to use allegations of secession against them. This effectively ended the Federalists' influence.

Peace

Test-Taking Strategy

Be sure to remember the significance of the War of 1812 for the new nation.

- The **Treaty of Ghent** ended the War of 1812 but did not settle the problems of neutrality, impressment, and boundaries between the two nations. The issue of the border with Canada was sent to a commission to resolve. After the war, however, Native Americans in the Upper Midwest were no longer a threat to U.S. westward expansion. The war also changed the relationship between the United States and Great Britain. Although neither nation had won, the United States had held at bay the strongest nation in the world.

KEY PEOPLE

- John C. Calhoun, Henry Clay as War Hawks
- Francis Scott Key, "The Star-Spangled Banner"
- Meriwether Lewis, William Clark, Lewis and Clark expedition, York, Sacajawea, Columbia River
- Oliver Hazard Perry, battle for Lake Erie, "We have met the enemy and they are ours"

KEY TERMS/IDEAS

- Berlin and Milan decrees, French laws restricting trade with ships that carried British goods or entered British ports
- Nonintercourse Act, trade with nations other than Great Britain and France
- Orders of Council, British laws restricting trade by neutral nations unless they stopped in British ports first

SECTION 3. NATIONALISM: PROSPERITY AND CHANGE

The period from 1815 to 1828 marked great changes for the new nation—both at home and abroad. **James Monroe's** two terms as president are known as the **"Era of Good Feelings,"** a time characterized by geographic expansion of the republic and, for a time, economic expansion. Monroe, a Republican from Virginia and Madison's former Secretary of State, made a tour of the country shortly after his election and spoke about national unity. He promised to look out for the interests of all Americans—New Englanders as well as Southerners and Westerners. This was one example of the growing spirit of **nationalism** that was an outcome of the War of 1812. The Republicans, over time, usurped the position of the Federalists so that for ten years, the Republicans were the only political party. As a result, Monroe ran unopposed for re-election in 1820.

FAST FACTS

Era of Good Feelings

- Even before Monroe took office, Congress was considering legislation that would spur economic growth in every section of the country as well as economic independence from other countries. Known as the **American System** and sponsored by **John C. Calhoun** and **Henry Clay,** the program included (1) a **protective tariff** for American manufacturing that had grown up during the embargo and the war; (2) **internal improvements,** a national system of roads and canals paid for by revenue from the tariff to aid commerce between farmers in the Southern and frontier states and their markets on the coast; and (3) authorization of a **Second National Bank.**

Review Strategy

See pp. 127–128 for the conflicts over the Second Bank.

- Expiration of the First Bank's charter in 1811 because of the opposition of Republicans had severely hampered efforts to finance the War of 1812. Without the National Bank, there was no stable national currency; people had little confidence in the state-chartered banks and in their currency. Because it was good for the country, Republicans approved a charter for the Second National Bank in 1816.

McCulloch v. *Maryland* (1819; principle of implied powers)

Case: In 1816, as part of a political fight to limit the powers of the federal government, Maryland placed a tax on all notes issued by banks that did business in the state but were chartered outside the state. The target was the Second Bank of the United States. In a test case, the bank's cashier, James McCulloch, refused to pay the tax. Maryland won in state court, and McCulloch appealed.

Decision: In upholding the constitutionality of the Second Bank, the Court cited the **"necessary and proper clause."** The Court ruled that the Bank was necessary to fulfill the government's duties to tax, borrow, and coin money.

Significance: The Court's opinion broadened the powers of Congress to include implied powers in addition to those listed in the Constitution. This ruling has had a major impact on the development of the government, allowing it to evolve as needed to meet new circumstances.

- Congress passed the **Tariff of 1816.** Westerners and people from the Middle Atlantic states supported the tariff. Even some of those, like Thomas Jefferson, who had opposed Hamilton's tariff plan in 1789, approved of this protective tariff. New Englanders were divided, with **Daniel Webster** arguing for no tariff. At this point, some Southerners, such as **John C. Calhoun**, expected that their region would develop manufacturing and were willing to live with the tariff.

Review Strategy

Track the issue of internal improvements as a factor in sectionalism.

- The plan for internal improvements was less successful. In 1806, Congress had approved money to build a road from Cumberland, Maryland, across the mountains into what today is West Virginia. The **National** or **Cumberland Road** was begun in 1811, and by Madison's administration had reached into Ohio. In 1816, Congress passed a bill for internal improvements at federal expense. Madison vetoed it because he did not believe the Constitution allowed expenditures to improve transportation. Later, Monroe also vetoed the bill.

The Panic of 1819

- The prosperity brought about by the post-war boom sparked a frenzy of borrowing to buy land and to build factories. Banks, eager to make money, were willing to offer loans with little collateral. In 1818, to stem the **speculation,** the Bank of the United States ordered its branch banks to tighten credit. Many of the state banks had been issuing their paper money without the gold or silver to back it, so the notes were worthless. Unable to back their paper, state banks closed; unable to repay their loans, farmers and manufacturers went bankrupt. A **depression** ensued that lasted for three years.

The Missouri Compromise

- The first serious controversy over slavery since the Constitution arose over admission of Missouri, part of the Louisiana Purchase, to the Union as a slave state. There were eleven free states and eleven slave states, with twenty-two votes each in the Senate. Admitting Missouri would tip the balance in favor of slave states.
- The House passed and the Senate rejected the **Tallmadge Amendment** which would have outlawed the further importation of slaves into Missouri and freed all people who were born into slavery after Missouri became a state on their twenty-fifth birthdays.

- Then, Maine petitioned to be admitted as a free state, thus restoring the balance of slave and free states. Henry Clay was able to reach a compromise in which (1) Maine would be admitted as a free state and Missouri as a slave state and (2) any future state created from the Louisiana Purchase north of the 36° 30' line would be free. Known as the **Missouri Compromise,** it only delayed resolution of the problem of slavery.

Foreign Policy Under Monroe

- After the War of 1812, the United States and Great Britain signed the **Rush-Bagot Agreement** by which they agreed not to keep warships on the Great Lakes. In 1818, they set the boundary between the Louisiana Territory and Canada at the 49th parallel. However, the issue of the boundary line for Oregon would continue unresolved until the 1840s.
- After the Revolutionary War, Spain received **Florida—East and West**—from Great Britain, and the areas remained under Spanish rule until 1819. In the thirty intervening years, many Americans had moved into the Floridas: white settlers, slaves escaping from servitude, Native Americans forced from their lands in the new states, and escaped criminals. They paid little attention to Spanish colonial government, and Spain, entangled in European wars, had few soldiers to send to Florida to subdue the settlers.

- In 1810, Americans in West Florida declared their independence and were admitted as a territory into the United States. When Madison offered to buy East Florida, the Spanish refused. In 1818, President Monroe sent **General Andrew Jackson** into East Florida, in what became known as the **First Seminole War**, to stop raids by Native Americans into U.S. territory. The following year, Spain agreed to give up East Florida in return for the U.S.'s abandonment of claims to Texas. The **Adams-Onis Treaty** also recognized U.S. claims to the Oregon Territory.

Review Strategy

See pp. 176–177 for the Roosevelt Corollary to the Monroe Doctrine.

- With the exception of Cuba and Puerto Rico, between 1810 and 1824, the Spanish colonies of **Latin America** had won or were in the process of winning their independence from Spain. As a result, both the United States and Great Britain had found profitable trading partners among these new nations. They did not wish to lose them if Spain regained its colonies, now that it was no longer bogged down in the long war against Napoleon. In addition, the United States was concerned about **Russia**'s activity along the Pacific Coast, where it was setting up trading posts and had claimed **Alaska**. The British urged the United States to join it in issuing a declaration (1) that opposed intervention by any European nation in the new nations of Latin America and (2) that agreed that neither Great Britain nor the United States would attempt to annex any part of the hemisphere. President Monroe consulted his Secretary of State John Quincy Adams, who advised issuing a statement alone, which Monroe did. The **Monroe Doctrine,** issued in 1823, was a warning to European nations to stay out of the affairs of the Western Hemisphere and, in turn, the United States would not interfere in European affairs. It was a bold statement by a nation that did not have the military power to back it up, but it showed the nation's desire to be considered a world power. Had the European nations decided to call the U.S.'s bluff, British warships would have intervened.

The Election of 1824

- Although by the election of 1824 the Federalist party was dead, the Republicans were split into several groups, usually along sectional lines so, that four Republicans ran for president in 1824. William H. Crawford of Georgia was picked by the Republican **caucus** to run for president. **John Quincy Adams** of Massachusetts, son of the second president, was the favorite son of New England. **Henry Clay,** building a reputation as the **Great Compromiser,** represented the West. Because of his role in the War of 1812, **Andrew Jackson** of Tennessee, also a Western state, was popular across all sections.

- When the election was over, Jackson had the most electoral votes (and popular votes) but not a majority. According to the Twelfth Amendment, the House of Representatives was to decide the election. Clay was disqualified because he had the fewest number

CHAPTER 3

of electoral votes. He threw his support to Adams, and Adams was elected president. When Adams made Clay his Secretary of State, Jackson and his supporters claimed that a **"corrupt bargain"** between Clay and Adams had cost Jackson his rightful victory. Clay had blocked Jackson's election to keep a rival Westerner from the presidency. Adams chose Clay because they shared certain beliefs, such as the necessity for a strong federal government and the importance of the American System.

Building a Transportation Network

- Although federally supported internal improvements had been voted down, the nation saw a **transportation revolution** in the 1800s. The **Canal Era** began with the building of the **Erie Canal** in New York State to connect the Northeast and the Great Lakes. By 1840, a network of canals linked the waterways of the Northeast with those of the newer states of the West. The Western parts of New York and Pennsylvania were joined with Eastern ports and with the Great Lakes, while canals in Ohio, Indiana, Kentucky, and Illinois linked the Ohio and Mississippi Rivers with the Great Lakes.

- In addition to speeding goods to customers, the canals created new markets. Canals made it possible for people—both the native-born who felt the older states were getting too crowded and the increasing waves of immigrants—to move quickly from the Eastern seaboard to the new frontier to settle. No canals were as financially successful as the Erie Canal, and the **Panic of 1837,** along with the advent of the railroad, ended the Canal Era.

- Although the first **railroads** were operating in the 1830s, a safe and reliable steam engine was needed before railroads could overtake canals, and that did not occur until the early 1850s. Railroads were a more satisfactory means of transporting goods and people than canals because (1) they did not rely on waterways for their routes, (2) they could operate in all kinds of weather, and (3) they were cheap to operate. Even more than canals, the railroads spurred the growth and settlement of the Western territories and the development of the nation's **market economy.**

www.petersons.com

118

Peterson's ■ *SAT II Success: U.S. History*

Gibbons v. *Ogden* (1824; interstate commerce)

Case: The case revolved around the Commerce Clause, Article 1, Section 8, Clause 3 of the Constitution. The state of New York had awarded Aaron Ogden an exclusive permit to carry passengers by steamboat between New York City and New Jersey. The federal government had issued a coasting license to Thomas Gibbons for the same route. Ogden sued Gibbons and won in a New York court. Gibbons appealed to the Supreme Court.

Decision: The Supreme Court ruled in Gibbons' favor. A state cannot interfere with Congress's power to regulate interstate commerce. It took a broad view of the term *commerce*.

Significance: Marshall, dealing a blow to the arguments of states' rights advocates, established the superiority of federal authority over states' rights under the Constitution. This ruling, which enlarged the definition of commerce, became the basis of the Civil Rights Act of 1964, prohibiting discrimination in public accommodations.

The Early Factory System

- The **factory system** replaced the **domestic system** in the United States in the early 1800s. A major impetus to this development was the embargo of 1807 and the War of 1812. The first mills were located in New England and operated by water power. Later, the large turbines were powered by coal or steam. Francis Cabot Lowell and his **Boston Associates** formed a corporation to build **Lowell, Massachusetts,** a company town whose factories produced textiles. In time, **entrepreneurs** learned how to transfer the factory system to other industries, such as manufacturing woolen goods and firearms. As a result, more and more jobs once done by skilled workers were taken over by machines. Areas in the Mid-Atlantic states with the same resources of energy and cheap labor as New England grew into industrial cities.

- The first workers in the textile mills were native-born women recruited from New England farms. They lived in supervised boarding houses and viewed millwork as a way (1) to help out their families by sending money home, (2) to save for their future marriage, or (3) to see something of the world before they married and settled down. The original **Lowell System** was an experiment in running factories without the abuses of the English factory system. By the 1830s, however, these women were being replaced by families of new immigrants, including children. Penniless, these families would work for less than the native-born women. Conditions in the mills deteriorated as mill owners demanded more work for a greater return on their investment. When times were bad, such as during the Panic of 1837, mill owners cut the already low wages.

- In the 1790s, the first **labor unions** organized skilled workers, such as printers. As early as the 1820s, factory workers organized to demand (1) higher wages, (2) a 10-hour workday, (3) better working conditions, and (4) an end to debtors' prisons. Several times in the 1830s and 1840s, the women workers in Lowell went out on **strike.** Each time, the mill owners threatened to replace them, and the women returned to work without winning their demands. The influx of immigrants beginning in the 1830s, and especially the large numbers of Irish in the 1840s, held back the growth of the labor movement.

Cotton Revolution in the South

Review Strategy

For more on the development of the South, see pp. 121–122.

- Because most labor, land, and capital in the South were dedicated to farming, little industry developed in that region. Because of the growing demand for cotton to feed the textile industry in the North and in England, the South had the potential to make money from cotton agriculture. However, removing cotton seeds from cotton bolls was labor intensive. With the invention of the **cotton gin** in 1793 by **Eli Whitney,** based on a suggestion by **Catherine Greene,** cotton bolls could be cleaned quickly. Raising cotton immediately became more profitable. As a result, cotton agriculture and **slavery,** which provided the labor, spread across the South.

KEY PEOPLE

Review Strategy

See if you can relate these people to their correct context in the "Fast Facts" section.

- **Richard Arkwright, Samuel Slater, spinning machine**
- **Edmund Cartwright, power loom**
- **De Witt Clinton**
- **Robert Fulton,** *Clermont*
- **Samuel F. B. Morse, telegraph**
- **Eli Whitney, interchangeable parts**

KEY TERMS/IDEAS

Review Strategy

See if you can relate these terms and ideas to their correct context in the "Fast Facts" section.

- **clipper ships, China trade; steamships**
- ***Commonwealth* v. *Hunt,* Massachusetts court ruling on legality of unions**
- **National Trades Union**
- **trade societies, closed shop**
- **Waltham System**

SECTION 4. SECTIONALISM

While the War of 1812 engendered a sense of nationalism in politicians and ordinary citizens alike, the economic changes that occurred after the war brought a growing sense of **sectionalism.** The nation was being divided by the economic self-interests of the Northeast, the South, and the quickly expanding Western states and territories.

FAST FACTS

The Southern Cotton Culture

- As a result of the cotton gin, **cotton agriculture** spread widely across the South from the coastal states to the Mississippi, the **Deep South.** Because of the need for large numbers of workers, **slavery** spread with it. Although the importation of enslaved Africans had ended in 1808, a thriving **internal market** in slaves developed between the old states and the new states of the South. By 1860, there were almost 4 million slaves, four times the number in 1808.

- Because slaves were considered property, slave owners thought nothing of selling individuals, thus splitting families apart. The worst fear was to be "sold down the river," meaning the Mississippi, to toil in the **"cotton factories"** of the **Deep South** (Alabama, Mississippi, Arkansas, Louisiana, and, later, Texas). Slaves worked from sunup to sundown in gangs supervised by a white **overseer** and a **slave driver**—often an African American— planting, hoeing, weeding, picking, and ginning cotton, depending on the season. Women and children worked alongside the men. A few slaves were trained as house servants to work in the planters' houses as butlers, cooks, or maids. A few learned skills such as blacksmithing and carpentry.

- From the earliest times, slaves had rebelled. In the 1600s and 1700s in New York and New England, slaves plotted against their owners but were caught and executed. Passage of a series of **slave codes** followed each incident. In the **Stono Uprising,** which took place in South Carolina in 1739, some twenty slaves tried to escape to St. Augustine in Spanish-held Florida but were captured. The Spanish were offering freedom to any slave who escaped to Florida. Other uprisings that frightened Southern slaveholders were (1) **Gabriel Prosser's Conspiracy** in Virginia, (2) **Denmark Vesey's Conspiracy** in South Carolina, and (3) **Nat Turner's Rebellion,** also in Virginia. In addition to outright rebellion, slaves used other ways to resist: they worked slowly and sabotaged tools and machinery.

- Although the phrase **"Cotton Kingdom"** has come to symbolize the **antebellum South,** in reality, the South was more than big cotton plantations. Virginia, Kentucky, Tennessee, and North Carolina raised tobacco; Louisiana's main crop was sugar; and the swampy areas of Georgia and South Carolina cultivated rice. There were only about 50,000 large plantations in the South, but hundreds of thousands of small farms that raised food crops and livestock, much of it for the farmers' own use. Most Southerners lived at the **subsistence level.**

- Because cotton was the major export of the South, the region had little industry—about 10 percent of the nation's total number of factories—few canals, major roads, or railroads and few large cities. Planters hesitated to put their money into factories because farming was more profitable. What industry existed, such as milling wheat or making iron tools, developed to satisfy local needs. These mills and factories were not part of any large national trading network, so there was little reason to build a transportation system. The economy of the South remained **rural** until the Civil War, so there was little reason to develop, or little need for, a number of large cities.
- The **"cotton culture"** gave rise to a rigid class system:

SOCIAL SYSTEM OF THE ANTEBELLUM SOUTH	
Planters	Owned from 20 to 200 slaves, lived on the best lands, were the leaders of the region
Small slaveholders	Owned fewer than 20 slaves and might own only 1 or 2, worked medium-size farms, had little influence
Small farmers	Owned no slaves, raised their own food and livestock, usually raised some **cash crop,** such as cotton or tobacco
Tenant farmers	Worked poor land, often exhausted soils that planters no longer could use, generally in debt
Poor whites	Frontier families living in the mountains on rocky soil that was difficult to farm, also hunted for food; might hire out as day laborers
Free blacks	Nearly half of all blacks in the United States; after 1830, Southern legislatures passed laws severely limiting their freedom (could not vote, have a trial by jury, testify against whites, attend public schools, or assemble in a group without a white person present); earned livelihoods as craftworkers
Slaves	No rights, considered **chattel**

- To the Southern way of thinking, a number of economic factors supported slavery: (1) the increasing demand for cotton, (2) the labor-intensive nature of cotton agriculture, (3) the cheap source of labor in slaves, and (4) the climate of the South, especially the Deep South, that allowed almost year-round farming, so slaves did not have to be supported during slack time. To justify their use of human beings as slaves, Southerners developed the argument that slavery actually helped slaves. According to the explanation, the system guaranteed slaves food to eat, a roof over their heads, clothes to wear, and a home in sickness and old age. Planters contrasted this secure life with the precarious existence of workers in Northern factories. Led by wealthy planters, this **pro-slavery argument** took hold in the antebellum South. Over time (1) small farmers who wanted to own more slaves, (2) farmers who hoped to own slaves some day, and (3) even those with no hope of owning slaves came to believe the rationale. It created a sense of who Southerners were and what they stood for.

Immigration

- The North during this period was developing into an urban, industrial region. Swelling **immigration,** especially from Ireland beginning in the 1840s, provided the labor to turn the engines of commerce. Between 1790 and 1815, about 250,000 Europeans immigrated to the new nation. Between 1820 and 1860, some 4.6 million came, mostly to port cities of the Northeast, where many stayed.

- Immigrants came for a variety of reasons. **Pull factors** included (1) economic opportunities created by industrialization, (2) the transportation revolution, and (3) westward expansion. Jobs and the possibility of owning land brought many people. **Push factors** depended on the immigrant group but, in general, included (1) lack of economic opportunities at home, including the inability to afford to own land; (2) crop failures; and (3) political instability.

- Immigrants were not always welcome. **Nativist** sentiment ran against immigrants because native-born Americans were concerned that the immigrants (1) would take their jobs, (2) were threats to the American way of life because they established their own separate communities, (3) were revolutionaries because of the revolutions of 1830 and 1848 in Europe, and (4) were Roman Catholics. **Anti-Catholic prejudice** was strong before the Civil War and directed mostly toward the Irish. Most other immigrant groups were Protestant, as were most native-born Americans.

Review Strategy

See pp. 134–138 for more information on the settling of the Far West, California, the Southwest, and Texas.

- Between 1790 and the 1820s, the **Western frontier** had been pushed from the Appalachians to the Mississippi River. The land between the Mississippi and the Rocky Mountains, the Great Plains, today the major farming area of the country, was considered the **Great American Desert** until after the Civil War. In the 1830s and 1840s, it was simply the area that settlers had to get through on their way to the **Oregon Territory.** The first Americans into Oregon had been **fur traders, Mountain Men** who blazed the **Oregon Trail.**

Settling the Upper Midwest

- By 1840, the fertile lands between the Ohio and Mississippi Rivers had been settled, and five states had been carved out of the

Northwest Territory (Michigan, Ohio, Indiana, Illinois, Missouri). Large farm families worked the land. In the beginning, the families were **self-sufficient,** but the invention of the **steel plow** and the **mechanical reaper** allowed them to raise **cash crops.** The Upper Midwest became the major grain-producing region of the United States. An efficient transportation system of waterways, canals, and, later, railroads developed to move goods to market. To serve these farmers who now had money to spend, villages and towns grew up, especially at the junction of transportation routes. A number of these towns grew into major commercial and industrial cities.

Native American Removal

- As white settlers moved into the land beyond the Appalachians, they came into contact with Native Americans already living there. As early as the 1790s, the nation had fought Native Americans in the Northwest Territory **(Battle of Fallen Timbers).** The **Treaty of Greenville** forced Native Americans to give up most of their lands, thus opening the area for white settlement. In 1831, as a result of the **Black Hawk War,** the **Sauk** and **Fox** were forced to move from Illinois and Wisconsin across the Mississippi to Iowa.

- In the 1820s and 1830s, the battle for Native American land shifted to the South and the **Old Southwest,** the area south of the Ohio River and between the Appalachians and the Mississippi (the modern states of Kentucky, Tennessee, Alabama, and Mississippi). The **Five Civilized Tribes,** as they were called because they had been converted to Christianity and had become farmers, stood in the way of settlers. The **Indian Removal Act of 1830** gave President Andrew Jackson the power to remove the Native Americans by force to the **Indian Territory,** what is now Oklahoma. One by one the nations were removed, sometimes forcibly. Even when they won, it made no difference to Georgians who wanted their land.

- In *Cherokee Nation v. The State of Georgia* (1831), the Cherokee Nation, besieged by white settlers who wanted their land, sued in Supreme Court to prevent the seizure of their land by the state of Georgia. The Court, under John Marshall, found that the Cherokee were not a sovereign nation but a dependent one and, as such, had no standing to bring a lawsuit to the Supreme Court. However, the Court found that they did have the right to their land. Georgia, supported by President Andrew Jackson, ignored the ruling.

- The Cherokee tried again to win recognition of their claims with *Worcester v. Georgia* (1832), citing treaties with the federal government. This time the Court, under John Marshall, agreed with the Cherokee and declared Georgia's laws in regard to the Cherokee unconstitutional. "The Cherokee Nation then is a distinct community, occupying its own territory . . . in which the laws of Georgia can have no force, and which the citizens of Georgia have no right to enter without the assent of the Cherokee themselves or in conformity with treaties and the acts of Congress." Again, Georgia—and Andrew Jackson—ignored the ruling.

- In 1838, **President Martin Van Buren** sent the army to move the Cherokee to Indian Territory, a journey known as the **Trail of Tears.**

KEY PEOPLE

Review Strategy

See if you can relate these people to their correct context in the "Fast Facts" section.

- **John Deere**
- **Charles Goodyear**
- **Cyrus McCormick**
- **Solomon Northup,** *Twelve Years a Slave*

KEY TERMS/IDEAS

Review Strategy

See if you can relate these terms and ideas to their correct context in the "Fast Facts" section.

- **American Colonization Society, Liberia**
- **Irish potato famine**
- **Know-Nothings, Order of the Star-Spangled Banner**

SECTION 5. THE AGE OF JACKSON, 1828–1848

The years between 1828 and the Mexican War of 1848 saw rapid change in both the political life of the country and its size. Sectional rivalries came to dominate politics and affect the nation's economy as well. The major change was in the size and nature of the electorate. The **"Age of Jackson"** has come to be synonymous with the **"Age of the Common Man."**

FAST FACTS

Increased Political Participation

Test-Taking Strategy

Think about which items on the list have had the most long-term significance of the United States.

- The election of 1828 was run not on issues but on the personalities of the candidates, **John Quincy Adams** and **Andrew Jackson.** The election is significant in that (1) for the first time, a candidate born west of the Appalachians was elected president; (2) the political center of the nation was shifting away from the Eastern seaboard; (3) leaders were no longer necessarily to be chosen from among the ranks of the educated and wealthy; (4) the number of voters increased threefold from the 1824 election; (5) the **Democratic Party** (supporters of Jackson) came into existence; and (6) the Republicans (the old Democratic-Republicans) were replaced by the **National Republicans** (supporters of Adams).
- The increased **political participation** evident in the election of 1828 came about because of the change in **voting requirements.**

The growth of the West, with its sense of social equality and the change in ways of making a living in all sections, prompted the states to drop property qualifications for voting. Religious tests were also dropped. Some states substituted the payment of a tax, but this, too, was eventually eliminated. By the 1820s, all free white male taxpayers could vote, and free black men could vote in some Northern states. Women and slaves were excluded. The removal of property requirements meant that **suffrage** was extended down into the middle and lower classes—**the common man.**

- **Jacksonian Democracy** manifested itself in other ways. People now expected their leaders to ask their opinions and represent their views. More offices became elective rather than appointive, especially local positions such as judge and sheriff. People took more interest in politics, and political parties began to organize at the **grassroots** level. Rather than use the **caucus** to choose candidates for public office, parties began to use **nominating conventions.** These changes led to **political patronage** and the **spoils system** ("to the victor belong the spoils"), which Jackson used widely to reward his friends with jobs in the federal government. But the changes also reflected a belief in the ability of ordinary people to govern—a logical outgrowth of the American Revolution.

New Political Parties

- During the election of 1828, Jackson's supporters began calling themselves **Democrats** after the Democratic-Republican Party of Jefferson. Jackson's appeal widened the traditional base of the party to include Westerners and ordinary people.
- The **Whig Party** was formed during the election of 1832 by the National Republicans and Jackson's opponents in the Democratic Party. Henry Clay was their presidential candidate. The party took its name from those who had opposed King George III; the new Whigs called Jackson **"King Andrew."** Jackson had very strong views of what the role of president should be, which his opponents regarded at times as a disregard for the law. The Whigs, in general, supported the protective tariff and the National Bank. Whig candidates were elected president in 1840 and 1844, but sectional differences (slavery and economic policy) divided the party. After the deaths of Clay and **Daniel Webster,** who had kept the party together, it disappeared in the 1850s.

States' Rights and Nullification

- The issue of **internal improvements** came up in Jackson's first term and became enmeshed with the issue of **states' rights.** Congress had passed a bill authorizing the expenditure of federal funds to extend the Cumberland Road within the state of Kentucky. Jackson appeared to support states' rights by vetoing the bill on the grounds that the Constitution did not allow the use of federal funds for local transportation. This became known as the **Maysville Road Veto.**

Review Strategy

The Kentucky and Virginia Resolutions and the Hartford Convention took the same stand.

- In the early 1820s, Northeastern manufacturers began to lobby for a higher tariff, arguing that the **Tariff of 1816** was not enough. Although Southerners had supported the earlier tariff, they opposed the **Tariff of 1824,** fearing that if Europeans could not sell their goods to Americans, they would stop buying raw materials from the South. The tariff was raised again in 1828 over their protests and was called by them the **Tariff of Abominations.** As Southerners feared, cotton exports fell, and some planters faced serious losses. In 1832, Congress passed a new tariff bill lowering the tax on some items. South Carolinians protested that the bill was not enough. They also believed that the tariff controversy showed that the federal government was becoming too strong, and that the next step would be the end of slavery. The South Carolina legislature called a convention and passed an **Ordinance of Nullification,** stating that the tariff was "null, void, and no law; nor binding upon this state, its officers, or its citizens." The state threatened to secede if the federal government attempted to collect the tariff in South Carolina.

- Based on the Maysville Road Veto, Southerners thought Jackson, a fellow Southerner and slave owner, would agree with the South Carolina position. However, Jackson stood behind the Constitution. While warning South Carolinians that secession was treason, he tried to persuade the leaders of Congress to pass a new tariff bill that would reduce taxes. He also requested that Congress pass the **Force Bill,** allowing him to use the army and navy to collect the tariff and put down any insurrection. **Henry Clay,** the **Great Compromiser,** negotiated a new tariff that was acceptable to South Carolina, and South Carolina repealed the nullification ordinance, thus ending the **Nullification Crisis.**

The Bank War

- Jackson distrusted the **Second Bank** because he believed it (1) was run by the wealthy for their own self-interests and (2) had too much influence on economic policy. The Bank's charter was to come up for renewal in 1836, but **Nicholas Biddle,** the Bank's president, requested early renewal in 1832, hoping to make the Bank a major issue in the election of 1832. **Henry Clay,** the presidential candidate on the Whig ticket, introduced the bill. Congress voted to recharter the Bank, but Jackson vetoed it. Congress could not override the veto. During the campaign, Clay, **Daniel Webster,** and the Bank's advocates called for renewal of its charter, arguing that the nation's economy depended on it. The voters, especially Westerners, Southerners, and the working class in the East, agreed with Jackson, and he was re-elected.

- Regardless of the law, Jackson destroyed the Bank in 1833 by having all federal money withdrawn from it. Jackson went through three Secretaries of the Treasury before one would agree to remove the funds. Jackson deposited the money in various state banks that the Whigs called **"pet banks,"** because they were supposedly run by loyal supporters of Jackson. Biddle countered by restricting credit to state banks and withdrawing money from circulation. As a result, credit dried up, and the nation teetered on the brink of an economic depression. Biddle sought to blame Jackson for the depression, while Democrats claimed that Jackson had been right to veto the Bank if it could cause so much damage. The people agreed with Jackson again, seeing his veto as an affirmation of democracy. Feeling the pressure from the fierce attacks, Biddle reissued credit to state banks.

The Panic of 1837

- Jackson turned to **Martin Van Buren** as his choice to succeed Jackson as president. Shortly after taking office, Van Buren found himself faced with the **Panic of 1837.** There were a number of causes for the panic and ensuing depression: (1) the **Specie Circular,** Jackson's attempt to halt the speculation and inflation that followed the release for sale of millions of acres of government land by requiring gold or silver, rather than bank notes to purchase the land; (2) the withdrawal of British investments as Great Britain suffered through its own economic hard times; and (3) the lack of a national banking system with stable currency.

- Van Buren did not want a central bank either, but he realized that the government's money had to be deposited somewhere. After having seen so many fail, he believed that small commercial banks were not safe. Van Buren proposed the **Independent Treasury Act** as a way to separate the federal treasury from the banking system. Vaults were installed in selected sites around the country to hold federal tax revenues, which were to be backed by gold. Congress approved the **Independent Treasury System** in 1840, repealed it in 1841, and reinstated it in 1846. The system ended in 1913 with passage of the **Federal Reserve Act.**

KEY PEOPLE/TERMS

Review Strategy

See if you can relate these people and terms to their correct context in the "Fast Facts" section.

- **Alexis de Tocqueville,** *Democracy in America*
- **Webster-Hayne Debate, public lands, issue of nullification**
- **wildcat banks**

SECTION 6. A CHANGING SOCIETY AND AN EMERGING CULTURE

The sense of nationalism apparent in politics found voice in an emerging cultural identity as well. Desirous of developing their own subjects and styles, American writers and artists set about creating an American culture. Mindful of the promises of the Declaration of Independence, some Americans also sought to reform a society that they felt was not living up to its founding ideals.

FAST FACTS

A Second Religious Revival

Review Strategy

Compare the First and Second Great Awakenings.

- Part of the impetus behind the reform movements was a resurgence in religion. Like the Great Awakening of the mid-1700s, the **Second Great Awakening,** which began in the 1790s, was accompanied by revival meetings, the erection of new churches, and the founding of colleges and universities.

Public Education

- The growth in political participation both encouraged the **movement for public education** and was an outgrowth of increased educational levels. Before the 1830s, only New England supported public elementary schools to any extent. Reformers called for public schools (1) to educate future voters and (2) to prevent social ills like poverty and crime. However, not everyone agreed with the reformers. Levying taxes to pay for public schools was an issue in part because of a dislike of taxes and in part because some religious groups that ran their own schools did not see why they had to pay to send other people's children to public school. If and how to educate African Americans remained an issue. Some people, especially in the West, saw no particular need for anything but the basics of education.

- By the 1850s, most free states had established public school systems. The **Northwest Ordinance** had required that every township set aside land for a school, so free public education grew quickly in the Midwest. In the South, because it was an agrarian society, little headway was made in establishing free public education. The children of planters, merchants, and professionals had tutors, or their sons were sent to private schools. While Americans might have supported elementary schools, there was little support for public high schools, although private **academies** for secondary education thrived.

Utopian Communities

- Some reformers wanted to remake all of society. These **Utopian experiments** were small groups of like-minded individuals who lived apart from society in self-sufficient communities. Some groups were based on the principles of **socialism;** that is, all members would work together and own all property in common. Other groups, like the **Mormons,** based their communities on religious principles.

- The Mormons, or the **Church of the Latter-Day Saints,** had communities in Ohio, Illinois, and Missouri before settling in Utah. In each location, they were resented by their neighbors (1) who took offense at the Mormon teaching that they had received revelations from God **(Book of Mormon),** (2) who did not approve of the Mormon practice of **polygamy,** and (3) who feared the Mormons would oppose slavery (Missouri). After an attack on their community of Nauvoo, Illinois, the Mormons went West, settling in Utah, which was still under Mexican control. After the Mexican War, the Mormons requested statehood but were caught in the controversy over slavery. Utah did not become a state until 1896.

Transcendentalism

Test-Taking Strategy

Emerson, author of Nature, *which defined transcendentalism, and Thoreau, who wrote* Walden *and* Civil Disobedience, *are significant figures in American letters.*

- **Transcendentalism** was very much an American literary movement. Centered in New England, Transcendentalists emphasized (1) the unity and divinity of human beings and nature, (2) the value of intuition over reason, (3) self-reliance, and (4) individual conscience. Authors such as **Ralph Waldo Emerson, Henry David Thoreau, Bronson Alcott,** and **Margaret Fuller,** who edited their journal *Dial*, were prominent Transcendentalists.

Development of a National Literature and Art

- Transcendentalism also influenced the development of such literary greats as **Herman Melville, Nathaniel Hawthorne,** and, later, **Walt Whitman.** The writers of the 1820s, 1830s, and 1840s created a **national literature**—that is, a literature that took its themes, its settings, and its characters from the new nation. The purpose was, in the words of one historian, "to reform America's attitude toward itself." No longer would Americans think of themselves as poor relations of Europeans when it came to culture.

- **James Fenimore Cooper** used the recent frontier past to create heroic figures. **Washington Irving** turned the Dutch history of the Hudson River Valley into literature, while Nathaniel Hawthorne used Puritanism as the backdrop for his stories. **Romanticism** played a role in the development of American literature of this period, but the context was purely American.

- The art of the period used American themes and subjects and was also inspired by romanticism. The **Hudson River School** used the landscape of the river valley for its paintings, just as the **Knickerbocker School** used the area for its literary themes. Among its most famous artists are **Thomas Cole** and **Asher B. Durand.** Earlier artists of the 1800s, such as **John Trumbull, Gilbert Stuart,** and **Charles Wilson Peale,** used the battles and heroes of the Revolutionary War as the subject matter for their paintings. Later painters **George Caleb Bingham** and **George Catlin** used the new frontier's Native Americans and ordinary people, such as fur traders floating down the Missouri River, as subjects for their paintings.

Women's Rights

- A major reform movement of the nineteenth century dealt with **women's rights.** At that time, (1) education for girls was limited, especially for poor girls; (2) women could not train for a profession other than teaching, and that only because women were more likely to work for less than men; (3) married women could not own property, although single women could; (4) mothers had no legal rights to their children; (5) married women could not make a contract or sue in court; (6) married women who worked outside the home had no right to their wages; (7) women could not vote; (8) women could not hold public office; (9) public speaking in front of an audience of men and women was not considered proper for women, although they could work in reform movements under the direction of men.
- At the **Seneca Falls Convention** in 1848, the first **women's rights conference, Lucretia Mott** and **Elizabeth Cady Stanton** led the delegates in drafting the **Declaration of Sentiments and Resolutions,** modeled after the Declaration of Independence. At mid-century, the reformers were able to effect few changes, although some states passed laws allowing women to own and manage property.

Abolition

Review Strategy

See pp. 138–139 for information on abolition and the Underground Railroad.

- There was a crossover between the women's rights movement and **abolition,** with many women active in both. **Sojourner Truth** spoke for both enslaved Africans and women, while **Frederick Douglass,** perhaps the best known of African American abolitionists, seconded Stanton's call for voting rights for women.
- In the early 1800s, the **antislavery movement** had supporters in all sections of the country, but as cotton became more profitable, fewer Southerners were willing to speak out against slavery. Abolitionist activities increased in the 1830s, and their petitions began to pour into Congress. To stop debate on these petitions, Southerners pushed through **gag rules** in both the House and the Senate in 1836 that rejected all petitions without debate. The gag rules were repealed in 1844.

Other Reform Movements

- The **temperance movement** developed in answer to the growing problem of drinking and drunkenness. Reformers laid the blame for such social ills as poverty, crime, and mental illness on heavy drinking. Reformers launched a campaign to convince people to give up drinking and to ask governments to **prohibit** the sale of alcohol. Temperance meetings resembled religious revival meetings, and, in fact, many of the movement's leaders were clergy. As a result of the clamor raised by the movement, a number of politicians supported it, and about a dozen states passed laws prohibiting the sale of alcohol. Other states passed laws giving local governments the option of banning the sale of liquor in their jurisdiction.

- Through the efforts of **Dorothea Dix** and like-minded reformers, a number of changes were made to help the mentally ill and criminals. When Dix began her work, those who were mentally ill went untreated and were sent to prisons with criminals. By the 1850s, (1) hospitals for the mentally ill had been opened in a number of states, (2) male and female prisoners were segregated, (3) youthful offenders were separated from adults, (4) the poor were no longer imprisoned for debt, and (5) the whipping of prisoners had been abolished by a number of states.

KEY PEOPLE

Review Strategy

See if you can relate additional people to their correct context in the "Fast Facts" section.

- Susan B. Anthony, Lucy Stone
- Catherine Beecher, Emma Hart Willard
- Thomas Gallaudet, hearing impaired, sign language
- Henry Highland Garnett; Theodore Weld, *American Slavery As It Is*
- William Lloyd Garrison, *Liberator,* New England Anti-Slavery Society, American Anti-Slavery Society
- Angelina Grimké, Sarah Grimké
- F. E. W. Harper (Frances Ellen Watkins), free African American abolitionist
- Samuel Gridley Howe, New England Institution for the Blind
- Knickerbocker School
- James Russell Lowell, Henry Wadsworth Longfellow
- Horace Mann, Secretary of Education, Board of Education, Massachusetts, normal schools to train teachers, professionals
- Herman Melville, Edgar Allan Poe
- Sarah Peale, John James Audubon
- Shakers
- Joseph Smith, Brigham Young

KEY TERMS/IDEAS

Review Strategy

See if you can relate these terms and ideas to their correct context in the "Fast Facts" section.

- **American Temperance Union**
- **Brook Farm, Transcendentalists**
- **higher education for the professions such as medicine and law, apprenticeships**
- **Lincoln University, first African American college**
- **Mount Holyoke Female Seminary, Mary Lyon**
- **New Harmony, Indiana; Robert Owen, social experiment**
- **Oneida Community, New York; religious experiment; considered themselves the family of God; very successful manufacturing business**

Chapter 4

REVIEWING THE EVENTS LEADING TO THE CIVIL WAR AND ITS AFTERMATH

The study of U.S. history in the nineteenth century revolves, to a large extent, around the events leading to the Civil War, fighting the war, and then Reconstruction of the South. Chapter 4 provides a brief review of these developments. Remember that 40 percent of the questions on the SAT II: U.S. History Test will be drawn from the period between 1790 and 1898. Consider that a number of the questions will deal with the years from 1845 to 1877 and the people and events that brought about the Civil War and its resolution.

SECTION 1. TERRITORIAL EXPANSION AND SECTIONAL CRISIS

By 1840, the United States had enjoyed more than two decades of peace. The frontier had been pushed back to the Mississippi, and Americans eager for land and/or adventure were traveling through the **Great American Desert** to the Pacific Northwest. **Commercial agriculture** was coming to dominate the Midwest. The **transportation revolution** and the **factory system** had transformed the Northeast and Middle Atlantic states into centers of commerce. Cotton was king in the South. What next?

As the land between the Eastern seaboard and the Mississippi filled with people and farms and more immigrants came to the country, some people looked to move farther west. However, the British and the Spanish blocked the way. In 1845, an editor at the *New York Morning News* wrote that the nation had a "**manifest destiny** to overspread the continent allotted by Providence." Americans used this idea of manifest destiny as their justification for expansion into the Southwest and the Far West. It was also a sense of **mission,** what Providence had deemed the direction of their future to be, that drove Americans west.

FAST FACTS

Realizing the Nation's "Manifest Destiny"

- Between 1845 and 1853, the United States grew to its current size of the forty-eight contiguous states, adding Alaska and Hawaii later.

ACQUISITION	PRESENT STATES
Texas by resolution of Congress in 1845	Texas, parts of Oklahoma, Kansas, Colorado, and New Mexico
Oregon Territory by treaty with Great Britain in 1846	Oregon, Washington, Idaho, and parts of Montana and Wyoming
Mexican Cession by treaty with Mexico in 1848	California, Nevada, Utah, Arizona, and parts of Colorado, Wyoming, and New Mexico
Gadsden Purchase from Mexico in 1853	Parts of Arizona and New Mexico
Alaska purchased from Russia in 1867	Alaska
Hawaii annexed by the United States in 1898	Hawaii

Annexation of Texas

- Mexico had achieved its independence from Spain in 1821. With few Mexicans living in Texas, Mexico was interested in settling the vast area. The Mexican government accepted **Moses Austin's** request to settle in East Texas, provided that the settlers (1) became Roman Catholics and (2) obeyed Mexican law, including the ban on slavery. Under the leadership of his son, **Stephen Austin,** some 300 families immigrated to Texas in 1822. By 1830, when Americans outnumbered Mexicans in Texas by six to one, the Mexican government (1) refused entrance to any more Americans and (2) restated the ban on slavery. This occurred because many Americans who had come to Texas were slave owners who brought their slaves to work cotton and sugar plantations. Austin protested and was jailed.

- When **General Antonio Santa Anna** became president of Mexico and assumed dictatorial powers, the Americans in Texas rebelled. Fighting broke out **(Battle of the Alamo),** but Santa Anna was unable to stop the rebels under **General Sam Houston (Battle of San Jacinto).** Santa Anna signed a treaty acknowledging Texas's independence but later refused to recognize it. However, the Mexicans could do nothing to stop Texas from declaring itself the **Lone Star Republic.**

Test-Taking Strategy

Be sure to track how slavery played a role in presidential elections.

- When Texans voted to ask the United States for admission as a state, Southerners readily agreed, but those who opposed slavery were against **annexation.** Jackson chose to delay the issue until after the 1836 election, and the new president, Martin Van Buren, refused to recommend annexation, thus delaying the issue again. By 1843, concern had grown that Texas would compete with the U.S. South as a source of cotton for British markets. The Senate defeated a bill to annex Texas, and **President John Tyler,** seeking reelection as a Whig, determined to make annexation a campaign issue. The antislavery Whigs, however, opposed annexation and nominated Henry Clay. The Democrats favored annexation of Texas and acquisition of Oregon, and their **dark horse** candidate, **James K. Polk,** running on a **platform of annexation,** won. By a **joint resolution** of Congress, Texas was annexed in 1845.

The Mexican War

- Annexation did not settle the question because Mexico and the United States claimed different boundaries for Texas. When U.S. troops in the disputed area were attacked by Mexican forces, the United States declared war. The **Mexican War** was waged on three fronts: Northern Mexico, New Mexico and California, and Mexico City. The **Treaty of Guadalupe Hidalgo** (1) settled the boundary between Mexico and the United States at the Rio Grande, (2) gave the United States territory known as the **Mexican Cession** in exchange for $15 million, and (3) settled claims against Mexico for $3.5 million.

Slavery as an Issue in the New Territories

- Fearing that the Mexican War would result in additional slave states, many Northerners opposed the war. **David Wilmot** from Pennsylvania proposed a bill in the House of Representatives banning slavery in any territory acquired from Mexico. **John C. Calhoun** vigorously opposed the **Wilmot Proviso** on the grounds that it was unconstitutional. Congress had a duty to protect the property rights of citizens, and that included slave owners' right to carry their property into new territory. The Senate rejected the bill.

- After 1821, the Mexican government gave away land in **California** to attract settlers, as it had in Texas. In the beginning, Americans adopted Spanish culture, became Mexican citizens, and married native-born Californians. By the 1840s, the Americans who came to California hoped for annexation by the United States. In 1845, President Polk offered to buy California from Mexico but was refused. Polk countered by encouraging the Americans in California to rebel. Once the Mexican War began, a group of Americans rose up in the **Bear Flag Revolt** and declared California independent. The Treaty of Guadalupe Hidalgo gave California to the United States as part of the Mexican Cession. The **gold rush** intervened, but in 1849, California drafted a constitution banning slavery and requested statehood.

- The debate over the admission of California sparked one of the most acrimonious disputes in Congress over slavery. There were then fifteen free and fifteen slave states. Admitting California as a free state would destroy this balance, and the nation would face the same problem every time a territory carved from the former Mexican lands requested statehood.

Test-Taking Strategy

Relate the Compromise of 1850 to the Missouri Compromise.

- **Henry Clay** proposed a compromise: (1) California would be admitted as a free state; (2) the people of New Mexico and Utah would decide by popular sovereignty whether they would be free or slave; (3) Texas would give up its claim to part of this territory in exchange for $10 million; (4) the slave trade, but not slavery, would be abolished in the District of Columbia; and (5) Congress would pass a Fugitive Slave Law. **John C. Calhoun** opposed the **Compromise of 1850** because he believed it would diminish the South's influence in national affairs. Both he and **President Zachary Taylor,** who also opposed the Compromise, died, and the new president, **Millard Fillmore,** supported it. Influenced by the arguments of **Daniel Webster,** who pleaded with Northerners to preserve the Union, and **Stephen A. Douglas**, the Compromise was passed.

Cultural Conflict

- In addition to the former Mexicans in Texas and California, there were Spanish-speaking settlers in the New Mexico Territory, which included the present states of Arizona and New Mexico. Altogether, about 75,000 Hispanics became citizens of the United States. Americans considered the Hispanic culture inferior. Because Hispanics spoke Spanish, they were considered "foreigners" in what had been their land first. All too often, their rights were ignored. Costly legal battles were fought to take their lands. Tensions remained high between Hispanics and Anglos throughout the 1800s.

Oregon Boundary Issue

- At one time, **Spain, Russia, Great Britain,** and the **United States** claimed **Oregon,** which stretched from the Northern border of California to the Southern border of Alaska. Spain gave up its claim in the **Adams-Onis Treaty,** and Russia withdrew as a result of the **Monroe Doctrine.** Great Britain and the United States held the area jointly. Originally an important source of furs, in the 1840s, Oregon became a destination for settlers and a political problem. Great Britain and the United States disagreed over the boundary. Polk offered to set the boundary at the 49th parallel, but Britain refused. Faced with the prospect of war (**"Fifty-four forty or fight!"**), Britain agreed to Polk's proposal, and Oregon was divided into the **Oregon** and **Washington Territories.**

Other Expansionist Efforts

- Additional land was acquired from Mexico in 1853 for $10 million. Known as the **Gadsden Purchase,** this strip of land allowed the United States to have a Southern route for a transcontinental railroad.
- In 1867, the United States bought Alaska from Russia. Secretary of State **William Seward,** a strong advocate of manifest destiny, pressed for the purchase because of the area's natural resources. At the time, however, it was called **"Seward's Folly."** In 1899, gold was found, and a new gold rush was on.

Key People

Review Strategy

See if you can relate these people to their correct context in the "Fast Facts" section.

- **Captain John C. Fremont, the Pathfinder, California**
- **General Zachary Taylor, Battle of Buena Vista**
- **Dr. Marcus Whitman, Narcissa Prentice Whitman, Henry Spalding, Elizabeth Hart Spalding, Samuel Parker**

KEY TERMS/IDEAS

Review Strategy

See if you can relate these terms and ideas to their correct context in the "Fast Facts" section.

- **Columbia River, fishing rights**
- **Mexican Borderlands**
- **Oregon Trail, Santa Fe Trail**
- **Sutter's Mill, Forty-Niners, three routes west**

SECTION 2. PRELUDE TO THE CIVIL WAR

Although the **Compromise of 1850** delayed the Civil War for eleven years, it settled nothing. Using **popular sovereignty** in Utah and New Mexico to decide whether the states would be slave or free did not address the central issue of whether slavery should be allowed to spread to new areas. Response to the **Fugitive Slave Law,** however, was immediate.

FAST FACTS

The Antislavery Movement

- The **Fugitive Slave Law** (1) authorized federal marshals to hunt escaped slaves and return them to their owners and (2) provided heavy fines against law officers and ordinary citizens who aided an escaped slave or failed to assist in the capture of one. The law was passed to undermine support for the **Underground Railroad.** However, the law drove many Northerners to join the **antislavery movement.** Angry Northerners sometimes went so far as to attack slave catchers and free their prisoners. Northern legislatures passed **personal liberty laws** that provided for trials to determine the status of apprehended blacks who might be fugitive slaves and forbid state officials to aid slave catchers. Southerners reacted angrily, claiming that Northerners were ignoring the Compromise of 1850 and the rights of Southern property owners.

- Based on information from escaped slaves, the novel **Uncle Tom's Cabin** by **Harriet Beecher Stowe** added fuel to the controversy. The book angered Southerners, who said it painted an unfair and untrue picture of plantation life. Northerners accepted it on face value. Published in 1852, some 300,000 copies had been sold within a year.

The Kansas-Nebraska Act

Review Strategy

See p. 116 for more on the Missouri Compromise.

- The **Kansas-Nebraska Act** added to the tensions. **Stephen A. Douglas** introduced the bill in 1854, claiming he was interested in (1) encouraging the settlement of the **trans-Missouri region,** (2) building a transcontinental railroad along a route from Chicago west to connect the nation (rather than on a southerly route using the land in the Gadsden Purchase), and (3) piercing the "barbarian wall" of Native Americans. The Act provided that (1) the trans-Missouri area be divided into Kansas and Nebraska, (2) popular sovereignty decide the issue of slavery, and (3) the ban on slavery north of the 36° 30', the **Missouri Compromise**, be repealed. Settlers, speculators, **proslavery** advocates, and **antislavery** forces rushed to control Kansas.

- When it came time to draft a constitution for Kansas, proslavery forces rigged the election for members to the constitutional convention and adopted a proslavery constitution, known as the **Lecompton Constitution.** Antislavery forces then held their own convention and drafted their own constitution. When the Lecompton Constitution was sent to Congress, **President James Buchanan** advised Congress to accept it, believing it would reinstate calm between North and South. His fellow Democrat Douglas argued strongly against it. Congress finally sent the constitution back to Kansas for a **popular referendum**, in which it was soundly defeated by a vote of ten to one.

Test-Taking Strategy

Check these off as consequences, or results, of the Kansas-Nebraska Act.

- Casualties of the Kansas-Nebraska Act were party unity and the Whig party itself. Southern Democrats and Southern Whigs voted for the bill, whereas Northern Democrats and Northern Whigs voted against it. The **Whigs** had been more a party of personalities—Henry Clay and Daniel Webster—than programs, and it could not mend its sectional split. After 1852, it ran no more presidential candidates. In 1854, in an effort to unite their forces, antislavery supporters from both parties, abolitionists, and members of the **Free-Soil Party** formed the **Republican Party,** taking its name from the Jeffersonian Democratic-Republican Party.

The Election of 1856

Review Strategy

The Republican Party made an important distinction between abolishing slavery where it existed and refusing to allow its extension into new territories.

- In the presidential election of 1856, the sectional divisions were very clear. The Democrats supported the Kansas-Nebraska Act and nominated James Buchanan, a Northerner who sympathized with the South. The new Republican Party ran on a platform that called for the prohibition of slavery but not its abolition. Their platform offered something for everyone (except Southerners): a protective tariff, free Western lands, and a national banking system. **John C. Frémont,** of Mexican War fame, was their candidate, winning 33 percent of the popular vote and two thirds of the free states' electoral votes. The Republicans were looking at the very real possibility that in the next election, a candidate with the backing of the free states alone could win the presidency.

Fueling North-South Tensions

- Another factor that added to the growing division between North and South was the **Dred Scott** case. Buchanan had hoped it would settle the issue of the legality of slavery in new territories, but it only inflamed the situation.

Scott v. *Sanford* (1857)

Case: Dred Scott was a slave of Dr. John Emerson, a doctor in the U.S. Army who moved from army post to army post. During his postings, Scott accompanied him and had lived in a free state and a free territory, although they had returned to Missouri, a slave state, before Emerson's death. Scott sued his owner's widow in Missouri court for his freedom, contending that he had been freed when he was transported into a free state and free territory to live. A lower court agreed with Scott, but the Missouri Supreme Court ruled against him, as did a lower federal court. His lawyers appealed to the Supreme Court.

Decision: The Southern majority on the Court held that Congress had no power to forbid slavery in U.S. territories. The Court also ruled that a person descended from a slave had no rights as a citizen and, therefore, could not sue in court.

Significance: This ruling struck down (1) the Missouri Compromise, by which Congress had determined which states would be free and which slave, and (2) the Kansas-Nebraska Act, which used the principle of popular sovereignty to determine whether the two territories would be admitted to the Union as free or slave states.

The Lincoln-Douglas Debates

- The Republicans' opposition to the decision in the Dred Scott case attracted new members, including **Abraham Lincoln,** a lawyer in Illinois. The Illinois Republican Party nominated him to run against Stephen A. Douglas for senator in the 1858 election. A clever debater, Lincoln challenged Douglas to a series of seven debates throughout the state.

- In the debates, Lincoln denied being an abolitionist. He said that Republicans would not interfere with slavery where it already existed, but that Republicans would not allow slavery to spread into new territories. He asked Douglas if he supported popular sovereignty or the Dred Scott decision, a question that put Douglas on the spot.
- In the **"Freeport Doctrine,"** Douglas chose to answer in a way that he thought would cause him the least damage. He said that by failing to pass **slave codes,** a territorial legislature could discourage slavery, thus, in effect, rendering the Dred Scott decision null and void.
- The debates attracted national attention, and although Lincoln lost the election, he had made a reputation for himself as a leader of the Republican Party. Douglas's answer probably cost him the support of Southern Democrats and the presidency in the election of 1860.

The Election of 1860

- In 1860, realizing that popular sovereignty did not guarantee that a territory would allow slavery, Southern Democrats refused to endorse Douglas for president because he ran on a platform supporting popular sovereignty. They wanted a platform that supported the Dred Scott decision and federal protection of slavery in the territories. Northern Democrats and Southern Democrats met separately; Northern delegates nominated Douglas and Southern Democrats chose Buchanan's vice president, **John C. Breckinridge** from Kentucky.
- The **Constitutional Union Party** avoided the issue of slavery, and its candidate, **John Bell** of Tennessee, ran on the Union, the Constitution, and enforcement of U.S. laws.
- Republicans chose Lincoln and a platform that would appeal to Western farmers and Northern workers. It pledged to continue slavery where it existed but to stop its spread into new territories. Lincoln won in both popular vote and electoral vote, carrying all eighteen free states.

Secession

- South Carolina had warned that if Lincoln were elected, it would secede. In December 1860, South Carolina passed an **ordinance of secession** and a statement explaining its reasons: (1) abolitionist propaganda, (2) the Underground Railroad, (3) Northern personal liberty laws, and (4) the formation of the Republican Party. Other reasons that have been given for the Civil War are (5) states' rights versus a strong central government, (6) the struggle for political power between the North and the South, and (7) ending slavery.

- After the November election results were known, South Carolina, Georgia, Louisiana, Mississippi, Florida, Alabama, and Texas had seceded. In February 1861, the states had formed the **Confederate States of America (CSA),** written a constitution, and chosen **Jefferson Davis** as president. Lame-duck President Buchanan claimed that secession was unconstitutional but did nothing.

- Lincoln became president on March 4, 1861, and in his inaugural address, he said that no state can decide on its own to leave the Union. He appealed to the Southern states to reconsider. When South Carolinians surrounded **Fort Sumter** in Charleston harbor and attacked a federal ship coming to supply the fort, the Civil War had begun. Four more states, Virginia, Tennessee, Arkansas, and North Carolina, seceded and joined the Confederacy.

KEY PEOPLE

- **John Brown, raid on Harper's Ferry, Northern abolitionist financial support, Southern outrage**
- **Franklin Pierce**
- **Charles Sumner, Preston Brooks, Andrew Butler**
- **Harriet Tubman, "Go Down, Moses"**

KEY TERMS/IDEAS

Review Strategy

See if you can relate these terms and ideas to their correct context in the "Fast Facts" Section.

- **American Party, election of 1856, ex-Whigs and Know-Nothings, anti-immigrant party**
- **"Bleeding Kansas," burning of Lawrence, John Brown, Emigrant Aid Society**
- **Ostend Manifesto, Cuba, manifest destiny, Southern interest in acquiring additional slave territory**

SECTION 3. THE CIVIL WAR

The **Union** had a strong government already in place to conduct the war, whereas the **Confederacy** had to build its government. The Union also had a population of 22 million. Slightly more than one third of the Confederacy's 9 million people were slaves. The North had many more advantages, especially economic, than the South, but the war was not the short, easy victory that either side expected before the fighting began.

FAST FACTS

Mobilizing the Union and the Confederacy

- Both sides faced the problems of **mobilization** and **financing** the war. The North (1) had twice as many soldiers though its army was small, (2) had a small navy, and (3) needed to invade and conquer the South to win. The Confederacy (1) had more and better officers, (2) had to use private ships for its navy, but (3) had only to fight a defensive war.

Review Strategy

Compare and contrast the actions of the Union and the Confederacy. Making a chart is a good way to see differences and similarities.

- At first, both the North and the South used volunteers who were paid a **bounty** to fight, but eventually, both sides passed **draft laws.** The South allowed draftees to hire substitutes, and anyone who owned twenty or more slaves was exempted. New draft laws in 1863 and 1864 eliminated the substitutes and some of the exemptions. The age limits were also changed from 18 to 35 to 17 to 50 as the supply of able-bodied men dwindled. The Union also allowed a draftee to hire a substitute or to pay $300 to the government. **Draft riots** broke out to protest the unfairness of the law but soon turned to racial violence.

- The Union did not accept African Americans into the army and navy until 1862, when it was becoming difficult to recruit enough white soldiers. Black soldiers found discrimination in pay, training, medical care, and the work assigned to them. They were often cooks, drivers, or laborers rather than soldiers. When white soldiers refused to serve with blacks, a few states, like Massachusetts, formed all-black regiments, often led by white officers. Altogether, some 186,000 African Americans served in the army and 29,000 in the Union navy. In addition, about 200,000 of the half million slaves, called **contrabands,** who escaped to the Union lines worked as laborers, cooks, and teamsters. The **Confiscation Act of 1861** provided a uniform policy regarding slaves who escaped from their owners to the Union lines; they were to be free forever.

- The Confederacy did not enlist slaves in its army, but it did force them to work on war-related construction projects, such as building fortifications and producing munitions. Slaves also worked as teamsters, cooks, and ambulance drivers for the army.

Financing the War

- The Union (1) had 80 percent of the industry in the United States; (2) had almost all its deposits of coal, iron, copper, and gold; (3) had the better railroad system since almost all tracks ran outside the Confederacy; (4) was the center for almost all banking and finance; and (5) continued throughout the war to trade with European nations. The Confederacy was still an agrarian economy in 1860. Its ability to sell its cotton for English goods was severely hampered by the Union blockade.

- The Union financed the war by (1) raising the **tariff,** (2) levying **excise** and **income taxes,** (3) issuing paper money, and (4) selling government **bonds.**

- The Confederacy (1) levied a **direct tax** on slaves and land, (2) passed an excise tax, (3) adopted a tax to be paid in goods rather than cash, and (4) printed paper money. These taxes raised little money, and unlike the Union, the Confederacy found it difficult to raise money by selling bonds. Most Southern capital was tied up in land and slaves. Foreign investors were doubtful about the future of the Confederacy. Although **inflation** became a problem in the North, it was far worse for the Confederacy. By the end of the war, the value of Confederate money was about 5 cents on the dollar.

The Confederate Constitution and States' Rights

- Although based on the U.S. Constitution, the **Confederate Constitution** had several provisions that addressed the issues of the prewar Southern position. Among them were the ideas that (1) the sovereignty of the individual states was paramount over the central government, (2) slave property was protected, and (3) protective tariffs and internal improvements were banned.

- The issue of states' rights came up quickly. North Carolina refused to obey the draft law, arguing that the Confederate government had no right to force the citizens of a state to serve in the military. At one point, Jefferson Davis suspended **habeas corpus,** and the courts denied his right to do so. South Carolina and, later, Georgia talked about seceding from the Confederacy.

Foreign Policy

- Achieving recognition of the **C.S.A.** as a sovereign nation was the focus of Confederate **foreign policy,** while the Union worked to deny the Confederacy this recognition. For the first two years of the war, both Great Britain and France were sympathetic to the Confederacy, hoping that if the Confederates won (1) they would be a source of cotton and other raw materials without, in turn, imposing tariffs on imported manufactured goods and (2) that the Northeastern and Mid-Atlantic commercial interests would be less of a competitive threat. In addition, Lincoln's claim at the war's beginning that he wanted to preserve the Union rather than free the slaves put off many Europeans who had abolished slavery earlier in the century. Several incidents between Great Britain and the Union almost resulted in war, but the offending side always stepped back.

Fighting the War

Review Strategy

Remember that the details of the battles are not important, but the significance of the battles is.

- The Union had three military objectives: (1) to capture the Confederacy's capital, **Richmond;** (2) to gain control of the Mississippi; and (3) to **blockade** Southern ports. These three goals would (1) weaken Southern morale, which was a time-honored war strategy; (2) split the South and close an important route for carrying reinforcements and supplies from Texas and Arkansas to the rest of the Confederacy; and (3) keep the South from trading raw cotton for much-needed supplies from Europe. The South had little in the way of manufacturing before the war, and although the South had opened some factories to produce war matériel, it badly needed supplies from abroad.

- The Union Army was divided into two parts: an army east of the Appalachians and one west of the mountains. After the **First Battle of Bull Run (Manassas),** no major fighting took place until 1862. The army in the East battled for Richmond in a series of brutal engagements, with huge casualties on both sides. After a particularly costly defeat for the Union at **Chancellorsville, General Robert E. Lee,** in July 1863, took his Confederate troops into the North. At **Gettysburg,** they met Union forces, and in the ensuing battle, Lee was forced to retreat. This defeat showed that Lee's strategy of taking the war into the Union for a speedy end would not work. It is also significant because it ended any hope of assistance from the British.

- In pursuit of the second Union goal, **Admiral David Farragut,** who was Hispanic, captured New Orleans, Baton Rouge, and Natchez, putting the lower part of the Mississippi under Union control by the end of 1862. From May to July 1863, **General Ulysses S. Grant** laid siege to **Vicksburg** on the Mississippi. With its surrender, the Union was in control of all the Mississippi. The victory won Grant command of all army forces in the West. When he took **Chattanooga** later in the year, Lincoln put him in command of the entire Union Army.

- Grant moved east and engaged Lee's army in a series of battles. Lee stopped at **Petersburg** near Richmond, and Grant surrounded the city. In the meantime, **General William Sherman** burned **Atlanta** and made his victorious and ruinous **"march to the sea"** from Atlanta to Savannah, then turn north to Richmond. Lee moved out from Petersburg with Grant in pursuit. Richmond fell, and Lee surrendered at **Appomattox Court House** on April 9.

- The third goal, the blockade, was very effective in the last two years of the war, cutting the number of ships entering Southern ports from around 6,000 a year to around 200. Although some **blockade runners** operated, the Union navy was so successful that by the end of the war, Southern factories were melting church bells to make cannon.

The Emancipation Proclamation

- Lincoln was reluctant to make emancipation a war goal for the Union because (1) he was concerned that the **border states** would join the Confederacy, (2) he knew that Northern workers feared the loss of their jobs to ex-slaves who they thought would work for less, and (3) he believed that slave owners should be paid for the loss of their property.

- By 1862, however, the pressure to declare emancipation, especially from **Radical Republicans,** was growing in order to (1) punish the Confederacy, (2) incite a general slave insurrection that would quickly end the war, and (3) ensure that the British, who had outlawed slavery, would not support the Confederacy.

- In September 1862, Lincoln announced the **Emancipation Proclamation,** declaring that on January 1, 1863, all slaves in states or parts of states still in rebellion would be free. In reality, the Proclamation freed no one. Slaves in border states or in Union-occupied areas were unaffected, as were slaves in Confederate territory. Lincoln's purpose was to try to end the war by pressuring the rebellious states to make peace before January 1.

The Election of 1864

- For the election of 1864, Democratic supporters of the war joined the Republicans to form the **Union Party.** They nominated Lincoln and, for vice president, Andrew Johnson, a Democrat and the only Southern senator who had not joined the Confederacy. The Democrats chose war hero **General George McClellan.** McClellan refused to run on the Democrats' platform that called the war a failure and demanded it be stopped.

- Lincoln believed he would win or lose depending on how well the Union Army was doing. When **General William Sherman** captured Atlanta, many people thought the war would end soon.

- The Republicans had also managed to run the nation while managing the war: (1) the tariff had been raised in 1861, with some rates as high as 40 percent; (2) the banking system had been strengthened; and (3) vast amounts of **cheap Western land** had been made available—something for every section in the Union. Lincoln won reelection easily.

KEY PEOPLE

- **Clara Barton, American Red Cross; Dr. Elizabeth Blackwell**
- **Copperheads, Northern Democrats**
- **Dorothea Dix, supervised all Union Army nurses**
- **Hinton Helper,** *The Impending Crisis of the South*
- **John Slidell, James M. Mason, HMS** *Trent*

- Clement Vallandigham, critical of Lincoln, *Ex parte Vallandigham;* Lincoln's violation of civil liberties
- Stand Watie, Cherokee, Brigadier General, Confederacy, Cherokee Mounted Rifles

KEY TERMS/IDEAS

Review Strategy

See if you can relate these terms and ideas to their correct context in the "Fast Facts" Section.

- Central Pacific, Union Pacific, transcontinental railroad, northern route, land grants
- Ex parte Milligan, presidential war powers
- Homestead Act of 1862, 160 acres, resident and work requirements
- *Monitor, Merimac,* ironclads
- Morrill Land Grant Act of 1852, federal land grants, establish colleges of agriculture and mechanical arts
- National Banking Act of 1863

SECTION 4. RECONSTRUCTION

At the end of the Civil War, the South lay in ruins. One in twenty whites had been either wounded or killed. Yankee soldiers had taken, destroyed, or burned anything they could find that might have been useful to the Confederates. Two thirds of the Southern railroad system was unable to operate because of track damage. **Inflation** was as high as 300 percent, and Confederate-issued war bonds were worthless. The federal government confiscated any cotton left in warehouses, so there was nothing to export. All this affected not just white Southerners but also their former slaves. At the same time, the nation needed to determine how to readmit the former Confederate states to the Union and how to deal with their leaders.

FAST FACTS

Freedmen's Bureau

- The **Freedmen's Bureau** was set up under the control of the War Department in March 1865 to help Southern blacks who were homeless and jobless because of the war. The bureau (1) helped them find homes and jobs, (2) negotiated labor contracts between African Americans and their employers, (3) built hospitals, (4) set up schools and provided teachers, and (5) provided legal help. Because a provision in the law that set up the bureau stated that former slaves could rent land that was abandoned or confiscated by the federal government for failure to pay taxes and, after three years, buy it, blacks believed that the government was going to give them **"forty acres and a mule."** In the fight with Congress over Reconstruction, Johnson ordered all land returned to its former owners.

Lincoln's Reconstruction Plan

Review Strategy

Compare and contrast the three plans for Reconstruction.

- Before the war was over, Lincoln announced his plan for **Reconstruction:** (1) A state could be readmitted when the number of men who had taken a **loyalty oath** to the Union equaled one tenth the number of voters in the 1860 presidential election (**"ten percent plan"**). (2) Most ex-Confederates would be granted **amnesty** if they took the loyalty oath. (3) High-ranking ex-Confederate officials would have to ask the president for a **pardon** to be granted amnesty. (4) The new state constitutions had to ban slavery. (5) States had to provide free public education to blacks. Once readmitted, a state would have to (1) form a government, (2) hold a constitutional convention, and (3) write a new constitution. Under Lincoln's plan, Tennessee, Arkansas, Virginia, and Louisiana set up new governments before the end of the war. Although not in his original plan, Lincoln came to believe that the right to vote should be given to African Americans who had fought for the Union or had some education.

- Congress refused to allow the newly elected members of Congress from these four states to take their seats. In 1864, the **Radical Republicans** had introduced their proposal for Reconstruction, the **Wade-Davis Bill.** (1) The South would be placed under military rule. (2) A majority of those who had voted in the 1860 election would have to take the loyalty oath for a state to be readmitted. (3) Only those white men who had not fought voluntarily against the Union could vote and attend their state's constitutional convention. (4) The new constitutions had to ban slavery. (5) Former Confederate officials would not be allowed to vote. Lincoln used a **pocket veto** on the bill. He based his veto on the argument that Reconstruction was part of the war effort, and as commander in chief, according to the Constitution, it was the president's duty to deal with it.

- The Radical Republicans and others, like Northern business interests, differed with Lincoln for a variety of reasons: (1) The conditions of readmission were not harsh enough. (2) Reconstruction was Congress's job, not the president's. (3) Southern white electorate would become Democrats. (4) Former Confederate members of Congress might vote against Republican programs. (5) The president's program did not address the rights of newly freed slaves.

Johnson's Reconstruction Plan

- After Lincoln's assassination, **Vice President Andrew Johnson,** who had been the only Southern senator not to leave Congress after secession, became president. He was a Jacksonian Democrat who favored states' rights and the interests of the small farmer, which he had been. He believed that it would be the small Southern farmer who would remake the South into a democratic region that was loyal to the Union.

- While Congress was in recess, he went ahead with Reconstruction, following Lincoln's plan for the most part with a few changes: (1) Amnesty was offered to all former Confederates except the highest officials and those whose property was worth more than $20,000. (2) These men were prohibited from voting or holding state or federal office unless they asked the president for a pardon. (3) The ordinances of secession had to be revoked. (4) Confederate war debts could not be collected. (5) The states had to ratify the **Thirteenth Amendment.**

- In January 1865, Congress had passed the Thirteenth Amendment outlawing slavery, and by December, the necessary twenty-seven states had ratified it.

- While Congress was in recess, all of the former Confederate states except Texas had followed the steps of Johnson's Reconstruction plan and were ready to seat their members in Congress when Congress reconvened in December 1865. However, none of the states had provided for voting rights for former slaves. The Radical Republicans refused to accept the supposedly reconstructed states.

- The Radicals argued that only Congress had the power to make laws and that many of the new members had been officials of the Confederacy, including fifty-eight members of the Confederate Congress and **Alexander H. Stephens,** the Confederacy's vice president. Congress appointed a committee to investigate whether the Southern states should be reinstated. The committee reported that **Presidential Reconstruction** was not working, and that Congress should oversee the process.

Civil Rights for Newly Freed Blacks

Test-Taking Strategy

Think about the significance of these new black codes and why they were considered an attempt to reinstate slavery.

- One of the actions of the South that had enraged Radical Republicans and others in the North was the passage of **black codes** by Southern legislatures in 1865 and 1866. These laws in reaction to the Freedmen's Bureau and the Thirteenth Amendment varied from state to state but in general:

  1. allowed former slaves to
     - marry fellow blacks
     - own personal property
     - sue and be sued
  2. forbade former slaves to
     - serve on juries
     - vote
     - carry weapons without a license
     - hold public office
     - own land
     - travel without a permit
     - be out after curfew
     - assemble in groups without a white person in attendance

3. required a former slave to buy a license to work in a craft
4. authorized the arrest and fining of unemployed blacks
5. allowed an employer to pay the fine of an unemployed black in exchange for the person's labor.

The South claimed that it needed these powers to enforce public safety. Northerners saw them as an attempt to reinstate slavery by ensuring a supply of cheap, unskilled labor that plantations still required.

- In response, Congress passed the **Civil Rights Act of 1866** and the Fourteenth Amendment. The Civil Rights Act (1) granted citizenship to all people born in the United States and gave African Americans the rights to (2) testify in court, (3) own land, (4) make contracts, and (5) exercise all the rights of white Americans. Johnson vetoed the bill, arguing that it violated the rights of the states. Moderate Republicans joined Radical Republicans and overrode the president's veto.

Review Strategy

See Chapter 2 for more on the Constitution.

- Johnson was not alone in considering the Civil Rights Act unconstitutional. To avoid the possibility of having it struck down by the Supreme Court, Congress passed the **Fourteenth Amendment.** It provided that (1) all persons born in the United States or naturalized were citizens of the United States and of the state in which they lived, (2) states were forbidden to deny citizens their rights without **due process of law,** (3) all citizens were to enjoy **equal protection under the law,** (4) a state that denied voting rights to any adult male would have its representation in Congress reduced in proportion to the number of citizens who had been denied the vote, (5) former Confederate officials could not hold federal or state office unless pardoned by a two-thirds vote of Congress, (6) Confederate debts would not be paid, and (7) former slave owners could not sue for payment for loss of their slaves.

- Congress added the **Fifteenth Amendment** in 1869. This amendment replaced part of the Fourteenth Amendment by removing from the states the power to deny the right to vote based "on race, color, or previous condition of servitude."

Radical Reconstruction

- Johnson made the Fourteenth Amendment the major issue of the Congressional elections of 1866. He urged the Southern states not to ratify it, and except for Tennessee, none did. Voters agreed with the Republicans and sent more than a two-thirds majority of Republicans to both houses, enough to overturn presidential vetoes. The Radical Republicans now established **military Reconstruction** using a series of **Reconstruction Acts.** (1) Except for Tennessee, which had ratified the Fourteenth Amendment, the other ten state governments were declared illegal. (2) The ten states were divided into five military districts. (3) The army could use force in these districts, if necessary, to protect civil rights and maintain the peace. (4) Each state was to call a convention to write a new constitution. (5) The members of the constitutional convention were to be elected by all adult males—white and African American. (6) Former Confederate officials could not participate in the conventions (a provision similar to the Fourteenth Amendment). (7) The new constitutions were to guarantee **suffrage** to African American males. (8) The former Confederate states had to ratify the Fourteenth Amendment, which accorded the rights of citizens to African Americans.

- Congressional Reconstruction called for the military governor of each district to oversee the organization of state governments. (1) The governor was to see that former slaves were able to vote for members of the new constitutional conventions and that ex-Confederate officials were not. (2) The new constitutions were to guarantee the right to vote to African Americans. (3) Voters in each state had to approve their new constitution. (4) Congress would then vote on the constitution. (5) The state legislature would ratify the Fourteenth Amendment. Once these conditions were met, the state could apply for readmission to the Union. By 1868, six of the states had been readmitted, and by 1870, Texas, Georgia, Mississippi, and Virginia had been reinstated. These last four states had to ratify the Fifteenth Amendment also.

The Impeachment of Johnson

Test-Taking Strategy

Know the difference between the stated and unstated reasons for Johnson's impeachment.

- During this battle for power, Congress passed the **Tenure of Office Act** in 1867, which required the president to get Congressional approval before removing any federal official, including Cabinet members who had been approved by the Senate. The president vetoed the bill, but Congress overrode his veto. Johnson then fired **Edward Stanton,** Secretary of War, who had opposed Johnson's Reconstruction plan and supported the Radical Republicans. The House voted to **impeach** Johnson for violating the Tenure of Office Act. The Senate trial lasted six weeks, and in three separate votes, the Senate was always one vote short of conviction. Johnson was acquitted, but his political career was effectively over.

Southern Government Under Reconstruction

- While former Confederate officials were banned from holding office, many Southern men who would have been political leaders had been killed during the war. Other Southerners refused to cooperate with the federal government and resented its support for the rights of blacks. Three groups then were primarily involved in reconstructing state governments in the South: (1) Northerners who wanted to help the newly freed slaves or who were interested in what they could gain for themselves, (2) Southern whites who were originally **Unionists** or were interested in what they could gain for themselves by working in the new governments, and (3) free-born and newly freed African Americans. Some African Americans were well educated, but most were poor, uneducated, and lacking in political experience.

- With the exception of South Carolina, where blacks controlled the lower house until 1874, no other state legislature—upper or lower house—was controlled by blacks. No African American was ever elected a governor. Most important offices were held by Northerners or by Southern whites.

- The record of the Reconstruction governments is mixed. While there was certainly corruption, considered in the context of **"Boss" Tweed** in New York, the **Whiskey Ring** in St. Louis, and scandal in the federal government, it was not unusual for the period. Tax rates rose dramatically, but 80 percent of state monies was put to use rebuilding the South's transportation networks. In addition, state governments (1) in an area that had had little public education built schools to educate not just white children but black children also, (2) allowed black and poor white men to vote and hold office for the first time, (3) abolished imprisonment for debt, and (4) built hospitals and orphanages. However, Reconstruction did not help freed slaves to improve their economic status. In time, even the political rights that African Americans had gained were lost.

The End of Reconstruction

- By the early 1870s, Northerners were tiring of Reconstruction. (1) The tales of corruption and **graft** spread by Southern newspapers were turning some Northerners against it. (2) **Moderate Republicans** who had gained ground in Congress did not agree with the Radicals' harsh approach. (3) Radicals lost influence with the deaths of **Charles Sumner** and **Thaddeus Stevens,** two major supporters, and the departure from office of Andrew Johnson who had angered many politicians. (4) The **Panic of 1873** shifted the attention of some Northerners from concern for the rights of Southern blacks, who had now been free for eight years, to financial concerns. (5) Northern business interests wanted to regularize business with the South.

- The end of Reconstruction began with passage of the **Amnesty Act** in 1872, which returned the right to vote and hold office to most ex-Confederates. By 1876, only Louisiana, Florida, and South Carolina remained under Reconstruction governments.

- For the presidential election of 1876, the Republicans had nominated **Rutherford B. Hayes** and campaigned on **"the bloody flag."** Democrats nominated **Samuel B. Tilden** and ran on a platform to end corruption in the federal government. Tilden had apparently won, but the Republican leaders in Florida, Louisiana, and South Carolina challenged a number of votes in their states, and Hayes was ultimately declared the winner in those states. A committee of eight Republicans and seven Democrats was appointed to investigate. The committee compromised, the **Compromise of 1877.** In exchange for (1) an end to Reconstruction, (2) a Southern appointee to the Cabinet, and (3) money to build the Texas and Pacific railroad, Hayes was declared the winner.

KEY PEOPLE

Review Strategy

See if you can relate these people to their correct context in the "Fast Facts" section.

- **Blanche K. Bruce, African American, senator, Mississippi**
- **Ulysses S. Grant, president, 1868–1876, corruption in government**
- **P.B.S. Pinchback, African American, lieutenant governor, Louisiana**
- **Hiram Revels, African American, senator, Mississippi**

KEY TERMS/IDEAS

Review Strategy

See if you can relate these terms and ideas to their correct context in the "Fast Facts" Section.

- **conquered provinces, Stevens' theory; seceded states were not even territories**
- **Force Acts, federal laws, combat anti-black groups in the South**
- **Ku Klux Klan, Knights of the White Camellia, terrorist groups opposed to Reconstruction**
- **scalawags, carpetbaggers, myths**
- **rebellion of individuals, Lincoln's theory; since individuals had rebelled, the president could use his pardon power to reinstate Southern states**
- **state suicide theory, Sumner's view; in secession, Southern states became similar to any unorganized territory and, therefore, Congress had the power to establish terms for readmission**

Chapter 5

REVIEWING HOW THE NATION BECAME AN URBAN AND INDUSTRIAL POWER

Test-Taking Strategy

The nation's shift from agrarian to industrial/urban is an important concept to learn.

The study of the history of the latter portion of the nineteenth century is usually divided into the building of the New South, the settling of the Plains, the growth in immigration, the rise of cities, and the emergence of the United States as an industrial power. Chapter 5 describes the shift of the United States from an agrarian to an industrial nation.

As you read and review for the SAT II: U.S. History Test, look for trends and the significance of events and people, analyze and determine cause-and-effect relationships, and compare and contrast motives and outcomes. Knowing the how and why is important for this test.

SECTION 1. THE NEW SOUTH

The period from 1865 to 1866 is called "Confederate" Reconstruction by some because presidential plans for Reconstruction called for ex-Confederates to remake their governments themselves. At the same time, Southern whites began their campaign of terror against African Americans and their white supporters. The **Freedmen's Bureau** was singled out for attack. The **Ku Klux Klan** and other white supremacist groups, like the **Knights of the White Camellia,** sprang up. When Radical Reconstruction took over and ousted the former Confederates from office—replacing them with Northerners, Southern "scalawags," and African Americans—the Klan and similar groups increased their activities.

FAST FACTS

Government in the New South

- It was against this background of terror and racism that the **Fifteenth Amendment** was drafted and ratified, and the **Enforcement Acts of 1870** and **1871** were passed. These two acts made it a federal crime to interfere with any man's right to vote. However, the ability of the Klan to terrorize African Americans and their supporters made the laws ineffective.

- By the end of Reconstruction in 1877, **Redeemers** had taken over the state governments in all the former Confederate states. "Redeemer" was the name that Southern whites gave to those politicians who restored white supremacy in the South. Most Redeemers were businessmen, not old-time Southern plantation owners, and making money was their goal. They reduced taxes, such as corporate income taxes, on the private sector and cut spending on the public sector, such as funding universal public education.

African Americans in the New South

- While Southern whites rejoiced at the end of the federal occupation of the South, Southern African Americans faced a bleak future—economically, politically, and societally. Although the end of slavery meant that African Americans were no longer bound to a plantation, it also meant that they were on their own to find employment, food, shelter, and clothing. Generally, they had no education and little understanding of contracts and commercial transactions, so white farmers and shopkeepers were able to take advantage of them. Immediately after the war, the Freedmen's Bureau helped blacks for a time, but it was closed down in 1872. By the 1880s, the **sharecropping system** had replaced slavery as the dominant socioeconomic institution in the South.

- After the war, because Southern planters had little cash, they could not pay workers. Yet field hands, both blacks and poor whites, needed to work. The Freedmen's Bureau worked out a system in which the landowner would give the sharecropper (and his family) land, tools, a mule, seed, and a shack in which to live. The sharecropper would work the land and give one third to one half of the harvest to the landowner. This was known as the **crop lien system.** In theory, the sharecropper would be able to save enough over time to buy land. The system turned out to be very different in practice.

- The sharecropper's plot was usually too small to grow much surplus. Repeated use of the land without any knowledge of good farming practices resulted in poor yields and exhausted soil. As a result, there was little to return to the landowner as rent for the use of the land, seed, tools, mule, and house. In addition, the sharecropper had to repay a shopkeeper, who was often the landowner, for food, clothing, and other supplies that the sharecropper and his family had bought on credit, in hopes of a good harvest. Often, the sharecropper found he had nothing left once he had repaid his debts. The cycle began all over again as he borrowed to keep his family fed over the winter.

- African Americans' options were few. Attempting to get legal redress in a Southern white community was futile. Even if African Americans could save enough money to buy land, most white landowners would not sell land to them. Bargaining for better terms for sharecropping was impossible because white landowners in many areas joined together to determine the terms they would offer to sharecroppers. Because white workers would not work alongside African Americans, the latter were barred from employment in the new mills and factories of the industrialized South. The threat of hiring blacks often was enough to end any strike threat by white workers.

- Politically, African Americans continued to vote and hold public office during Radical Reconstruction. However, beginning in 1890 in Mississippi, the Southern states began to write new constitutions and new laws that effectively kept African Americans from voting. The new laws did not violate the Fifteenth Amendment but used other means to bar blacks from the voting booth: **poll tax, literacy test, grandfather clause, property requirement,** and the **direct primary.** The grandfather clause was declared unconstitutional in 1915.

- The **Civil Rights Act of 1875** had established that all persons within the United States regardless of "race and color . . . [and] previous condition of servitude" were eligible to the "full and equal enjoyment" of public accommodations. In 1883, the Supreme Court declared the Act unconstitutional on the basis that the Fourteenth Amendment applied only to states.

- Any hope for social equality ended with **Jim Crow.** The first Jim Crow law, requiring separate railway cars for African Americans and whites, had been passed in 1881 in Tennessee. After the Supreme Court ruling on the Civil Rights Act of 1875, other Southern legislatures followed with similar laws until railroad stations, streetcars, schools, parks, playgrounds, theaters, and other public facilities across the South were segregated. In 1896, the Supreme Court institutionalized segregation with its ruling in *Plessy* **v.** *Ferguson.*

Plessy **v.** *Ferguson* **(1896; principle of separate but equal)**

Case: In a test of the Jim Crow laws, Homer Plessy, an African American, was arrested in Louisiana for riding in a whites-only railroad car. Plessy was found guilty in state court, and appealed to the U.S. Supreme Court on the basis of the Fourteenth Amendment's "equal protection under the law" guarantee.

Decision: The Court ruled that as long as the facilities were equal, it was not unconstitutional to segregate whites and blacks.

Significance: The Court's ruling led to new and more comprehensive segregation laws across the South.

- African Americans responded by developing their own communities and their own businesses. Mutual aid societies, insurance companies, funeral parlors, and banks sprang up. Black churches became a focal point of life and would become, along with the NAACP, the base for civil rights activities in the next century.

- White supremacist groups continued to spread terror among African Americans. **Lynching** was a favored weapon. **Ida Wells Barnett,** a former teacher turned journalist, campaigned to end "lynch law." **Frederick Douglass** emerged to lead protests against the treatment of African Americans in the South.

The Economy of the New South

- While African Americans were struggling to survive, the general economy of the **"New South"** was slowly improving until, by 1890, cotton production and the amount of railroad track were twice what they had been in 1860. The latter aided the South in developing its industrial base. One of the factors that had caused the end of Radical Reconstruction had been the desire of business interests to get back to business. Northern financiers and Southern businessmen joined together to provide capital to rebuild the South's infrastructure and to develop industry.

- Southern industrial production quadrupled between 1860 and 1900. Birmingham, Alabama, and Chattanooga, Tennessee, became centers of the Southern iron and steel industry. Tobacco processing developed in North Carolina and Virginia. Cotton textile mills appeared in South Carolina and Georgia, and sugar refineries appeared in Louisiana. All that an area needed for some industry to develop was a mix of (1) water power; (2) a supply of cheap labor; (3) raw agricultural products or (4) natural resources, such as coal and iron deposits; and (5) access to transportation. Because of the distance to Northern markets and the amount of competition for Southern goods, wages were usually low, and unions made little progress because of the threat to hire African American workers.

Key People/Terms

Review Strategy

See if you can relate these people and terms to their correct context in the "Fast Facts" section.

- **Henry Grady, term "New South"**
- **Exodusters, disenfranchisement, Henry Adams, Benjamin "Pap" Singleton**

SECTION 2. THE LAST FRONTIER

While the South was rebuilding itself, settlers were finding that the **Great American Desert** was, in reality, a vast fertile plain. The region around the Mississippi had been settled, and people were looking for new land. As miners, ranchers, sheepherders, and farmers moved into the Great Plains and the mountains beyond, they came up against the claims of the Native Americans who had lived there for centuries.

FAST FACTS

Government Aid for Westward Expansion

- While conducting the Civil War, Lincoln and his Republican Congress had also passed legislation that was important to the development of the Great Plains. Settlers needed two things to move west: cheap land and access to cheap land. The **Homestead Act of 1862** provided the cheap land. The Act granted plots of 100 acres to individuals—citizens or immigrants—who would live on and work the land for five years.

- **The Pacific Railway Acts of 1862** and **1864** subsidized the **Central Pacific** and the **Union Pacific** to build the first **transcontinental railroad.** The companies were given vast tracts of land along their routes to divide and sell to pay for laying the track. Work did not begin until 1865, and the two branches of the railroad met at Promontory Point, Utah, in 1869. Additional railroads were built, including the **Southern Pacific,** along a right-of-way through the land bought from Mexico in the **Gadsden Purchase.**

Native Americans' Last Stand

- In the early days of the Republic, the federal government had forced Native Americans in the Upper Midwest to sign treaties that ceded large tracts of land to the United States. The Native Americans were then confined to small reserves. Beginning in the 1830s with the establishment of the **Indian Territory** in what is today Oklahoma, Native Americans from the Southeast were moved onto **reservations** in the Indian Territory.

- Around 1850, the **Bureau of Indian Affairs (BIA)** adopted a policy known as **concentration.** Native Americans were to be confined to certain areas of the West, away from settlers travelling to California and Oregon. The Native Americans would be free to continue their own ways of life.

- As more settlers came, the BIA decided to resettle all Native Americans on the Plains and in the Southwest on **reservations.** Reservations greatly restricted the traditional way of life of Native Americans. Some of the lands they had been removed to were suited to farming, but much of it was poor. In addition, most groups were **hunters and gatherers,** not farmers. By the late 1880s, the buffalo were gone from the Plains. As a result, Native Americans had to rely on the BIA for food, clothing, and shelter. Bureau agents were often corrupt. Sometimes they stole the food and supplies meant for the Native Americans and resold them, and sometimes Indian agents took bribes from suppliers to accept shoddy goods.

- Among the leaders who resisted resettlement were **Chief Joseph** of the **Nez Perce; Mangas Coloradas, Cochise,** and **Geronimo** of the **Chiricahua Apache; Black Kettle** of the **Cheyenne; Red Cloud** and **Crazy Horse** of the **Oglala Sioux;** and **Sitting Bull** of the **Hunkpapa Sioux.** The last major battle between Native Americans and the U.S. Army was the massacre at **Wounded Knee,** South Dakota, in which the army, in a surprise attack, charged a camp of men, women, and children at dawn, killing several hundred Native Americans.

- Two voices raised in protest were **Sarah Winnemucca,** a Paiute, who wrote and lectured about the government's mistreatment of the Paiute, and **Helen Hunt Jackson,** who wrote *A Century of Dishonor,* outlining the government's mistreatment of Native Americans and the corruption in the BIA. The book also sought to correct the many stereotypes that whites had about Native Americans.

Review Strategy

Compare the purpose of the Act with the reality.

- In an effort to quiet the protests that arose with the publication of Jackson's book, the federal government passed the **Dawes Act.** It (1) broke up reservations; (2) gave 160 acres of land to the head of each household and lesser amounts to bachelors and women; (3) restricted the sale of the land or use of it for collateral for twenty-five years in an effort to protect Native Americans from unscrupulous land speculators; (4) granted citizenship after twenty-five years to those who received land; and (5) sold to whites any land not given to Native Americans, the proceeds of which were to be used to educate Native American children.

- An attempt to assimilate Native Americans into white culture, the Dawes Act failed for several reasons: (1) many Native Americans were not farmers; (2) the land was often poor; (3) many families sold their land, and when the money was gone, they had nothing to live on; and (4) many were cheated out of their land. In time, Native Americans lost their own culture, traditions, much of their lands, and their means of financial support—without being accepted into the dominant white culture. Native Americans remained wards of the government and increasingly dependent on it for their means of survival.

Settling the Plains

- The **open-range** cattle industry began on the Texas plains in the 1840s and 1850s with cattle that had been driven up from Mexico. The land the cattle ranged over was unfenced government property that the cattle ranchers neither rented nor owned. By the 1870s, cattle ranching had spread to the Northern Plains. The early cattle drives had either New Orleans or the gold fields in California as their destination. After the Civil War, the cattle drives moved across several trails to railheads in Kansas and Nebraska, where the cattle were sold and shipped to meat-packing plants in Chicago. With the building of rail lines south into Texas in the 1870s, the long cattle drives were over.

- By 1890, open-range cattle ranching itself was over, coincidentally the year the Census Bureau declared the **frontier** closed. As early as the 1860s, farmers and, in the 1880s, sheepherders were moving onto the Plains, buying up land, building **barbed-wire** fences, and damming rivers. When a decline in the price of beef in the 1880s, combined with two winters of blizzards and severe cold and a summer of drought between 1885 and 1887, many ranchers were forced into bankruptcy. To combat these problems, ranchers (1) formed cooperative associations, (2) bought or rented government land to end the range wars that had erupted with farmers and sheepherders, (3) introduced sturdier **Hereford** cattle, (4) kept herds small to keep prices up, and (5) grew hay to feed cattle in severe weather.

- Farmers began moving onto the Plains after the Civil War. Some were African Americans escaping the black codes and hoping to own their own land. Others were newly arrived immigrants. Farming on the Plains involved a number of problems: (1) less than 20 inches of rain a year, (2) low yield per acre, (3) free-roaming cattle, and (4) a lack of trees for fencing. The problems were solved by the (1) development of "dry" farming techniques; (2) invention of various farming implements, such as steel plows and threshing machines combined with harvesters, that made possible the cultivation of vast acres of land; and (3) and (4) invention of barbed-wire for fencing.

KEY PEOPLE

Review Strategy

See if you can relate these people to their correct context in the "Fast Facts" section.

- **Buffalo Soldiers**
- **James J. Hill, Great Northern, "empire builder"**
- **Leland Stanford, Collis Huntington**
- **Frederick Jackson Turner, historian who wrote about the U.S. frontier, individualism, democracy in *The Frontier in American History***

KEY TERMS/IDEAS

Review Strategy

See if you can relate these terms and ideas to their correct context in the "Fast Facts" section.

- **Ghost Dance, Sioux, celebration of traditional way of life**
- **Indian Territory, Oklahoma Land Rush**
- **Morrill Land-Grant Act**
- **Treaty of Fort Laramie, 1868, Great Sioux Reservation**

SECTION 3. INDUSTRY, LABOR, AND BIG BUSINESS

Test-Taking Strategy

The real number of people engaged in agriculture may have been greater, but they represented a smaller proportion of the population.

- While the South was rebuilding and the West was being settled, the Midwest and Northeast were growing quickly as a result of new inventions and new industries. Industrial growth was fueled by a wave of immigrants from Southern and Eastern Europe and by rural Americans looking for opportunity. During the last part of the nineteenth century, the United States changed from a rural, agrarian society to an industrial, urban one.

FAST FACTS

Industrial Development

- For the **Industrial Revolution** to take hold and develop in the United States, certain requirements had to be met. The nation needed (1) a national transportation system; (2) large deposits of iron and coal and, later, oil; (3) new sources of power, such as **electricity, steam turbines,** and **diesel engines;** (4) surplus agricultural production for textile factories, meat-packing plants, and canneries; (5) a supply of labor; (6) capital for investment; and (7) a stable banking system.

Review Strategy

For more on railroads and their pricing polices, see Chapter 3.

- The late 1800s saw a consolidation in the **railroad industry.** Until then, railroads were small independent lines meant to link relatively small areas. For example, when the **Pennsylvania Railroad** began to absorb competitors, it bought up several hundred companies. Because of the number of companies, there was no uniformity in rail widths. With the consolidation of lines, a standard for rails was set. (1) The merging of rail lines, (2) the building of several transcontinental lines, (3) the standardization of rails, and (4) the establishment of three standard time zones helped to bring about a **national rail system.** The growth of railroads made it possible to move raw materials to factories and finished goods to markets easily—but not cheaply.

- The early factories had been powered by water wheels. The **industrial revolution** required vast amounts of energy and the flexibility to build factories close to raw materials or transportation hubs. **Coal** to power the new **steam turbines** was one answer. The United States had the largest deposits of anthracite coal in the world and large fields of bituminous coal as well. Coal mining became big business in the second half of the nineteenth century, especially to feed the furnaces of the growing steel industry.

Social Theorists and Industrialism

- **Social Darwinism** applied to human society the theories of natural selection and evolution that **Charles Darwin** developed while observing nature. According to Darwin, a constant competition for survival exists in the natural world in which the weak vie for a place with the strong who always win, thus ensuring the continuity of the species. Social Darwinists transferred this competition to the human species and pointed to successful businessmen as proof. The poor were poor because they were unfit and, therefore, had to suffer the consequences. The most notable Social Darwinist was English philosopher and social theorist **Herbert Spencer.**

- Social Darwinism greatly influenced social thinking in the late 1800s. Its supposed reliance on science and scientific fact provided proof for the rightness of the principle of **laissez-faire government.** Social Darwinism suggested that poverty and failure were the result of laziness, inefficiency, and lack of ability. (There was a certain similarity to Puritanism in the belief that hard work and success were a sign of being one of the chosen.) Because of this rationale, government should not interfere in the workings of society by providing assistance to the poor or to failing businesses. Competition—even cutthroat competition—should be applauded because it showed that the fittest were winning and ensuring the survival of the nation. With this philosophy as a backdrop, neither the federal government nor state governments attempted to check the ruthless competition and exploitation of the industrial era.

- **Andrew Carnegie** was a social Darwinist who allowed his managers to cut wages and demand 70-hour workweeks. But he also espoused what is known as the **"Gospel of Wealth."** He believed that those who made great sums of money had a duty to use part of that money to help those who would help themselves to better their lives. True to his word, he established the Carnegie Foundation that today continues to provide philanthropy to a wide variety of organizations such as public libraries and research institutions.

- One dissenting voice was the **Social Gospel** movement that developed among Protestant churches around the turn of the century. Proponents believed that the desire to achieve heaven did not rule out improving life on earth. Christians had a sacred duty to work toward the end of social and economic abuses in society. Social Gospelers advocated an end to child labor, a shorter workday, and a six-day workweek.

Labor Organizations

- The **Knights of Labor** was founded as an **industrial union** in 1869 to organize all skilled and unskilled workers in an industry. African Americans were welcome and made up about 10 percent of the membership. Women and immigrants were also members. Under **Terence V. Powderly,** the Knights worked for an 8-hour workday and health and safety regulations, including limits on the kinds of jobs that children could perform. Powderly believed in the power of negotiation rather than the strike. The **Haymarket Riots** severely damaged the Knights, and they rapidly lost members. By 1900, the union had disappeared.

LABOR UNREST	CAUSES	RESULTS
Haymarket Riots, Chicago, 1886	Began as a general strike in support of the 8-hour day for all trade unions in the city; after three days of peaceful demonstrations, crowd at an outdoor meeting ordered to disperse; bomb thrown, killing seven police officers and four workers	• Eight anarchists tried and convicted; four hanged • Effectively kills the Knights of Labor; nation horrified by violence and fearful of labor
Homestead Strike, Carnegie Steel Company, Homestead, Pennsylvania, 1892	Strike of Amalgamated Association of Iron, Steel, and Tin Workers to protest wage cut and 70-hour workweek demanded by management	• Pinkerton guards called in to break up strike; ten die; national guard called in by order of President Harrison; strike broken • Effectively kills unionism in steel industry until 1930s • Tarnishes reputation of Carnegie and Harrison
Pullman Strike, Pullman Palace Car Company, Pullman, Illinois, 1894	Strike by Pullman workers and American Railway Union to protest wage cut and dismissal of union workers who had protested wage cut	• Stops railway traffic in and out of Chicago for two months; twenty-seven states affected; twenty-two workers killed • Company owners granted **injunction;** workers in violation of **Sherman Antitrust Act** • Federal troops ordered in by President Cleveland; strike broken; adds to public's fear of labor

- The **American Federation of Labor (AFL)** was organized during the year of the Haymarket Riots and was led by **Samuel Gompers** for thirty-seven years. It was an affiliation of **craft unions** for skilled workers, thus leaving out women, immigrants, and African Americans, most of whom were unskilled. Each craft union within the AFL bargained for its own workers and managed its own affairs. The central organization lobbied for an 8-hour workday and a six-day workweek, higher wages, better working conditions, protection for workers on dangerous jobs, and compensation for workers and their families for work-related injuries or death.

- There were a number of strikes in the late 1800s, but three were especially damaging to labor. The strike was not a particularly effective bargaining tool until strikers began using the **sit-down strike** in the 1930s.

- All of these strikes, plus others like the **Baltimore and Ohio Railroad Workers Strike** in 1877, hurt organized labor. A major weapon used by company owners was the **injunction.** According to the courts at this time, union members, in determining to strike, entered into "a conspiracy in restraint of trade." This violated the Sherman Antitrust Act of 1890. The fact that the Act had been written to regulate big business rather than unions was ignored. In general, the courts and governments favored business over labor.

Test-Taking Strategy

The specific acts are less important than the trend to protect workers.

- Despite the negative impact of strikes and hostile court rulings, labor made a number of gains in the years between 1877 and 1917. Government employees won the 8-hour workday in 1892, and the eight-hour workday was extended to railroad workers in 1916. The Erdman Act, passed in 1898, provided for arbitration of labor disputes involving interstate carriers. Ten years later, the Employers' Liability Act made railroads responsible for employees' injuries while on the job. States, often pressured by progressives, also passed laws protecting workers.

KEY PEOPLE/TERMS

Review Strategy

See if you can relate these people and terms to their correct context in the "Fast Facts" section.

- **Horatio Alger, Jr,** *Ragged Dick,* **"poor boy works hard and makes good"**
- **Bessemer process; open-hearth process; skyscrapers**
- **J. Pierpoint Morgan, J.P. Morgan & Co.; Northern Securities Company**
- **John D. Rockefeller, Standard Oil**
- **Cornelius Vanderbilt, New York Central; "Commodore"**

SECTION 4. URBAN SOCIETY

As the introduction to Section 3 noted, the late 1800s saw the nation shift from an agrarian and rural society to an urban and industrial one. Because the Northeast was the oldest region of the nation, it had the most cities and the most industry. The fastest-growing cities were in the Midwest, where rail lines fed the growing factories with both raw materials and workers. The railroads also aided in the building of Western cities. Southern cities grew more slowly because industrial development played less of a role in the South.

FAST FACTS

The Growth of Cities

Review Strategy

See p. 171 for more on the Panic of 1873.

- A variety of reasons sent people to the cities: (1) farm workers lost their jobs to the new farm equipment, (2) small farmers could not afford to buy the new equipment and without it could not compete with large **commercial farms,** (3) farmers lost their land during the **Panic of 1873,** (4) African Americans were escaping from Jim Crow, and (5) immigrants were looking to make a better life for themselves. Many of the immigrants had been farmers in their native countries and were tired of trying to scrape by on too little land with too few resources. The excitement, bright lights, educational and cultural opportunities and the freedom that cities seemed to offer also lured some restless rural people to the big city. The isolation and loneliness of rural life pushed others.

- The quality of urban life depended on whether a person was wealthy, middle class, or poor; and white and native-born, African American, or an immigrant. Being poor, African American, or an immigrant consigned a person to life in a **tenement** in the **slums,** while the middle class and the wealthy moved farther and farther from a city's downtown as **cable cars** and **electric streetcars** made it possible to commute from the outskirts of a city.

- With the growth of the cities came numerous problems and some solutions. In the place of horse-drawn streetcars and cabs came elevated trains, cable cars, and subways to carry workers along the crowded streets. Because business transactions demanded fast communications, telephone and telegraph systems developed locally and then nationwide. To light the now-crowded streets and to take advantage of as much working time as possible, some form of illumination was needed. The dynamo, electricity, the arc light, and Edison's light bulb together solved the problems. The safe water, disposal of sewage, and adequate housing problems were less easily solved.

Immigration

- Most immigrants who came to the United States from the first days of the republic to 1890 were from Northern and Western Europe, the largest number from Germany. In the ten years between 1890 and 1900, however, 70 percent of all immigrants came from **Eastern** and **Southern Europe:** Italians, Russians, Austro-Hungarians, Poles, Bulgarians, Serbs, Romanians, Greeks, and Turks.

Test-Taking Strategy

Compare the push and pull factors of early immigration with those of the late nineteenth century.

- Economic reasons caused many of these people to leave their homelands. Large landholdings across much of the regions had been subdivided into tenant farms that were too small for farmers to support their families. Austria-Hungary suffered an economic depression in 1873. Italy saw its markets for fruit and wine sharply decline in this period. Political reasons also figured in the **push factors** that sent people to the United States. Poland had been carved up and ceased to exist. Polish Catholics and Russian Jews emigrated because of religious persecution in their native lands. Although some immigrants moved to the Plains to farm and others found jobs as miners or on construction crews, most became city dwellers and went to work in factories and **sweatshops.**

Review Strategy

See Chapter 6 *for information on social reforms in the early twentieth century.*

- Social reformers opened **settlement houses** to help immigrants make the transition to their new lives more easily. **Lillian Wald,** through New York's **Henry Street Settlement House,** and **Jane Addams,** with Chicago's **Hull House,** provided (1) classes to teach immigrants to read and write English, (2) health care for families, and (3) recreational, sports, and cultural activities.

Urban Politics

- One of the first people that a new immigrant family would probably meet was the local **ward boss.** He would help a family find housing and work and see they were taken care of if they got sick. The ward leader would help them navigate the American legal system, including filing for citizenship. In exchange, the male members of the family were expected to vote the way the ward leader told them to.

Review Strategy

See Chapter 6 *for political reforms brought about by the progressives.*

- The ward boss was at the bottom of the city and/or state **political machine.** The period from the late 1860s to the turn of the century was marked by political corruption at the local, state, and federal government levels and in both the Republican and Democratic Parties. The **party boss** for a city or state (1) controlled his party, (2) decided who would run for office, (3) influenced the decisions and actions of officials once elected, and (4) doled out **patronage** jobs. At the city level, Democrat **William "Boss" Tweed** in New York was one of the most corrupt party bosses in the country. As Superintendent of Public Works, he took millions of dollars in bribes in exchange for awarding city contracts.

KEY PEOPLE/TERMS

Review Strategy

See if you can relate these terms to the correct context in the "Fast Facts" section.

- **Jacob Riis, journalist, social reformer**
- **spoils system, merit system**

SECTION 5. INTELLECTUAL AND CULTURAL MOVEMENTS

The period after the Civil War brought about many changes not only to the South but to the Northeast, Midwest, and Far West. Not the least of these changes had to do with the intellectual and cultural life of the nation. There was greater access to higher education simply because there were more colleges and universities. Great advances were made in science and technology, much of it related to practical applications for business, industry, and the home. A new phenomenon—**leisure time**—developed among the middle class.

FAST FACTS

Broadening Educational Opportunities

- As the nation entered the **Industrial Age,** some people saw the need for a new kind of education. Responding to the need to train people for office work, the number of high schools increased by tenfold between 1870 and 1900. High school courses of study included such practical business subjects as bookkeeping, typing, and manual arts. The natural sciences were also added to the curriculum. Education also began earlier, with the introduction of **kindergarten** in 1873.

- The **Morrill Act** resulted in the building of a number of so-called **land-grant colleges,** which were to teach agricultural and mechanical arts. These new colleges and universities admitted women and African Americans. Established colleges like Princeton and Harvard added more science and foreign languages other than classical Greek and Latin to their traditional courses of study. Law and medicine became professional courses of study. In the past, new doctors and lawyers were trained through apprenticeships. Several all-black institutions of higher education were also founded during this post–Civil War period, among them **Tuskegee Institute,** Howard University, and Bethune-Cookman College. While **co-education** in higher education was typical west of the Appalachians, in the Northeast, women were founding all-women's colleges, such as Vassar, Mount Holyoke, and Bryn Mawr.

Practical Uses of Science

- The late 1800s saw Americans making great advances in science and the practical applications of scientific discoveries. Among the discoveries and inventions of this period were the harnessing of electricity, the light bulb, the telephone, the elevator, the escalator, air brakes for trains, the linotype machine for setting type, and the ballpoint pen. Driven by the needs of industry, most of the discoveries that occupied American scientists were in the field of **applied science** rather than pure science.

Cultural Developments

Test-Taking Strategy

Specific individuals are less important to know than the movements and trends.

- **Realism** and, to a lesser extent, **naturalism** were the predominant influences on U.S. writers at the end of the nineteenth century. Among the realists were **Hamlin Garland, Frank Norris, Willa Cather,** and **William Dean Howells. Stephen Crane** and **Theodore Dreiser** were naturalists who had been influenced by Howells. There were also **regional,** or **local color,** writers, among whom **Mark Twain** was the best known. Others in the genre were **Edward Eggleston, Sarah Orne Jewett,** and **Joel Chandler Harris.** Nonfiction writers of note were **Oliver Wendel Holmes,**

Henry Adams, and **Edward Bellamy.** Bellamy is of particular note for his work *Looking Backward,* which described a benevolent socialism. Writers of the period who transcended labels were the poet **Emily Dickinson** and writers **Henry James** and **Edith Wharton.**

- **Impressionists** and **realists** vied for the attention of the art world during the late 1800s. **Mary Cassatt** and **James McNeil Whistler** were well-known American impressionists who studied and worked in Europe. Among the realists were **John Singer Sargent, Thomas Eakins,** and **Henry Ossawa Tanner.** Sculptors of the period were **Edmonia Lewis, Daniel Chester French, Augustus Saint-Gaudens,** and **Frederic Remington.**

- In many cities in the late 1800s, general interest newspapers, foreign-language newspapers, and newspapers for African American readers were being published. Magazines developed as a response to a better-educated middle class with more time for leisure activities. Women's magazines, such as the ***Ladies Home Journal*** and ***Godey's Lady's Book,*** appeared along with ***Atlantic Monthly, Harper's Weekly,*** and ***McClure's.*** These magazines published articles that highlighted the serious problems of the day and called for social and political reforms.

- At the end of the nineteenth century, about 12 percent of the nation's families controlled about 88 percent of the nation's wealth. However, a growing middle class found that they, too, had a little **discretionary income** and time to enjoy themselves. In addition to reading newspapers and magazines, people attended vaudeville shows and nickelodeons. Baseball, basketball, and football became major spectator sports. In rural areas and farm states, people went to state fairs, had square dances, and attended quilting bees.

KEY PEOPLE

Review Strategy

See if you can relate these people to their correct context in the "Fast Facts" section.

- **George Washington Carver, impact on Southern farming**
- **John Dewey, "learn by doing"**
- **Thomas Edison, light bulb, phonograph**
- **William Randolph Hearst, social reform**
- **Joseph Pulitzer, human-interest stories**

SECTION 6. THE GILDED AGE

The term **"Gilded Age"** was coined from the title of a novel by Mark Twain and C.D. Warner. The term came to represent the period from around 1877 to the 1890s. It was a time characterized by corruption in government and unbridled competition in business.

FAST FACTS

The Nature of the Presidency

- As one historian has noted, this was a time of undistinguished occupants of the White House. Presidents tended to be "of modest intellect, vision, and resourcefulness." **Party men,** they were elected by conservative financial and business interests who wanted the status quo maintained. In general, the five men who sat in the president's seat between 1877 and 1897 (Rutherford B. Hayes, James A. Garfield, Chester A. Arthur, Grover Cleveland, and Benjamin Harrison) were conservatives in fiscal policy, foreign affairs, and social reform. Although, like Ulysses S. Grant, they were personally honest, they were heedless of the corruption and **"influence-peddling"** that went on in their administrations.

The Divisive Tariff Issue

Review Strategy

The tariff is an important issue throughout American history.

- A major issue of the 1880s was the **tariff.** As Arthur took office, a number of people, from politicians to ordinary citizens, thought the time had come to lower tariff rates on certain items. These people were not arguing against using import duties to protect infant industries, but they saw no need to protect industries that were among the largest in the world. In fact, advocates of lower tariff rates argued that the lack of competition from foreign companies was enabling some U.S. manufacturers to charge higher prices. Republicans balked, however, when the commission that was established to study the issue recommended a general reduction in tariff rates.

- The **Tariff Act of 1883,** also known as the **Mongrel Tariff,** was the result. It offered little relief to consumers. The significance of the law, however, lay in the division it created between the Republican and Democratic Parties. After passage of this Act and until the latter part of the twentieth century, the Republicans consistently defended high tariffs and the Democrats opposed them. From the Civil War until 1883, there had been little difference between the two parties on the tariff.

Antitrust Activities

- By the end of the 1870s, larger companies—manufacturing, railroad, and financial—began to find ways to reduce their competition. Sometimes, they acquired smaller companies in **mergers.** The mergers might result in **horizontal combinations** or **vertical combinations,** depending on the nature of the businesses bought. In some industries, competing companies banded together in **pools** to restrain competition among themselves. Because there was no way to enforce these **"gentlemen's agreements,"** they were not very satisfactory. In the 1880s, beginning with **John D.**

Rockefeller's Standard Oil, companies turned to **trusts** to formalize their agreements to act together in such a way as to remove competition. In practice, trusts became **monopolies.** Having crushed their competitors, monopolies felt free to raise prices, break labor unions, and exploit the nation's natural resources.

- In response to the public outcry against trusts, both the Republicans and the Democrats promised in the election of 1888 to curb trusts. The **Sherman Antitrust Act of 1890** was the result. It declared illegal "every contract, combination in the form of a trust . . . , or conspiracy, **in restraint of trade** or commerce." Unfortunately, the lawmakers did not define terms such as trust and combination, so it was difficult to enforce the law. Some historians view the passage of the Sherman Antitrust Act as a way to placate the public, while others see it as a way to control labor unions. The law is important because it established the principle of federal regulation of big business.

The Agrarian Revolt of the Late 1800s

- Scandals like **Crédit Mobilier, manipulation of railroad stocks,** discrimination in the establishment of **freight rates, free passes, pooling,** and **rebates** finally pushed farmers into organizing to protest the practices of the railroads. For farmers, the issue was not only the cost of shipping their grain, but also the high fees the railroads charged to store grain in railroad-owned elevators and warehouses. The railroads insisted that the farmers store their grain with them as a condition of shipping.

- During the 1870s, the **National Grange,** an organization of farmers, began the **Granger Movement** to organize farmers in the South, West, and Midwest to fight railroad monopolies and their storage businesses. The Grange used political clout to elect sympathetic members to several state legislatures, who then passed what were known as **Grange laws** to regulate the business practices of the railroads, such as rebates and discriminatory practices in setting rates. The railroads fought the laws in the courts in what became the basis of the **Granger cases.**

- The railroads argued that they were being deprived of their property without **due process** in violation of the Fourteenth Amendment. In *Munn v. Illinois,* one of six **Granger cases,** the U.S. Supreme Court upheld the right of the people to regulate railroads, which in effect had become **public utilities.** The Court ruled that property in which the public had an interest must expect to be controlled by the "public interest."

- While *Munn* was a victory for the National Grange, the Supreme Court ruled in the 1886 **Wasbash Case** that the states had no power to regulate traffic that crossed state boundaries. The ruling ended all attempts by states to regulate railroad traffic. In response, Congress passed the **Interstate Commerce Act,** establishing the

Test-Taking Strategy

Look for the twofold significance of the Act.

Interstate Commerce Commission, the nation's first federal regulatory agency. The Act also declared illegal (1) pooling, (2) rebates and lower rates to favored customers, (3) charging higher fees for short hauls than for long hauls on the same line, and (4) charging unreasonable rates. Railroads had to post their rates and give ten days' notice when changing rates. The Act, however, had little practical effect because the Commission had no power to enforce its provisions other than filing lawsuits. In sixteen cases brought before the Supreme Court in eighteen years, the decisions in fifteen cases favored the railroads. The law is important, however, because it established the principle of federal regulation of business.

Test-Taking Strategy

Compare the Omaha Platform to the reforms achieved in the next twenty years.

- Another organization that supported farmers was the **Populist Party**, which was formed by the **Southern Alliance** and the **Northwestern Alliance** of farmers. In the election of 1892, the Populists drafted what is known as the **Omaha Platform.** It called for (1) government ownership of railroads; (2) free and unlimited coinage of silver at the rate of 16-to-1 with gold; (3) direct election of U.S. Senators; (4) the secret ballot, also known as the Australian ballot; (5) a graduated income tax; (6) government storage of crops and advances to farmers' on the price of those crops until farm prices improved **[subtreasury];** (7) an 8-hour workday; and (8) limits on immigration. The last two planks were meant to attract urban workers to the party. James B. Weaver, the Populist candidate for president, won one million popular votes and twenty-two electoral votes. Much of the vote appeared to be in response to the Party's monetary plank.

The Silver Issue and Cheap Money

- Beginning in the 1850s, miners trickled and then flooded into the Rockies and the Southwest looking for silver and gold. In 1891, Cripple Creek, Colorado, marked the last big gold and silver strike. In the approximately thirty-five years of the mining bonanza, many towns and cities had grown from tent cities. Although few miners struck it rich, many people stayed to build new lives and make their living from selling goods and providing services to their fellow townspeople and the outlying farmers and ranchers. A number of large cities developed from mining camps; for example, Virginia City, Denver, and Helena, Montana.

- By the end of the century, mining had shifted from the solitary gold panner to big business. In addition to gold and silver for currency, the nation needed metals like copper, tin, and lead for industry.

- In the aftermath of the **Panic of 1873,** people who owed debts wanted to expand the currency supply, thus reducing the value of the dollar and their debts. Although interest in **greenbackism** as a remedy faded, **free and unlimited coinage of silver** at the ratio of 16-to-1 with gold took its place. Farmers united with Western miners, who were suffering from an oversupply of silver as a result of various silver strikes, to lobby Congress. Congress, however, fearful of a glut of silver coins, had **demonetized** silver, that is, had ordered the coinage of silver halted. To advocates of free silver, this became known as the **Crime of 1873.**

- In 1878, Congress passed the **Bland-Allison Act,** ordering the purchase and coining of two- to four-million dollars worth of silver a month. The law had little effect on the money supply and provided little relief to debtors or miners.

- In 1890, Congress passed the **Sherman Silver Purchase Act,** which required the purchase of 4.5 million ounces of silver every month. To pay for the silver, the Treasury had to issue new notes. This Act provided cheap money and satisfied the Populists. In the **Panic of 1893,** President Cleveland asked Congress to repeal the law, and the Populists reacted angrily when Congress agreed with the president. Cleveland lost more support among farmers when he negotiated with J.P. Morgan and other Wall Street financiers for a bailout of the government. Gold reserves had dipped to a dangerous low level during the depression that followed the Panic of 1893—the worst the nation had seen.

- The silver controversy became the central issue in the election of 1896. Democrats chose **William Jennings Bryan** after his rousing **"Cross of Gold"** speech. He ran on a platform similar to the Populists' Omaha Platform. Populists split over whom to back but eventually supported Bryan. Republicans nominated William McKinley, who ran on a platform supporting a high tariff, the gold standard, annexation of Hawaii, and a strong foreign policy. Dissident Republicans bolted from the party, formed the National Silver Republicans, and supported Bryan. Although Bryan did well in the South and West, McKinley held the Northeast and won.

- The Populist Party declined and collapsed after the 1896 election. Many of the ideas of the Populists were realized through the activity of the major political parties and the progressives: (1) adoption of the secret ballot, (2) enactment of a graduated income tax through passage of the Sixteenth Amendment, (3) direct election of U.S. senators through the Seventeenth Amendment, (4) reorganization of the monetary policy of the nation through the Federal Reserve Act of 1913, (5) adoption of the Warehouse Act of 1916 based on the subtreasury principle, and (6) the strengthening of the Interstate Commerce Commission and Sherman Antitrust Act.

Key People

Review Strategy

See if you can relate additional people to their correct context in the "Fast Facts" section.

- **"goldbug" Democrats and Republicans**
- **Greenback Party, Greenback Labor Party, cheap money, unbacked currency**
- **Mark Hanna**

KEY TERMS/IDEAS

Review Strategy

See if you can relate these terms and ideas to their correct context in the "Fast Facts" section.

- bimetalism
- Clayton Antitrust Act, 1914, labor unions
- Dingley Tariff of 1897
- holding company
- interlocking directorate
- Hepburn Act, 1906, railroad regulation
- McKinley Tariff of 1890
- Specie Resumption Act of 1875, greenbacks "as good as gold"
- Wilson-Gorman Tarriff Bill, House-Senate conference bill, Cleveland's reaction, farmers' support

Chapter 6

REVIEWING THE NATION'S GOALS AND IDEALS, THE 1890S TO THE 1920S

This chapter reviews U.S. history from the end of the nineteenth century to the end of the 1920s. As the nation became used to its new industrial wealth, it turned its political interests outward and began to flex its muscles in the arena of world affairs. The global expansion of the late 1890s marked the end of almost a century of isolation. However, the horrors of World War I combined with the Russian Revolution revived isolationist tendencies in the United States. At home, these thirty years saw social reforms engineered by the progressives, Prohibition, women's suffrage, the Harlem Renaissance, the first Catholic to run for president, and a soaring stock market.

According to the College Board, 40 percent of the questions on the SAT II: U.S. History Test will be drawn from 1898 to the present. As you read and review for the test, focus on the why as much as the who and what. Be sure you make note of trends and significant people and events. To track trends, make connections between people and events over time.

SECTION 1. THE NATION ABROAD, 1898–1914

In 1867, Secretary of State **William Seward** succeeded in buying **Alaska** from Russia for the United States. It was almost thirty years before the nation added more territory. Between the end of the Civil War and 1900, the nation was occupied with settling the West, rebuilding the South, developing industrial power, and becoming an urban nation. It was a time of **isolationism.** However, by the end of the nineteenth century, a new sense of manifest destiny in the form of **imperialism** was catching hold. This desire for territories abroad was fueled by the need for raw materials and new markets for manufactured goods and farm products. It was also an attempt to show Europe that the United States had come of age as a world power.

FAST FACTS

Annexation of Hawaii

- By 1887, American planters controlled the Hawaiian legislature. When **Liliuokalani** became queen four years later, she attempted to wrest control from the planters. The planters demanded that she renounce the throne. When she refused, the planters set up their own government and asked the United States to annex **Hawaii.** Cleveland, who opposed imperialism, declined. The change in the presidency from Cleveland to McKinley, who embraced imperialism, opened the way for annexation in 1898.

The Spanish-American War

Review Strategy

Keep track of the events that resulted from the U.S.'s acquiring territory in the Spanish-American War.

- The year 1898 also saw the short-lived **Spanish-American War.** Fired up by the **yellow journalism** of competing New York newspapers, many Americans demanded that the United States stop Spain's abuses in Cuba. When the U.S.S. *Maine* blew up in Havana harbor, the United States declared war. After an easy victory in the "summer war," the United States and Spain negotiated the **Treaty of Paris.**

- Senate debate over ratification focused on the Philippines. Americans were not concerned about tiny Guam, and Puerto Rico was close to the mainland, but the Philippines were 8,000 miles away. Arguments against the treaty included (1) the fear that the United States might be dragged into a war in Asia to defend the Philippines, (2) the problems that would be created by trying to integrate Filipinos into American society if they were granted citizenship and allowed to emigrate to the United States without restriction, (3) the competition that Filipino products would create in U.S. markets if import duties were waived, (4) the concern that the Philippines would request statehood, and (5) the idea that **colonialism** was not compatible with the Constitution.

- Supporters of the treaty rejected the notion that **"the Constitution follows the flag."** There was no obligation on the part of the United States, they said, to establish a process that would lead to statehood for the Philippines. The treaty's advocates won ratification.

- After the war, the United States made Cuba a **protectorate** and passed the **Platt Amendment** to the Cuban constitution. The Amendment (1) forbade interference by any foreign nation in Cuba and (2) stated that the United States had the right to maintain order in Cuba. Cuba became an independent nation in 1934 and the Platt Amendment was withdrawn.

- In 1900, the United States made Puerto Rico a U.S. territory under the **Foraker Act,** which established (1) that trade between Puerto Rico and the United States would not be subject to tariffs and (2) that Puerto Ricans would not pay federal taxes. The **Jones Act,** in 1917, gave U.S. citizenship to Puerto Ricans.

U.S. Policy in China

- The **Open Door policy** of **John Hay** was a clever maneuver to ensure that U.S. business interests in China would be honored. Parts of China had been turned into **spheres of influence** by Russia, Germany, Great Britain, France, and Japan. These nations ran their **foreign concessions** for their own commercial benefit, which concerned U.S. businesses.

- Hay sent the same note to the American ambassador in each of the capitals of the nations that held a concession in China. The ambassadors were to ask for assurances that the foreign power (1) would not interfere with the privileges accorded other concessions, (2) would not favor their own nationals over others in the fees charged for harbor duties and railroad rates, and (3) would allow the Chinese to continue to collect customs duties. All the foreign powers refused to give Hay these assurances. Hay, however, announced that they had. Rather than be seen as threatening China's independence, the foreign powers remained silent in the face of Hay's lie.

Roosevelt's Policies in Latin America

Review Strategy

See Chapter 7 *for Franklin Roosevelt's Latin American policy.*

- With the annexation of Hawaii and the addition of Guam and the Philippines to U.S. territory, the United States had a renewed interest in seeing a canal built between the Atlantic and the Pacific Oceans. In 1902, President Roosevelt offered **Colombia** $40 million to pay for the work that a French company had already done on a canal. When Colombia refused to sell, Roosevelt aided a rebellion by Panamanians against Colombia. In exchange for guaranteeing the independence of the new nation, the United States signed the **Hay–Bunau-Varilla Treaty** with **Panama,** giving the United States control of the **Panama Canal Zone.**

- Because of growing U.S. business interests in Latin America and the U.S. investment in the Panama Canal, any European intervention in Latin America became an issue for the United States. When several European nations attempted to collect their debts from Venezuela by sending warships, Theodore Roosevelt issued the **Roosevelt Corollary** to the **Monroe Doctrine.** In essence, Roosevelt made the United States the self-appointed policeman of the Western Hemisphere, promising to use force if necessary to keep order and prevent chronic "wrongdoing" by any nation in the hemisphere. Roosevelt took action to counter the **Drago Doctrine,** which asked that the forcible collection of a nation's debts be made a violation of international law.

- Roosevelt invoked the Corollary shortly afterward for the first time to seize customs houses in the Dominican Republic and restore the nation's economic stability so that it could repay its debts to European nations.

Taft's "Dollar Diplomacy"

- Taft pursued a policy in China and Latin America known as **"dollar diplomacy."** The purpose was (1) to block European and Japanese efforts to take over more of China and (2) to help U.S. businesses invest in China and Latin America. The outcomes were (1) heightened resentment of the United States on the part of European and Latin American nations and Japan and (2) little in the way of profits for U.S. businesses.

Wilson's Policy of "Moral Diplomacy"

- In contrast to Roosevelt's "big stick" and Taft's fistful of dollars, **Woodrow Wilson** began his first term declaring his foreign policy would be based on **"moral diplomacy."** The **Mexican Revolution** tried Wilson's policy, and it was found wanting.
- Although U.S. business interests supported **General Victoriano Huerta,** Wilson abhorred Huerta's brutal tactics and refused to recognize his government. When the Mexicans did not overthrow Huerta, Wilson, on a pretext, sent U.S. marines to seize Veracruz. Wilson had expected that if the Mexican people were given support, they would opt for democracy and oust Huerta. Instead, Mexicans rioted against the United States. European and Latin American nations condemned Wilson's action, and he agreed to mediation by the **ABC powers** (Argentina, Brazil, and Chile).

KEY TERMS/IDEAS

Review Strategy

See if you can relate these terms and ideas to their correct context in the "Fast Facts" section.

- **American Samoa**
- **"big stick" policy; "Walk softly and carry a big stick"; U.S. intervention in the Caribbean and Latin America**
- **Boxer Rebellion**
- **Chinese Exclusion Act of 1882, 1920 ban on all Chinese immigration**
- **Gentlemen's Agreement, school segregation in San Francisco, denial of passports to Japanese laborers**
- **Insular Cases, Congress would determine whether an acquired territory was put on the path to statehood**
- **Nicaragua, "dollar diplomacy," "big stick" policy, Taft**
- **Root-Takahira Agreement, promises not to interfere with each other's territories**
- **Rough Riders, Battle of San Juan Hill, Roosevelt as war hero**
- **Russo-Japanese War, Treaty of Portsmouth; lack of an indemnity, anti-American rioting**
- **Taft-Katsura Memorandum, U.S. recognition of Japanese dominance in Korea, Japanese promise not to attack the Philippines**

SECTION 2. THE PROGRESSIVE ERA

The **progressives** sought reform, improvement, and progress through government action. Progressivism was both an attitude and, for a brief time in 1912, a political party. The progressives were repelled by the (1) corruption and **graft** in government, (2) the cutthroat competition in business that reduced the ordinary working family to poverty, and (3) the exploitation of the nation's natural resources.

FAST FACTS

Differing Approaches to Reform

- A certain amount of the goals of the progressives could be traced to the **Populist Party,** but there were important differences.

PROGRESSIVES	POPULISTS
Farmers, factory workers, small business owners; college-educated middle- and upper-class urbanites	Farmers, factory workers, small business owners
Urban base	Agrarian base
Progressive Party (1912); worked through established political parties	Basically a political party
Each group had its own issues, such as government reform, regulation of big business, relief for the poor	Tariff and cheap money as major issues
Some success at state and local levels	Issues co-opted by major parties

- The need for reform was publicized through the works of the **muckrakers,** a group of journalists and writers who exposed (1) corruption in government, (2) the evils of big business practices, and (3) the conditions of the cities. Among the muckrakers were **Lincoln Steffens (*Shame of the Cities*), Ida M. Tarbell (*History of the Standard Oil Company*), Upton Sinclair (*The Jungle*), Ray Stannard Baker (*Following the Color Line*), John Spargo (*The Bitter Cry of the Children*),** and **Gustavus Myers (*History of the Great American Families*).**
- Progressive reforms had some success at the local level and then moved up to the state level. It was only when Theodore Roosevelt became president that the movement was able to accomplish reforms at the national level. Among the changes the progressives brought about were:

1. experiments with different types of city government: **city commission** and **city manager, home rule**
2. adoption of ways to improve government: **direct primary, direct election of U.S. senators (Seventeenth Amendment); initiative, recall,** and **referendum; Australian,** or secret ballot
3. adoption of a **graduated income tax (Sixteenth Amendment)**
4. **Prohibition (Eighteenth Amendment)**
5. granting of **women's suffrage (Nineteenth Amendment)**
6. more aggressive regulation of big business, including public utilities
7. greater protection for workers
8. regulation of the food and drug industries
9. institutionalization of the **conservation** movement.

- **Socialism** presented an alternative for some, in part because of Edward Bellamy's book *Looking Backward 2000–1887.* After his arrest and imprisonment during the **Pullman Strike, Eugene V. Debs** organized the **American Socialist Party.** The **Industrial Workers of the World (IWW, Wobblies)** was a radical labor union formed to take control of business. Whereas the Wobblies believed in confrontation, most socialists were more moderate and worked through the system. Debs, for example, ran for President of the United States five times.

African Americans Find Their Voices

- The period from the Civil War to the 1920s was very difficult for African Americans in the South. Beginning around 1910 and lasting until 1930, the **Great Migration** of African Americans out of the South occurred. They were pushed by (1) the **boll weevil,** a pest that had laid waste to 85 percent of the South's cotton fields by the early 1920s; (2) several seasons of extreme weather; (3) severe poverty as a result of the **sharecropping system;** (4) fear of **lynching;** and (5) the refusal of white factory owners to hire African Americans.

- In Northern cities, various organizations developed to serve the newly arrived African Americans. Among them were black churches, newspapers, the **National Urban League,** and the **National Association for the Advancement of Colored People (NAACP).** The latter developed out of the **Niagara Movement** that was organized by **W.E.B. Du Bois.** The **Nation of Islam** also began around this time.

- Three major figures of this period were **Booker T. Washington,** Du Bois, and **Marcus Garvey.**

WASHINGTON	DU BOIS	GARVEY
Born a slave	Born free	British subject from Jamaica
Founded **Tuskegee Institute**	• Founded Niagara Movement • Founded NAACP	Founded **Universal Negro Improvement Association (UNIA)**
Appealed to ordinary African Americans	Appealed to **Talented Tenth**	Appealed to ordinary African Americans
Worked for economic equality, but not social or political equality	Believed in confrontation to achieve complete equality	**Back-to-Africa** movement
• Noted for **Atlanta Compromise** • Was influential among whites	• Noted for writing in the *Crisis* magazine • Shared interest in African heritage	Noted for **Pan-Africanism**

How Roosevelt Earned His Reputation

Review Strategy

See Chapter 5 *to review business organizations and their practices.*

- Theodore Roosevelt earned the title **"trust buster"** as he set out to rein in big business. His administration brought suit against the **Northern Securities Company** and won when the Supreme Court ruled that the **holding company** restrained trade and was, therefore, in violation of the **Sherman Antitrust Act.** In all, Roosevelt's administration prosecuted forty lawsuits against business combinations.

- Roosevelt was also responsible for Congress' passing of the **Elkins Act (1903)** and the **Hepburn Act (1906)** to strengthen the **Interstate Commerce Commission.** Congress also passed the **Pure Food and Drug Act**, which helped to establish the precedent that protecting the public welfare was the legitimate business of the federal government.

- In the coal miners' strike of 1902, Roosevelt became the first president to intervene in a strike on behalf of labor. Rejecting the opportunity to use the Sherman Antitrust Act against the miners, he attempted to mediate. The attempt failed, but the strike ended soon after both parties agreed to arbitration.

- Roosevelt built his reputation as a **conservationist** on policies such as (1) his withdrawal from sale of 200 million acres of public land, (2) the **Newlands Reclamation Bill** to finance irrigation projects, (3) the establishment of the **Inland Waterways Commission,** and (4) the **White House Conservation Commission.**

The Progressives' Split with Taft

- In the election of 1908, the Republicans had pledged tariff revisions. The **Dingley Tariff of 1897** was still in effect, and many people blamed the tariff for rising prices. Although the Republican Party had favored high tariffs since the election of 1883, Taft had said he would reduce tariffs. After an unsuccessful fight to defeat the bill that led in the Senate by progressive **Robert La Follette,** the **Payne-Aldrich Tariff** reached Taft's desk. The bill reduced some rates but raised thousands of others. Taft, who had done little to fulfill his campaign promise, signed the bill, praising it as the best tariff bill that the Republicans had ever passed. He was concerned that vetoing it would hurt the chances for passage of other legislation that he wanted.

- Claiming that Roosevelt had overstepped his authority, **Richard Ballinger,** the new secretary of the interior under Taft and a lawyer, reopened for public sale some of the lands Roosevelt had closed. **Gifford Pinchot,** the chief forester, criticized Ballinger publicly and provided information to the muckraking press about Ballinger's activities. Both a presidential investigation and a Congressional committee found Ballinger innocent of any wrongdoing. Taft fired Pinchot. The progressives in the Republican Party were furious at both the appointment of Ballinger and the firing of Pinchot. This controversy and the Payne-Aldrich Tariff led to a split in the party.

- The split in the Republican Party led to the founding of the **Progressive Party,** or **Bull Moose Party,** which nominated Theodore Roosevelt in the election of 1912. His opponents were Taft, who was renominated by the Republican Party; **Woodrow Wilson,** the nominee of the Democratic Party; and Eugene V. Debs of the Socialist Party, who made a strong showing by capturing two million votes.

Wilson's Efforts at Domestic Reform

- The Democrats had promised to revise tariff rates downward if elected. Wilson called a special session of Congress to consider what became known as the **Underwood-Simmons Tariff of 1913.** The bill became locked in debate in the Senate, and Wilson appealed directly to voters. His reprimand of the lobbyists for big business started a Congressional investigation, and the bill was passed, substantially reducing tariffs for the first time since 1857.

- Wilson also introduced a reform of the banking and currency system. After the **Panic of 1907** forced the closure of a number of banks because they were undercapitalized, Congress had established the **Aldrich Commission** to study the nation's monetary practices. In 1913, the Commission reported that (1) the nation's banks lacked stability, (2) the nation's currency supply needed to be more flexible so that it could expand or contract as required by the volume of business, (3) there was no central institution to oversee and regulate banking practices, and (4) Wall Street (New York City) had too much power over the nation's banking capital. Wilson's answer was the **Federal Reserve Act** that (1) provided money to banks in temporary trouble, (2) eased the inflexibility of the money supply by providing currency in exchange for promissory notes from businesses, and (3) and (4) set up twelve Federal Reserve banks in twelve regions of the country supervised by a Board of Governors, whose headquarters were in Washington D.C., thus removing the power from Wall Street.

Test-Taking Strategy

Connect the Clayton Anti-trust Act with the Sherman Antitrust Act to see why the exemption is significant.

- Among Wilson's efforts to regulate big business were creation of the **Federal Trade Commission** and passage of the **Clayton Antitrust Act.** The former could (1) investigate businesses suspected of illegal practices and (2) issue cease-and-desist orders for businesses found guilty of practices such as mislabeling and adulterating goods and engaging in combinations to fix retail prices. The major significance of the Clayton Antitrust Act was that it specifically exempted labor unions and agricultural cooperatives from antitrust regulations. The law also forbade (1) **interlocking directorates,** (2) **holding companies** for the purpose of creating **monopolies,** (3) **tying contracts,** and (4) price discrimination for the purpose of creating a monopoly.

KEY PEOPLE/TERMS

Review Strategy

See if you can relate these people and terms to their correct context in the "Fast Facts" section.

- **Joseph ("Uncle Joe") G. Cannon**
- *McClure's*
- **New Freedom, Wilson's philosophy, government should intervene in private business to assert the public interest**
- **New Nationalism, Roosevelt's promise in the election of 1912**
- **Old Guard Republicans, conservatives**
- **"Square Deal," Roosevelt's 1904 campaign promise**

SECTION 3. WILSON AND WORLD WAR I

At the beginning of the war in Europe, **President Woodrow Wilson** declared the nation's **neutrality.** While grateful for the expanse of the Atlantic Ocean between the United States and Europe, Americans were still concerned about the fate of Great Britain and France. As time went on, those who had supported the Germans began to revise their views and become **pro-Ally,** and support for the British and the French intensified.

FAST FACTS

The Problems of Neutrality

- The declaration of neutrality did not stop private U.S. companies from selling weapons and supplies and making loans to Great Britain and France. This economic activity helped raise the United States out of a recession. Because the British controlled the sea lanes, the Germans could not do business with U.S. companies.

- Both the British and the Germans challenged U.S. neutrality. The British put into effect a series of policies, including laying mines in the North Sea and seizure and search of neutral ships, that endangered U.S. merchant ships and violated their rights under international law. The Germans declared the waters around Great Britain a **war zone** and announced that their submarines, known as **U-boats,** would sink enemy merchantmen on sight. Because British ships sometimes flew the U.S. flag, the Germans said they could not ensure the safety of U.S. ships.

- Wilson protested to both nations, but little came of his protests until a U-boat sank the British passenger ship *Lusitania.* The Germans agreed that in the future, U-boats would provide for the safety of the passengers and crew of any ships they sank. After another incident in 1916, the Germans issued the **Sussex Pledge,** stating that they would not sink merchant ships without warning. However, things were going badly for the Germans. In an effort to raise morale and to cut off supplies to the European **Allies,** the Germans decided to resume **unrestricted submarine warfare** in 1917. The Germans realized that this would probably bring the United States into the war, but the Germans decided that they could starve the Allies into defeat before the United States could **mobilize.**

- The backdrop to all this was an internal debate in the United States waged by **pacifists** versus those who advocated **preparedness.** Among the former were **progressives,** who feared that their reform program would collapse, and those of German and Irish descent, who did not want to see the United States fight on the side of Great Britain. Among the latter were **nationalists,** who thought that Wilson should be stronger in his response to Germany.

- Wilson, himself, wished to keep the nation out of the European war and campaigned in 1916 on the slogan **"He kept us out of war."** However, in 1915, he also asked Congress to authorize a modest **preparedness program.** Faced with harsh opposition from the progressives, Wilson took his campaign to the people and won approval of his proposal.

Declaration of War

Red Alert!

The battles may be interesting, but you won't find them on the test.

- In early 1917, when the secret **Zimmerman Note** was published asking Mexico to join the German effort and promising to help it recapture Texas, Arizona, and New Mexico, a wave of anger swept the United States. By April 1917, the resumption of unrestricted submarine warfare had severely curtailed shipping; the Allies were nearly exhausted. Wilson called Congress into special session and asked for a declaration of war.

- The nation began to mobilize. The **Selective Service law** was passed, instituting the **draft.** The **War Industries Board,** created to handle the purchasing of materials for the Allies, was one of several such **war boards** that were established to oversee the management and allocation of industry, labor, and raw materials. To finance the war, the government decided to sell **war bonds,** known as **Liberty bonds,** and organized **Liberty Loan drives** to sell them. Wilson was also given authority to take over industries, requisition supplies, and control distribution in order to prosecute the war.

Wilson's Fourteen Points

- At the peace conference that ended World War I, Wilson unveiled his **Fourteen Points,** a set of proposals to eliminate the causes of war. A very moral man, Wilson believed that morality should underlay the conduct of government. His plan called for the following:

  1. Open rather than secret diplomacy
  2. Freedom of the seas
  3. Removal of as many tariffs and other trade barriers as possible
  4. Reduction of national armaments to a level consistent with domestic safety
  5. Settlement of colonial claims that recognize the interests of the colonial peoples and the occupying nation
  6. Evacuation of all Russian territory by foreign powers
  7. Evacuation of Belgium and restoration of its sovereignty
  8. Restoration of Alsace-Lorraine to France
  9. Readjustment of the Italian border to recognize nationality
  10. Autonomy for the peoples of Austria-Hungary
  11. Autonomy for Serbia, Montenegro, and Romania—the Balkan states
  12. Autonomy for the subject peoples of the Ottoman Empire
  13. Independence for Poland
  14. An international organization of world nations

Test-Taking Strategy

If you were a question writer, what would you ask about Wilson and the peace conference?

- The most important point to Wilson was the fourteenth—a **League of Nations.** Determined to win approval for his plan, Wilson went to the peace conference. Some historians believe that Wilson would have been better able to judge the domestic opposition to his plan had he stayed in Washington. They also believe that he would have had a better chance of winning his points at the conference had he been away from the political pressures of the negotiating table. Wilson might also have been wise to include a prominent Republican or two on his negotiating team in order to win over the opposition or at least to dampen it.

- As it was, Wilson attended the conference to find that, while he wanted peace that would not lead to another war, his Allies wanted revenge and the territories that they had secretly agreed to divide up when they won the war. Most of Wilson's Fourteen Points were ignored. His biggest loss was the Allies' insistence that Germany pay **reparations.** This insistence would lead to (1) the worldwide depression of the 1920s, (2) the emergence of **Adolf Hitler,** and (3) World War II. Wilson, however, won his League of Nations.

Opposition to the League of Nations

- When Wilson returned with the **Treaty of Versailles,** he faced a fight, not only in the Senate but also in the nation. **Isolationists** denounced the League because they feared it would force the United States to go to war to preserve other nations' boundaries. Some thought that Great Britain would dominate the League or that the United States would give up its sovereignty to a superstate League. Others thought the Treaty was unjust, especially those who supported Germany or one of the nations that lost territory in the settlement. Some Republicans feared that Wilson would use a victory for the League as an issue in a campaign for a third term.

- When a number of Republican senators and senators-elect came out against the League, Wilson publicly denounced them. He took his campaign to the nation in a cross-country tour, but he collapsed partway through the tour and suffered a stroke. The Senate twice refused to ratify the Treaty as it stood and negotiated separate treaties with the **Central Powers.**

The Red Scare

- The end of the war saw the rise of intolerance and a phenomenon known as the **"red scare."** The Russian Revolution of 1917 had stirred fears in the United States that radicals were trying to take over the government. A series of mail bombs in the early part of 1919 that were addressed to prominent Americans, some of whom had spoken out against subversives or for restrictions on immigration, confirmed for many that these fears had merit. Attorney General **A. Mitchell Palmer** launched an investigation of **Bolsheviks**—raided Communist meetings, seized records, and arrested some 6,000 people, without regard to their rights. The courts released most of the accused for lack of evidence.

***Schenck* v. *United States* (1919; principle of a clear and present danger)**

Case: Under the Espionage Act of 1917, Charles Schenck, General Secretary of the Socialist Party in the United States, was convicted of printing and distributing leaflets that urged men to resist the draft during World War I. The Espionage Act forbade people from saying, printing, writing, or publishing anything against the government. Schenck appealed on the grounds that the First Amendment's guarantee of freedom of speech protected him.

Decision: The Court ruled against Schenck, holding that during peacetime, the First Amendment would have protected him, but during wartime, his words presented a danger to the nation.

Significance: This decision meant that the First Amendment does not protect freedom of speech when it presents an immediate danger that it will incite a criminal action.

- One of the factors that motivated the red scare was the increasing strength of **labor unions.** During the war, **collective bargaining** had helped to keep the war industries humming, but once **reconversion** was underway, cooperation between business and labor faltered. Prices went up, but wages did not. A series of strikes, 3,600, swept the nation in 1919, some accompanied by violence. The press carried hostile coverage of the strikes, and some Americans came to see organized labor as un-American, an invitation to **anarchy.**

KEY PEOPLE

Review Strategy

See if you can relate these additional people to their correct context in the "Fast Facts" section.

- **William Jennings Bryan, Theodore Roosevelt as opponents**
- **Eugene V. Debs, "Big Bill" Haywood, deprivation of civil liberties**
- **Henry Cabot Lodge, Sr.; William E. Borah, Republican opponents**
- **General John J. Pershing, commander of U.S. troops**

KEY TERMS/IDEAS

Review Strategy

See if you can relate these terms and ideas to their correct context in the "Fast Facts" section.

- **airplane as a weapon of war, trench warfare**
- **Article 10, mutual guarantee of political boundaries**
- **Committee on Public Information, propaganda, anti-German**
- **Espionage Act, Sedition Act**
- **Food Administration, War Labor Board, War Labor Policies Board, Fuel Administration, Railroad Administration**
- **National Defense Act, 1916; modest increase in the armed forces**
- **"peace without victory"**

SECTION 4. THE 1920s

The **roaring twenties** coincided with the **"return to normalcy"** that was promised in the 1920 election by **Warren G. Harding.** It was a time of glittering prosperity— mixed with a dark strain of intolerance and injustice.

FAST FACTS

The Business Climate of the Early 1920s

- Normalcy in business meant a **laissez-faire** attitude toward regulating business but a probusiness attitude (1) in passing the **Fordney-McCumber Tariff,** (2) in promoting foreign trade through providing huge loans to the postwar Allied governments who returned the favor by buying U.S.-produced goods and foodstuffs, and (3) by cracking down on strikes. The Supreme Court helped with a number of rulings that were favorable to big business, such as (1) allowing antitrust laws to be used as the basis for suits against unions, (2) declaring boycotts by labor to be illegal, and (3) nullifying the minimum wage for women.

Review Strategy

See Chapter 7 *for how the Depression affected farmers.*

- For a time after World War I, farmers participated in the prosperity of the 1920s, but when the federal government cut loans to the Allies early in the decade, the agricultural boom ended. The high tariffs levied by the United States and the Allies' insistence on repayment of war debts hurt the world economy and the market for U.S. farm products. In addition, during the war, farmers had been encouraged to grow as much as they could. Once the war was over, farmers continued and were left with surpluses. Farmers lobbied for the federal government to buy the excess inventory, but Coolidge vetoed the bill twice. He claimed it would create artificial prices and promote overproduction. In 1929, Congress established the **Farm Board** to buy surpluses and maintain prices, but farmers continued to grow as much as they wanted.

- The Harding administration is remembered for its scandals from Harding's attorney general who sold pardons and paroles to the **Teapot Dome Scandal,** named after a reserve in Wyoming. The reserve land that was rich in oil deposits had been set aside under the jurisdiction of the Navy Department for years. The scandal involved a member of Harding's Cabinet, two oil speculators, and large bribes to open the reserve for drilling.

Flowering of African American Culture

- The decade of the twenties was also known as the **Jazz Age.** Jazz is a musical form that is unique to the United States. It began in the South around the turn of the twentieth century and moved North. It blends West African rhythms, African American spirituals and blues, and European harmonies. After the war, some jazz musicians and singers found less racial discrimination in Europe and moved abroad.

- The **Great Migration** had transformed parts of some Northern cities into all-black neighborhoods. One of these neighborhoods was Harlem in New York City. It became the center of a flowering of African American culture called the **Harlem Renaissance.** The **National Urban League,** the **NAACP,** and the **Universal Negro Improvement Association** (led by **Marcus Garvey**) were headquartered there. Harlem attracted African American writers, artists, and musicians from around the nation to what was known as the **New Negro Movement.**

Prohibition

Review Strategy

See Chapter 3 *for the reform movements of the nineteenth century.*

- The **Temperance Movement** could trace its beginnings to the reform movements of the early nineteenth century. By 1917, two thirds of the states had passed laws prohibiting the consumption of alcohol, and several others had approved **local-option** laws. With the entrance of the United States into World War I, prohibitionist forces cloaked themselves in the mantle of patriotism to argue that (1) prohibition would shift thousands of tons of grain from liquor manufacture to war uses; (2) alcoholism led to drunkenness, and a drunken man was of no use to the war; and (3) most breweries and whiskey distilleries were owned by Germans. In 1917, Congress passed the **Eighteenth Amendment,** and the states ratified it by 1919.

- The amendment was difficult to enforce because most Americans did not believe in it, including a succession of occupants of the White House. Wilson vetoed the **Volstead Act,** which was meant to enforce the amendment, but Congress passed it over his veto. Americans tired of the self-sacrifice of the war years circumvented the law through **bootlegging.** The large-scale manufacture and smuggling of alcohol became the business of organized crime. **Prohibition** was repealed in 1933.

Women's Suffrage

- By 1913, **suffragists** were able to count nine states in which women could vote. All nine states were in the West. To speed the process of enfranchisement, women like **Carrie Chapman Catt** and **Alice Paul** continued the fight for an amendment to the Constitution. Such an amendment had been introduced into Congress every year since 1878—and defeated every year. Congress finally passed the amendment in 1918, and the necessary states ratified the **Nineteenth Amendment,** so women could vote in the 1920 elections.

Nativism

- The "red scare" at the end of war also resulted in legislation restricting immigration. Up until the late 1800s when the first immigration law was passed, people could freely enter the United States. With the exception of Chinese and Japanese people, this remained true until 1921. In that year, the **Immigration Restriction Act** was passed and in 1924, the **National Origins Act.** These laws were aimed at restricting immigrants from Southern and Central Europe and Asia. Buoyed by the patriotism generated by the war and fearful of anarchists and Bolsheviks, Americans pressured lawmakers for these laws to keep America for Americans.

- This **nativist** attitude also resulted in a resurgence of the **Ku Klux Klan.** This **white supremacist** organization from the South now spread north and west and added Jews and Catholics to its targets. The organization's goal was to protect white, Anglo-Saxon Protestant America from African Americans and foreigners.

The Election of 1928

- Anti-Catholic sentiment was a factor in the 1928 election, in which **Al Smith,** the Democratic candidate and a Catholic, faced Herbert Hoover. Smith had other liabilities in addition to this Catholicism. He was a product of the New York City political machine and not from a rural background, as Democratic candidates had been up until then. He was also against Prohibition. Hoover ran on his record of public service and on Republican prosperity.

- Although Smith lost the **"Solid South,"** he managed to resurrect the Democratic Party from its long eclipse under the Republicans. He also attracted a new constituency to the party. In this election, membership shifted from rural and small-town to urban, Catholic, immigrant, and working-class.

KEY PEOPLE

Review Strategy

See if you can relate these people to their correct context in the "Fast Facts" section.

- **African American artists: Romare Bearden, Sargent Johnson, Augusta Savage**
- **expatriates, "lost generation," alienation, Ernest Hemingway, F. Scott Fitzgerald, Gertrude Stein**
- **African American music: Billie Holiday, Duke Ellington, Jelly Roll Morton, Bessie Smith, William Grant Still**
- **African American writers and poets: Langston Hughes, Countee Cullen, Zora Neale Hurston, James Weldon Johnson**

KEY TERMS/IDEAS

Review Strategy

See if you can relate these terms and ideas to their correct context in the "Fast Facts" section.

- anti-Semitism
- consumer culture: the automobile, radio, movies, sports
- Sacco-Vanzetti case
- Scopes trial, evolution, William Jennings Bryan; religious fundamentalism

Chapter 7

REVIEWING THE GREAT DEPRESSION, WORLD WAR II, AND THE POSTWAR NATION

This chapter describes the weaknesses in the nation's economy that led to the 1929 stock market crash, the efforts of the Roosevelt administration to end the Great Depression, the worsening events in Europe and Asia, the eventual declaration of war, and the changes in the nation that were brought about by World War II. The presidencies of Herbert Hoover, Franklin Roosevelt, Harry Truman, and Dwight Eisenhower are covered.

As you review for the SAT II: U.S. History Test, remember that you are unlikely to find questions about the battles of World War II. You will find questions about social, economic, cultural, and intellectual history, although the largest percentage of questions—32 to 36 percent—will be about political history.

Red Alert!

For basic information about the SAT II: U.S. History Test, see the Red Alert! section, pp. 2-5.

SECTION 1. THE GREAT DEPRESSION

When Herbert Hoover took office in 1928, there were a number of weaknesses in the U.S. economy that he was either unaware of or ignored. The most visible was the amount of **speculation** in the stock market, but there were a number of problems.

FAST FACTS

The Stock Market Crash

Review Strategy

See Section 2 of this chapter for how Roosevelt's policies dealt with the weaknesses in the economy.

- Among the weaknesses in the U.S. economy were (1) the amount of stock being bought **on margin;** (2) depressed agricultural prices because of large surpluses; (3) the unequal distribution of wealth, so that 5 percent of the population provided the nation's investment capital and the majority of its purchasing power; (4) the tax policies of Andrew Mellon, Secretary of the Treasury, that contributed to the unequal distribution of wealth; (5) the expansion of businesses in response to rapidly increasing profits; (6) easy-to-get **installment credit** for consumers; (7) the size and influence on segments of the economy of **holding companies;** (8) the weakness of the banking system because of many small and mismanaged banks; (9) high tariffs that closed off foreign markets for U.S.

goods; and (10) the Allies' insistence on collecting war debts that depressed foreign trade, especially for U.S. foodstuffs.

- Andrew Mellon believed that the rich should not be so heavily taxed because heavy taxation discouraged them from investing in businesses and, thus, stimulating the economy. Congress abolished the excise and excess profits taxes that had been instituted during World War I. Taxes on income were reduced by more than 50 percent. Still, many people thought that the tax burden fell unequally on the middle class and poor, in part because the reduction in taxes meant a reduction in services for the poor.

- By the end of the decade, that part of the 95 percent of the population that was buying on credit had overextended its credit or had bought all that it wanted. The larger part of that 95 percent, however, could never afford to buy the new luxury goods of the 1920s. **Overproduction** and **underconsumption** joined to create financial problems for businesses that now found themselves with surplus inventory and their own loans to meet.

- All these factors came together in the late 1920s to create the backdrop for the **Stock Market Crash of 1929.** By the fall of 1929, more than $7 billion had been borrowed to buy stocks on margin. Based on the profits that the companies were earning, many stocks were hugely overvalued. When professional speculators began to cash out of the market in September, it was only a matter of time before **Black Tuesday** and the end of the **Roaring Twenties.**

- After the Crash, many stocks were worthless. People lost their life savings, their jobs, and their homes. Banks foreclosed on loans and mortgages. When their borrowers could not repay their loans, the banks went under. Businesses went bankrupt as inventories piled up because people could not afford anything but necessities—if even those. People relied on family members who were better off to take them in. As more businesses closed and more people lost their jobs, the **Great Depression** worsened.

Hoover's Policies

- Hoover believed (1) that helping the unemployed was the responsibility of churches, private agencies, and local and state governments; (2) that giving a handout to the unemployed would destroy their self-respect and individual initiative; (3) that a federal relief program would bankrupt the nation; and (4) that a federal relief program would dangerously enlarge the power of the federal government and create a bloated bureaucracy.

- Hoover believed that the Depression would be short-lived. Although he did not believe that the federal government should help the unemployed, he did authorize the funding of the **Home Loan Bank Act** and the **Reconstruction Finance Corporation,** the latter to help businesses.

- Hoover acted to shore up farm prices by ordering the **Farm Board** to buy surplus farm products to keep prices up. But as warehouses filled, prices fell and the Farm Board stopped buying surpluses in 1931.

- In 1932, some 20,000 unemployed veterans descended on Washington, D.C., demanding immediate payment of bonus certificates that were not to come due until 1945. The **Bonus Marchers** set up a **Hooverville** just outside the city or camped in empty buildings on Pennsylvania Avenue to await Congress's vote. When Congress rejected the bill, many veterans went home, but some stayed because they had nowhere else to go. After two weeks, Hoover sent the capital police to remove the veterans from the abandoned buildings. Somehow, shots were fired and a mob scene followed. **General Douglas MacArthur,** who had been told to stand ready in case of trouble, ordered troops and tanks into the shanty town The veterans were routed, and the army burned the Hooverville. The sight of unarmed veterans fleeing before U.S. Army tanks hurt Hoover's already damaged credibility.

KEY TERMS/IDEAS

Review Strategy

See if you can relate these additional terms and ideas to their correct context in the "Fast Facts" section.

- **"self-liquidating projects,"** Reconstruction Finance Corporation's idea that projects should earn back loans
- **Smoot-Hawley Tariff of 1930,** raised tariffs drastically, European nations retaliated, U.S. agriculture and industry suffered

SECTION 2. THE NEW DEAL

Roosevelt's policies to deal with the Great Depression can be categorized as **"relief, recovery, and reform."** The fifteen programs enacted in the first **"Hundred Days"** were meant to provide relief and begin the nation's recovery. Although some measures in this period dealt with reform of the banking and securities businesses, most reform measures came later.

FAST FACTS

New Deal Legislation

- The following table lists some of these major bills and provisions. One agency that was created as the result of a direct order by Roosevelt was the **Civil Works Administration (CWA).** Overseen by **Harry Hopkins,** who also headed **FERA** and the later **WPA,** the CWA pumped a billion dollars into the economy between late 1933 and spring 1934 by providing **work-relief** for more than four million people—from building roads to teaching adult school.

NEW DEAL LEGISLATION

ACT	SOME PROVISIONS
Emergency Banking Act, 1933	• Allowed inspection of bank records to enable financially stable banks to reopen; validated **"bank holiday"** • Permitted **Reconstruction Finance Corporation (RFC)** to buy stocks of banks in trouble, thereby giving the banks an infusion of new capital, an example of **"pump priming"**
Glass-Steagall Banking Act, 1933	Established **Federal Deposit Insurance Corporation (FDIC)** to insure bank deposits (and stabilize the banking system)
Federal Emergency Relief Administration (FERA), 1933	Provided work on projects, such as building roads and airports, schools and playgrounds, and parks
Civilian Conservation Corps (CCC), 1933	Provided jobs related to conservation of natural resources to men between the ages of seventeen and twenty-five
Agricultural Adjustment Act (AAA), 1933	• In order to raise prices, limited farm production by paying **subsidies** to farmers to withhold land from cultivation • Declared unconstitutional in 1936 • Replaced with **Soil Conservation and Domestic Allotment Act** (1936) and second **Agricultural Adjustment Act** (1938) to keep surpluses in check and prices of agricultural commodities and farm incomes up

National Industrial Recovery Act (NIRA), 1933	• Created **National Recovery Administration (NRA)**
	  • Administered codes of fair practices for businesses and industry
	  • Declared unconstitutional in *Schechter Poultry Corp.* v. *United States* (Section 7A)
	• Created **Public Works Administration (PWA)** to provide money for construction or improvement of the **infrastructure** and public buildings

Securities Act, 1933	• Gave Federal Trade Commission power to supervise new issues of stock • Required statement of financial information to accompany new stock issues • Made company directors liable—civilly and criminally—for misrepresentation

NEW DEAL LEGISLATION

ACT	SOME PROVISIONS
Tennessee Valley Authority (TVA), 1933	• Bought, built, and operated dams • Generated and sold electrical power • Planned flood control and reforestation projects • Withdrew poor land from farming • Used TVA rates as a yardstick to gauge rates charged by private utilities controversial
Farm Credit Administration (FCA), 1933	Provided funding for farm mortgages
Home Owners Loan Corporation (HOLC), 1933	Provided funding for home mortgages
Securities and Exchange Act, 1934	• Provided for federal regulation of securities exchanges • Established the **Securities and Exchange Commission (SEC)**
Banking Act of 1935	Reorganized the **Federal Reserve System** to give the **Federal Reserve Board** control over **open-market operations**
National Youth Administration (NYA), 1935	• Provided work-relief, training, and employment to people between the ages of sixteen and twenty-five who were not full-time students • Provided part-time employment for students to enable them to stay in school
Works Progress Administration (WPA), 1935	• Provided employment on infrastructure projects, such as dredging rivers and building highways • Created projects for artists, writers, actors, and musicians
Social Security Act of 1935	• Established unemployment compensation fund • Established old-age pension fund • Set up grants to states for care of needy dependent children, the physically disabled, and women and children in poverty • Did not cover all jobs, such as farmers, farm workers, and domestics, and, therefore, excluded some 80 percent of all African Americans
National Labor Relations Act (also known as **Wagner Act**), 1935	Authorized the **National Labor Relations Board (NLRB)** to oversee union elections and define and prohibit unfair labor practices
Fair Labor Standards Act (also known as **Wages and Hours Act**), 1938	Set maximum of a forty-four hour workweek and a minimum wage of twenty-five cents an hour for workers engaged in interstate commerce or in the production of goods involved in interstate commerce

- In his annual address to Congress in 1935, Roosevelt announced the **Second New Deal.** Admitting that recovery had not helped everyone, Roosevelt ended attempts to balance the budget and shifted the focus of his programs in an attempt to form a new coalition to support both his programs and the Democratic Party. Because of the NRA, business was hostile, so he courted labor, farmers, and African Americans. They joined the traditional backbone of the Democratic Party—Southerners and Northern political machines. The legislative and executive activities of the Second New Deal reflected many of their interests.

- The National Recovery Administration (NRA), one of the alphabet agencies of the New Deal, had been established under the National Industrial Recovery Act (NIRA). It was extremely unpopular with the public—large employers, small business owners, consumers, and labor alike. In *Schechter Poultry Corp.* **v.** *United States* (1935), the Supreme Court found the law unconstitutional because, among other reasons, under Section 7A, the law attempted to regulate intrastate commerce, a violation of the commerce clause of Article I.

- Critics of the New Deal ranged from those who thought it did not do enough to those who thought it did too much. On the left were **Father Charles E. Coughlin,** who attacked Roosevelt for moving too slowly to resolve the unequal distribution of the nation's wealth; **Huey Long,** a senator from Louisiana, who championed the rural poor and built a national reputation attacking Roosevelt; and **Dr. Francis Townshend,** who proposed a national pension for the elderly. On the right, business leaders concerned by increasing federal power and the cost of New Deal programs formed the **American Liberty League** to work against Roosevelt and his policies, which they believed were leading the nation into socialism and bankruptcy. Conservative Northern and Western Republicans and conservative Southern Democrats would increasingly oppose Roosevelt's programs as being too liberal.

- In an effort to offset inflation in 1937, Roosevelt ordered cuts in federal spending, especially in the WPA and in the PWA's pump-priming activities. In addition, workers and businesses were now paying Social Security taxes. This contraction in **purchasing power** resulted in a **recession** that dragged on into 1938, almost wiping out the economic advances since 1935. By mid-1938, Roosevelt asked for a new spending program, and Congress agreed. The recession ended, but no new large-scale relief programs were passed by a Congress that was now controlled by conservatives.

"Court Packing"

- One of the least successful of Roosevelt's actions was the so-called **court-packing** scheme to put judges who were more sympathetic to the New Deal on the **Supreme Court.** Having had both the AAA and the NIRA and several smaller bills declared unconstitutional, Roosevelt worried about the fate of the NLRA and the Social Security Act.

- Early in his second term, Roosevelt asked Congress, in the interest of making the federal judiciary more efficient, to allow him to add judges for those members who chose not to retire at age seventy. He wanted to add no more than forty-four judges to the Circuit Court and six justices to the Supreme Court. The scheme was a blunder on the part of an unusually adept politician. Roosevelt had not paved the way for his proposal by making it a campaign issue in 1936 or even mentioning it to his own party. Roosevelt had played into the hands of the Republicans who criticized him for seeking too much power. Congress voted down Roosevelt's proposal. The issue evaporated when the Court began handing down rulings that upheld New Deal legislation, and aging justices began to retire.

Native Americans and the New Deal

- The **Wheeler-Howard Indian Reorganization Act** (1) ended the practice of dividing reservations into individual landholdings; (2) restored to the nations those lands not already given to individuals; (3) guaranteed a measure of self-government for each Native American nation, although real power remained with the secretary of the interior; (4) allowed the practice of traditional customs, beliefs, and crafts; (5) guaranteed the rights of Native Americans to enter into contracts and to sue and be sued in court; (6) established a fund to give loans to Indian corporations for economic development; and (7) provided information on soil conservation and improved methods for raising and selling crops and livestock. Little came of the last or of any of the provisions of the act. Native Americans still lived in poverty.

African Americans and the New Deal

- While Roosevelt's record on African Americans is mixed, his was the first administration since Reconstruction to show concern for them. African Americans participated in FERA, WPA, CCC, and the NYA. However, while federal policy forbade discrimination in New Deal programs, local officials ignored it and placed African Americans in segregated groups and did not allow them to do certain jobs.

- **Mary McCleod Bethune** was the Director of Negro Affairs for the NYA and a member of Roosevelt's informal advisory body, known as the **Black Cabinet**.

- The TVA hurt rather than helped black tenant farmers.

- Roosevelt did not work for passage of antilynching laws or the end of the poll tax.

A New National Labor Organization

Review Strategy

See Chapter 3 *for more on early labor organizations.*

- The **AFL** had been organized in the late 1800s for **craft workers** and had never attempted to organize the vastly larger group of **industrial workers.** Some members of the AFL believed that the labor reforms of the New Deal provided an opportunity for organizing industrial workers. When the leadership of the AFL disagreed, **John L. Lewis** and others founded the **Committee of Industrial Organizations** (later **Congress, CIO**) and began organizing industrial workers, including African Americans. The newly founded CIO was successful in winning contracts from U.S. Steel, General Motors, and the Chrysler Corporation. The CIO used **sit-down strikes** against the two auto makers.

KEY PEOPLE/TERMS

Review Strategy

See if you can relate these people and terms to their correct context in the "Fast Facts" section.

- **Mexicans, repatriation, Hoover administration**
- **Mexican Americans,** *mutualistas,* **migrant labor, urban jobs and relief programs**
- **Eleanor Roosevelt**
- **sharecroppers, Arkies, Okies, unintended victims of AAA**
- **"soak-the-rich" tax, Share the Wealth Clubs**

SECTION 3. DIPLOMACY IN THE 1920S AND 1930S

The diplomacy of the 1930s under Franklin Roosevelt was a dance to ensure that Great Britain and the other nations of Europe who were being menaced by **Adolf Hitler** and **Nazi Germany** were supported, while not antagonizing **isolationists** in Congress and among the voters.

FAST FACTS

Attempts at Disarmament and Peace

- There had been several attempts at **disarmament** prior to Roosevelt's first administration. In the **Five-Power Treaty,** signed at the **Washington Conference** in 1921 by the United States, Great Britain, France, Italy, and Japan, the nations agreed to limit their navies to 1921 levels and not to build any large warships for ten years. After that, they would only replace ships that were twenty years old. Although this and other agreements signed at the Washington Conference appeared to create an atmosphere of mutual cooperation and a desire for peace, no limitations were set for the size of land forces or for building smaller warships and submarines.

- When Japan overran **Manchuria** and set up **Manchukuo,** Secretary of State **Henry L. Stimson** urged President Hoover to issue economic sanctions against Japan. Hoover did not believe that the Japanese were any threat to the United States and refused. He agreed to allow Stimson to issue the **Stimson Doctrine,** which stated that the United States would not recognize any territorial changes or treaties brought about in violation of American rights or by force. The occupation of Manchuria violated the **Nine-Power Treaty,** and, therefore, the United States would not recognize Japan's right to the territory. Other nations did not support the Doctrine, and it did not prevent the Japanese from further military actions.

- The **London Naval Conference** of 1931 extended the ban on shipbuilding that was imposed in the Five-Power Treaty until 1936 and included smaller ships in the ban. The **World Disarmament Conference** in 1932 accomplished nothing. With the rise of Nazism and the aggression of Japan, it was apparent that disarmament's time had passed.

The Good Neighbor Policy

Test-Taking Strategy

Be sure you know the Monroe Doctrine, the Roosevelt Corollary, and "dollar diplomacy" as well as the Good Neighbor Policy. What is the significance of each? How does each show a shift in U.S. foreign policy?

- Roosevelt's articulation of the **Good Neighbor Policy** in 1933 was an effort to enlist the nations of the Western Hemisphere on the side of the United States should war come. The policy was meant to erase the longstanding history of intervention by the United States in the affairs of Latin American nations. The change had begun under Warren Harding and was solidified in the **Clark Memorandum** of Calvin Coolidge's administration. At the **Montevideo Conference,** the United States stated unequivocally that no nation had the right to intervene in the affairs of another state in the Western Hemisphere.

- In 1936, Roosevelt attended the **Inter-American Conference** in **Buenos Aires** to rally support for the part of the **Monroe Doctrine** that pledged nations to resist attacks from abroad. The Roosevelt Corollary was, in effect, repudiated.

Neutrality Legislation

- Influenced by the **Nye Report** which laid the entrance of the United States into World War I on manipulation by international bankers and arms makers, Congress passed a series of **Neutrality Acts** beginning in 1935. Among other things, the Acts (1) forbade the United States to sell or ship arms to nations declared in a state of war and (2) banned loans to belligerents. The president (3) could also declare an embargo on arms and ammunition, require belligerents (4) to pay cash for these goods, and (5) transport them on their own ships.

- Critics of these laws pointed out that the laws did not distinguish between friendly nations and enemy nations. Advocates of the laws believed that the affairs of Europe and the Pacific did not constitute a danger to the security of the United States, as long as the nation remained neutral. They also believed that if the **profit motive** for entering into a war was removed, there would be less manipulation of the public interest.

Appeasement and Aggression

- In an effort to avert war in Europe, the leaders of France and Great Britain followed a policy of **appeasement** toward Hitler and **Mussolini**. The climax of French and British concessions was the agreement signed at the **Munich Conference** to allow Hitler to take the part of Czechoslovakia that had a large German population. In exchange, Hitler agreed that he would not interfere with Czechoslovakian sovereignty again. Within six months, he had seized the rest of the nation.
- Talk of neutrality, isolationism, and appeasement was taking place against a backdrop of aggression by what would soon become the **Axis Powers**—Germany, Italy, and Japan.

AXIS AGGRESSION		
GERMANY	**ITALY**	**JAPAN**
• **Prewar aggression:** Austria, Czechoslovakia, Rhineland • **Wartime invasions:** Poland, Denmark, Norway, Luxembourg, Belgium, the Netherlands, France	• **Prewar aggression:** Albania, Ethiopia • **Wartime invasions:** France	• **Prewar aggression:** Manchuria, northern China, most of China's coastal areas • **Wartime invasions:** Indo-China, Guam, Wake Island, Thailand, Singapore, Malaysia, Philippine Islands

U.S. Efforts to Aid Great Britain

Test-Taking Strategy

What were the two reasons that Lend-Lease was significant?

- Although Roosevelt declared the neutrality of the United States when Britain and France declared war on Germany and Italy, he wanted to help the Western European nations. He found two ways, the **destroyer deal** and **Lend-Lease.** In exchange for fifty old World War I destroyers, the United States received the right to build a string of air and naval bases in British territory in the Western Hemisphere. In the latter deal, the United States would lend Great Britain war matériel rather than the money to buy it. While there was little opposition to the destroyer deal, isolationists considered Lend-Lease a way to pull the United States into war, but they lost their fight against the bill. The program provided some

$50 billion worth of supplies to Great Britain and helped to mobilize U.S. industry for war production.

- The **Atlantic Charter,** signed by Roosevelt and **Winston Churchill,** provided a statement of Anglo-American war aims: (1) no extension of territory by either nation, (2) territorial self-determination, (3) the destruction of Nazism, and (4) the establishment of an international organization to promote world peace. The two also promised the **Four Freedoms:** freedom from war, from fear, and from want and freedom of the seas.

Japanese Attack on Pearl Harbor

- The attack on **Pearl Harbor** came after months of trying to find a diplomatic solution to differences between the two nations. Japan would not provide assurances that it would end its aggression in Asia. In that event, the United States would not promise that it would not go to war against Japan.

- When the Japanese overran Indo-China, Roosevelt stopped almost all trade with Japan, including the sale of petroleum, upon which a resource-poor Japan depended. The Japanese had expected some small retaliatory action from the United States. They did not expect anything so forceful, provocative, or damaging as ending oil shipments.

- Japanese military leaders began to prepare for war against the United States. Diplomatic talks continued as a cover for these preparations. The U.S. Army had cracked the Japanese code, so the government knew that a Japanese attack would come somewhere in the Pacific once diplomatic talks broke down. But it did not know where or when, until Japanese bombers roared in over Pearl Harbor on December 7, 1941.

KEY TERMS/IDEAS

Review Strategy

See if you can relate these terms and ideas to their correct context in the "Fast Facts" section.

- **Allies**
- **blitzkrieg**
- **Kellogg-Briand Pact,** renounced "war as an instrument of national policy"
- **Neutrality Act of 1939,** "unrestricted submarine warfare"
- **phony war**
- **Quarantine Speech,** major break with isolationists
- **Russo-German Pact,** nonaggression pact
- **Washington Conference, 1921,** additional agreements: Four-Power Treaty, Nine-Power Treaty

SECTION 4. WORLD WAR II

Once war was declared, the United States had to **mobilize.** The army had some 1.6 million men in uniform, and the government instituted a **draft,** eventually registering all men between the ages of eighteen and forty-five. Women were allowed to volunteer in special women's branches of the armed forces. African Americans, Hispanics, Native Americans, and Japanese Americans enlisted or were drafted. African Americans in the navy often found themselves assigned to jobs as cooks and stewards. In the army, African Americans served in segregated units. Some six million women took jobs in industry to fill the positions that these men gave up to enter the armed forces. **"Rosie the Riveter"** became the symbol of these women.

FAST FACTS

On the Home Front

- Shortly after the declaration of war, about 100,000 Japanese Americans, some two thirds of whom had been born in the United States, were evacuated from their homes in California and **interned** in camps in Wyoming, Arizona, and Colorado. Some Americans, including members of the War Department, feared that these Japanese Americans would aid Japan in an invasion of the mainland, so they wanted the Japanese Americans removed from strategic areas. Later, it came to light that some of the Californians who pressed for internment had economic motives for wanting the Japanese Americans removed.

- *Korematsu* **v.** *United States* (1944) is one of several cases that dealt with the internment of American-born citizens of Japanese descent. In May 1942, all Japanese people in California were ordered to report to evacuation centers for relocation to internment camps. Fred Korematsu, intending to move to the Midwest voluntarily, did not report. However, when the authorities found him in California at the end of the month, they arrested him. He was convicted for ignoring the evacuation order. On appeal, the Supreme Court upheld the conviction. They found that the evacuation was a lawful exercise of the war powers granted to the president and Congress under the Constitution.

- Managing the nation's economic resources came under the authority of the **War Production Board.** It was responsible for mobilizing industry to retool assembly lines to produce war matériel rather than consumer goods. The war was paid for through tax increases and the sale of **war bonds.** As a result, the national debt rose sixfold from 1940 to 1949.

On the Battle Front

- The war was fought on two fronts, **Europe/North Africa** and the **Pacific.** There was concern that Great Britain might fall if the Germans defeated the Soviet Union and took the Suez Canal. The Allies, therefore, adopted a strategy to defeat Germany and its ally Italy before turning to the Japanese in the Pacific. Short-term goals to accomplish this strategy were (1) control of the sea lanes to keep war matériel moving to Europe, (2) effective use of the Allies' superior air power, and (3) supplying Soviet forces to fight the Nazi assault on the Eastern front.

- Between summer 1942 and May 1943, the Allies had forced the Afrika Korps to surrender, thus ending the war in North Africa. By winter 1941–1942, the Soviets had stopped the German advance into Russia and were on the counterattack. In July 1943, the Allies invaded Italy. On June 6, 1944, the Allies began **Operation Overlord,** their major offensive in Europe. The timing of this invasion had been an area of contention with Stalin since the beginning of the war. Within eleven months, Paris was liberated, U.S. troops fought their way into Germany, Soviet troops continued their advance westward, Hitler committed suicide, and the war in Europe ended on May 7, 1945.

- The Allies developed a two-pronged strategy to defeat the Japanese in the Pacific. **General Douglas MacArthur** would **"leap-frog" islands,** fighting for control of important islands and going around others on a course from New Guinea to the Philippines. **Admiral Chester Nimitz** would drive through the Central Pacific toward Japan. By 1945, U.S. bombing raids were battering the Japanese home islands.

- Allied military experts believed that it could be another year before Japan was conquered, and the fighting could take the lives of another one million U.S. troops. Japan, at this point, was divided between a civilian government, supported by Emperor **Hirohito,** that was willing to make peace, and the military that wanted to continue fighting. Through the Soviets, the civilian government offered to end the war but would not accept **unconditional surrender.**

- When nothing came of the feelers, President Truman ordered the use of the **atomic bomb.** On August 6, 1945, a U.S. plane dropped an atomic bomb on **Hiroshima.** Three days later, in the face of the Japanese government's continuing refusal to surrender, the United States dropped an atomic bomb on **Nagasaki.** The USSR entered the war as promised. Japan surrendered.

Wartime Diplomacy

- While Roosevelt and, to a lesser extent, Churchill believed that the time had come to adopt Wilson's idea for an international organization to ensure the sovereignty of all nations, Stalin had other ideas. However, in order to gain time and war matériel for the Eastern front, Stalin went along with the planning for a **United Nations.** (1) This future organization, (2) the more immediate concerns of European governance after the war, and (3) the conduct of the war itself were the topics of a series of conferences during World War II. The divisions of the **Cold War** could already be seen in the decisions the **Big Three** made.

- When the "secret agreements" were made known after Roosevelt's death, many critics faulted Roosevelt and Churchill for abandoning Poland, East Germany, the rest of Eastern Europe, and **Nationalist China** to communism. In truth, Soviet forces already occupied **Eastern Europe.** Short of another war, there was little that the Western powers could do to force Stalin to live up to his promises in Europe. In February 1945, the United States and Great Britain were still fighting the war in the Pacific, and British and U.S. troops had not yet entered Germany.

WORLD WAR II CONFERENCES	
CONFERENCE	**PURPOSES**
Moscow Conference of Foreign Ministers, October 1943 (Great Britain, USSR, United States)	• Agreed to an invasion of France in 1944 • Discussed the future of Poland but reached no agreement • Set up a committee to draft policy for postwar Germany • Agreed to set up an international peace-keeping organization
Teheran, November 1943 (Churchill, Stalin, Roosevelt)	• Agreed on timing of D-Day to coincide with Russian offensive • Renewed promise from Stalin that USSR would join war in Asia after the defeat of Germany • Agreed, in vague terms, to giving USSR some concessions in Asia for joining the war against Japan • Discussed structure of international peace-keeping organization
Bretton Woods, July 1944 (Forty-four nations represented)	Set up **International Monetary Fund**
Dumbarton Oaks, August–October 1944 (Representatives of China, Great Britain, USSR, United States)	Drafted plans for United Nations, including a **Security Council** as the seat of permanent peace-keeping responsibilities

WORLD WAR II CONFERENCES

CONFERENCE	PURPOSES
Yalta, February 1945 (Churchill, Stalin, Roosevelt)	• Agreed to divide Germany into **four military zones of occupation** (France would administer the fourth zone) • Agreed to **free elections** in Poland "as soon as possible" but also agreed to accept the Soviet-dominated **Lublin Committee** as the interim government • Agreed to "broadly representative" interim governments throughout Europe (Communist-backed governments in the areas the Soviets controlled) • Worked out voting procedures in the proposed United Nations for the sixteen Soviet territories • Agreed to call a conference in San Francisco on April 25, 1945, to write a charter for the new international organization
	"Secret Agreements" In exchange for entering the war against Japan and signing a treaty of friendship and alliance with China, Stalin asked for and received • Recognition of the independence of the Mongolian People's Republic under Soviet protection • Possession of the Kurile Islands, part of Sakhalin Island, an occupation zone in Korea, and rights in Manchuria
Potsdam, July–August 1945 (Churchill replaced by the new Prime Minister, Clement Atlee; Stalin; Truman)	• Agreed to policies for the occupation and administration of Germany, including disarmament, "denazification," democratization, and payment of reparations • Issued **Potsdam Declaration,** demanding Japan's unconditional surrender

• As World War II ended, the United States found itself in a new role as a world power. Between World Wars I and II, the United States had adopted a policy of **isolationism.** That was no longer possible in the new postwar world. As soon as the common enemies were vanquished, the cracks in the wartime alliances began to show. To maintain its own security, the United States had to decide how to (1) safeguard its security and national interests against powerful and unfriendly nations; (2) help protect the sovereignty of nations in Europe, Latin America, and Asia without provoking hostile reactions from them or from the **Communist bloc**; (3) establish ties to the newly independent nations of Asia and Africa; and (4) balance the cost of domestic programs with defense needs.

KEY PEOPLE

Review Strategy

See if you can relate these people to their correct context in the "Fast Facts" section.

- A. Philip Randolph, Brotherhood of Sleeping Car Porters; March on Washington, 1941; Executive Order 8802, Committee on Fair Employment Practices
- Navajo codetalkers
- Nisei
- Tuskegee Airmen

KEY TERMS/IDEAS

Review Strategy

See if you can relate these terms and ideas to their correct context in the "Fast Facts" section.

- Axis
- bracero program
- Holocaust, concentration camps, anti-Semitism
- price controls, rationing, shortages
- United Nations Charter, General Assembly, veto power
- United Nations Relief and Rehabilitation Administration (UNRRA), relief for Europe and Asia after World War II
- Universal Declaration of Human Rights
- Zoot suit riots, Mexicans, Mexican Americans

SECTION 5. TRUMAN AND THE BEGINNING OF THE COLD WAR

Review Strategy

See Section 2 of this chapter for the beginnings of this conservative coalition.

The major domestic issues that **Harry S Truman** faced after the war were **demobilization** and **reconversion.** Carrying out policies was made more difficult because Truman was faced with a Congress that was controlled by a conservative coalition of Northern Republicans and Southern Democrats.

FAST FACTS

Demobilization

- Some 12.5 million members of the armed forces needed to be returned to civilian life, and industries needed to be retooled to produce consumer goods. During the war, six million women had entered the labor force in defense industries. Many of these women still needed to work or wanted to continue working, but they often found themselves out of a job in favor of a returning veteran. However, the trend toward women working outside the home has continued since World War II.

Reconversion

- During the war, unions had made few wage demands on employers. Once the war was over and the pent-up demand for consumer goods could be satisfied by the items rolling off assembly lines, workers began to demand higher wages. When their demands were not met, a series of strikes in the steel and auto industries occurred in 1945–1946. When the **United Mine Workers** under **John L. Lewis** threatened a strike, Truman seized the mines. He then seized the railroads when railway workers threatened to strike. In the end, workers in both industries won most of their demands.

- Although Truman appeared tough on unions with these actions, he vetoed the **Taft-Hartley Act,** which (1) outlawed the **closed shop,** (2) provided **cooling-off periods** before a strike could be called, (3) gave the president the power to ask for an **injunction** to prevent a strike that could be dangerous to the health or safety of the nation, (4) forbade union practices considered unfair (**jurisdictional strikes,** refusal to bargain in good faith, union contributions to political campaigns), and (5) required unions to file annual financial reports. The Act also provided direct benefits to employers by allowing employers (1) to present their side during organizing drives, (2) to ask the **National Labor Relations Board (NLRB)** for elections to determine bargaining agents, and (3) to sue unions for breach of contract. The conservative coalition in Congress passed the bill over Truman's veto, but the Act did not damage unions as badly as had been feared. The Act did, however, cement unions' support for Truman.

African Americans and the Fair Deal

Test-Taking Strategy

Track civil rights activities to see the changes over time. Note the significance of each.

- A liberal Democrat, Truman had come to see the problems that the nation's racism created, not only at home, but in dealing with the newly emerging nations of Asia and Africa. He also understood the changing demographics of the nation. As African Americans moved from the South to the North and the West, they provided a large bloc of voters that was already sympathetic to the Democratic Party of Roosevelt. Truman set up a series of committees and used their reports to ask Congress (1) to establish a permanent civil rights commission; (2) to set up a permanent **Fair Employment Practices Commission;** (3) to end segregation in schools, transportation, and public accommodations; and (4) to make lynching a federal crime. The conservative coalition in Congress blocked Truman's proposals.

- In the election of 1948, party bosses in Northern and Western states were able to add a strong **civil rights plank** to the Democratic platform. They expected that Truman would lose, but they hoped that the civil rights plank would persuade African Americans to vote for lesser Democratic candidates. Truman campaigned hard on this plank, and African Americans responded by reelecting him and electing many other Democrats.

- Truman then began to fulfill his campaign promise. Although blocked in Congress, Truman used other avenues to promote civil rights, including directing federal agencies to end segregation and to award no federal contracts to businesses that discriminated in employment. He also issued **Executive Order 9981** to end segregation in the armed forces.

Truman's Foreign Policy

- In foreign affairs, Truman adopted the policy of **containment.** According to this idea, the Soviet Union and its **satellites,** if left alone, would change and possibly collapse from internal economic and political pressures. The **free world** only had to keep the Soviet Union from expanding.

- This policy of containment was the basis for the **Truman Doctrine.** When Great Britain announced that it could no longer provide economic and military aid to Greece and Turkey to fight Communist takeovers, Truman asked Congress for $400 million in aid. Mindful of the fine line between support and interference, he did not ask for military intervention, stating, "I believe that it must be the policy of the United States to support free people who are resisting attempted subjugation by armed minorities or by outside pressures." Without aid, Greece and Turkey would most probably have fallen to the Communists, and the Soviet Union could then have dominated the Eastern Mediterranean.

- Secretary of State **George Marshall** proposed a program that came to be known as the **Marshall Plan** to help European nations rebuild after the war. The Soviet Union and its satellites rejected the offer, but Western European nations agreed to draft a common recovery plan. The Plan was met with heated resistance in Congress. Opponents claimed it (1) would end any possibility of working with the Soviet Union, (2) would reestablish the United States as an imperialist power, (3) would bankrupt the nation, (4) could be a waste of money or could set up European nations as competitors for American markets, and (5) should be aimed at Asia, not Europe. **Senator Arthur Vandenberg,** a Republican, rose to the defense of the Plan and argued that it was in the nation's self-interest to ensure that Europe did not fall to communism. The Plan was approved.

- In an effort to sabotage the creation of a financially strong, independent, and democratic West Germany, the Soviets manufactured the **Berlin Crisis.** Access to the Western occupation zones of Berlin was through Soviet territory, and there was a written agreement from the Soviets that the way would remain open. However, in June 1948, the Soviets closed the land routes, intending either to force the French, British, and Americans to make concessions or to give the Soviets all of Berlin. Instead, the Western powers decided to institute a massive **airlift** of supplies into Berlin. The Soviets were correct in assuming that the Western Powers did not wish to go to war, but neither did they intend to give up Berlin or their efforts to support a rehabilitated West Germany. The Western Powers believed that the stability of Europe depended on their standing up to the Soviets at this first challenge. The blockade was lifted in 1949.

- In 1949, ten European nations, Canada, and the United States signed a **mutual defense pact** to form the **North Atlantic Treaty Organization (NATO).** Its purpose was to guard Europe, the North Atlantic, and the Mediterranean from Communist attack. Most of the personnel, money, and supplies to support the organization came from the United States. General Dwight Eisenhower was the first commander. The Soviet Union countered in 1955 by forming its own mutual defense organization, the **Warsaw Pact,** with its Communist satellites.

- Once World War II was over, civil war broke out in China between the **Nationalist Chinese,** led by **Chiang Kai-shek,** and the Communists, or **Kuomintang,** led by **Mao Zedong.** In 1949, the Nationalists fled to **Taiwan** and established what they contended was the government of China, while Mao proclaimed the **People's Republic of China (PRC)** on the mainland. The United States continued to support Chiang and in 1950 broke off diplomatic and trading ties with the PRC.

The Korean War

- After World War II, **Korea** was partitioned. In 1948, the United States oversaw free elections in South Korea and pulled out its troops once the new government was installed. Also in 1948, the Soviets installed their own Communist government in North Korea and pulled out. In 1950, North Koreans overran the **38th parallel,** the dividing line between the two nations, and invaded the South. The Soviet Union was boycotting the Security Council because of the United Nations' refusal to admit the PRC, so the Council was able to approve the sending of UN troops to support the South Koreans. Ninety percent of the troops and support personnel were from the United States. U.S. General Douglas MacArthur commanded the forces.

- The fighting moved back and forth, with the North Koreans winning ground and then the South Koreans driving them back. MacArthur was ordered to destroy the North Korean armed forces but not to move into China or the Soviet Union. The UN forces began to move north across the 38th parallel. Within a month, the Chinese had eight divisions in North Korea and began to move south. MacArthur never agreed with the concept of a **"limited war,"** and he publicly disagreed with the president.

- When Truman removed him from command, MacArthur returned to the United States to plead his case before Congress for total victory, even if that meant war with China. The Joint Chiefs of Staff warned Congress of the danger of war in Asia, and MacArthur's support collapsed. Negotiations to end the war began in mid-1951 and were at a standstill when Eisenhower became president in 1953. Stalin died shortly thereafter, and the North Koreans became more flexible in their demands. An armed truce went into effect, and the fighting ended without a peace treaty.

KEY TERMS/IDEAS

Review Strategy

See if you can relate these terms and ideas to their correct context in the "Fast Facts" section.

- **Arab-Israeli War, Palestinian refugee camps**
- **baby boom**
- **Point Four Program, technical assistance, capital investment, poor nations of the world**
- **Full Employment Act, Council of Economic Advisers**
- **G.I. Bill of Rights, Servicemen's Readjustment Act**
- **Iron Curtain, cold war**
- **"Solid South," Dixiecrats**

SECTION 6. THE EISENHOWER YEARS

A hero of World War II, **Dwight D. Eisenhower** was drafted in 1952 by the Republican Party to run for president. A conservative in domestic affairs, he had liberal views in world affairs. Although a believer in the free enterprise system and an opponent of enlarging the role of the federal government, Eisenhower made no attempt to undo any of the New Deal legislation.

FAST FACTS

McCarthyism

- When Eisenhower took office, **Senator Joseph McCarthy** was still hard at work investigating subversives and **fellow travelers** in the government. McCarthy, a Republican from Wisconsin, had achieved notoriety when he claimed he could identify the country's top spy. When a Senate investigation into his allegations proved them to be groundless, he went after Senator Millard Tydings, a conservative Democrat and the committee chair of the investigation, in his reelection bid. With outside money, McCarthy was able to engineer Tydings' defeat as well as that of another senator who had bucked him. Suddenly, McCarthy had supporters across the Republican Party. Eisenhower was incensed at McCarthy's accusations that former General George Marshall was **"soft on communism,"** but he counseled patience. Eisenhower believed that McCarthy would eventually "hang himself." The **Army-McCarthy hearings** proved McCarthy's undoing. The Senate **censured** him, and **McCarthyism** gradually subsided.

Civil Rights

Review Strategy

See pp. 215–218 for civil rights activities during Lyndon Johnson's term in office.

- During the 1952 campaign, Eisenhower supported the civil rights ideas of liberal Republicans. Once in office, he began to make changes such as desegregating schools on military bases. In 1956, he sent a civil rights bill to Congress, and although it passed the House, conservative Southern Democrats rejected it in the Senate. Eisenhower tried again in 1957, and this time, advocates managed to win approval with the support of **Lyndon Johnson,** the majority leader and Democratic senator from Texas. **The Civil Rights Act of 1957,** the first federal civil rights legislation since 1875, (1) established a permanent Civil Rights Commission, (2) appointed an assistant attorney general for civil rights in the Justice Department, and (3) authorized the federal government to issue injunctions in cases where citizens had been denied the right to vote. Little came of the law.

- The **Civil Rights Act of 1960** was meant to expand voting rights protection for African Americans by setting up a procedure for adding African Americans to voting rolls, but little came of this law either.

- One notable Supreme Court ruling was the decision in ***Brown* v. *Board of Education of Topeka, Kansas***. The Supreme Court overturned the **"separate but equal"** decision in ***Plessy* v. *Ferguson***.

***Brown* v. *Board of Education of Topeka, Kansas* (1954; equal protection under the law)**

Case: African Americans had won several Supreme Court cases that involved segregation in colleges and universities but needed a case involving public elementary and secondary schools. In 1954, Thurgood Marshall and the National Association for the Advancement of Colored People (NAACP) found their case in *Brown* v. *Board of Education of Topeka, Kansas,* filed in behalf of Linda Brown by her father. According to the law, Linda could not attend her neighborhood school, which was all-white, but had to go across town to an all-black school. Marshall based his argument on expert testimony that demonstrated that segregated schools damaged the self-esteem of African American children. As such, segregated schools violated the equal protection clause of the Fourteenth Amendment.

Decision: The Warren Court agreed with Marshall's argument.

Significance: The Court ordered schools to desegregate "with all deliberate speed." It would take court orders, more laws, and the civil rights movement to desegregate public education in the South and the North. This ruling reversed *Plessy* v. *Ferguson*.

Eisenhower's Foreign Policy

- Eisenhower chose **John Foster Dulles** as his Secretary of State. Dulles took a hard line against communism, and his policy became known as **brinksmanship.** His rhetoric called for **massive retaliation** against the Soviets. While Dulles may not have believed in containment and limited war, his conduct of foreign affairs was not much different from that of the Truman administration, except that under the Eisenhower administration, the arsenal of nuclear weapons increased.

Review Strategy

See pp. 220–221 for Vietnam.

- In the 1950s, the United States found itself filling the vacuum in the Middle East that was created by Great Britain's departure. After the **Suez crisis,** Eisenhower issued what became known as the **Eisenhower Doctrine:** (1) It promised economic and military aid to countries of the Middle East. (2) It also promised that it would consider intervening with military force if the sovereignty of any nation were endangered by Communist forces.

Review Strategy

See pp. 219–220 for information on the Bay of Pigs invasion.

- When **Fidel Castro** came to power in **Cuba** in 1959, the U.S. government guardedly hoped that he would launch democratic reforms and revive the Cuban economy. Instead, he (1) held a series of circus-like trials of former associates of **Fulgencio Batista,** (2) nationalized foreign-owned industries and properties without compensating the owners, (3) mounted an anti-American campaign, (4) signed a series of aid agreements with the Soviet Union, and (5) supported revolutionary activities in several Latin American nations. The United States finally cut all diplomatic and trade relations with Cuba.

- Another **Berlin crisis** occurred between November 1958 and May 1959 when **Nikita Khrushchev** offered the Western Powers two alternatives for the future of Berlin. Eisenhower responded that the United States would not agree to any change in the status of Berlin that was dictated by the Soviets. The United States would stand by its obligations under the **NATO treaty.** It appeared as though the two nations were prepared to go to war. However, the deadline passed without any comment from Khrushchev, and the crisis was over.

Society at Mid-Century

- A major social phenomenon of mid-century America was the growth of the **suburbs.** This was made possible by the expansion of the **highway system** under Eisenhower and the proliferation of **tract housing** such as **Levittown, New York,** the first planned suburban development after World War II.

- The nation was enjoying great prosperity as a result of (1) its natural resources, (2) its educated workforce, (3) its efficiently managed industries, (4) its expanded transportation system, (5) the application of advances in science and technology to industry, and (6) the productivity of its agricultural sector. With a high level of productivity came lower unemployment and higher wages, which led to the development of a **consumer culture.**

KEY PEOPLE

Review Strategy

See if you can relate these people to their correct context in the "Fast Facts" section.

- Beat Generation
- Alger Hiss, Julius and Ethel Rosenberg, witch hunts, Communist Control Act

KEY TERMS/IDEAS

Review Strategy

See if you can relate these terms and ideas to their correct context in the "Fast Facts" section.

- arms race, long-range ballistic missiles, nuclear warheads
- Nixon's "goodwill tour" of Latin America
- Organization of American States
- Southeast Asia Treaty Organization (SEATO)
- space race, *Sputnik;* National Aeronautics and Space Administration (NASA), *Explorer,* Mercury Project, astronauts
- U-2 spy plane incident

Chapter 8

REVIEWING THE KENNEDY TO THE BUSH ADMINISTRATIONS

This chapter summarizes the 1960s through the beginning of the twenty-first century. This was a period of intense activity in civil rights—not only among African Americans but also among Hispanics, women, Asians, gays, and lesbians. Other ethnic groups also began to rebel against the "melting pot" theory of the American experience. In world affairs, that symbol of post-World War II aggression, the Berlin Wall, fell, and the Soviet Union collapsed. Buoyed by a roaring economy, the United States entered the twenty-first century as the undisputed leader of the world.

The College Board states that 40 percent of the questions on the test will be taken from the period from 1899 to the present. However, because test questions go through several years of revision, you probably won't find much about the last ten years on the test. Study the high points, and know the trends.

SECTION 2. THE KENNEDY/JOHNSON YEARS

John F. Kennedy became the first Roman Catholic and the youngest man ever elected president. In a very tight race, he defeated **Richard Nixon,** the incumbent vice president. Kennedy's administration became known as the **New Frontier.** He sought to continue the kinds of domestic programs and reforms that Roosevelt had created in the **New Deal.** Conservative Southern Democrats and conservative Northern Republicans blocked or watered down many of Kennedy's proposals. Some, like **Medicare,** were approved after his **assassination** through the efforts of the new president, **Lyndon Johnson.**

FAST FACTS

Domestic Policy

- When Kennedy assumed office, the nation was mired in a recession. Kennedy requested passage of the **Area Redevelopment Act** to provide (1) grants and loans to communities with chronic economic problems and (2) funding to retrain the unemployed. With this and similar measures, the economy revived but began a downturn again in 1962. Kennedy then sought tax cuts and tax credits in an effort to stimulate the economy. His requests bogged down in Congress. After Kennedy's assassination, Johnson, using the powers of persuasion and negotiating skills he had developed as **Senate majority leader,** was able to win passage of a **tax cut** bill that promised $11 billion in personal and corporate tax relief to boost spending.

Test-Taking Strategy

Truman had advocated a similar Medicare program, but conservatives in Congress had rejected it. Track how conservative interests have affected American policy in the twentieth century.

- Johnson's own domestic program was called the **Great Society.** Major legislation included (1) the **Economic Opportunity Act** that launched the **"war on poverty,"** (2) **Medicare,** (3) **Medicaid,** and (4) the **Elementary and Secondary Education Act of 1965.**

- In time, the escalating **Vietnam War** drained Johnson's energy and strained the national budget. The trade-off symbolized by the phrase **"guns or butter"** became a reality. To push a tax cut through Congress to ease the growing **federal deficit,** Johnson slashed the funding for social programs and effectively, the "war on poverty."

Civil Rights

- One of the most far-reaching of Johnson's acts was his issuance of an Executive Order in 1964 that all contractors working on federal projects "take **affirmative action**" to ensure that they did not discriminate in hiring or promoting members of minority groups. This Order was meant to enforce the provisions of the **Civil Rights Act of 1964** for federal projects. The concept became institutionalized when President Nixon set specific goals, or quotas, for federally financed construction projects.

- During these years, a number of significant pieces of legislation were passed and Supreme Court decisions handed down that expanded civil rights.

CIVIL RIGHTS LEGISLATION	
LEGISLATION/RULING	**SIGNIFICANCE**
Civil Rights Act, 1964	• Prohibits discrimination in public accommodations • Authorizes the U.S. attorney general to intervene on behalf of victims of discrimination • Forbids employers and unions to discriminate against minorities • Enables the federal government to withhold funding from projects in which discrimination exists • Forbids the use of different standards for whites and African Americans applying to register to vote
Twenty-Fourth Amendment	Outlaws the use of a poll tax or any tax to keep African Americans from voting in federal elections

CIVIL RIGHTS LEGISLATION

LEGISLATION/RULING	SIGNIFICANCE
Voting Rights Act, 1965	Allows the federal government to register voters in localities where literacy tests and similar restrictions were in effect as of November 1, 1964, and where less than half the eligible voters had registered and voted in the 1964 federal election (most of the South)
Heart of Atlanta **v.** *United States*	Upholds the use of the commerce clause as the basis for civil rights legislation
Wesbery **v.** *Sanders*	Ends pattern of overrepresentation of rural districts and underrepresentation of cities in legislatures; **"one man, one vote"**

Heart of Atlanta Motel **v.** *United States* **(1964; interstate commerce)**

Case: In 1964, Congress, using its power to regulate interstate commerce under Article I, Section 8, passed the Civil Rights Act banning discrimination in public accommodations and in employment. A motel owner challenged the law on the basis that his business was local—even though it was convenient to exits for an interstate—and, therefore, should not be regulated under interstate commerce.

Decision: The Warren Court ruled against the owner. It based its decision on the theory that public accommodations, places that sell lodging (hotels, rooming houses, etc.), food (restaurants, lunch counters, etc.), and entertainment (movie theaters, auditoriums, etc.) serve transients and/or have moved a large portion of their goods by interstate commerce. In its opinion, the Court found "overwhelming evidence of the disruptive effect [of] racial discrimination" on commerce.

Significance: The Court's ruling upheld Congress's use of the commerce clause as the basis for civil rights legislation.

Wesbery v. *Sanders* (1964; one man, one vote)

Case: As a result of the 1960 Census, Georgia's ten Congressional districts were reapportioned. The Fifth District had more than 800,000 people, while the other nine districts had just under 400,000 on average. Several members of the Fifth Congressional District joined in a suit against Sanders, their representative, claiming that the size of the district deprived them of equal representation.

Decision: The Court, citing Article I, Section 2, ruled that the difference in size of the population of the ten Congressional districts violated the Constitution.

Significance: This case was one in a series of cases dealing with apportionment of state and Congressional seats that the Court agreed to hear. The decisions in these cases, known collectively as "one man, one vote," ended the pattern of rural overrepresentation and urban underrepresentation in legislatures.

- The most prominent civil rights activist of the late 1950s and 1960s was the **Reverend Martin Luther King Jr.** Head of the **Southern Christian Leadership Conference (SCLC),** he preached **nonviolence** and led a series of demonstrations and marches to protest racial discrimination—until his assassination in 1968. Similar in approach was the **Congress of Racial Equality (CORE)** which was founded by **James Farmer.**
- The **Student Nonviolent Coordinating Committee (SNCC)** began with similar objectives and tactics but changed under the leadership of **Stokely Carmichael,** who championed **Black Power.** This caused a split between SNCC and more mainline organizations like the SCLC and the **NAACP.** Carmichael defined Black Power as a call to African Americans "to unite, to recognize their heritage, to build a sense of community."
- The following were major civil rights' activities of the 1950s and 1960s:

CIVIL RIGHTS MOVEMENT

ACTIVITY	SIGNIFICANCE
Montgomery bus boycott, 1955	• Protested segregation in public buses; lasted more than a year; Supreme Court found bus segregation unconstitutional • Launched Martin Luther King Jr., as most prominent member of the **Civil Rights Movement**
Desegregation of **Little Rock High School, Arkansas**, 1957	• Governor Orval Faubus blocked enforcement of ***Brown*** v. ***Board of Education*** by calling out the Arkansas National Guard to stop students. • Eisenhower took over National Guard and ordered admission of black students.

CIVIL RIGHTS MOVEMENT

ACTIVITY	SIGNIFICANCE
Greensboro, North Carolina, Sit-in, 1960	• A group of integrated college students take over a lunch counter at Woolworth's and request service, which is denied. • Sit-ins spread across the South to protest segregation in public accommodations.
Freedom rides, 1961	• Groups of students rode interstate carriers to protest segregation on interstate buses and in bus terminals. • President Kennedy ordered federal marshals to accompany riders into the **Deep South.** • Federal government issued tougher regulations against segregation on interstate transit.
March on Washington, 1963	Some 250,000 Americans—black and white—marched in Washington to protest segregation. Pressed Congress to pass the civil rights bill that President Kennedy sent to Congress.
Freedom Summer, 1964	• Four civil rights organizations joined to lead a **voter registration drive** in the South. • Three volunteers were murdered, and seven **Ku Klux Klan** members were tried and convicted.

- The 1960s also saw the emergence of a civil rights movement among Mexican Americans or **chicanos/chicanas.** Led by **César Chávez** and **Dolores Huerta,** Mexican farm workers formed the **National Farm Workers Association (NFWA)** and organized a nationwide boycott of table grapes.
- The **women's movement** emerged in the mid-1960s, seeking equal pay for equal opportunity. A major force was the publication of *The Feminine Mystique* by **Betty Friedan.** The **National Organization for Women (NOW),** founded in 1966, worked for passage of the **Equal Rights Amendment (ERA),** but the amendment was never ratified by the required number of states. Some opponents feared that it would cause women to lose some of the protection they already had under existing laws. Conservatives equated the law with everything from federal funding for abortion to unisex toilets.
- The Supreme Court also handed down a number of rulings that expanded civil liberties.

Gideon v. *Wainwright* (1963; right to be represented by counsel)

Case: Clarence Earl Gideon was charged with robbing a Florida pool hall—a felony. Penniless, Gideon asked for a court-appointed lawyer and was denied. Convicted and sentenced to five years in jail, Gideon crafted his own appeal and sent it to the Supreme Court.

Decision: The Court overturned the conviction, stating that the **due process clause of the Fourteenth Amendment** protects individuals against state encroachments on their rights. Represented by counsel, Gideon was retried and acquitted.

Significance: Florida, as well as other states, had to release prisoners who had not been represented by an attorney. As a result of *Gideon,* everyone accused of a crime must be represented by an attorney. If a person is too poor, then the state must provide one. This is one of several cases dealing with the rights of the accused that the Warren Court agreed to hear. Many of the decisions have been controversial among conservatives, because they think the Warren Court was soft on criminals.

Miranda v. *Arizona* (1966; Miranda Rule)

Case: Ernesto Miranda was arrested on charges of kidnapping and rape and was identified by the victim. He was not informed of his right to have an attorney present during questioning. After 2 hours of interrogation, Miranda confessed and voluntarily signed a confession, which was later used in court. Miranda was convicted and appealed. His lawyer argued that Miranda's right under the Fifth Amendment to avoid self-incrimination was violated when he was not informed of his right to have a lawyer present.

Decision: The Warren Court reversed the conviction in a 5–4 decision. It ruled that a suspect must be "read his rights:" the right to remain silent, that anything that the suspect says may be used against him/her in a court of law, the right to have an attorney present during questioning, the right to have a court-appointed attorney if the person cannot afford one, and the right to end questioning at any time.

Significance: The Warren Court stated that the Court would not uphold any convictions on appeal if the suspects had not been informed of their constitutional rights before questioning. Conservatives criticized the ruling for tying the hands of the police, although many law enforcement officials said that by setting rules, it made everyone aware of what was expected and how the police needed to do their jobs.

Cuba

- Shortly after taking office, Kennedy was confronted with the dilemma regarding continued support for an invasion of Cuba by 1,500 **anti-Castro Cubans.** The **Central Intelligence Agency (CIA),** with Eisenhower's approval, had begun the project. Kennedy decided to provide weapons and ships to transport the exiles but to provide no military support. The CIA and the **Cuban exiles** expected Cubans to take up arms and oust Castro, but the insurrection never materialized. All the exiles were killed or captured. The United States took a great deal of criticism from around the world, especially from Latin American nations, for what became known as the **Bay of Pigs** invasion.

- Kennedy dealt more successfully with the **Cuban Missile Crisis.** The **Soviet Union,** an ally of Castro, had secretly constructed missile sites in Cuba, some 90 miles from the U.S. mainland. Kennedy ordered the U.S. Navy to throw up a **blockade** around the island and turn back Soviet ships steaming toward Cuba with nuclear missiles to arm the sites. After a week, **Nikita Khrushchev,** the Soviet premier, ordered the ships to return to the USSR without delivering the missiles.

The Escalating Vietnam Conflict

Review Strategy

See p. 222, for the end of the Vietnam War.

- After World War II, France reluctantly gave up its claim to **Vietnam,** and the nation was divided into North and South Vietnam, with Communists in power in the North. **Ngo Dinh Diem** refused to hold free elections in the South in 1956 for fear that the Communists would win. When his regime did not topple but seemed instead to be gaining strength, the Communist **Viet Cong** began a guerrilla campaign to take the South.

- Eisenhower and then Kennedy, believing in the **domino theory,** sent military advisers to help the government of South Vietnam. Under Kennedy, the United States engineered the ouster of the Diem family and the installation of a civilian as the head of the government. Power would change several more times before the war was over. While the well-organized and highly disciplined Viet Cong were finding support in the countryside, the government in Saigon seemed unable to achieve stability.

- Johnson manufactured the crisis that allowed him to ask Congress to approve the **Gulf of Tonkin Resolution.** (The **War Powers Resolution** that was passed in 1973 was in direct response to the use of presidential powers in the Vietnam War.) Also believing in the domino theory, Johnson ordered an **escalation** of the war by bombing North Vietnam and sending more U.S. ground troops. Underestimating the resolve of **Ho Chi Minh** and the Communists, Johnson expected this show of force and determination on the part of the United States to force the Viet Cong to sue for peace within the year. However, the Communists had their own theory that they could outwait the Americans, who would tire of the war and the antiwar demonstrations at home.

- In January 1968, to coincide with the Vietnamese New Year (Tet), the North Vietnamese and Viet Cong staged the **Tet offensive.** This was a group of attacks on cities and U.S. bases in South Vietnam and even the U.S. embassy in Saigon.

- The number of U.S. troops in Vietnam continued to grow and, with it, **antiwar protests** in the United States. These mirrored the dissension and confusion in Congress with **hawks** against **doves.** Ultimately, the escalating war in Vietnam cost Johnson both his Great Society programs and his presidency. Faced with challenges by antiwar Senators **Eugene McCarthy** and **Robert F. Kennedy,** Johnson (1) ended bombing raids over most of North Vietnam, (2) refused to send any more troops, and (3) withdrew from the 1968 presidential election.

KEY PEOPLE

Review Strategy

See if you can relate these people to their correct context in the "Fast Facts" section.

- **Black Panthers**
- **Rachel Carson,** *Silent Spring*
- **Malcolm X, Black Nationalism, Nation of Islam**
- **Michael Harrington,** *The Other America*
- **Ralph Nader,** *Unsafe at Any Speed*
- **Rosa Parks, Montgomery, NAACP**
- **"silent majority"**

KEY TERMS/IDEAS

Review Strategy

See if you can relate these terms and ideas to their correct context in the "Fast Facts" section.

- **Alliance for Progress, stop the spread of communism, Latin America**
- **American Indian Movement (AIM)**
- **Berlin Crisis, Berlin Wall**
- **Brown Power**
- **Communications Satellite Act, Telstar communications satellite system, private corporation**
- **counterculture, youth culture, antimaterialistic, utopian communes, "Never trust anyone over 30"**
- **Food for Peace**
- **"Letter from a Birmingham Jail," Dr. Martin Luther King Jr.**
- **NASA; Mercury, Gemini, Apollo space programs**
- **Peace Corps**
- **reverse discrimination, white backlash**
- **VISTA (Volunteers in Service to America)**
- **Watts riots**

SECTION 2. THE NIXON YEARS

After his defeat in the 1960 presidential election by **John F. Kennedy, Richard Nixon** returned to California. When he lost his 1962 bid for the California governorship, he vowed to leave politics forever. However, within two years, Nixon was back on the political scene. He methodically restored his old party ties and won the Republican nomination for president in 1968. The Democrats nominated **Hubert Humphrey.** The presence of third-party candidate **George Wallace** made the outcome uncertain, but Nixon won in a very close race. Had Wallace won a few more electoral votes, the election could have been thrown into the House. Then Nixon might have had to negotiate with Wallace for his votes, thus making him beholden to Wallace.

FAST FACTS

Foreign Policy

- With **Henry Kissinger** as his **National Security Adviser,** Nixon set about leaving his mark on world affairs. Impatient with the time involved and the maneuverings inherent in the regular diplomatic channels, Nixon and Kissinger carried on their own high-level negotiations without including the secretary of state or normal government channels. The two men believed that the U.S.'s reputation in world affairs had suffered as the Soviet Union had become more powerful. Rather than continue a foreign policy based on moral principles, the United States needed to consider the realities of power and develop policies on a pragmatic basis.

- Nixon, with Kissinger's aid, embarked on finding a solution to the Vietnam War. He announced his **Vietnamization** policy while carrying on a series of negotiating sessions with the North Vietnamese. The talks continued throughout 1970 and 1971, while U.S. troops were withdrawn from Vietnam. On February 27, 1973, after massive bombing of the North, North and South Vietnam and the United States signed a **cease-fire agreement.** A month later, the last of the U.S. troops was gone. The South Vietnamese hung on for another year, but, in 1975, the government collapsed, and the North Vietnamese proclaimed a single unified nation. Cambodia and Laos also fell to Communist-backed governments.

- Once a strong supporter of **Nationalist China (Taiwan),** Nixon made an overture to the **People's Republic of China** to establish friendly relations. The United States had severed all diplomatic and trading ties with mainland China when the PRC was established in 1949. Nixon visited the mainland, and both nations agreed to a policy of **peaceful coexistence.** Additional outcomes were (1) resumption of trade between the two nations, (2) agreement by the United States that Taiwan was part of China, (3) withdrawal of U.S. troops from Taiwan, but (4) continuation of U.S. diplomatic and trade relations with Taiwan.

- Pursuing a policy known as **détente,** Nixon eased tensions with the Soviet Union. As early as 1969, the two nations had signed a **nuclear nonproliferation treaty.** The Soviet Union was interested in relaxing tensions with the United States to strengthen its own position against the PRC and to buy U.S. wheat to ease its food shortages caused by poor harvests. Nixon visited Russia, and

Test-Taking Strategy

Track the various programs and policies that the United States adopted to counteract the rise of the Soviet Union after World War II.

(1) signed the first round of the **Strategic Arms Limitation treaties (SALT I),** limiting the spread of antiballistic missiles, and (2) agreed to cooperate in health research, space exploration, trade, and pollution control.

Domestic Policy

- In domestic policies, Nixon launched the **New Federalism,** aimed at reducing big government and returning more power to state and local governments. His major tool was **revenue sharing,** which returned to states and municipalities some of the revenue from income taxes. This was in place of the federal government's paying directly for programs. A significant provision of revenue sharing was that programs that received the funds could not engage in racial or ethnic discrimination. (Opposition from Reagan and the worsening federal budget deficit killed revenue sharing in 1987.

The Supreme Court

Review Strategy

For more on interpretations of the Constitution, see Chapter 2.

- Nixon had the opportunity to change the nature of the Supreme Court while president. When Chief Justice **Earl Warren** retired in 1969, Nixon nominated **strict constructionist Warren E. Burger** to replace him. Nixon's next two nominees were rejected as unfit, but, ultimately, Nixon replaced three additional justices, thus turning the court from **judicial activism** to a more conservative reading of the law.
- However, the Supreme Court during Nixon's administrations still handed down decisions that were controversial. One of the most controversial and vigorously opposed by conservatives and others was *Roe* v. *Wade.*

Roe v. _Wade_ (1973; right to privacy)

Case: Looking for a case to test state laws against abortion, advocates found it in *Roe* v. *Wade*. A Texas law banned all abortions except those to save the life of the mother. An unwed pregnant woman sought an abortion and was denied. Her case was appealed to the Supreme Court.

Decision: In their opinion, the justices ruled that the state may not ban abortions in the first six months of pregnancy. A fetus is not a person and, therefore, not protected by the Fourteenth Amendment. However, the amendment does protect a woman's right to privacy, and, therefore, the state may not interfere in a woman's decision to have an abortion. At the same time, the right to an abortion is not absolute. After the first trimester, the state may regulate abortion procedures to protect women who elect to have the procedure. During the final three months, the state may regulate and even ban abortions in the interest of the unborn, except in cases to save the life of the mother.

Significance: The Court's decision expanded the right to privacy, which is not explicitly stated in the Constitution. The Court based its opinion on personal property rights that are found in the Fourteenth Amendment. The decision sparked a campaign to add an anti-abortion amendment to the Constitution.

Watergate

- Nixon was brought down by the **Watergate Scandal.** It began early in the 1972 election as an attempt to bug Democratic Party National Headquarters in the Watergate office complex. Surprised in the act, the seven "burglars" were arrested, tried, and convicted. The trail led back to the **Republican campaign committee to reelect Nixon.** Top administration officials began to resign as the details of a **cover-up** unfolded. It was learned that Nixon had routinely taped conversations in the Oval Office, and a court fight ensued over the tapes. When transcripts of some of the tapes were made public, it appeared certain that Nixon had participated in the cover-up.

- Impeachment proceedings began in the House, and the **House Judiciary Committee** voted to send three **articles of impeachment** to the House for formal debate. The articles accused the president of (1) obstructing justice in the Watergate cover-up, (2) abusing presidential power, and (3) attempting to block the impeachment process by withholding evidence. Tapes played during the debate showed that Nixon had approved the cover-up six days after the burglary.

- Nixon then admitted publicly that he had known about the cover-up, but he said that it did not merit impeachment. With urging by Republican Party leaders in Congress, Nixon resigned.

- In addition to the cover-up, Nixon had been found to have (1) evaded taxes, (2) used tax information against political "enemies," and (3) bugged the telephones of some members of Congress and the press. The attempt to wiretap Democratic Party headquarters was an attempt to subvert the electoral process.

KEY PEOPLE

Review Strategy

See if you can relate these people to their correct context in the "Fast Facts" section.

- **Archibad Cox, special prosecutor, "Saturday Night Massacre"**
- **John Dean, president's counsel, testimony on wiretapping**
- **Sam Ervin, senator, Ervin Committee**
- **Leon Jaworski, special prosecutor**
- **John Sirica, judge**

KEY TERMS/IDEAS

Review Strategy

See if you can relate these terms and ideas to their correct context in the "Fast Facts" section.

- *Regents of University of California* v. *Bakke,* **affirmative action**
- **Kent State, National Guard, incursion into Cambodia, continued unrest and protests in the United States**
- **shuttle diplomacy to find a solution to Vietnam**
- **"peace with honor," extrication of United States from Vietnam**

SECTION 3. THE UNITED STATES SINCE 1974

A major phenomenon of the late 1970s and 1980s was the emergence of the **New Right.** Members of the movement believe that **liberalism** is responsible for much of the nation's current social problems. According to them, liberals had taken over the federal government, corporations, the banking system, the media, and labor unions and were wielding their power to make and enforce policies that weakened the moral and social fabric of the nation as well as its political and economic well-being. The election of Ronald Reagan to the presidency in 1980 and 1984 was brought about in large part by a coalition of the New Right and **fundamentalist groups** with whom he shared certain views, such as reversing the right to abortion and enacting legislation that would allow **school prayer.**

The defeat of George Bush for a second term as president was in large measure because of the poor economy. However, his opponent, Arkansas governor Bill Clinton, also appealed to the political center. Known as a **centrist,** Clinton took over a number of Republican ideas, such as welfare reform and a balanced budget, and made them work. His reelection in 1996 was a confirmation of the roaring economy and his appeal to moderates and independents as well as the Democratic Party faithful.

FAST FACTS

Ford/Rockefeller Term

Study Strategy

See Chapter 2 *for the Twenty-Fifth Amendment.*

- Among the important facts to remember about the **Gerald Ford/ Nelson Rockefeller** administration are:
  - Gerald Ford and Nelson Rockefeller are the only two unelected president and vice president to serve in those offices. Ford was nominated and confirmed to replace Nixon's vice president, **Spiro Agnew.** When Nixon resigned, Ford became president and nominated Nelson Rockefeller as vice president.
  - Ford granted Nixon an **unconditional pardon** for all crimes he may have committed while in office. Ford said this would save the nation the agony of a trial; critics protested. It would be a number of years before Nixon began the process of rehabilitating his reputation.
  - The relations between Ford and the Democratic-controlled Congress were tense from the beginning but worsened over differences in how to fight the **recession.** While Ford's concerns were inflation and dependence on foreign oil, Congress worried about unemployment and the low level of the **GNP** (gross national product; now referred to as the **GDP,** gross domestic product).
  - Ford continued the policy of **détente,** signed the **Helsinki Accords,** and watched helplessly while Congress refused to aid Cambodia and South Vietnam, both of which fell to Communist-led insurgents.

Carter/Mondale Term

- Among the important facts to remember about the **Jimmy Carter/ Walter Mondale** administration are:
  - Faced with rising oil prices as a result of actions by the **Organization of Petroleum Exporting Companies (OPEC)** and a genuine concern about Americans' consumption of oil, a nonrenewable resource, Carter declared an **energy crisis** and tried to enlist Americans in a **"moral war"** against energy consumption. His approach failed with the public and with Congress when he asked for a tax on oil imports and the authority to impose gasoline rationing.
  - Rising energy prices brought on **double-digit inflation**. When the **Federal Reserve Board** raised interest rates to curb inflation, a recession resulted. Unemployment and prices continued to rise during Carter's presidency.
  - A major foreign policy coup was the **Camp David Accords** that brought peace between Egypt and Israel. The two nations agreed to (1) the establishment of diplomatic relations, (2) a phased withdrawal of Israeli forces from the Egyptian Sinai, and (3) further discussions to resolve the question of Palestinian self-rule.

- A major problem was the **Iranian hostage crisis.** The United States had supported the Shah of Iran during his thirty-eight-year reign. Forced to flee after a year of increasingly violent antigovernment demonstrations, the Shah sought refuge in the United States for cancer treatment, and Carter agreed. In retaliation, a mob of Iranians stormed the U.S. Embassy in Teheran and took sixty-three American employees hostage. A series of negotiations and an attempted military rescue failed. After agreeing to accept $8 billion dollars in Iranian assets that had been frozen in the United States, the Iranian government released the hostages some thirty minutes after Carter left office in January 1981.

- Other important elements of Carter's foreign policy were (1) recognition of the People's Republic of China; (2) the signing of **SALT II (Strategic Arms Limitation Treaty),** although the Senate did not ratify it; (3) an embargo on grain shipments to the USSR and a boycott of the Summer Olympics in Moscow in retaliation for the Soviet invasion of Afghanistan; and (4) treaties abolishing the **Panama Canal Zone** and turning over control of the area to Panama.

Reagan and Bush Administrations

- Some of the major facts to remember about the two terms in office of **Ronald Reagan/George Bush** are:

- In 1980, voters rejected Carter's policies and elected Ronald Reagan, an optimist who played well against Carter's view of the **national malaise.** Reagan's election in 1980 was significant because it showed the shift to **conservatism** among the nation's voters, including many blue-collar Democrats. It was the first election of a conservative to the presidency since Calvin Coolidge. Americans who related to Reagan's call for smaller government gave him a Republican-controlled Senate and so large a number of Republican representatives that Democrats retained only a slim margin in the House.

- Faced with the continuing recession, Reagan called for tax reductions and spending cuts. He based his policies, called **Reaganomics,** on **supply-side economics.** Many people objected to his cuts in social programs like food stamps and Medicare. However, with the support of Southern Democrats, Reagan's measures were passed. An economic recovery began and unemployment dropped.

- While advocating cuts in social programs, Reagan pushed for increases in the defense budget, especially for the development of a space-based antiballistic missile defense system, the **Strategic Defense Initiative (SDI, "Star Wars").** Democrats refused to agree to Reagan's cuts in social programs. Because of the cost of social programs coupled with Reagan's defense requests, the **federal budget deficit** mushroomed. Few social programs actually ended during Reagan's administration, and some, like Medicare, were actually strengthened and expanded.

- In foreign affairs, Reagan signed the **Intermediate Nuclear Force (INF) Treaty** with the Soviet Union. However, he opposed a **nuclear freeze.**

- The **Iran-contra affair** was, to a degree, a result of Reagan's "hands-off" management style. **Sandinistas,** socialist revolutionaries, had overthrown the dictatorship in **Nicaragua** and set up a government. Reagan backed a second revolutionary group, the **Contras**, who opposed the Sandinistas. Members of Congress who disagreed with Reagan's policy passed a measure banning aid to the Contras. Several high-level members of Reagan's staff continued to supply the Contras with money. They sold weapons to so-called Iranian moderates to obtain the release of three hostages and used the profits for the Contras. (1) The arms sale violated U.S. policy. (2) The financial support to the Contras violated the Congressional ban. (3) Several administration officials were charged with conspiracy, fraud, lying, and withholding information.

Deregulation

- During both the Carter and Reagan administrations, a number of industries were **deregulated,** beginning with the airline industry in 1978 and including interstate bus companies and financial institutions. The trend continued into the 1990s with the telecommunication industry among others. The goals of deregulation were to (1) increase competition, (2) cut the costs associated with the enforcement of regulation, and thereby (3) decrease consumer prices.

Ethnic Groups

- Although more African Americans and Hispanics were elected to public office on the state and local levels, little headway was made on the national level in the 1980s. **Bilingual education** and **affirmative action** became major social and political issues of the 1980s and 1990s.

- **Hispanics** became the fastest-growing ethnic group in the United States in the late 1980s and 1990s. Most Hispanics are of **Mexican descent.**

- The **1986 Immigration and Reform and Control Act** naturalized illegal aliens. The **1990 Immigration Act** revised past quotas and loosened restrictions for those with special employment skills.

Bush and Quayle Term

- The major achievements of the **George Bush/Dan Quayle** administration were in foreign affairs. Bush seemed to lack the experience or the skill to deal successfully with domestic issues. The wrangle over **"no new taxes"** and the ever-worsening federal deficit created the impression among voters that Bush's domestic programs had little direction. In the election of 1992, **Bill Clinton** combined his own appeal to the **Baby Boomers** with Bush's economic problems to win a close election.

  - The **Persian Gulf War** brought together a coalition of nations to oust Iraq from Kuwait. In **Operation Desert Storm,** the coalition bombarded military installations in Iraq and in Kuwait. After six weeks, the international force began an invasion. While the Iraqi were forced from Kuwait, which was returned to its former status as an independent state, **Saddam Hussein** remained in power.

  - President Bush continued to try to find a peaceful solution to the Arab-Israeli conflict. As a result of the Persian Gulf War, Israel, Lebanon, Jordan, Syria, and the Palestinians met for the first direct peace conference.

  - Beginning in the mid-1980s, **Mikhail Gorbachev** began dismantling the Communist system in the Soviet Union and allowed Eastern European nations to overthrow their Communist-led governments. In 1990, the division of East and West Germany ended, and the Berlin Wall fell. Bush and Gorbachev declared the end of the **Cold War** in 1991.

  - Among the laws and other changes made during the Bush term were (1) tighter controls on air pollution and (2) **the savings and loan bailout.**

Clinton and Gore Years

- Some of the major facts to remember about the two terms in office of **Bill Clinton** and **Al Gore** are:

Review Strategy

According to the Constitution, the House is empowered to decide whether there is enough evidence of misconduct on the part of the president (or certain other government officials) to warrant turning the person over to the Senate for trial. To impeach does not mean to convict a person of alleged wrongdoing.

  - Clinton's impressive record as president will be forever clouded by the spectacle of his impeachment. Only the second president in the nation's history to be impeached by the House, Clinton was acquitted by the Senate in February 1999 of two charges related to his attempt to cover up his affair with a young White House intern.

  - While Andrew Johnson's impeachment and trial revolved around who would set the rules for the reconstruction of the South after the Civil War and Richard Nixon's impeachment hearings focused on his attempts to subvert the electoral process for his own gain, the Clinton trial supposedly revolved around his extramarital relationship with Monica Lewinsky and his efforts to cover it up. However, there were many who felt that the roots of the attempt to discredit Clinton lay in his political ideals and in the Nixon resignation. Clinton's advocacy of gun control, civil rights, gay and lesbian rights, abortion rights, and national education reform, among other policies, created diehard opponents. There were some political analysts who thought that the impeachment of Clinton was the Republicans' payback for the Democrats' pursuit of Nixon.

- While Congress debated impeachment, the voters went to the polls in November 1998 and gave the Democrats an impressive victory in the off-year election. The trend since 1934 in off-year elections had been to return fewer members of the president's party to the House and Senate. In 1998, however, Democrats picked up seats rather than lost them. The Republicans still had a margin of 11 seats in the House (222 to 211) and 10 seats in the Senate (55 to 45), though not the necessary two-thirds majority (60). The people seemed to be saying that they had had enough of the scandal and impeachment.

- Speaker of the House **Newt Gingrich,** who had become the symbol of the Republicans' drive to cut social programs and to "get" Clinton, resigned. Gingrich's **Contract with America,** the name given to the collection of social and economic policies that had propelled the Republicans into control of both the House and the Senate for the first time since 1930, was at an end.

- Among the laws and other changes enacted during Clinton's two terms in office were (1) the **Family and Medical Leave Act** (1993), requiring companies with more than 50 employees to allow employees up to 12 weeks of unpaid leave for family emergencies; (2) "don't ask, don't tell" policy in the military regarding gays and lesbians; (3) **Taxpayer Relief Act** (1997), the first tax cut in 16 years; (4) a plan, negotiated with the Republicans, to balance the budget and reduce the federal deficit; (5) adoption of a policy of **engagement** with China to stimulate the Chinese economy and encourage the government to observe human and civil rights in China; and (6) the **North American Free Trade Agreement (NAFTA),** removing trade barriers with Mexico.

- Congress passed a **line item veto** bill, giving the president the power to remove items from the federal budget. When President Clinton used the line item veto in 1997, several affected localities appealed to the courts. In 1998, the Supreme Court ruled against the law. According to its reading of the Constitution, the Court held that the president must accept or veto a bill in its entirety.

- An ongoing problem for both political parties was **campaign finance reform.** The costs of running political campaigns for statewide and national office had skyrocketed during the 1990s. In the 1996 election, both parties had used questionable tactics in raising campaign financing. The issues of **PACS (Political Action Committees)** and **soft money** dogged the parties.

Blocked by Republicans in Congress, no effective campaign finance reform law could be passed. Cleaning up the system proved to be an effective message for Senator John McCain in the 2000 election when he seemed at one point in the primaries close to toppling Republican party-backed candidate George W. Bush, the governor of Texas and son of former President George Bush.

The Election of 2000

- Although running for president during a time of peace and eight years of prosperity, Vice President Al Gore was unable to catch fire with the electorate. In a surprisingly hard-fought early primary season, Gore defeated former Senator Bill Bradley and went on to win the Democratic nomination easily. However, his unwillingness to embrace the record of the Clinton administration for fear he would be tainted by Clinton's misdeeds, questions about Gore's own truthfulness and his fundraising activities along with what was considered a stiff demeanor cost him votes. What damage Gore did not do to himself, the Republicans did by fixing him with the familiar label of "a tax-and-spend Democrat."

- On the Republican side, Governor George W. Bush of Texas, son of former President George Bush, won the nomination after a hard-fought campaign against Senator John McCain of Arizona. Although McCain appeared to be more conservative than Bush, his "straight talking" persona and his accessibility to the press created a media phenomenon that appealed to many primary voters. In the end, he could not match the money and Republican organization that backed Bush.

- Come election night, after a premature awarding of Florida's electoral votes to Gore, the final tally showed a Florida popular vote too close to call. Florida state law provided for a statewide recount in such an event. The votes in several counties as well as absentees ballots cast by service people and Americans abroad became an issue as Democrats and Republicans jockeyed to score public relations points. Both sides appealed decisions to the Florida Supreme Court that upheld the recount in disputed counties as requested by the Democrats. The Republicans also appealed to the U.S. Supreme Court. Ultimately, the U.S. Supreme Court upheld the appeal of George W. Bush, halted the recounts, and handed the election to Bush.

The Bush and Cheney Administration

- The first months of George W. Bush's administration were rocky. The economy continued to weaken, and efforts to boost it through rate cuts by the Federal Reserve Bank and a large tax cut passed by Congress did not halt the downturn. By the end of 2001, economists declared that the nation had indeed entered a recession in March of that year. Those who had invested in dot.com businesses suffered heavy losses on the stock market as the Internet bubble burst. Opponents of Bush's tax cutting policies claimed that the huge tax cut that returned approximately $300 to individuals and $600 to families was too little to make a difference in anything but the federal deficit. The huge surpluses of the last few years of the Clinton administration were wiped out, and the nation again faced a budget deficit for the 2003 fiscal year.

- The deficit was not caused solely by the weakened economy. The aftermath of the September 11, 2001, terrorist attack on the United States also played a significant role. Nineteen terrorists hijacked four commercial airliners bound for the West Coast from airports in the Northeast. Three of the planes hit their targets—the two World Trade Towers and the Pentagon. The hijackers of the fourth plane, with 40 passengers on board, were apparently overcome by the passengers. That plane crashed in a rural area in Pennsylvania. Government officials surmised that its target might have been one of Washington's federal buildings, perhaps the Capitol. Within 90 minutes of the crashes, both towers collapsed. Some 2,800 people were lost in the two buildings and another 180 at the Pentagon. The nation was stunned as New York City was "locked down," F-16 fighters flew over New Jersey on reconnaissance, and national landmarks, federal buildings, dams, and nuclear plants across the country were sealed off. Terrorists operating under the Al Quaida network of Osama bin Laden were identified as the hijackers. President Bush vowed an all-out war on terrorism, and within a month, U.S. warplanes and missiles were on the attack in Afghanistan. Although Afghanistan's Taliban government, which had harbored bin Laden and Al Quaida, were routed from Afghanistan by year's end and a new Afghan government was installed by early 2002, bin Laden eluded capture. His terrorist network suffered serious setbacks throughout Europe, however, as European governments began arresting and bringing to trial suspected terrorists. President Bush promised to take the fight against terrorism to any nation that sponsored it, specifically naming Iran, Iraq, and North Korea.

KEY PEOPLE

Review Strategy

See if you can relate these people to their correct context in the "Fast Facts" section.

- Jesse Jackson, presidential bids, Rainbow Coalition
- Menachem Begin, Anwar Sadat, Camp David Accords
- George W. Bush
- Bill Bradley, John McCain

KEY TERMS/IDEAS

Review Strategy

See if you can relate these terms and ideas to their correct context in the "Fast Facts" section.

- El Salvador, human rights, civil war
- *glasnost, perestroika*
- Gramm-Rudman Act, across-the-board federal spending cuts
- human-rights policy, Carter
- War Powers Act, reassertion of Congressional power, backlash to Vietnam
- Chads, "butterfly ballot"

PRACTICE TEST 1

While you have taken many standardized tests and know to completely blacken the ovals on the answer sheets and to completely erase any errors, you will need to indicate on the answer key which test you are taking. The instructions on the answer sheet will tell you to fill out the top portion of the answer sheet exactly as shown.

1. Print *U.S. HISTORY* on the line to the right under the words *Subject Test (print).*

2. In the shaded box labeled *Test Code*, fill in four ovals: —Fill in oval 2 in the row labeled V.
   —Fill in oval 5 in the row labeled W.
   —Fill in oval 5 in the row labeled X.
   —Fill in oval C in the row labeled Y.
   —Leave the ovals in row Q blank.

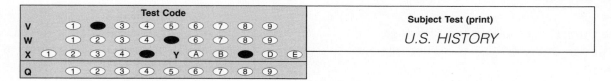

There are two additional questions that you will be asked to answer: How many semesters of U.S. history have you taken? Have you taken courses in government, economics, geography, psychology, sociology, and/or anthropology? The College Board is collecting statistical information. If you choose to answer, you will use the key that is provided and blacken the appropriate ovals in row Q. You may also choose not to answer, and that will not affect your grade.

When everyone has completed filling in this portion of the answer sheet, the supervisor will tell you to turn the page and begin. The answer sheet has 100 numbered ovals on the sheet, but there are only 90 (or 95) multiple-choice questions in the test, so be sure to use only ovals 1 to 90 (or 95) to record your answers.

GO ON TO THE NEXT PAGE →

PRACTICE TEST 1—*Continued*

Directions: Each of the questions or incomplete statements below has five suggested answers or completions. Choose the response that is best and then fill in the corresponding oval on the answer sheet.

1. A major characteristic of the Anasazi culture in what is today the U.S. Southwest was

   (A) the building of large mounds for burial grounds

   (B) potlatch ceremonies to display one's wealth

   (C) sheepherding

   (D) the erection of long houses

   (E) the building of cliff dwellings

2. The primary reason that the British government was interested in chartering Georgia was to

   (A) earn profits for its proprietors who were friends of the king

   (B) provide a buffer between South Carolina and Spanish Florida

   (C) establish a colony for the poor who were imprisoned for debt

   (D) establish a colony of small farms rather than slave-run plantations

   (E) experiment with rice agriculture

3. Which of the following is generally true about immigration to the British colonies in North America?

   (A) Most immigrants in the 1600s were non-English.

   (B) Religion was not a factor in the immigration of non-English colonists.

   (C) By the time of the Revolutionary War, the colonies were still predominantly English.

   (D) The New England colonies had the least diverse population in the 1600s.

   (E) The largest group of non-English immigrants over time were French.

4. The major stumbling block between the colonies and Great Britain was

   (A) King George's refusal to believe that the colonists were loyal subjects

   (B) Parliament's insistence on the theory of virtual representation

   (C) the Boston Tea Party

   (D) the Townshend Acts

   (E) the Proclamation of Rebellion

5. The development of the United States as an industrial giant was implicit in the policies of

   (A) Hector St. John de Crèvecoeur

   (B) Thomas Jefferson

   (C) Alexander Hamilton

   (D) John C. Calhoun

   (E) Patrick Henry

6. All of the following were elements of U.S. foreign relations with Great Britain in the first half of the nineteenth century EXCEPT

   (A) Rush-Bagot Agreement

   (B) War of 1812

   (C) settlement of the boundary dispute over Oregon

   (D) purchase of Alaska

   (E) Webster-Ashburton Treaty

PRACTICE TEST 1—*Continued*

7. During the Civil War, all of the following were true of the Union policy toward African Americans EXCEPT

   (A) many African Americans saw duty only as teamsters, cooks, and laborers

   (B) the Union refused to allow African Americans to enlist until there was a shortage of recruits

   (C) African Americans fought in segregated units

   (D) the Union commissioned some African Americans as officers, but most black troops fought under white officers

   (E) African Americans were integrated into white regiments

8. "The working class and the employing class have nothing in common. There can be no peace so long as hunger and want are found among millions of working people and the few, who make up the employing class, have all good things in life."

   The above quotation is most likely from the constitution of the

   (A) Greenback Party

   (B) Knights of Labor

   (C) Grange

   (D) Industrial Workers of the World

   (E) CIO

9. Which actions were part of Theodore Roosevelt's "big stick" foreign policy?

   I. Platt Amendment
   II. support of Panamanian rebels seeking independence from Colombia
   III. intervention in Mexico

   (A) I, II, and III

   (B) I and II only

   (C) II and III only

   (D) I only

   (E) II only

10. The Harlem Renaissance can best be described as a period in which

    (A) a wide audience was exposed to jazz

    (B) white as well as black audiences became interested in African American literature, art, and music

    (C) the concept of the "New Negro" underlay African American cultural works

    (D) poets and novelists wrote about black pride and black protest

    (E) African American painters and sculptors exhibited their works to appreciative audiences

11. Which of the following was NOT created during Roosevelt's first "Hundred Days" in office?

    (A) Public Works Administration

    (B) Agricultural Adjustment Administration

    (C) Civilian Conservation Corps

    (D) Social Security Administration

    (E) Tennessee Valley Authority

12. All of the following were elements of Richard Nixon's foreign policy EXCEPT

    (A) the "two China" policy

    (B) détente with the Soviet Union

    (C) cease-fire agreement with the North Vietnamese

    (D) nuclear nonproliferation treaty with the Soviet Union

    (E) Marshall Plan

GO ON TO THE NEXT PAGE →

PRACTICE TEST 1—*Continued*

13. All of the following are true about the Albany Plan of Union EXCEPT

(A) each colonial legislature would select representatives to a Grand Council

(B) it was based on the Iroquois League of Six Nations

(C) the plan was the first step toward uniting the colonies

(D) a purpose of the Union was to organize and act together for common defense

(E) the Grand Council would elect the governor-general

14. Alexander Hamilton advocated all of the following policies EXCEPT

(A) a protective tariff

(B) a national banking system

(C) an excise tax on whiskey

(D) an income tax on the wealthy

(E) assumption of all state debts arising from the Revolutionary War

Questions 15 and 16 relate to the following map.

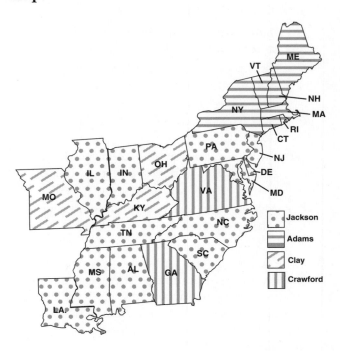

15. In the election of 1824, which two candidates won the Western states?

(A) Adams and Jackson

(B) Clay and Crawford

(C) Adams and Clay

(D) Clay and Jackson

(E) Crawford and Jackson

16. In which region of the country was Adams the strongest?

(A) Western

(B) Southern

(C) New England

(D) Middle Atlantic

(E) Frontier

PRACTICE TEST 1—*Continued*

17. All of the following contributed to the growth of U.S. industry between 1800 and 1850 EXCEPT

    (A) the availability of a large pool of immigrant labor
    (B) the introduction of the factory system
    (C) the introduction of the cotton gin
    (D) a series of protective tariffs
    (E) passage of federal internal improvements bills

18. Which of the following men is NOT correctly paired with the policy he advocated?

    (A) Stephen Douglas: advocated allowing people in a territory to decide for themselves whether to approve the extension of slavery into their territory
    (B) Abraham Lincoln: advocated allowing slavery to continue in the South while banning its extension into the Western territories
    (C) Henry Clay: advocated allowing California and the New Mexico and Utah Territories to decide for themselves whether to allow slavery
    (D) John C. Calhoun: advocated secession if the North would not agree to extending slavery into Western territory
    (E) David Wilmot: advocated outlawing slavery in any territory acquired from Mexico

19. Andrew Johnson vetoed the Civil Rights Act of 1866 primarily because he believed

    (A) its provisions were already covered in the Fourteenth Amendment
    (B) it violated states' rights
    (C) it should have included women's rights
    (D) it would be unnecessary once Reconstruction went into effect
    (E) it was not strong enough to counteract the black codes

20. Which of the following did NOT contribute to the Great Depression?

    (A) buying stocks on margin
    (B) consumer installment buying
    (C) underconsumption of goods
    (D) underproduction of goods
    (E) U.S. insistence on collecting its war debts

21. The Alliance for Progress can best be described as an attempt to

    (A) counteract among other Latin Americans the appeal of Fidel Castro's Cuban communism
    (B) provide arms to rebel forces in Nicaragua
    (C) intervene in Chilean elections
    (D) establish economic and social programs across Latin America
    (E) establish a process for turning over control of the Panama Canal to Panama

22. All of the following were elements of the "war on poverty" EXCEPT

    (A) Voting Rights Act of 1965
    (B) Office of Economic Opportunity
    (C) Medicare
    (D) Elementary and Secondary School Act
    (E) Volunteers in Service to America (VISTA)

GO ON TO THE NEXT PAGE

PRACTICE TEST 1—*Continued*

23. Jimmy Carter won the 1976 election for all of the following reasons EXCEPT

    (A) his ability to put together a coalition of the industrial Northeast and the South

    (B) his strategy of campaigning as an outsider

    (C) the Watergate scandal

    (D) his promise to balance the budget

    (E) his promise to lower inflation by raising employment

24. " . . . We whose names are underwritten, . . . having undertaken, for the glory of country, a voyage to plant the first colony in the Northern parts of Virginia, do . . . solemnly and mutually in the presence of God, and one of another, covenant and combine ourselves together into a civil body politic . . . ; and by virtue hereof to enact, constitute, and frame such just and equal laws, ordinances, acts, and constitutions, and offices, from time to time, as shall be thought most meet and convenient for the general good of the Colony. . . ."

The above statement was most probably written by the founders of

    (A) Massachusetts Bay

    (B) Maryland

    (C) Plymouth Colony

    (D) Pennsylvania

    (E) Georgia

25. Which of the following rebellions was caused by frontier settlers and landless former indentured servants angered by the policies of Virginia's government?

    (A) the Stono Uprising

    (B) Nat Turner's Rebellion

    (C) the Whiskey Rebellion

    (D) Shays's Rebellion

    (E) Bacon's Rebellion

26. The purpose of the Declaratory Act is best summarized by which of the following statements?

    (A) Loyal subjects of George III should oppose rebellion in the colonies.

    (B) All colonists should weigh the need to separate themselves from Great Britain.

    (C) Parliament has the right to make laws for the colonists in all matters.

    (D) The colonists should resist the Townshend Acts.

    (E) As the precursor to the Declaration of Independence, the act lists all the basic rights of the colonists as British subjects.

27. The Judiciary Act of 1789

    (A) established the principle of judicial review

    (B) designated the Supreme Court as the court to hear disputes involving federal laws

    (C) established the office of Attorney General and the Department of Justice

    (D) created the federal court system

    (E) was invoked by Andrew Jackson in the dispute over *Worcester* v. *States of Georgia*

28. The Monroe Doctrine was issued primarily

    (A) to protect U.S. business interests in Latin America

    (B) to warn that the United States would not tolerate any attempt by European nations to intervene in affairs of their former colonies in the Western Hemisphere

    (C) to assert that the United States had the right to ensure that acceptable governments were in place in nations of the Western Hemisphere

    (D) as part of the recall of troops from Nicaragua and Haiti

    (E) to forestall a similar declaration by Great Britain

PRACTICE TEST 1—*Continued*

29. To reconstruct life on a Southern plantation, which type of record would be LEAST useful?

    (A) plantation account books
    (B) local school-attendance records
    (C) oral traditions of the families of the plantation's former slaves
    (D) diaries of the plantation's owners and their families
    (E) records of auction houses and merchants who sold Africans to the plantation

30. All of the following added to the growing tension between the North and the South prior to the Civil War EXCEPT

    (A) *Uncle Tom's Cabin*
    (B) *Plessy* v. *Ferguson*
    (C) raid on Harper's Ferry
    (D) California's request for statehood
    (E) Underground Railroad

Questions 31 and 32 relate to the following cartoon.

31. The large cartoon figures represent Wall Street giants. Who does "Jack" represent?

    (A) Herbert Hoover
    (B) William McKinley
    (C) Franklin Roosevelt
    (D) Theodore Roosevelt
    (E) Warren G. Harding

32. What would be the most appropriate label for the sword?

    (A) In God We Trust
    (B) In the Public Service
    (C) Silver
    (D) Gospel of Wealth
    (E) Social Darwinism

GO ON TO THE NEXT PAGE

PRACTICE TEST 1—*Continued*

33. Because of isolationist opinions, Roosevelt developed which of the following strategies to help the Allies?

(A) Good Neighbor Policy

(B) gunboat diplomacy

(C) Neutrality Act of 1935

(D) Roosevelt Corollary

(E) Lend-Lease

34. Medicaid is

   I. a federally funded program

   II. a private insurance program

   III. a state-funded program

(A) I and II

(B) I, II, and III

(C) I and III only

(D) II and III only

(E) I only

35. The Great Society was the name given to the domestic policies of

(A) John F. Kennedy

(B) Lyndon Johnson

(C) Richard Nixon

(D) Ronald Reagan

(E) George Bush

36. The significance of the Fundamental Orders of Connecticut was that it

(A) established representative government through election to the House of Burgesses

(B) provided that any white man owning property could vote

(C) separated church and state

(D) established the Great Court

(E) outlawed slavery in the colony

37. American policy toward France during Washington's administration can best be described as an attempt to

(A) honor the commitment to France that the new nation had made in 1778 when the two became allies

(B) play France off against Great Britain

(C) keep the United States out of a war that it was ill-equipped to fight

(D) protect U.S. trade with Great Britain

(E) placate Napoleon in order to purchase Louisiana

38. Which of the following statements best describes the Lowell experiment of the 1820s?

(A) The Boston Associates were more interested in profits than in the well-being of their workers.

(B) Native-born women workers were replaced by lower-paid Irish immigrants.

(C) The Boston Associates attempted to operate Lowell without the labor abuses of the English factory system.

(D) Lowell women mill workers organized into successful unions.

(E) Lowell was one of the earliest mills to use water power.

PRACTICE TEST 1—*Continued*

39. "The people of Massachusetts have, in some degree, appreciated the truth, that the unexampled prosperity of the State—its comfort, its competence, its general intelligence and virtue—is attributable to the education, more or less perfect, which all its people received. . . . Education, then, beyond all other devices of human origin, is the great equalizer of the conditions of men—the balance-wheel of the social machinery."

    The above statement was most probably written by:

    (A) Benjamin Franklin
    (B) Woodrow Wilson
    (C) Frederick Douglass
    (D) Dorothea Dix
    (E) Horace Mann

40. "Manifest destiny" was a term coined to apply to the

    (A) principle of popular sovereignty
    (B) theory of Social Darwinism
    (C) belief that the United States should extend across the continent from the Atlantic to the Pacific
    (D) extension of slavery into the newly acquired Western territories
    (E) U.S.'s entrance into World War I

41. Reconstruction ended in the South as a direct result of

    (A) the collapse of the remaining carpetbag governments in Florida, South Carolina, and Louisiana
    (B) ratification of the Fifteenth Amendment
    (C) increased activities of white supremacist groups
    (D) Democrats' acceptance of Hayes as president in exchange for the withdrawal of troops from the South
    (E) general Northern fatigue with the programs of the Radical Republicans

42. The Roosevelt Corollary to the Monroe Doctrine was first applied

    (A) to the British and German blockade of Venezuela
    (B) in recognizing Panama's independence
    (C) to the withdrawal from Nicaragua of U.S. troops who had been sent to collect debt payments
    (D) to Cuba when the military occupation ended in 1901
    (E) in the Dominican Republic when the United States assumed responsibility for collecting Dominican debts to pay off creditors

43. Which of the following movies was controversial at the time because of its portrayal of African Americans?

    (A) *The Jazz Singer*
    (B) *Gone With the Wind*
    (C) *Inherit the Wind*
    (D) *Birth of a Nation*
    (E) *On the Road*

44. Which of the following did NOT occur on the home front during World War II?

    (A) There was little internal migration in the nation because of the rationing of gas and tires.
    (B) Japanese nationals and Japanese Americans were interned in detention camps in the United States.
    (C) Wage and price controls were established.
    (D) Women in record numbers took over men's jobs in industry.
    (E) The Fair Employment Practices Commission was established to end discrimination in hiring in the defense industry.

GO ON TO THE NEXT PAGE ➡

PRACTICE TEST 1—*Continued*

45. Which of the following was part of U.S. foreign policy immediately after World War II?

    I. Marshall Plan
    II. "dollar diplomacy"
    III. Point Four

    (A) I only
    (B) II only
    (C) I and II only
    (D) II and III only
    (E) I and III only

46. The Gulf of Tonkin Resolution was based on what false information?

    (A) The North Vietnamese were sending troops into South Vietnam.
    (B) North Vietnam had fired on U.S. destroyers that were aiding South Vietnam in electronic spying of the North.
    (C) The Vietcong had little or no support in rural areas and, therefore, could be easily subdued.
    (D) North Vietnam had fired on two destroyers in an unprovoked attack.
    (E) The North Vietnamese were using napalm against U.S. soldiers.

47. Which of the following colonies was self-governing?

    (A) Maryland
    (B) Pennsylvania
    (C) Rhode Island
    (D) Georgia
    (E) New York

48. The revenue from which of the following acts was to be used to pay the salaries of the royal governors, thus negating the power of the purse?

    (A) Tea Act
    (B) Stamp Act
    (C) Sugar Act
    (D) Currency Act
    (E) Townshend Act

49. Which of the following statements about the Declaration of Independence is NOT true?

    (A) The Declaration was based on the philosophy of the Enlightenment.
    (B) All references to George III's part in the slave trade were deleted in the final version.
    (C) By declaring independence, the new nation established that the rules of war had to be observed, thus protecting its soldiers.
    (D) The Declaration listed various ways in which George III had taken away the rights of the colonists.
    (E) The Declaration established the organization of the new nation.

50. Which of the following was adopted to resolve the issue of representation in the House and Senate?

    (A) Three-Fifths Compromise
    (B) New Jersey Plan
    (C) direct election of senators
    (D) Great Compromise
    (E) Virginia Plan

PRACTICE TEST 1—*Continued*

51. The American System favored all of the following EXCEPT

(A) development of U.S. industrial capacity

(B) relaxation of the quota system for immigrants

(C) lessening of sectional divisions

(D) a charter for the Second Bank

(E) a protective tariff

52. "What good man would prefer a country covered with forests and ranged by a few thousand savages to our extensive Republic, studded with cities, town, and prosperous farms embellished with all the improvements which art can devise or industry execute, occupied by more than 12,000,000 happy people . . ."

The above statement would most likely have been written in support of

(A) Confederate secession

(B) *Cherokee Nation* v. *The State of Georgia*

(C) the Indian Removal Act of 1830

(D) establishment of the Indian Territory

(E) a request for Oklahoma statehood

53. The Missouri Compromise was nullified in effect by the

(A) Dred Scott decision

(B) Emancipation Proclamation

(C) Wilmot Proviso

(D) Gadsden Purchase

(E) black codes

54. All of the following were part of Congressional Reconstruction EXCEPT

(A) the Southern states were organized into five military districts

(B) the Southern states had to ratify the Fourteenth Amendment

(C) the governments of the Southern states except for Tennessee were declared illegal

(D) the Southern states were to write new constitutions to guarantee suffrage to African American men

(E) former Confederate officials could participate in the state conventions if they paid a fine

55. The Crédit Mobilier scandal involved

(A) an attempt by Congress to raise its own pay and to collect two years' back pay

(B) a bribe by an Indian trader to William Belknap, the Secretary of State

(C) "Boss" Tweed and the building of a courthouse in New York City

(D) the awarding of construction contracts on the Union Pacific Railroad by a group of stockholders to their own company at inflated prices

(E) a ring of whiskey distillers and blackmailers who had been defrauding the federal government of taxes on whiskey

GO ON TO THE NEXT PAGE ➤

PRACTICE TEST 1—*Continued*

Questions 56 and 57 refer to the following charts.

Year	U.S. Exports to Europe	U.S. Exports to Asia
1890	684	20
1891	705	26
1892	851	20
1893	662	17
1894	701	22
1895	628	18
1896	673	26
1897	813	39
1898	974	45
1899	937	49

Source: *Historical Abstract of the United States*

56. In which year did the value of U.S. exports to Europe increase while the value of U.S. exports to Asia declined?

(A) 1895
(B) 1894
(C) 1893
(D) 1892
(E) 1891

57. The trend in trade with Asia, as shown on the graph, appears to demonstrate the wisdom of

(A) the Roosevelt Corollary
(B) John Hay's Open Door policy
(C) the Panama Canal Treaty
(D) the annexation of the Philippines
(E) a favorable balance of trade

58. A major policy difference between Truman and Congress was

(A) raising the minimum wage
(B) passage of the National Housing Act of 1949
(C) establishing farm price supports
(D) expansion of the Reclamation Bureau's work in flood control and the building of hydroelectric plants
(E) enactment of national health care

59. All of the following occurred during Eisenhower's two terms in office EXCEPT

(A) the war in Korea ended in a stalemate
(B) approval of economic aid and military assistance to Middle Eastern nations in an attempt to thwart Communist plans in the region
(C) Alaska and Hawaii were admitted to statehood
(D) the National Aeronautics and Space Administration (NASA) was created
(E) Eisenhower sent troops to Little Rock, Arkansas, to keep peace and end the crisis over desegregation of the high school

60. Which of the following helped England become a major power in the Americas?

(A) exploration of North America by Frobisher, Hudson, and Cabot
(B) the exploits of "sea dogs", like Sir Francis Drake, against the Spanish
(C) the defeat of the Spanish Armada
(D) the rivalry between Spain and France
(E) the triangular trade route

PRACTICE TEST 1—*Continued*

61. The major significance of the delegated powers listed in the U.S. Constitution is

    (A) the powers correct areas of weakness in the Articles of Confederation

    (B) Congress is given the power to levy and collect taxes

    (C) the delegated powers relate to matters of common concern across the states

    (D) the states reserve some powers to themselves

    (E) the Tenth Amendment asserts that powers not given to the states reside with the federal government

62. The unstated purpose of the Alien and Sedition Acts was to

    (A) unite the nation in time of danger

    (B) deport immigrants who were becoming too numerous

    (C) protect freedom of the press from misuse by Anti-Federalists

    (D) silence advocates of states' rights

    (E) weaken the Democratic-Republican Party

63. Martin Van Buren's belief during the Panic of 1837 that "the less the government interferes with private pursuits, the better for the general prosperity" could also be attributed to

    (A) Franklin Roosevelt

    (B) John Maynard Keynes

    (C) Theodore Roosevelt

    (D) Herbert Hoover

    (E) Grover Cleveland

64. Because of Cleveland's stand on tariffs and silver, which of the following groups generally supported him?

    (A) Western farmers and miners

    (B) Eastern big business

    (C) Eastern big business, farmers, shop owners, and workingmen

    (D) Southern Democrats

    (E) Southern and Western Democrats

65. Which of the following statements best describes the United States at the end of the nineteenth century?

    (A) The nation had shifted from an agrarian, rural economy to an industrial, urban one.

    (B) The development of a vast transportation system was a major factor in the industrialization of the Midwest.

    (C) The closing of the frontier marked the end of the era of manifest destiny.

    (D) Cities had undergone a vast change with the growth of urban services and infrastructures.

    (E) Widespread use of the telegraph and telephone had created a giant communications network that linked the nation.

GO ON TO THE NEXT PAGE ▶

66. All of the following are true about Latinos' experiences in World War II EXCEPT

    (A) unlike African Americans, Latinos fought in integrated units

    (B) Latino youths were the target of Zoot Suit riots in several major U.S. cities

    (C) Puerto Ricans were not allowed to enlist in the U.S. armed forces

    (D) through the bracero program, Mexicans were brought to the United States to work in agriculture.

    (E) Latinos and Latinas found work in defense industries as a result of the Fair Employment Practices Commission

67. Which of the following is NOT true about the establishment of NATO?

    (A) NATO was based on the principle of collective security.

    (B) The first commander of NATO's forces was U.S. General Dwight Eisenhower.

    (C) The United States supplied most of the money, arsenal, and troops for defense.

    (D) Nuclear weapons were not part of NATO's arsenal.

    (E) The Soviet Union established the Warsaw Pact to counterbalance NATO.

68. "I have never been a quitter. To leave office before my term is completed is abhorrent to every instinct in my body, but as president I must put the interests of America first. America needs a full-time president and a full-time Congress, particularly at this time, with the problems we face at home and abroad."

    This statement was most probably made by

    (A) Franklin Roosevelt

    (B) Bill Clinton

    (C) Andrew Johnson

    (D) Richard Nixon

    (E) Lyndon Johnson

69. What policy of the Federal Reserve Board to curb inflation in the late 1970s resulted in a severe business recession?

    (A) The Fed "primed the pump."

    (B) The Fed took no action.

    (C) The Fed raised interest rates.

    (D) It imposed a windfalls-profit tax.

    (E) It discouraged borrowing.

70. The most significant result of the French and Indian War was that

    (A) France gave Spain the Louisiana Territory in payment for its debts

    (B) France lost its remaining territories in North America

    (C) the Native Americans in the Ohio Valley lost their French allies

    (D) the colonists learned to work together and realized the benefits of cooperation

    (E) Pontiac's Rebellion

71. Which of the following was NOT true of the British position in the American Revolution?

    (A) The war was unpopular in Great Britain.

    (B) The hit-and-run tactics of the Americans made it difficult for the British to plan and execute their strategies.

    (C) The British were well supplied by both their navy and by Loyalist farmers.

    (D) Secure in their empire, the British were able to focus their resources and attention on the American Revolution.

    (E) The British had a well-trained army led by professional soldiers.

PRACTICE TEST 1—*Continued*

Question 72 refers to the following table.

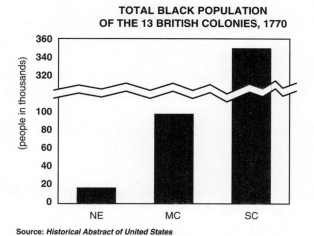

TOTAL BLACK POPULATION OF THE 13 BRITISH COLONIES, 1770

Source: *Historical Abstract of United States*

72. The above table best supports which of the following statements?

   (A) One in five people in the British colonies in 1780 were of African descent.

   (B) The number of blacks represented on the graph includes both free and enslaved persons.

   (C) Whereas there were few plantations in the Southern Colonies in relation to the overall population, plantations accounted for most of the black population.

   (D) Fewer blacks worked on farms in the Middle Colonies than in New England because of the climate of the Middle Colonies.

   (E) Automated cotton agriculture accounted for the vast numbers of slaves in the Southern Colonies.

73. The major reason Great Britain agreed to relinquish its claim to territory between the 49th parallel and the Columbia River was that

   (A) most of the beaver in the area had been trapped out

   (B) the United States did not want to fight Great Britain and Mexico

   (C) the British government wanted to end the Hudson's Bay Company's monopoly on the fur trade

   (D) U.S. settlers were moving into the area, staking out claims, and challenging the British

   (E) beaver hats had gone out of fashion

74. The Webster-Hayne debate

   (A) centered on the issue of slavery

   (B) resulted in a rebuttal of the Freeport Doctrine

   (C) shifted from discussing a limit on Western land sales to the protective tariff

   (D) shifted from discussing a limit on Western land sales to states' rights and nullification

   (E) was settled in a compromise by the Force Bill

75. The system of laws and customs in Southern states from the 1800s to the 1950s that segregated African Americans from whites is known as

   (A) Jim Crow

   (B) black codes

   (C) *Plessy* v. *Ferguson*

   (D) New South

   (E) *de facto* segregation

GO ON TO THE NEXT PAGE ▶

76. All of the following are true about the report of the Nye Committee EXCEPT that it

    (A) contributed to Congress's resolve to look at ways to limit U.S. economic aid to belligerents

    (B) fed isolationist fears

    (C) was a factor in the passage of the Neutrality Acts of 1935, 1936, and 1937

    (D) was a factor in Roosevelt's adoption of the Good Neighbor Policy

    (E) blamed U.S. entrance into World War I on U.S. bankers and weapons manufacturers

77. "No matter how long it may take us to overcome this premeditated invasion, the American people in their righteous might, will win through to absolute victory. I believe that I interpret the will of the Congress and the people when I assert that we will not only defend ourselves to the uttermost but will make it very certain that this form of treachery shall never again endanger us."

    The above statements were made in response to

    (A) Pancho Villa's raids into the United States

    (B) the explosion of the *Maine* in Havanna harbor

    (C) the Japanese attack on Pearl Harbor and U.S. territories and bases in the Pacific

    (D) attacks by Boxers on U.S. leaseholds in China

    (E) German invasion of Poland

78. All of the following were elements of Ronald Reagan's policies EXCEPT

    (A) the Persian Gulf War

    (B) supply-side economics

    (C) the Iran-contra affair

    (D) the Tax Reform Act

    (E) increased deregulation of industry

79. Anglicanism was the established church in

    (A) Pennsylvania

    (B) Maryland

    (C) Massachusetts Bay

    (D) Connecticut

    (E) Georgia

80. In his Farewell Address, George Washington counseled Americans to avoid foreign alliances because

    (A) they would make it difficult to carry on trade with a nation at war with a U.S. ally

    (B) foreign alliances could lead to domestic insurrection over the issue of slavery

    (C) foreign alliances could lead to curbs on U.S. exports and an unfavorable balance of trade for the United States

    (D) the United States, in time, would be strong enough to choose its own course in foreign affairs without the need to rely on allies

    (E) foreign alliances could revive the issue of mercantilism

PRACTICE TEST 1—*Continued*

Question 81 refers to the following map.

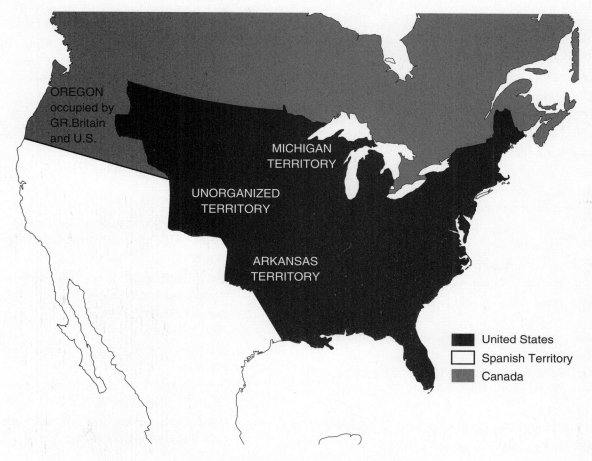

81. The above map shows the United States in

    (A) 1789
    (B) 1800
    (C) 1820
    (D) 1848
    (E) 1850

GO ON TO THE NEXT PAGE ➡

PRACTICE TEST 1—*Continued*

82. One notable way to become president has been to use a successful military career as a steppingstone to the White House. Which of the following presidents was a general and a military hero before becoming president?

(A) William Henry Harrison

(B) Jimmy Carter

(C) James Buchanan

(D) James K. Polk

(E) John Tyler

83. In the economy of the New South, it is generally true that

(A) most African Americans found jobs in factories

(B) discrimination against African Americans lessened because there was more wealth

(C) most African Americans found they had no place in the South and moved North

(D) most African Americans remained tenant farmers

(E) African Americans found it easier to find work in a variety of jobs

84. The Pendleton Act was passed to regulate

(A) the banking system

(B) civil service

(C) railroads

(D) tariffs

(E) foreign policy toward Latin America

85. Rebates and pooling were abusive practices of

(A) the canal industry

(B) the railroad industry

(C) the oil industry

(D) farmers on the Great Plains

(E) the steel industry

86. The Dawes Act can best be described as a

(A) well-organized effort to strip Native Americans of their land

(B) bureaucratic plan to resettle and civilize Native Americans based on a false assumption that all Native Americans were farmers

(C) well-meaning attempt to rectify the wrongs of U.S. Indian policy

(D) policy of extermination

(E) get-rich-quick scheme for U.S. Indian agents

87. The most significant change in higher education at the end of the nineteenth century was

(A) the introduction of courses in the social and natural sciences

(B) the widespread introduction of the elective system

(C) the founding of colleges devoted to technical training

(D) the building of state university systems, often through the Morrill Act

(E) coeducation as a common practice in colleges and universities

88. *Living Well Is the Best Revenge* would be an appropriate title for a literary work about which of the following movements?

(A) romanticism

(B) the Beat Generation

(C) realism

(D) the Lost Generation

(E) nationalism

PRACTICE TEST 1—*Continued*

89. In *Regents of the University of California* v. *Bakke* the Supreme Court ruled

(A) that affirmative action programs were unconstitutional

(B) that President Johnson had erred in issuing his executive order requiring those who received federal money to hire and promote members of minorities

(C) that while strict racial quotas were unconstitutional in determining admissions, race could be taken into consideration

(D) that bilingual education was not mandatory

(E) that the Civil Rights Act of 1964 prohibiting discrimination in hiring and firing, wages, and promotion based on sex, race, religion, or place of birth was constitutional

90. The major issue that cost George Bush the election in 1992 was

(A) his relaxed manner of conducting the presidency

(B) a backlash over the invasion of Kuwait

(C) his ineffective domestic war on drugs

(D) the inability to solve the Palestinian problem

(E) the economy

S T O P

If you finish before the hour is up, you may review your work on this test only. You may not turn to any other test in this book.

ANSWERS AND EXPLANATIONS

QUICK-SCORE ANSWERS

1. E	11. D	21. A	31. D	41. D	51. B	61. C	71. D	81. C
2. B	12. E	22. A	32. B	42. E	52. C	62. E	72. B	82. A
3. D	13. E	23. E	33. E	43. D	53. A	63. D	73. D	83. D
4. B	14. D	24. C	34. C	44. A	54. E	64. C	74. D	84. B
5. C	15. D	25. E	35. D	45. E	55. D	65. A	75. A	85. B
6. D	16. C	26. C	36. B	46. D	56. D	66. C	76. D	86. C
7. E	17. E	27. D	37. C	47. C	57. B	67. D	77. C	87. D
8. D	18. C	28. B	38. C	48. E	58. E	68. D	78. A	88. D
9. B	19. B	29. B	39. E	49. E	59. A	69. C	79. E	89. C
10. B	20. D	30. B	40. C	50. D	60. C	70. D	80. D	90. E

EXPLANATION OF ANSWERS

Test-Taking Strategy

The key words are primary *and* British government.

Test-Taking Strategy

When you see the words generally true, *look for a generalization, a statement that pulls together common themes or ideas behind a number of specific facts and examples.*

Test-Taking Strategy

The key words are the major stumbling block.

1. **The correct answer is (E).** The Mound Builders of the Midwest and Southeast built large mounds, some of which were used for burial purposes, choice (A). The Native Americans of the Northwest used the potlatch ceremony to display their wealth, choice (B). The Navaho of the Southwest became sheepherders, choice (C). The Iroquois of the Northeast Woodlands built long houses, choice (D).

2. **The correct answer is (B).** Spanish Florida was a problem because Native Americans staged raids into South Carolina from there and slaves escaped into La Florida, as it was known. Having a population center closer to La Florida would make it easier to defend British interests. Although choices (A), (C), and (D) were goals of the proprietors, they were not goals of the British government. Choice (E) is incorrect.

3. **The correct answer is (D).** While New England had the least diverse population, the Middle Colonies had the most diverse. The population of the Southern Colonies was mainly English and African. Choice (A) is incorrect because most immigrants to the colonies in the 1600s were English. Choice (B) is incorrect because religion was a factor in the immigration of other groups such as the Pennsylvania Dutch. By the time of the Revolutionary War, less than half the population was English, making choice (C) incorrect. The largest group of non-English immigrants to the colonies were German, not French, making choice (E) incorrect.

4. **The correct answer is (B).** The underlying premise of all Parliament's dealings with the colonies was the theory of virtual representation, that is, the House of Commons was sworn to represent every person, voter and nonvoter alike, in England and the empire. The

colonists, on the other hand, believed in direct or actual representation. Although choice (A) was true—and with good reason—it was
not the basic issue. Choices (C) and (D) were results of the conflict,
but neither was a cause. George III issued the Proclamation of
Rebellion, choice (E) to rally his loyal supporters in the colonies; it
was not a proclamation issued by the colonists as you may think
from the title.

5. **The correct answer is (C).** Choice (A) was a writer and farmer
who wrote *Letters from an American Farmer,* which described
rural life in the late eighteenth century. Jefferson, choice (B),
believed that the nation should be one of yeoman farmers. Calhoun,
choice (D), championed policies that would aid the agrarian South.
Choice (E) is incorrect.

6. **The correct answer is (D).** The United States bought Alaska in
1867 from Russia for $7.2 million. Choice (A) agreed to the mutual
disarmament of the Great Lakes by the United States and Canada.
Choice (C) refers to the Treaty of 1846, and choice (E), to the
settlement of the boundary between Maine and New Brunswick
Province.

7. **The correct answer is (E).** It was not until 1862 that African
Americans were allowed to enlist, choice (B). Lincoln had been
against black enlistment, fearing that it would drive the border states
into the Confederacy, and many whites considered it a "white man's
war." Even when they joined, African Americans had to protest to
be allowed to fight, choices (A) and (C), and to be paid the same as
white soldiers. Only 75 to 100 African Americans became officers,
choice (D).

8. **The correct answer is (D).** Clues are the phrases *working class*
and *employing class* and the aggressive tone of the quotation.
Choice (A) was made up largely of farmers, so it can be eliminated.
Choice (B) was a conservative labor union that believed in the use
of arbitration rather than strikes, so it can be eliminated. Choice (C)
was a cooperative farm organization and not a labor union. Choice
(E) can be eliminated because the CIO was not organized until
1935, and this question fits between the 1860s and 1919. The Industrial Workers of the World (IWW) was organized by socialist radicals
in 1905 and championed revolution rather than reform. Its slogan
was "Workers of the World, Unite!"

9. **The correct answer is (B).** Item III was part of Woodrow Wilson's
foreign policy, not Theodore Roosevelt's. Any answer choice with
item III as a part is incorrect, so choices (A) and (C) can be eliminated. Both items I and II were part of Roosevelt's foreign policy, so
choices (D) and (E) are only partially correct and, thus, incorrect.

10. **The correct answer is (B).** Choices (A), (B), (C), (D), and (E) are
all true about the Harlem Renaissance, but choice (B) incorporates
all the elements of the other four. It includes the music—jazz,
choice (A); the "New Negro," choice (B); the subject matter of
poets and novelists, choice (D); and the interest in the arts, choice

(E). In addition, it mentions the audience for the works of the Harlem Renaissance.

11. **The correct answer is (D).** The programs of the first "Hundred Days" were dedicated to relief and recovery by getting people back to work and stimulating the economy. Reform programs like Social Security, choice (D), came later.

12. **The correct answer is (E).** Nixon initiated and pursued a "two China" policy, People's Republic of China and Taiwan, choice (A), whereas his predecessors had not recognized the People's Republic of China. Nixon also took advantage of the Soviet Union's interest in relaxing tensions with the United States to pursue détente and treaties on nuclear weapons, choices (B) and (D). One of his campaign promises—"peace with honor"—had been to end the war in Vietnam, choice (C). Choice (E) was part of Truman's foreign policy.

13. **The correct answer is (E).** The Albany Plan of Union, proposed by Benjamin Franklin, called for choices (A), (B), (C), and (D), but the Crown would appoint the governor-general, so choice (E) is the correct answer. If the question had asked for the significance of the Albany Plan of Union, then choice (D) would have been correct.

14. **The correct answer is (D).** Hamilton's policies included choices (A), (B), (C), and (E), but not choice (D). Choice (A) was never acted upon by Congress because most members did not see the need for it. Choice (B) became law as the First Bank of the United States. An excise tax was passed on whiskey, choice (C), and resulted in the Whiskey Rebellion. The Assumption Bill accomplished choice (E), thus reassuring the new nation's creditors and potential creditors of its creditworthiness.

15. **The correct answer is (D).** Besides the map, logic would tell you that, as Westerners, Clay and Jackson would probably have carried the frontier states.

16. **The correct answer is (C).** Again, logic will tell you that as a New Englander, Adams would have won New England.

17. **The correct answer is (E).** After passage of the bill to begin construction of the National Road, later appropriations were defeated because of the issue of states' rights. Choice (C) aided industrial development by making possible large supplies of raw cotton to feed the growing capacity of textile mills. Choice (D) raised the cost of imported goods, thus making U.S.-made goods cheaper and more attractive to U.S. consumers.

18. **The correct answer is (C).** Clay wanted California to be admitted as a free state, and New Mexico and Utah to decide for themselves whether to allow slavery, so choice (C) is incorrect. Don't be fooled by choice (B). For much of his political life, Lincoln did not advocate the end of slavery; he held to the Republican Party line against extending slavery into the new territories. Stephen Douglas's policy, choice (A), was known as popular sovereignty. John C. Calhoun articulated the position of those who believed in states' rights,

Test-Taking Strategy

For not/except questions, ask yourself if the answer is true. If it is, cross it off and go on to the next answer.

Test-Taking Strategy

Be sure all parts of an answer are correct. A partially correct answer is a partially incorrect answer— and a quarter-point deduction.

choice (D). David Wilmot gave his name to the Wilmot Proviso, choice (E).

19. **The correct answer is (B).** Choice (A) is true, but the Fourteenth Amendment was not drafted and ratified until after the Civil Rights Act was passed over Johnson's veto. Because others shared Johnson's concern that the act was unconstitutional, Congress drafted the amendment. Choices (C), (D), and (E) are incorrect.

20. **The correct answer is (D).** The problem was overproduction, not underproduction, choice (D), combined with underconsumption, choice (C). Early in the 1920s, people had used installment credit, choice (B), to purchase big-ticket items, and by the end of the decade, the demand was decreasing but not the supply. Factories were turning out more than Americans could buy, and the high tariffs (Fordney-McCumber) along with the U.S.'s insistence on collecting its war debts, choice (E), decreased foreign markets. The amount of loans made to cover stocks bought on margin, choice (A), caused professional speculators to begin to sell their stocks, and the downward economic spiral began.

21. **The correct answer is (A).** Choice (D) was the goal of the Alliance for Progress, but the underlying purpose for the program and, thus, the best description for what it hoped to accomplish is choice (A). Choice (B) relates to the Iran-Contra affair under Ronald Reagan. Choice (C) relates to efforts under Richard Nixon to keep Salvador Allende from becoming president of Chile in 1970. While the United States did turn over control of the Panama Canal to Panama, it was not part of the Alliance for Progress and it occurred in 1999, not between the 1930s and late 1960s, based on the time frame of the question.

22. **The correct answer is (A).** Choice (A) had a political rather than economic purpose: to enforce the voting rights of African Americans. Choice (D) was part of the "war on poverty" because it gave federal aid to public and parochial schools to improve educational opportunities for all children, including the poorest and African Americans.

23. **The correct answer is (E).** Carter became the first Southerner, choice (A), elected president since Zachary Taylor. Choice (E) is the correct answer because in a time of high inflation, Carter campaigned on a promise not to decrease inflation by allowing unemployment to increase. Typically, increasing employment tends to make inflation rise rather than decline.

24. **The correct answer is (C).** The clue is *first colony in the Northern parts of Virginia.* Of the five choices, only the Pilgrims set out to establish a colony, Plymouth, choice (C), in northern Virginia. This quotation is from their Mayflower Compact. Another way to eliminate three choices is to consider that choices (B), (D), and (E) all had proprietors and, therefore, the colonists would not be drawing up an agreement about governing themselves. Choice (A) might

be true, but the clue and the fact that Plymouth was the first colony to establish self-government would rule out choice (A).

25. **The correct answer is (E).** Bacon's Rebellion helped convince Virginia planters that Africans enslaved for life would be less trouble than indentured servants, who might not be able to make a living after they were free. Both choices (A) and (B) were rebellions of enslaved blacks. The Stono Uprising, choice (A), occurred in 1739 near Charleston, South Carolina, and resulted in the deaths of twenty or thirty whites and most of the twenty slaves involved. In 1831, Nat Turner, choice (B), led some sixty slaves in rebellion in Virginia, and they killed some sixty whites before they were captured. The Whiskey Rebellion, choice (C), occurred on the Pennsylvania frontier in response to the excise tax on whiskey levied as part of Alexander Hamilton's fiscal program for the new nation. Shays's Rebellion, choice (D), occurred in Massachusetts during the Confederation period in response to high taxes and the practice of foreclosing and imprisoning debtors.

26. **The correct answer is (C).** Choice (A) refers to the *Proclamation of Rebellion* issued by George III. Choice (B) relates to Lee's Resolution, which was introduced into the Second Continental Congress and debated while the Declaration of Independence was being written. Choice (D) relates to the Circular Letter, and choice (E) to the Declaration of Rights and Grievances.

27. **The correct answer is (D).** *Marbury* v. *Madison* established the principle of judicial review, choice (A). The Constitution established choice (B). The first Congress created the office of Attorney General, but the Justice Department was not created until 1870, choice (C). Choice (E) is incorrect; Jackson ignored the Supreme Court's ruling in that case.

28. **The correct answer is (B).** For the time period, choice (A) is incorrect. Choice (C) relates to the Roosevelt Corollary issued by Theodore Roosevelt. Choice (D) refers to the Good Neighbor Policy of Franklin Roosevelt. Choice (E) is incorrect; Great Britain was interested in issuing a joint declaration with the United States, but Secretary of State John Quincy Adams convinced President James Monroe to issue the statement in the name of the United States alone.

29. **The correct answer is (B).** Slaves were not allowed to learn to read and write. The female children of plantation owners were taught at home, as were young male children. Older sons were sent away to boarding schools. Choices (A), (C), (D), and (E) are all useful tools for recreating the life of a Southern plantation.

30. **The correct answer is (B).** *Plessy* v. *Ferguson* is the post-Civil War (1896) landmark case establishing "separate but equal" facilities for African Americans. *Uncle Tom's Cabin,* choice (A), by Harriet Beecher Stowe, was an antislavery novel that provoked the South with its portrayals of the odious Simon Legree and the faithful Uncle

Tom. Choice (C) refers to John Brown's raid on the arsenal at Harper's Ferry and his plan to arm a slave insurrection in Virginia. Choice (D) set off the fiercest debate in Congress yet over the admission of slave and free states and resulted in the Compromise of 1850. Choice (E) was a continual source of ill feeling and occasional violence.

Test-Taking Strategy

Put your visual skills to work. The figures in this cartoon have mustaches and haircuts of the late nineteenth century rather than the 1920s or 1930s.

31. **The correct answer is (D).** Theodore Roosevelt is known as the "trust buster." McKinley, choice (B), running on a platform of high tariffs and the gold standard, was elected through the efforts of Republican party boss Mark Hanna and big business interests. Harding's policies of normalcy, choice (E), meant little government regulation of business, high tariffs, and strikebreaking, so choice (E) is illogical. Hoover, choice (A), was a traditional pro-business Republican. Franklin Roosevelt, choice (C), courted business in the first New Deal, but he abandoned it in the second phase to build a coalition of traditional opponents of big business for the Democratic Party.

32. **The correct answer is (B).** Silver, choice (C), as a political issue died out with the election of 1896. Choice (D) was the philosophy of big business philanthropists, so it is illogical as the tool of the president. Choice (E), a belief in the inevitability of social inequalities, would seem to contradict trust-busting. Choice (A) is irrelevant.

33. **The correct answer is (E).** Through Lend-Lease, Roosevelt was able to lend, sell, lease, and transfer to the Allies more than $50 billion in food, machinery, and supplies. The program continued through the war. Choice (A) was a Roosevelt policy of the 1930s to improve relations with Latin America; among other things, he agreed to a resolution that "no state has the right to intervene in the internal affairs of another." Choice (C) was one of several laws that banned the sale or transfer of arms to belligerents. Choice (D) was Theodore Roosevelt's addition to the Monroe Doctrine, which said that the United States could intervene to punish nations that were chronic wrongdoers in the Western Hemisphere.

34. **The correct answer is (C).** Item II is incorrect, so any answer that contains II is incorrect. That eliminates choices (A), (B), and (D). Medicaid is funded by both the federal government and the state governments, so choice (E) is incorrect. It pays for medical assistance for the poor—those under 65 and eligible for welfare as well as poor children, pregnant women, and the elderly who are not eligible for welfare.

35. **The correct answer is (D).** Not all presidencies are categorized by programs or calls to action. However, John F. Kennedy's administration, choice (A), was known as the New Frontier.

Test-Taking Strategy

The chronological shift indicates a new set of questions.

36. **The correct answer is (B).** Several of these responses are important and correct, but they do not relate to Connecticut. Choice (A) relates to Virginia, choice (C) to Rhode Island, and choice (D) to Massachusetts. Choice (E) is incorrect.

37. The correct answer is (C). The key words are *best be described.* There is some truth to both choices (B) and (D), but the most inclusive answer is choice (C). Choice (A) restates the argument that Jefferson made to Washington at the beginning of the French Revolution and with which Washington did not agree. Choice (E) is incorrect.

38. The correct answer is (C). Choice (E) is true but of less importance in the larger context than choice (C). In the beginning, native-born women workers lived in supervised boardinghouses, were served healthful meals, and had opportunities in the evening and on Sundays for recreation and to improve themselves. Wages were adequate for the time, and children were not employed. Choice (A) became true of factory owners in general in the late 1830s and 1840s, and choice (B) was also true of that period. Lowell workers organized unions in the 1840s, choice (D), but they were not successful.

39. The correct answer is (E). One clue word is *Massachusetts.* Horace Mann was the Secretary of the Massachusetts State Board of Education from 1837 to 1848 and campaigned for universal education. Although Dorothea Dix, choice (D), was also a reformer of the period, her work was in the area of mental health. Choices (A) and (B) can be eliminated because Franklin lived in the 1700s, and Wilson was the president of Princeton University in the 1900s before becoming president of the United States. While Douglass, choice (C), championed education, he would have no reason to single out Massachusetts.

40. The correct answer is (C). A newspaper editor coined the term in 1845, and it came to stand for a policy of expansionism. Choice (A), championed by Stephen Douglas, allowed residents of the new Western territories to decide for themselves whether to allow slavery. Social Darwinism, choice (B), applied Darwin's theories from the biological world to social institutions and explained social inequalities as the result of the survival of the fittest. Choice (D) is a partial explanation of the principle of popular sovereignty, choice (A). Choice (E) is incorrect.

41. The correct answer is (D). Although choice (E) was a contributing factor, the deal reached to make Hayes president, choice (D), was the direct cause of the end of Reconstruction. Choice (A) occurred once the military had moved out of Florida, South Carolina, and Louisiana. States that did not have reconstructed governments by 1870 had to ratify the Fifteenth Amendment as well as the Fourteenth, but choice (B) had no bearing on the end of Reconstruction, nor did choice (C).

42. The correct answer is (E). The British and German blockade of Venezuela, choice (A), in an attempt to collect debts for their citizens, was one cause of the Roosevelt Corollary. Choice (C) occurred under Coolidge; the troops had been sent originally under Taft to install a pro-U.S. government and force the

Test-Taking Strategy

The key phrase is best describes.

Test-Taking Strategy

The key word is direct.

Test-Taking Strategy

The key word is first.

Nicaraguans to accept a loan from New York bankers. Choices (B) and (D) are both incorrect.

43. **The correct answer is (D).** The movie by D.W. Griffith played on all the stereotypes and myths of Reconstruction and was picketed by the NAACP for its pro-Ku Klux Klan message. Choice (A) was the first talkie and showed Al Jolson in blackface as a minstrel, but neither it nor choice (B), with its stereotypes of happy enslaved African Americans, was rabidly racist. Choice (C) is a later film about the Scopes trial and the teaching of evolution, and choice (E) is the title of a book by Jack Kerouac of the 1950s Beat Generation.

44. **The correct answer is (A).** One in five Americans moved from one part of the country to another during World War II, usually for better job opportunities.

45. **The correct answer is (E).** Item II is a reference to the foreign policy of William Howard Taft and is, therefore, incorrect. Any answer choice with item II is incorrect, so choices (B), (C), and (D) can be eliminated. Choice (A) is incorrect because it is only partially correct.

46. **The correct answer is (D).** Choice (A) did not occur until after the Gulf of Tonkin Resolution was passed. Choice (B) is the real reason the North Vietnamese fired on one or possibly two U.S. destroyers. Choice (C) is the opposite of the true situation; the strongest support for the North Vietnamese was in the countryside. The Unites States used napalm, so choice (E) is incorrect.

47. **The correct answer is (C).** Rhode Island and Connecticut were the only two self-governing colonies. Unlike Maryland, choice (A); Pennsylvania, choice (B); Georgia, choice (D); and, for a time, New York, choice (E), the two were not governed by proprietors. Rhode Island and Connecticut had been founded by dissenters from Massachusetts Bay, and each colony elected its own governor and representatives to the upper and lower legislative houses.

48. **The correct answer is (E).** The power of the purse was the only hold that the colonies had over the royal governors' actions. The purpose of choice (A) was to give the East India Company a monopoly on the tea trade in the colonies. The significance of choice (B) was that it placed a tax on goods made and sold in the colonies, and, therefore, was not part of traditional mercantilist policies. The significance of choice (C) was in Great Britain's announcement that it would be strictly enforced; it meant that Great Britain was abandoning its policy of salutary neglect. Choice (D) tightened Great Britain's financial hold on the colonies by requiring that all taxes be paid in gold or silver and by forbidding the colonies to print their own money.

49. **The correct answer is (E).** The Second Continental Congress managed the government of the states during the early days of the war and oversaw the establishment of a new government under the Articles of Confederation, which took effect in 1781. Choice (B)

Test-Taking Strategy

Be sure all parts of an answer are correct. A partially correct answer is a partially incorrect answer—and a quarter-point deduction.

occurred because the delegates to the Continental Congress were afraid that any references to the slave trade would diminish Southerners' support.

50. **The correct answer is (D).** According to the Great or Connecticut Compromise, there would be two legislative houses. In the lower house, each state would have representation based on population, whereas in the upper house each state would have two representatives. Choice (A) refers to the compromise about counting slaves as part of the population, and choice (B), to a plan for allotting the same number of representatives for each state. Choice (E) was a plan to base representation on state population.

51. **The correct answer is (B).** Like Hamilton's financial program, Clay and Calhoun's American System favored choices (A), (D), and (E). The two Congressmen hoped that choice (C) would be an outcome of their program. Choice (B) is the correct answer because the first immigration law was not passed until 1875.

52. **The correct answer is (C).** The clues are *savages* and *12,000,000.* Choice (A) can be eliminated because Confederate secession does not have anything to do with Native Americans, whom the writer calls savages. If you did not know the population of the United States at any given time, you could still eliminate choices (D) and (E) because both came after 1850, the time frame for the next question. Time frame will also eliminate choice (A). The question prompt asks you to identify the answer that the quotation supported. Choice (B) ruled against the Cherokees' standing to bring a case to the Supreme Court but upheld their right to their lands, so choice (B) is incorrect because the writer of the quotation opposed the right of Native Americans to the land. Choice (C), then, is correct; the quotation was written by Andrew Jackson seeking support for the Indian Removal Act.

53. **The correct answer is (A).** By ruling in *Scott* v. *Sanford* that Congress had no power to forbid slavery in U.S. territories, the Supreme Court nullified both the Missouri Compromise by which Congress had determined which states would be free and which slave, and the principle of popular sovereignty. Choice (B), the Emancipation Proclamation issued by Abraham Lincoln, decreed that slaves in territories still held by Confederates on January 1, 1863, would be considered free. The Wilmot Proviso, choice (C), offered by Representative David Wilmot but not approved by Congress, sought to outlaw slavery in the new territories acquired from Mexico. Choice (D) completed the acquisition of territory from Mexico. Choice (E) is incorrect.

54. **The correct answer is (E).** According to the Congressional Reconstruction plan and the Fourteenth Amendment, former Confederate officials could not participate in the state constitutional conventions or vote. Any state that had not organized a new government by 1870 also had to ratify the Fifteenth Amendment to be readmitted.

55. **The correct answer is (D).** All five choices describe actual scandals of the post-Civil War period, but only choice (D) describes Crédit Mobilier. Choice (A) was known as the "salary grab." Belknap, choice (B), wanted to award the lucrative Indian trading rights at Fort Sill, Oklahoma, to a friend, but the current trader offered a bribe to both Belknap and the friend to keep his trading rights. "Boss" Tweed, choice (C), and his Tammany Hall machine were responsible for much of the graft and corruption in New York City government, including ballot stuffing, kickbacks for city jobs, and bribery. The "whiskey ring," choice (E), operated to blackmail distillers who found it cheaper to pay blackmail than to pay federal taxes on whiskey.

56. **The correct answer is (D).**

57. **The correct answer is (B).** The Open Door Policy recognized the rights of all nations to trade in China. Choice (A) related to the Western Hemisphere and reserved to the United States the right to police chronic malefactor nations. Trade with Asia may have resulted in choice (E), but choice (E) would have been an effect, not a cause. Choices (C) and (D) are unrelated.

58. **The correct answer is (E).** It was not until Lyndon Johnson's presidency that a national medical care program—for the elderly, the disabled, and the poor—was signed into law as Medicare and Medicaid. Choices (A), (B), (C), and (D) were part of Truman's Fair Deal program and were passed by Congress.

59. **The correct answer is (A).** The war was at a stalemate when Eisenhower took over the presidency from Truman. Eisenhower put pressure on the North Koreans to resume negotiations, and a truce was reached by mid-1953. Choice (B) was known as the Eisenhower Doctrine and stated that the United States would intervene if any Middle Eastern nation came under attack by Communist forces.

Test-Taking Strategy

Knowing the time frame will help you eliminate choice (E).

60. **The correct answer is (C).** Although the facts in choices (A) and (B) are true, neither is the main reason that England became a major power. The defeat of the Spanish Armada greatly hindered Spain's ability to keep English ships off the seas. Knowing that the trans-Atlantic triangular trade did not begin until the 1600s will help you eliminate choice (E). Choice (D) is irrelevant.

Test-Taking Strategy

The key words are major significance.

61. **The correct answer is (C).** Choices (A), (B), (C), and (D) are true, but choice (D) does not relate to the delegated powers, so it can be eliminated. Of the other three choices, choices (A) and (B) are very specific. Choice (C) is a general view of delegated powers and, thus, a better answer. Choice (E) is the opposite of what the Tenth Amendment says. All powers not specifically delegated to the federal government reside with the states.

Test-Taking Strategy

The key word is unstated.

62. **The correct answer is (E).** Choice (A) was the stated purpose of these acts, but choice (E) was the Federalists' underlying goal. The acts were aimed at French immigrants, most of whom joined the Democratic-Republican Party that favored U.S. intervention in the

European wars on the side of France. Federalists may have used choice (C) as a rationalization, but the Sedition Act interfered with both the freedom of the press and freedom of speech. Both choices (B) and (D) are incorrect.

63. **The correct answer is (D).** As the Depression worsened, Hoover followed his theory of "rugged individualism" and "decentralized local responsibility." Franklin Roosevelt, choice (A), on the other hand, with the advice of Keynes, choice (B), believed in "priming the pump"—putting government money into the economy to provide relief and jobs. Theodore Roosevelt, choice (C), as a progressive, also believed that government should help people. As the Panic of 1893 worsened, Cleveland, choice (E), accepted the offer of J.P. Morgan and a group of bankers to lend the federal government money to shore up the sagging dollar.

Test-Taking Strategy

In choosing an answer with multiple elements, be sure all the elements are correct.

64. **The correct answer is (C).** First, you need to know that Cleveland opposed "free and unlimited silver," which choice (A) supported. Choice (B) is only partially correct. The groups in choice (C) feared unlimited silver coinage as a Western threat to stability and supported Cleveland. Choices (D) and (E) supported the Populist program of silver and cheap money.

Test-Taking Strategy

The key words are best describes.

65. **The correct answer is (A).** While choices (A), (B), (D), and (E) are true of the period, choice (A) is the most inclusive choice. It contains the elements of the other three answers. Widespread transportation and communications networks, the growth of industries and markets for industrial goods, and large-scale urban development that provided workers—all transferred the center of power, influence, and wealth from farms to cities. Choice (C) is arguably true of the period but irrelevant to the question. Americans shifted from a belief in manifest destiny on the U.S. continent to a philosophy of imperialism, or worldwide colonialism.

66. **The correct answer is (C).** Puerto Ricans had been made U.S. citizens in 1917 under the Jones Act. Puerto Ricans served in World War I and another 65,000 served in World War II. Although choice (A) is true, Latinos often served in units that originated in states with high concentrations of Latinos, such as New Mexico.

67. **The correct answer is (D).** The United States committed nuclear weapons as well as conventional weapons, troops, and money, choice (C). But the nuclear missiles were under the sole authority of Eisenhower, who served as the first commander of NATO, choice (B).

Test-Taking Strategy

Be sure to read the quotations carefully. Underline or circle key words.

68. **The correct answer is (D).** Remember that the time frame for this question is the second half of the twentieth century, so that eliminates choices (A) and (C). Choice (B), Bill Clinton, always maintained he would not resign. While it is true that Johnson decided not to run for a second term, this statement does not fit with someone announcing his decision not to run for office. Johnson would still have been a full-time president for the remainder of his term. The reference to full-time president and full-time Congress is to the

amount of time and resources that the Watergate investigation was taking; this is from the resignation speech of Richard Nixon, choice (D).

69. **The correct answer is (C).** Raising rates normally lowers inflation, but for much of the 1970s, the action of the Fed caused stagflation. Inflation continued, and economic growth declined. Choice (A) means putting government money into circulation through loans and federal programs to get the economy moving. Only Congress can levy taxes, so choice (D) is incorrect. Choice (E) was an outcome of choice (C); rising interest rates discourages people from borrowing because of the amount of money they would have to pay back. Choice (B) is incorrect.

70. **The correct answer is (D).** All five choices are correct, but choice (D) is the most important in terms of the larger context of U.S. history. Spain had to cede the Louisiana Territory back to France at the end of the American Revolution, choice (A), so there is little long-term importance to this. Choice (B) was important to France, but not particularly to the British colonies or to the later United States, which dealt with Great Britain rather than France. Choice (C) was important to settlers on the frontier, but during the American Revolution and for a time afterwards, the British armed the Native Americans, so the long-term importance of choice (C) was minimal. Choice (E) was a contributing factor to the development of colonial resistance to Great Britain but not as lasting as the ability of colonists to work together.

71. **The correct answer is (D).** One of the reasons that the British imposed extra taxes on the colonies and began to enforce the Navigation Acts after the French and Indian War was to force the colonies to pay for the war. The British empire stretched around the globe, and the British government was faced with subduing and governing large parts of the world that did not wish to be governed as colonies. Its resources were overextended.

72. **The correct answer is (B).** The information in choices (A) and (C) are correct, but they do not relate to the information on the table. Choice (D) is incorrect. There were fewer blacks in New England than in the Middle Colonies because the climate and terrain of New England were unsuited to large-scale cash-crop agriculture. Time frame eliminates choice (E); the data on the table is for 1770, before the invention of the cotton gin.

73. **The correct answer is (D).** Choices (A), (D), and (E) are correct, but the most important reason why Great Britain agreed to a compromise was because it did not want to fight the United States. Choice (B) is a reason why the United States on the brink of the Mexican War did not want to fight Great Britain, but is irrelevant as a factor in Great Britain's decision. Choice (C) is incorrect.

74. **The correct answer is (D).** What began as a debate about limiting the sale of Western land in order to keep factory workers in the

Test-Taking Strategy

The key words are most significant.

Test-Taking Strategy

Read the answer choices carefully. On a quick reading, choice (B) might make sense until you realize that the question is asking about Great Britain, not the United States.

Northeast turned into a full-scale discussion of states' rights and nullification, with Webster upholding the Union. Choice (C) is partially correct in that the debate shifted to tariffs but then shifted again to states' rights, and that was the greater significance of the debate. Choices (A) and (B) are incorrect. The Force Bill, choice (E), did not represent a compromise and relates to a later tariff and secession attempt by South Carolina.

75. **The correct answer is (A).** The same name, "black codes," choice (B), was given to laws passed before and after the Civil War in the South to regulate the rights of blacks. After the Civil War, the laws were one cause of the imposition of Congressional or Radical Reconstruction. Choice (D) is the name given to the reconstructed South. Choice (E) is segregation that exists not by law but by custom and economic conditions; *de jure* segregation is segregation by law.

76. **The correct answer is (D).** Isolationism was strong in the United States in the 1930s, and the conflicts in Europe fed those fears, choice (B). Roosevelt adopted the Good Neighbor Policy in an attempt to better relations with other nations in the Western Hemisphere should war be declared, choice (D). His actions, however, were not a direct consequence of the Nye Report; they were a consequence of the policy of intervention that the United States had adopted earlier in the century.

77. **The correct answer is (C).** The question is placed between one about the 1930s and one about the 1980s, so choices (A), (B), and (D) can be eliminated because they deal with events in 1916, 1898, and 1900. Choice (E) can be eliminated because the quotation talks about an invasion, the American people, and "defend ourselves."

78. **The correct answer is (A).** The Persian Gulf War occurred during the term of Reagan's successor, George Bush. Supply-side economics, choice (B), and the Tax Reform Act of 1986, choice (D), are signature elements of Reagan's domestic policies.

79. **The correct answer is (E).** Established religion, in this sense, means the religion that is supported by the state. Pennsylvania, choice (A), was set up as a haven for Quakers, and there was no established religion. Maryland, choice (B), practiced religious tolerance. Congregationalism was the state-supported religion in Massachusetts Bay, while Connecticut had no established religion. Georgia was chartered by George II and became a royal colony. The Church of England is Anglican.

80. **The correct answer is (D).** Although choices (A) and (C) may seem reasonable, Washington was less concerned about trade than about the future of the nation. Choice (B) might be a possibility, except that in the late 1700s, slavery was not a very divisive issue. Choice (E) is illogical because the United States was an independent nation, not a colony.

Test-Taking Strategy

Knowing time frame would help you to eliminate choices (A), (B), and (D).

---

81. **The correct answer is (C).** If choice (A) were correct, the Spanish would still be in possession of the center portion of what would become the United States. If choice (B) were the correct answer, the French would now claim the central portion of the continent in place of the Spanish who ceded the area to French in 1800. Choices (D) and (E) would both show Texas as a state.

82. **The correct answer is (A).** Other generals and war heroes who became president are George Washington, Andrew Jackson, Zachary Taylor, Ulysses S. Grant, and Dwight Eisenhower. Jimmy Carter, choice (B), was a Navy officer before going into private business and serving as governor of Georgia. Choices (C), (D), and (E) were career government officials and politicians. Tyler succeeded Taylor as president when the latter died shortly after taking office.

83. **The correct answer is (D).** Choices (A), (B), and (E) are incorrect, and the opposite of what occurred. Some African Americans did find jobs as laborers or street cleaners, menial jobs that white men did not want. In some areas blacks were not allowed to work in factories. Blacks could not move off their tenant farms until they had paid off their debts. This was the time of lynch law and Jim Crow. The migration North began toward the end of 1800s, choice (C), but it was only a trickle compared to what occurred after 1910.

84. **The correct answer is (B).** As a result of the growth of the spoils system (begun by Andrew Jackson), the rampant corruption in the Grant administration, and the assassination of President Garfield by a disappointed office seeker, Congress passed the Pendleton Act, which authorized the Civil Service Commission and the reform of the system.

85. **The correct answer is (B).** The time frame for question 84 is the late 1800s, so the canal industry, choice (A), cannot be the correct response since the usefulness of canals was eclipsed by railroads in the 1850s. Logic says that choice (D) is incorrect because the farmers in the late 1800s were the victims of industry, not the perpetrators of abuses. A rebate was a refund to a favored shipper of part of the advertised rate that the shipper paid. Pooling was the practice whereby railroads in an area agreed to maintain high prices for shipping goods. Some pools even divided the profits among members' railroads. Choices (C) and (E) are incorrect.

86. **The correct answer is (C).** The Dawes Act was meant to end the extermination policy of the military, so choice (D) is incorrect. Some Indian agents turned the provisions of the act into choices (A) and (E), but that was not the intent of the law. Choices (B) and (C) are both true, but choice (C) is the more inclusive answer of the two and reflects the concerns of the reformers who pushed for the law.

87. **The correct answer is (D).** All five responses are correct, but choices (A), (B), (C), and (E) would not have been widespread without the building of state university systems, such as the University of California and Michigan State.

88. **The correct answer is (D).** The title is from a work about two members of the Lost Generation, Sara and Gerald Murphy, rich Americans whose only claim to fame was knowing and entertaining authors like Ernest Hemingway and F. Scott Fitzgerald. Romanticism, choice (A), is a literary and artistic style of the mid-nineteenth century that focused on emotion, intuition, imagination, and individualism. The "Beats," choice (B), were writers of the 1950s who protested what they saw as smug, self-satisfied, middle-class American life. Realism, choice (C), is a style of the late nineteenth century that described people in realistic detail. Nationalism, choice (E), inspired the cultural developments of the new nation in the early nineteenth century.

89. **The correct answer is (C).** The *Bakke* decision had a limited application and was not applied to all affirmative action programs, so choice (A) is incorrect. Choice (B) is incorrect; the decision did not overrule Johnson's executive order. Choice (D) is incorrect and does not relate to affirmative action. Choice (E) is incorrect; the constitutionality of the law was not questioned.

90. **The correct answer is (E).** Choice (A) made Bush popular, so choice (A) is incorrect, as is choice (B). Choices (C) and (D) are both true, but Bush was not the only president to have difficulty solving these problems. It was the rapidly building deficit, slowing economic growth, and Bush's reneging on his promise of "no new taxes" that cost him supporters.

PRACTICE TEST 2

While you have taken many standardized tests and know to completely blacken the ovals on the answer sheets and to completely erase any errors, you will need to indicate on the answer key which test you are taking. The instructions on the answer sheet will tell you to fill out the top portion of the answer sheet exactly as shown.

1. Print *U.S. HISTORY* on the line to the right under the words *Subject Test (print)*.

2. In the shaded box labeled *Test Code*, fill in four ovals: —Fill in oval 2 in the row labeled V.
    —Fill in oval 5 in the row labeled W.
    —Fill in oval 5 in the row labeled X.
    —Fill in oval C in the row labeled Y.
    —Leave the ovals in row Q blank.

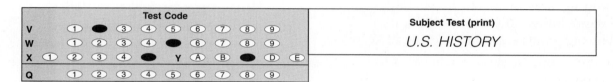

There are two additional questions that you will be asked to answer: How many semesters of U.S. history have you taken? Have you taken courses in government, economics, geography, psychology, sociology, and/or anthropology? The College Board is collecting statistical information. If you choose to answer, you will use the key that is provided and blacken the appropriate ovals in row Q. You may also choose not to answer, and that will not affect your grade.

When everyone has completed filling in this portion of the answer sheet, the supervisor will tell you to turn the page and begin. The answer sheet has 100 numbered ovals on the sheet, but there are only 90 (or 95) multiple-choice questions in the test, so be sure to use only ovals 1 to 90 (or 95) to record your answers.

GO ON TO THE NEXT PAGE ➤

PRACTICE TEST 2—*Continued*

Directions: Each of the questions or incomplete statements below has five suggested answers or completions. Choose the response that is best and then fill in the corresponding oval on the answer sheet.

1. Pueblo people adapted to the environment of the

   (A) Northeast Woodlands
   (B) Great Plains
   (C) Southeast
   (D) Southwest
   (E) Pacific Northwest

2. In writing an essay about the establishment of Massachusetts Bay Colony, all of the following points should be included EXCEPT

   (A) the colony began as a joint-stock company
   (B) Separatists were a major portion of the colony's population
   (C) the General Court was a representative body that governed the colony
   (D) the right to vote and to hold public office was limited to church members
   (E) the General Court passed the first set of laws in the English colonies

3. The Proclamation of 1763 contributed to growing tensions between the colonies and Great Britain primarily because the Proclamation

   (A) forbade settlers from moving into the land west of the Appalachians until treaties could be signed with the Native Americans
   (B) set the boundary between Canada and Maine, Vermont, and New York
   (C) outlawed land speculation in the trans-Appalachians but not the purchase of land by settlers
   (D) declared martial law on the Western frontier of the thirteen colonies
   (E) established the presence of a standing British army in the colonies

4. The views of which of the following men influenced the writing of the Declaration of Independence?

   (A) Thomas Paine
   (B) John Locke
   (C) John Milton
   (D) Alexis de Tocqueville
   (E) Edmund Burke

5. The structure and duties of which of the following is NOT described in detail in the Constitution?

   (A) House of Representatives
   (B) Senate
   (C) Supreme Court
   (D) federal court system
   (E) the presidency

PRACTICE TEST 2—*Continued*

6. Hamilton's financial program and the American System had all of the following in common EXCEPT

(A) money for internal improvements

(B) a protective tariff

(C) programs for each of the sections of the country in order to draw them together

(D) regulation of labor unions

(E) a national bank

7. Which of the following events contributed to the increase in westward migration primarily in the 1830s and 1840s?

(A) building of the transcontinental railroad

(B) the Gadsden Purchase

(C) completion of the Erie Canal

(D) completion of the Panama Canal

(E) the invention of interchangeable parts

8. Which of the following authors is correctly paired with a literary work?

(A) Henry David Thoreau: *Walden*

(B) James Fenimore Cooper: *The Scarlet Letter*

(C) Upton Sinclair: *Nature*

(D) Ralph Waldo Emerson: *The Jungle*

(E) Nathaniel Hawthorne: *Leather-Stocking Tales*

Question 9 refers to the following photograph.

9. All of the following are most likely true about the people in the picture EXCEPT that the workers

(A) illustrate the truth of the doctrine of Social Darwinism

(B) are recent immigrants

(C) are doing piecework

(D) are nonunion

(E) are working in a sweatshop

GO ON TO THE NEXT PAGE ➤

PRACTICE TEST 2—*Continued*

10. The cause of U.S. isolationism after World War I was primarily because of

    (A) the belief that Great Britain was strong enough to check any war advances by Germany and Japan

    (B) disillusionment with the results of World War I

    (C) a belief that World War I had been "the war to end all wars"

    (D) the desire to collect U.S. war debts and, therefore, an unwillingness to see the reality of the situation in Europe and Asia

    (E) the belief that neutrality would protect the nation

11. Which of the following was a direct consequence of U.S. involvement in Vietnam?

    (A) The United States ended diplomatic relations with China.

    (B) Nixon authorized an action that ended as the "Saturday Night Massacre."

    (C) Nixon authorized the Iran-Contra activities.

    (D) Congress passed the War Powers Act of 1973 over Nixon's veto.

    (E) The Cold War ended.

12. It is generally true that Native American cultures

    (A) combined hunting with some settled agriculture

    (B) had little or no trading network

    (C) did not make clay pots or other items that were breakable

    (D) were mainly nomadic hunters

    (E) had a variety of ways of providing food

13. The most significant effect of the Navigation Acts was

    (A) that they increased the price of goods coming into the colonies

    (B) that they ensured a supply of goods for England

    (C) that they shut out Dutch merchant ships

    (D) that they provided a monopoly for colonial tobacco growers

    (E) that they signaled an end to Britain's policy of salutary neglect

14. Which of the following statements is TRUE about Pinckney's Treaty?

    (A) Canada and the United States agreed to a mutual disarmament of the Great Lakes.

    (B) The United States received the right of deposit at New Orleans.

    (C) Native Americans were banished from the Upper Midwest.

    (D) It set a boundary between Maine and New Brunswick, Canada.

    (E) The British agreed to leave their forts in the Old Northwest.

15. Congress passed gag rules in 1836 to prevent

    (A) free blacks from testifying in court

    (B) publication of Frederick Douglass' *North Star*

    (C) the organization of suffragist groups

    (D) debate on antislavery petitions

    (E) filibusters

PRACTICE TEST 2—*Continued*

16. Which of the following best describes the principle of popular sovereignty used to deal with slavery?

(A) No state admitted after 1850 would be allowed to legalize slavery.

(B) Settlers within a territory had the right to determine for themselves whether the territory would be slave or free.

(C) A slave taken from a slave state to a free state was free.

(D) Congress as the representative of the people would decide whether a state would be free or slave.

(E) A territorial legislature could refuse to pass slave codes and, thus, keep slave owners out.

17. Which of the following writers used a style known as "local color" or "regional"?

(A) Stephen Crane

(B) Theodore Dreiser

(C) Mark Twain

(D) Joseph Pulitzer

(E) Thomas Eakins

18. The primary issue in Reconstruction about which Lincoln and Congress disagreed was

(A) Lincoln's veto of the Wade-Davis Bill

(B) Congress's division of the South into five military districts

(C) Congress's refusal to honor Lincoln's promise of "forty acres and a mule"

(D) Lincoln's recognition of state governments without Congressional approval

(E) Lincoln's assertion that Reconstruction was part of the war effort and, therefore, his responsibility as commander in chief

19. The principle of separate but equal was established by

(A) *Brown* v. *Board of Education*

(B) *Wesbery* v. *Sanders*

(C) *Plessy* v. *Ferguson*

(D) *Regents of University of California* v. *Bakke*

(E) *Heart of Atlanta Motel* v. *United States*

20. Which of the following was the direct cause of the Progressives' abandoning their support of President Taft?

(A) Taft's support of Speaker of the House "Uncle Joe" Cannon

(B) the annexation of Hawaii

(C) Taft's signing of the Payne-Aldrich Tariff

(D) Taft's selection of Richard Ballinger as head of the Department of the Interior

(E) the Taft administration's record in prosecuting antitrust suits against big business

21. Voter 1: He doesn't seem to care much for the little guy. Look at what he did to those veterans.

Voter 2: He talks about acting decisively if he's elected, but he's pretty vague about what he'll do.

Voter 3: I don't know if I believe that the problem is the American economy. It might be the aftermath of the war.

The above discussion most likely would have occurred during which presidential election?

(A) 1920

(B) 1928

(C) 1932

(D) 1948

(E) 1952

GO ON TO THE NEXT PAGE

PRACTICE TEST 2—*Continued*

22. Which of the following was a victory for organized labor?

    (A) Taft-Hartley Act

    (B) AFL strike against US Steel in 1919

    (C) Wagner Act

    (D) Sherman Antitrust Act

    (E) Bonus Army

23. In the 1950s, all of the following resulted in long-term social change EXCEPT

    (A) the development of rock and roll

    (B) the development of suburbia

    (C) *Brown* v. *Board of Education of Topeka*

    (D) shift from permissiveness to more traditional practices of child-rearing

    (E) the baby boom

24. Which of the following resulted in peace between Israel and Egypt?

    (A) *perestroika*

    (B) recognition of Palestine's right to exist

    (C) Camp David Accords

    (D) assassination of Anwar Sadat

    (E) invasion of Kuwait

25. The introduction of tobacco as a cash crop probably saved which colony from collapsing?

    (A) Massachusetts Bay

    (B) Pennsylvania

    (C) North Carolina

    (D) Virginia

    (E) Kentucky

Question 26 refers to the following chart.

State	Voting For	Voting Against
1. Delaware	30	0
2. Pennsylvania	46	23
3. New Jersey	38	0
4. Georgia	26	0
5. Connecticut	128	40
6. Massachusetts	187	168
7. Maryland	63	11
8. South Carolina	149	73
9. Rhode Island	34	32
10. New Hampshire	57	47
11. Virginia	89	79
12 New York	30	27
13. North Carolina	194	77

26. Which two states ratified the Constitution with the narrowest vote?

    (A) New York and Pennsylvania

    (B) Rhode Island and New Hampshire

    (C) Virginia and New Hampshire

    (D) New York and Rhode Island

    (E) New Hampshire and New York

PRACTICE TEST 2—*Continued*

27. How many states were needed to ratify the Constitution in order for it to become law?

(A) seven

(B) all thirteen states

(C) nine

(D) the four most populous states

(E) three quarters of the states

28. Passage of the Twelfth Amendment was a direct result of the

(A) controversy that arose when the election of 1824 was settled in the House of Representatives

(B) difficulties that resulted from not having separate presidential and vice presidential elections in the electoral college in the election of 1800

(C) revolution of 1800

(D) one-man, one-vote system of the electoral college

(E) loss of the 1888 presidential election by Grover Cleveland to Benjamin Henry Harrison

29. "We hold these truths to be self-evident; that all men and women are created equal. . . . Now, in view of this entire disfranchisement of one half of the people of this country, their social and religious degradation . . . and most fraudulently deprived of their most sacred rights, we insist that they have immediate admission to all the rights and privileges which belong to them as citizens of the United States."

This was most probably written in behalf of

(A) free blacks

(B) enslaved blacks

(C) women

(D) Native Americans

(E) Mexicans in the Southwest

30. Division of labor in factories resulted in

(A) the manufacture of interchangeable parts

(B) the factory system

(C) mass production of goods

(D) the Bessemer steel process

(E) development of the electric dynamo

31. All of the following were results of the Spanish-American War EXCEPT

(A) interest in having a U.S. naval presence in the Pacific as well as the Atlantic Ocean

(B) renewed interest in building a Panama Canal

(C) establishment of a protectorate in Cuba

(D) the Supreme Court ruling that unincorporated possessions, such as Puerto Rico, were not directed toward statehood

(E) the Monroe Doctrine was modified

32. In the election of 1912, Theodore Roosevelt wanted Progressives to abandon which of the following beliefs?

(A) The federal government should use its resources to aid the needy.

(B) The federal government should strike down all legal challenges to free-market competition.

(C) The tariff system should be reformed to aid workers.

(D) Monopolies are never in the public interest.

(E) The federal government should prohibit child labor through federal law.

GO ON TO THE NEXT PAGE

33. All of the following were criticisms of the nation's banking and currency system before enactment of the Federal Reserve Act EXCEPT

    (A) during crises, the banking system lacked stability

    (B) the amount of currency in circulation was not pegged to the investment needs of the country

    (C) the money supply should be backed by gold

    (D) no central bank set banking practices

    (E) Wall Street controlled too much bank capital

34. The Howard-Wheeler or Indian Reorganization Act was the LEAST successful in

    (A) raising the living standards of Native Americans

    (B) restoring tribal ownership to those reservation lands that had not been divided into individual parcels

    (C) returning local self-government to nations who wished it

    (D) ridding the reservations of squatters

    (E) re-establishing traditional beliefs, crafts, and customs

35. About of a third of the colonists were Loyalists. A major reason for their desire to maintain British rule was

    (A) fear among the wealthy that law and order would end with the end of British control

    (B) lack of belief in the Patriot cause

    (C) fear of a slave revolt across the South

    (D) fear by landowners of the loss of their property

    (E) fear of Native American attacks on frontier settlements

36. The two-party political system in the United States was primarily the result of

    I. the fight over ratification of the Constitution waged by the Federalists and the Anti-Federalists

    II. conflicts in Congress over Hamilton's financial proposals

    III. conflicts within Washington's Cabinet over Hamilton's financial proposals

    (A) I only

    (B) II only

    (C) III only

    (D) I and II only

    (E) II and III only

37. The most significant result of the invention of the cotton gin was

    (A) the mechanization of the process of cleaning the raw cotton once it was picked

    (B) the increase in the slave trade

    (C) an oversupply of cotton

    (D) the increase in cotton agriculture

    (E) the wearing out of the soil in the older Southern states

38. Both the Force Bill and the Tariff Act of 1833 were passed to deal with the crisis that developed over

    (A) the Webster-Hayne Debate

    (B) South Carolina's Ordinance of Nullification

    (C) *South Carolina Exposition*, published anonymously by John Calhoun

    (D) Tariff of Abominations

    (E) the Maysville Road veto

PRACTICE TEST 2—*Continued*

39. The Kansas-Nebraska Act nullified part of the

(A) Compromise of 1850
(B) Great Compromise
(C) Wilmot Proviso
(D) Missouri Compromise
(E) Dred Scott decision

40. Which of the following is NOT an accurate description of the Knights of Labor?

(A) The Knights championed the abolition of child labor.
(B) Women, African Americans, and immigrants were admitted.
(C) The Knights were organized into separate unions by crafts.
(D) Because of the Haymarket Riot, the Knights became identified with radicalism.
(E) The Knights advocated arbitration rather than strikes.

41. All of the following were "push" factors for Southern and Eastern European immigrations in the last half of the nineteenth century EXCEPT

(A) tenant farms too small to support a family
(B) financial panic and economic depression
(C) high tariffs on foodstuffs
(D) religious persecution
(E) industrial development

42. The significance of the Open Door Policy for the United States lay in its

(A) providing a use for the Philippines as a way station between China and the United States
(B) moving the American public away from isolationism and toward the view of the nation as a world power
(C) keeping Japan from annexing Formosa
(D) guarantees from leasehold nations that they would keep their Chinese ports open to all nations
(E) obtaining the right to build a railroad in China

43. The right to privacy was expanded in

(A) *Heart of Atlanta* v. *United States*
(B) *Roe* v. *Wade*
(C) Fourteenth Amendment
(D) Civil Rights Act of 1964
(E) Fair Credit Reporting Act of 1970

44. Why was the election of Ronald Reagan in 1980 of major significance?

(A) It demonstrated the importance of the economy in presidential elections.
(B) It signaled a shift among voters to conservatism.
(C) It reawakened interest in Richard Nixon's presidency.
(D) It was the first time a movie star had been elected president.
(E) It showed a weariness with Jimmy Carter's leadership style.

GO ON TO THE NEXT PAGE

45. Which of the following colonies established the principle that local communities have a duty under the law to establish schools?

    (A) Rhode Island
    (B) Connecticut
    (C) Georgia
    (D) Pennsylvania
    (E) Massachusetts

46. The western boundary of British territory in 1763 in what would become the United States was the

    (A) Ohio River
    (B) Pacific Ocean
    (C) St. Lawrence River
    (D) Mississippi River
    (E) Lake Superior

47. The significance of the Annapolis Convention lay in its

    (A) agreement on uniform trade regulations for the new states
    (B) decision to send troops to end Shays's Rebellion
    (C) ratification of the Northwest Ordinance
    (D) decision to request another convention to discuss the weaknesses of the Articles of Confederation
    (E) nomination of George Washington for president

Questions 48 and 49 refer to the following bar graph.

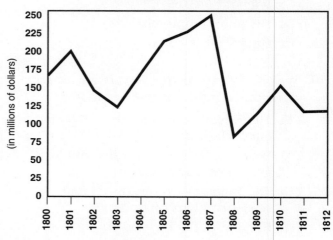

U.S. FOREIGN TRADE, 1800–1812

Source: *Historical Abstract of United States*

48. The drop in trade in 1808 can be attributed to

    (A) the Embargo Act
    (B) the actions of the Barbary states
    (C) Neutrality Proclamation
    (D) Nonintercourse Act
    (E) impressment of U.S. seamen

49. Which section would have suffered the most from the decline in trade?

    (A) Southern states
    (B) New England
    (C) frontier states
    (D) Middle Atlantic states
    (E) Old Northwest

PRACTICE TEST 2—*Continued*

50. "Fifty-four forty or fight!" was the rallying cry of

(A) those who wanted to annex Texas

(B) proslavery supporters in Kansas

(C) supporters of the Oregon Territory

(D) Copperheads

(E) supporters of a larger area for the Indian Territory

51. Agriculture prospered during the Civil War as a result of all of the following EXCEPT

(A) rising prices for farm products

(B) the Homestead Act of 1862

(C) development of laborsaving machines, such as the McCormick reaper

(D) expansion of railroads

(E) contraction of the money supply

52. The major reason for the economic rebuilding of the South was

(A) high railway rates for freight

(B) the alliance between Southern businessmen and Northern financiers

(C) that Southern factory owners paid lower wages than Northern owners

(D) the large number of African Americans who were employed as sharecroppers

(E) the Supreme Court's attitude toward separate but equal accommodations

53. The Gilded Age can best be described as a period of

(A) intense political activity by the presidents

(B) political agitation by Western farmers

(C) labor unrest and combinations of businesses

(D) unchecked use of the spoils system and unregulated business competition

(E) *laissez-faire* attitude by government toward business

54. "I stand for the square deal. But when I say that I am for the square deal, I mean not merely that I stand for fair play under the present rules of the game, but that I stand for having those rules changed so as to work for a more substantial equality of opportunity and of reward . . ."

The above statement was most likely the words of

(A) Theodore Roosevelt

(B) Ronald Reagan

(C) Franklin Roosevelt

(D) Harry Truman

(E) John F. Kennedy

55. The most significant result of the Bonus Army March was the

(A) passage in 1936 of a law allowing World War I veterans to cash in their bonus certificates nine years early

(B) show of support that veterans received from the active army

(C) image it created of Hoover's apparent disregard for human suffering

(D) additional money the Reconstruction Finance Corporation gave to state governments for relief efforts

(E) demolition of the veterans' Hooverville

56. An important work that contributed to the awareness of the need for the "war on poverty" was

(A) Michael Harrington's *The Other America*

(B) Rachel Carson's *Silent Spring*

(C) Ralph Nader's *Unsafe at Any Speed*

(D) Hinton Helper's *The Impending Crisis in the South*

(E) John Kenneth Galbraith's *The Affluent Society*

GO ON TO THE NEXT PAGE ➤

PRACTICE TEST 2—*Continued*

57. Between 1820 and 1997, the largest number of immigrants to the United States have been

(A) Irish

(B) German

(C) Mexican

(D) Italian

(E) Chinese

58. Both the Democrats and the Republicans nominated presidential candidates in the twentieth century who did not represent the mainstream of political thought. Which of the following pairs of candidates were considered radical nominees by the majority of Americans?

(A) Barry Goldwater and George McGovern

(B) Richard Nixon and Jimmy Carter

(C) Thomas Dewey and John F. Kennedy

(D) Richard Nixon and Lyndon Johnson

(E) George Bush and Lyndon Johnson

59. All of the following statements about colonial politics are true EXCEPT

(A) the legislatures controlled taxes and expenditures

(B) voting rights were limited to white male property owners

(C) most colonies had bicameral legislatures

(D) each colony elected its own governor

(E) governors had limited authority

60. The weakening of the position of established churches was a significant result of

(A) the splitting off of groups of Congregationalists into new churches

(B) the temperance movement

(C) transcendentalism

(D) the Great Awakening

(E) the opening of institutions of higher education

61. The intent of the First Continental Congress was primarily to

(A) stir up among the colonists the desire to separate from Great Britain

(B) establish Committees of Correspondence

(C) oversee the conduct of the war

(D) revive the nonimportation agreements

(E) demand the colonists' rights from Great Britain within the framework of British law and government

62. Which of the following is NOT true about the election of 1828?

(A) Property qualifications for voting had eased since the beginning of the nation so that more men were able to vote in 1828 than in previous elections.

(B) Small farmers crossed sectional lines to vote for Jackson.

(C) Jackson was the first president who was not from the wealthy elite of the Eastern seaboard.

(D) Jackson's reputation as a self-made man appealed to small business owners.

(E) Southern plantation owners did not vote for Jackson because of a personal dislike for the man.

63. In the presidential election of 1844, the principal issue was

(A) the qualifications of James K. Polk

(B) manifest destiny

(C) slavery

(D) the annexation of Texas

(E) Clay's refusal to promise to go to war against Mexico

PRACTICE TEST 2—*Continued*

Question 64 refers to the following map.

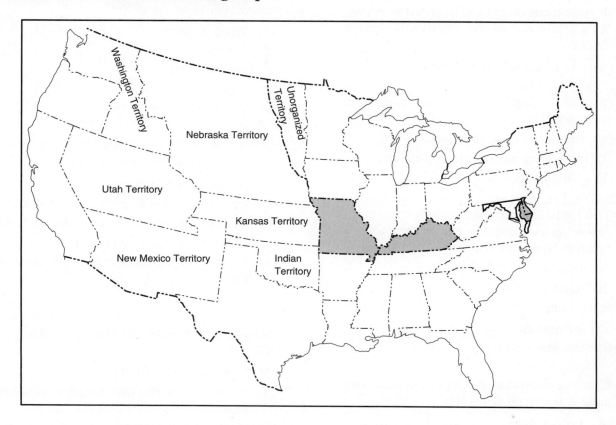

64. The four states shown on the map were

(A) the last four states to secede

(B) the so-called border states that remained in the Union

(C) the first four states to have reconstructed governments after the war

(D) the only four states in which slaves were freed by the Emancipation Proclamation

(E) states represented by Copperheads in Congress

GO ON TO THE NEXT PAGE

65. All of the following contributed to the development of the cattle industry in the West at the end of the nineteenth century EXCEPT

    (A) the replacement of longhorns by Herefords
    (B) the fencing in of the open range with barbed wire
    (C) the network of railroads
    (D) new methods of meat processing
    (E) the Morrill Act

66. The United States acquired which of the following as a result of the treaty ending the Spanish-American War?

    (A) Hawaii
    (B) Alaska
    (C) Panama
    (D) Hispaniola
    (E) the Philippines

67. Using economic means to achieve military aims was the purpose of

    (A) Lend-Lease
    (B) the Good Neighbor Policy
    (C) the Works Progress Administration
    (D) the Roosevelt Corollary
    (E) the Glass-Steagall Banking Act

68. The purpose of Freedom Summer was to

    (A) call attention to segregation on interstate buses and in bus terminals in the South
    (B) protest the Vietnam War
    (C) register black voters in the South
    (D) call attention to the segregation of public facilities in the South
    (E) prepare students to integrate Southern schools

69. The colony that recognized the land rights of Native Americans was

    (A) Massachusetts
    (B) Virginia
    (C) Pennsylvania
    (D) New Jersey
    (E) Maryland

70. In the early 1700s, the Spanish decided to establish settlements in Texas to

    (A) control the Apache
    (B) keep British from settling the Plains
    (C) keep the French from claiming the area
    (D) convert the Native Americans
    (E) provide steppingstones into the interior for expeditions to find Cibola

71. All of the following are true about the status of women in the mid-nineteenth century EXCEPT

    (A) women could not vote
    (B) women were discouraged from speaking in public
    (C) teaching was generally the only profession open to women
    (D) single women could not own property, but married women could
    (E) mothers had no legal rights to their children

PRACTICE TEST 2

PRACTICE TEST 2—*Continued*

72. Andrew Jackson opposed the Second Bank of the United States primarily because

(A) he believed the bank concentrated too much power in the hands of a few wealthy men in the Northeast

(B) he believed the bank did not provide a sound basis for a national currency

(C) the bank would not accept federal deposits

(D) he believed the bank created an economic climate that fostered land speculation

(E) the bank closed state banks, known as "pet banks," run by Jackson's supporters

73. The Freeport Doctrine of Stephen Douglas

(A) disagreed with the Dred Scott decision

(B) failed to address the rights of slave owners

(C) stated that a territorial legislature could discourage slavery by failing to pass slave codes

(D) restated the Republicans' position that slavery should not be allowed to spread

(E) repudiated popular sovereignty

74. The most significant aspect of state government under Radical Reconstruction was the

(A) physical rebuilding of the South

(B) establishment of statewide public education systems

(C) end of the plantation economy

(D) extension of civil and political equality to African Americans

(E) establishment of a system of railroads across the South

GO ON TO THE NEXT PAGE

Questions 75 and 76 refer to the following cartoon.

75. Which of the following statements best supports the message of the cartoon?

(A) Too many people are coming to the United States.

(B) The Statue of Liberty looks as if she is afraid of getting her skirt dirty.

(C) More people should be allowed to enter.

(D) The United States is becoming a dumping ground for Europe's unwanted people.

(E) The Statue of Liberty looks as if she wants to go back to France.

76. Which groups were experiencing the most restrictions on immigration in the late nineteenth and early twentieth centuries?

(A) Asians

(B) Southern Europeans

(C) Eastern Europeans

(D) Mexicans

(E) Southern and Eastern Europeans

PRACTICE TEST 2—*Continued*

77. ". . .[I]n the battle with the slum we win or we perish. There is no middle way. We shall win, for we are not letting things be the way our fathers did. But it will be a running fight, and it is not going to be won in two years, or in ten, or in twenty. For all that, we must keep on fighting, content if in our time we avert the punishment that waits upon the third and fourth generation . . ."

The person who wrote these words would most likely have been a

(A) Social Darwinist
(B) supporter of the "Gospel of Wealth"
(C) Populist
(D) Post-Modernist
(E) supporter of the gold standard

78. The fear of communism that McCarthyism spurred led to all of the following EXCEPT

(A) charges of communism in the U.S. Army
(B) the National Origins Act
(C) the Alger Hiss case
(D) charges of communism in high places in the government
(E) the blacklisting of supposed Communists in the movie industry

79. The meaning of "black power" can be best characterized as

(A) a call for separatism
(B) a demand for equality
(C) a political slogan with little meaning outside the African American community
(D) an appeal to black pride and for black leadership
(E) a variation on Garvey's black nationalism

80. The disagreement between the thirteen British colonies and Great Britain revolved around the issue of taxation. The two opposing theories were

(A) popular sovereignty and virtual representation
(B) direct representation and conquered provinces
(C) virtual representation and direct representation
(D) conquered provinces and rebellion of individuals
(E) popular sovereignty and rebellion of individuals

81. A number of Native American nations joined the British in the Revolutionary War primarily because the

(A) British promised them freedom
(B) Americans had broken the Iroquois Confederation
(C) British promised to leave the Ohio Valley if they won the war
(D) British enlisted Native Americans into the British army
(E) colonists opposed the Proclamation of 1763

GO ON TO THE NEXT PAGE ➡

PRACTICE TEST 2—*Continued*

82. The stated reason that the Mexican government gave for restricting the settlement of Americans in Texas was

(A) the settlers had brought slaves with them, which was in violation of Mexican law

(B) American settlers had attacked General Santa Anna's forces at the Alamo

(C) the U.S. government was agitating for control of East Texas

(D) Mexico was concerned that the settlers would demand independence

(E) Stephen Austin had protested the Mexican government's decision to collect customs duties on trade across the Texas-U.S. border

83. All of the following presidents acquired territory for the United States EXCEPT

(A) Andrew Jackson

(B) William McKinley

(C) James K. Polk

(D) James Monroe

(E) Andrew Johnson

84. The upturn in the economy around 1880 was significant because it

(A) put an end to lobbying for expansion of the currency system

(B) renewed pressure for free and unlimited coinage of silver

(C) resulted in passage of the Bland-Allison Act

(D) caused the decline of the Greenback Party

(E) demonetized silver

85. A person who agreed with the concept of the Talented Tenth would most likely have NOT agreed with

(A) Booker T. Washington

(B) George Washington Carver

(C) W.E.B. Du Bois

(D) Herbert Spencer

(E) Horace Mann

86. Which of the following was Theodore Roosevelt's most significant use of his "big stick" policy?

(A) The United States established a protectorate in Cuba after the Spanish-American War.

(B) The United States sent marines to occupy Veracruz and keep President Huerta from receiving weapons from Germany.

(C) Roosevelt legitimized the "big stick" policy by issuing the Good Neighbor Policy toward Latin America.

(D) The United States supported Panamanian rebels in their revolt against Colombia.

(E) The United States intervened in the internal affairs of the Dominican Republic when that nation could not repay its foreign debts.

87. Which of the following was NOT a result of Andrew Mellon's economic policies?

(A) Taxes took a disproportionate share of the wages of middle- and lower-class wage earners.

(B) The lack of places to invest large amounts of money contributed to an overheated stock market.

(C) The high tariff reduced markets for U.S. goods.

(D) A higher proportion of taxes was paid by the wealthy.

(E) Corporations and the rich accumulated large amounts of capital for investment.

PRACTICE TEST 2—*Continued*

88. Which of the following is NOT true about the Washington Conference?

    (A) The conference gave Americans a false sense of peace and security.

    (B) Through the Four-Power Treaty, the signatories agreed to respect one another's possessions in the Pacific.

    (C) The conference lessened the tensions in the Pacific in the short term.

    (D) Through the Nine-Power Treaty, the signatories agreed to respect one another's trading rights in China.

    (E) Agreements were reached on limiting land forces and the building of smaller warships like submarines.

89. Federal personal income taxes are

    (A) proportional
    (B) regressive
    (C) progressive
    (D) proportional and regressive
    (E) progressive and proportional

90. Who are the only two vice presidents to have gained office through the Twenty-Fifth Amendment?

    (A) Lyndon Johnson and Gerald Ford
    (B) Nelson Rockefeller and Harry Truman
    (C) Gerald Ford and Nelson Rockefeller
    (D) Theodore Roosevelt and Lyndon Johnson
    (E) Lyndon Johnson and Harry Truman

S T O P

If you finish before the hour is up, you may review your work on this test only. You may not turn to any other test in this book.

ANSWERS AND EXPLANATIONS

QUICK-SCORE ANSWERS								
1. D	11. D	21. C	31. E	41. E	51. E	61. E	71. D	81. E
2. B	12. E	22. C	32. D	42. B	52. B	62. E	72. A	82. A
3. A	13. E	23. D	33. C	43. B	53. D	63. B	73. C	83. A
4. B	14. B	24. C	34. A	44. B	54. A	64. B	74. D	84. A
5. D	15. D	25. D	35. A	45. E	55. C	65. E	75. D	85. A
6. D	16. B	26. D	36. E	46. D	56. A	66. E	76. A	86. D
7. C	17. C	27. C	37. B	47. D	57. B	67. A	77. B	87. D
8. A	18. E	28. B	38. B	48. A	58. A	68. C	78. B	88. E
9. A	19. C	29. C	39. D	49. B	59. D	69. C	79. D	89. C
10. B	20. D	30. C	40. C	50. C	60. D	70. C	80. C	90. C

EXPLANATION OF ANSWERS

1. **The correct answer is (D).** So named by the Spanish because they lived in villages (*pueblos*), Pueblo people still live in the Southwestern United States. Descended from the Anasazi cliff dwellers, the Pueblos were and continue to be sedentary farmers with great skill in basket weaving and pottery.

2. **The correct answer is (B).** Separatists were another name for the Pilgrims who settled Plymouth Colony south of Massachusetts Bay. The Pilgrims wished to separate themselves from the Church of England, while the Puritans wanted to purify the Church of practices they considered too close to Catholicism. While the General Court was a representative governing body, choice (C), the number of those who could vote and hold office was greatly limited, choice (D). In 1641, the General Court passed the Body of Liberties, the first set of laws in the English colonies, choice (E).

3. **The correct answer is (A).** Choices (B), (C), and (D) are incorrect. Choice (E) may sound familiar but is not quite correct. Pontiac's Rebellion, which resulted in the Proclamation of 1763, convinced the British that a standing army was needed in the colonies.

Test-Taking Strategy

Knowing time frame would have helped you eliminate choice (D). De Tocqueville wrote about the new nation in the 1830s, not about the colonies.

4. **The correct answer is (B).** Locke was an English philosopher whose works greatly influenced the Enlightenment. In writing the Declaration of Independence, Thomas Jefferson used Locke's theories of natural rights and the social contract. Choice (A), Thomas Paine, author of *Common Sense* and *The Crisis,* was influential in creating public support for the Revolution. John Milton, choice (B), was a poet and Puritan supporter in England in the 1600s. This is a distracter because his name probably seemed familiar to you.

Choice (D), Alexis de Tocqueville, was a French politician and visitor to the United States who wrote *Democracy in America* giving his observations of the country. Choice (E), Edmund Burke, was an Anglo-Irish politician and statesman who supported the colonies in the Parliament.

5. **The correct answer is (D).** The Constitution has only three sections and five clauses about the judicial branch of the government. In Section 1 on the federal courts it says only that "The judicial power of the United States shall be vested in one Supreme Court, and in such inferior courts as the Congress may from time to time ordain and establish." The Judiciary Act of 1789 filled in the structure of the federal court system.

6. **The correct answer is (D).** Labor unions were in their infancy at the beginning of the new nation.

7. **The correct answer is (C).** The Erie Canal linked New York to the Upper Midwest and by moving people and goods quickly and cheaply helped to stimulate the economic and physical development of both areas. Choice (A) was not begun until the 1860s and not completed until 1869. Choice (B) refers to the land the United States bought from Mexico in order to have a southern route for a transcontinental railroad. Choice (D) is incorrect; it was not built until the early 1900s. Choice (E) is incorrect, because in the 1830s and 1840s mass production had no relation to the available means of transportation.

8. **The correct answer is (A).** Thoreau was a writer, philosopher, and naturalist of the Transcendentalist movement. *Walden* relates his reflections on living alone with nature. The correct pairings are Cooper and *Leather-Stocking Tales,* Sinclair and *The Jungle,* Emerson and *Nature,* and Hawthorne and *The Scarlet Letter.* Cooper is important because he was one of the first novelists of the new nation and used themes from colonial history to build a national identify in literature. Sinclair was a muckraker, and Emerson, a transcendentalist and friend of Thoreau. Hawthorne, too, used themes from the colonial past and the new nation in his novels.

9. **The correct answer is (A).** Social Darwinism was a theory of the nineteenth century that sought to explain social inequalities by Darwin's theory of survival of the fittest. The workers in the photograph are most likely recent immigrants, doing piecework in a nonunion sweatshop, choices (B), (C), (D), and (E).

10. **The correct answer is (B).** Americans were disillusioned by the quarrels among European nations that occurred after World War I (known as the Great War), the tariff wars, and the Europeans' failure to disarm. The Nye Committee's report on the huge wartime profits by U.S. bankers and munitions makers was another cause of disillusionment. While choice (C) was the belief of many people, it was not a cause of isolationist feelings. Choice (A) is incorrect. Choice (D) is incorrect, although many in government and outside it

Test-Taking Strategy

Educated guessing could help you eliminate all the choices but (C).

Test-Taking Strategy

For a not/except question, ask yourself if the answer is true. If it is, cross it off and go on to the next answer.

insisted on collecting war debts and therefore, added to the world-wide depression. Choice (E) may have been a result of isolationism, but it was not a cause.

11. **The correct answer is (D).** In an effort to curb the "imperial presidency" and regain some of its power, Congress passed this bill giving the president 48 hours to notify Congress after sending combat troops abroad or engaging in military action; if Congress did not agree, the president had 60 days to withdraw the troops. Choice (B) is true; the attorney general and then his top assistant resigned before Nixon was able to find a Justice Department official willing to fire special prosecutor Archibald Cox. However, this was in relation to Watergate, not Vietnam. The United States recognized China during Nixon's administration, so choice (A) is incorrect. Iran-Contra, choice (C), occurred during the Reagan administration, and choice (E), during the Bush administration.

12. **The correct answer is (E).** There were a variety of ways that Native Americans supplied food. The Native Americans in the Pacific Northwest and along the Atlantic Coast, for example, fished. The nomadic Plains Native Americans hunted and gathered their food. Sedentary peoples in the Southwest, like the Pueblo and the Navaho, trapped small animals as well as farmed. While choice (A) is true, choice (E) is a more inclusive answer. Choices (B), (C), and (D) are incorrect. Many groups traded within their own nations, across nations, and with the French, British, Russians, and Americans. Choice (C) is mainly true of nomadic peoples because these items were likely to break as the people moved about, but sedentary peoples, such as the Pueblo, made pottery. Some nations were nomadic hunters, but some were not.

13. **The correct answer is (E).** All five choices are correct, but choice (E) was the most important in terms of consequences for the colonists. Imposition of the Navigation Acts meant that there would most likely be more such acts and limits on colonial rights.

14. **The correct answer is (B).** Choice (A) refers to the Rush-Bagot Agreement. Choice (C) is partially true of the Treaty of Greenville; the Native Americans had to give up much of their lands in the Old Northwest. Choice (D) refers to the Webster-Ashburton Treaty, and choice (E), to Jay's Treaty.

15. **The correct answer is (D).** Choice (E) relates to a legislative tactic used by a minority to prevent the adoption of a measure or procedure by holding the floor and blocking a vote. It is used mostly in the U.S. Senate and has been used to block civil rights legislation. It is incorrect here, as are choices (A), (B), and (C).

16. **The correct answer is (B).** Choice (D) is a good distracter but not the definition of the term. Choice (E) is Stephen Douglas's Freeport Doctrine stated in the Lincoln-Douglas Debates. The Dred Scott decision established the opposite of choice (C), which is incorrect as a definition of popular sovereignty. Choice (A) is a partial restatement

of the proposed Wilmot Proviso that would have outlawed slavery in lands ceded from Mexico.

17. **The correct answer is (C).** The novelists, Crane, choice (A), and Dreiser, choice (B), were realists. Pulitzer, choice (D), was the influential publisher of the New York *World* that practiced "yellow journalism." Eakins, choice (E), was a painter of the realist school.

Test-Taking Strategy

The key word is primary.

18. **The correct answer is (E).** Both choices (A) and (E) are correct, but Lincoln used the argument in choice (E) to justify his control of Reconstruction, preventing Congress's harsh stand. The Wade-Davis Bill was a Congressional plan for Reconstruction. Choice (B) occurred after Lincoln's death, as did choice (D)—Andrew Johnson recognized the Southern governments while Congress was in recess. Choice (C) is incorrect.

19. **The correct answer is (C).** Choice (A) is the landmark school desegregation case of the 1950s. Choice (B) is the "one man, one vote" case of the 1960s. Choice (D) is an affirmative action case relating to the use of race as an element in admissions policies in higher education. Choice (E) is a landmark interstate commerce case relating to serving African Americans.

Test-Taking Strategy

The key word is direct.

20. **The correct answer is (D).** The Ballinger-Pinchot controversy was the proverbial straw that broke the camel's back. While choices (A) and (C) damaged Taft's support among Progressives, the appointment of Ballinger, the resignation of Pinchot, and the resulting investigation and clearing of Ballinger turned the Progressives against Taft. Choice (E) is true and should have increased Taft's support among Progressives. Choice (B) is a distracter.

21. **The correct answer is (C).** Voter 1's opinion is based on Hoover's actions against the Bonus Army March in 1932, so choices (A) and (B) are illogical. Voter 2 is voicing an opinion about Roosevelt's campaign strategy in 1932. If you could not figure this out, Voter 3's opinion about the state of the economy would point you to 1932, choice (C).

22. **The correct answer is (C).** Also known as the National Labor Relations Act, the Wagner Act guaranteed the right to organize and bargain collectively. Choice (A) greatly limited union activities. Choice (B) was one of many strikes after World War I that failed. Choice (D) was an attempt to regulate big business but was unsuccessful. Choice (E) failed in its attempt to have the government cash certificates issued to veterans for service in World War I.

Test-Taking Strategy

For a not/except *question, ask yourself if the answer is true. If it is, cross it off and go on to the next answer.*

23. **The correct answer is (D).** Choice (D) is the opposite of what occurred. Parents turned away from traditional child-rearing practices and embraced permissiveness. The leading advocate of more liberal practices was Dr. Benjamin Spock who wrote *Common Sense Book of Baby and Child Care.*

24. **The correct answer is (C).** Choice (A) refers to the economic policy of Mikhail Gorbachev in the Soviet Union, so it is incorrect. It

was not until 1993 that Israel and Palestine signed a series of agreements recognizing the Palestinian right to self-rule in the Gaza Strip and parts of the West Bank, choice (B). Sadat had been one of the signatories to the Accords, so choice (D) is illogical. Choice (E) is irrelevant.

25. **The correct answer is (D).** Tobacco cultivation by the Virginia colonists began with local tobacco. In 1612, John Rolfe introduced better quality West Indian tobacco and a method for curing it that soon led to huge exports of tobacco to Europe and prosperity for the colony. Before this, the colonists at Jamestown had undergone what was known as the "starving time." They had been unable to provide food for themselves and relied on local Native Americans for food—often through force of arms. Massachusetts, choice (A), is illogical because tobacco agriculture requires a warm climate and large fields. Pennsylvania, choice (B), was one of the "breadbasket colonies" and raised mostly grains as cash crops. North Carolina, choice (C), exported mainly rice and indigo. Kentucky, choice (E), was not a colony.

26. **The correct answer is (D).**

27. **The correct answer is (C).** Although the Constitution would go into effect when nine states ratified it, supporters knew that the new nation would not succeed if all thirteen did not approve it. Debate in Virginia and New York was especially heated. When those states ratified, only North Carolina and Rhode Island remained outside the nation. Those states ratified in November 1789 and May 1790, respectively.

28. **The correct answer is (B).** The election of 1800 was determined in the House because both Aaron Burr and Thomas Jefferson had the same number of electoral votes. Although Burr had run for the vice presidency, he wanted to be president, but because there was no separate election, there was no way to distinguish votes. The election of 1824 was decided in the House because no candidate for president had a majority of electoral votes, choice (A); the issue was different because the Twelfth Amendment had been ratified by 1804. Choice (C) is a term given to the peaceful change in the political party in power in the election of 1800. Choice (D) is incorrect; each state's electoral vote is the sum of the number of its senators and members of the House. Choice (E) is the wrong time frame for the question.

29. **The correct answer is (C).** The clues are *women, one half of the people,* and *citizens.* If you did not recognize this quotation from the Seneca Falls "Declaration of Sentiments and Resolutions," you could eliminate several of the choices by educated guessing. The time frame for this question is after 1833 and before Reconstruction so that neither choices (B) nor (D) were citizens. Neither choices (A) nor (E) could account for "one half of the people of this country," even though free blacks could not necessarily vote, so choice (C) must be the answer.

Test-Taking Strategy

Knowing the time frame would have helped you to eliminate choice (E).

Test-Taking Strategy

Knowing the time frame will help you eliminate choices (B) and (D).

30. The correct answer is (C). First came the factory system, choice (B), and then the development of interchangeable parts, choice (A), by Eli Whitney, among others. These resulted in the division of labor that, in turn, resulted in the mass production of goods, choice (C). Mass production was facilitated by the development of the electric motor, choice (E). Choice (D) is irrelevant.

31. The correct answer is (E). President Theodore Roosevelt later issued the Roosevelt Corollary that modified the Monroe Doctrine to suit U.S. business interests in Latin America, but the Spanish–American War did not result in any changes to the Monroe Doctrine. Once in possession of territories in the Pacific, the United States realized that it needed to be able to defend them, and that realization resulted in choices (A) and (B). Choice (C) was a direct result of the war. The Insular Cases, choice (D), resulted in a ruling that unincorporated territories like Puerto Rico and the Philippines did not have the constitutional protection of incorporated territories such as Hawaii, but the residents were guaranteed due process.

32. The correct answer is (D). Roosevelt never wished to abandon choices (A), (C), or (E). He had come to believe, however, that monopolies were not inherently bad. Some actually could work for the benefit of consumers; for example, by using economies of scale to produce goods and thus lower prices. Also, combinations and big business enterprises were inevitable. Roosevelt believed that business needed to be policed, and he proposed a federal trade commission to oversee business practices. Wilson campaigned on choice (B).

33. The correct answer is (C). Choice C is incorrect and irrelevant; the money supply at the time was backed by gold reserves. The Federal Reserve Act established the Federal Reserve System (known as the Fed), the monetary side of the nation's economic policies, by setting up twelve Federal Reserve Banks in twelve regions around the nation. Through member banks, the Fed provided money to banks in temporary trouble, choice (A). It eased the inflexibility of the money supply, choice (B), by providing Federal Reserve notes in exchange for promissory notes from member banks. The Fed also controlled the amount of money in circulation, choice (D). The Federal Reserve Board that governed the system was appointed by the President and approved by the Senate for fourteen-year terms, thus resolving choice (E).

34. The correct answer is (A). Efforts were made to teach soil conservation and better ways to raise crops and livestock, but with little success. As a result, the program did not raise the standard of living of Native Americans on reservations, as had been intended. Choices (B), (C), and (E) were goals that were met. Choice (D) is incorrect.

35. **The correct answer is (A).** Choices (A) and (D) are true, but choice (A) includes choice (D), so it is the more inclusive answer. Some Loyalists may have rejected the Patriots' cause on philosophical terms, choice (B), but that was not the major reason that most Loyalists supported Great Britain. Choice (E) may have been true for some colonists who feared that the French were supplying Native Americans to fight against the colonies but that would not have motivated wealthy Loyalists in coastal towns and cities. Choice (C) was not a major concern at the time.

36. **The correct choice is (E).** Although men began to group themselves as Federalists and Anti-Federalists during the campaign to ratify the Constitution (I), real party lines were not drawn until the government was inaugurated (II and III). Choices (A) and (D) are incorrect because they both include item (I). Thomas Jefferson and his supporters opposed Alexander Hamilton's fiscal policies and his influence on George Washington. Choices (B) and (C) are incorrect because they contain only half of the correct answer.

37. **The correct answer is (B).** Choice (A) is correct, but it is the direct result of the invention of the cotton gin. Choice (D) is also correct and very specific, like choice (B). Look for a response that presents a larger concept. The increase in the slave trade, choice (B), had a very significant and long-term effect on U.S. history and, therefore, is the best answer. Choice (C) is incorrect; the invention of the cotton gin and the increase in cotton production led to an increase in demand for much of the period. Choice (E) occurred later than the time frame of this question, which is between the 1790s, question 36, and 1833, question 38.

38. **The correct answer is (B).** All five choices were part of a series of events that culminated in the Force Bill and the Tariff Act of 1833, but the direct cause of the two bills was choice (B). The Webster-Hayne Debate, choice (A), began as a discussion of limiting the sale of Western lands to keep workers in the Northeast and progressed to a discussion of the tariff. The Tariff of Abominations, choice (D), or the Tariff of 1828, angered South Carolinians who were faced with a depressed cotton market, and they blamed high tariff rates. They found voice in Calhoun's paper, choice (C). Jackson's veto of the Maysville Road bill in 1830, choice (E), on the grounds that it encroached on the sovereignty of a state seemed to signal to advocates of nullification that he would support states' rights in a showdown with South Carolina. However, Jackson issued a statement to South Carolina after it passed the Ordinance of Nullification, choice (B), that nullification was equal to treason. The Force Bill gave Jackson the power to use force in South Carolina to prevent dissolution, and a new tariff lowered rates, thus averting the crisis.

39. **The correct answer is (D).** The Missouri Compromise, choice (D), had set the Northern boundary for slavery at 36° 30', and Kansas and Nebraska lay north of this line, thus nullifying the law. Choice (A) did not deal with Kansas and Nebraska but did admit California

as a free state; prohibit the slave trade in Washington, D.C.; propose a stricter Fugitive Slave Law; defer the discussion of slavery in Utah and New Mexico until they requested statehood; and agree to pay Texas to give up much of its Western land to the federal government. Choice (B) refers to the compromise in the writing of the Constitution that resulted in two representatives from each state in the Senate and proportional representation in the House. Choice (C) is the proposal, never accepted, that would have banned slavery in any territory purchased as a result of the Mexican War. Choice (E) ruled that slave owners' right to their property (slaves) were protected.

40. **The correct answer is (C).** The slightly later American Federation of Labor (AFL), under Samuel Gompers, was organized into craft unions. The Knights were organized by industry, and this was one reason for their ultimate collapse, as was choice (D). Another difference between the two unions was the AFL's refusal to accept African Americans, women, and immigrants.

41. **The correct answer is (E).** Bulgarians, Hungarians, Romanians, and Poles emigrated after much of their nations were cut up into small tenant farms, choice (A). Choice (B) relates to Austria-Hungary in this period. High tariffs hurt Italian vineyards and orchard workers, choice (C). Polish Catholics and Russian Jews emigrated because of religious persecution. Choice (E) was a pull factor.

Test-Taking Strategy

The key word is significance.

42. **The correct answer is (B).** Choices (A), (B), and (D) are true about the Open Door Policy, but the importance of the policy lay in choice (B). Between the War of 1812 and the Spanish-American War of 1898, the United States had been able to rely on its location to keep it out of European conflicts. After the U.S.'s victory in the Spanish-American War and the acquisition of an overseas empire, the United States looked at itself as a world power. U.S. businessmen, fearing they would be forced out of China, demanded a change in policy. The Open Door Policy established terms in such a way that nations had to agree. Japan had already annexed Formosa in 1895, choice (C). The information in choice (E) is incorrect.

43. **The correct answer is (B).** Choice (A) upheld Congress's use of the commerce clause as the basis for civil rights legislation. Choice (C) defines the rights of citizens. Choice (D) prohibits discrimination in employment and created the Equal Employment Opportunity Commission. Choice (E) regulates the collection and dissemination of information about people's credit history, but it does not relate to the question.

Test-Taking Strategy

The key words are major significance. *To help you answer, ask yourself what this election says about the larger context of U.S. history.*

44. **The correct answer is (B).** Choices (A), (D), and (E) were all factors in the campaign, but the election's significance lay in the turn of many voters toward more limited government. Reagan was the first conservative elected president since Calvin Coolidge. Reagan campaigned on a platform of lower taxes, reduced government spending, and a strengthened military. Choice (C) is incorrect.

45. The correct answer is (E). The Massachusetts General School Act of 1647 established this principle.

46. The correct answer is (D). Choices (A), (C), and (E) all lay within British territory in 1763. Spanish territory lay between the Mississippi and the Pacific, making choice (B) incorrect.

47. The correct answer is (D). The Annapolis Convention was called to discuss trade regulations across the new states but ended in requesting a convention to address the weaknesses of the Articles, choice (D). No trade agreements were reached, so choice (A) is incorrect. The Confederation Congress accomplished choice (C). Massachusetts put down Shays's Rebellion, so choice (B) is incorrect. Choice (E) is incorrect.

48. The correct answer is (A). The Embargo Act was supposed to hurt British and French markets, but, instead, it badly damaged the fledgling U.S. economy. Shipping; businesses related to shipping, such as shipbuilding; manufacturing; and farming, saw their markets decline and their incomes dip. Choice (B) refers to the harassment of U.S. ships (and the ships of other nations) in the Mediterranean by Barbary Coast pirates. A fleet of U.S. and European warships subdued the pirates in 1815. Choice (C) was Washington's attempt to keep the United States out of the European wars. Choice (D), passed in 1809, replaced the Embargo Act and allowed Americans to trade with any nation except Great Britain and France. Choice (E) was a cause of the War of 1812.

49. The correct answer is (B). New England was the center of shipping and related industries in the early 1800s and would have been hit the hardest by the embargo on trade.

50. The correct answer is (C). "Fifty-four forty or fight!" was the slogan of those who wanted the United States to claim all of Oregon up to the 54° 40' north latitude. Officially, the United States had asked only for the area up to the 49th parallel. By telling the British that he now agreed with the demands for the larger area and that the United States would not renew the agreement to hold the land jointly, President Polk maneuvered the British into agreeing to a permanent boundary line at the 49th parallel. This led the way for Oregon's organization as the Oregon Territory in 1848. Choice (D) were a group of Northern Democrats who opposed the Civil War and wanted Lincoln to make peace with the Confederacy. Anyone who wanted more territory for Native Americans probably would not have advocated fighting for it, so choice (E) is illogical.

51. The correct answer is (E). During the Civil War, inflation—the opposite of a tight money supply—was a great problem, so choice (E) is the correct answer. If you were not sure of the answer, you could make an educated guess based on the fact that farmers, or any debtors, prefer cheap, or inflated, money, because they can repay their loans with money that is worth less than when they borrowed it.

Test-Taking Strategy

Educated guessing can help you eliminate choices when you are not sure of an answer.

52. The correct answer is (B). The alliance between Northern and Southern business interests provided capital for Southern factory owners. Choice (A) worked against development of the Southern economy and was one cause of the low wages that Southern factories paid, choice (C). The information in choices (D) and (E) is true but irrelevant.

53. The correct answer is (D). Choices (B), (C), (D), and (E) are all characteristics to a certain extent of the period from the end of the Civil War to 1880, but choice (D) is the most correct description of the term "Gilded Age." Although all the events in choices (B), (C), (D), and (E) occurred, the term refers to the political corruption and unrestrained business competition of the era. Choice (A) is incorrect; this period was notable for its lack of presidential leadership.

54. The correct answer is (A). The giveaway is the phrase "square deal." This is the name that came to symbolize Theodore Roosevelt's domestic policies. The phrases "fair play" and "rules of the game" also point to Theodore Roosevelt and his hardy, sportsman's view of life. Don't be confused by choices (C) and (D) because their domestic programs had similar titles. The term given to the domestic policies of Franklin Roosevelt, choice (C), was "New Deal." Harry Truman's policies, choice (D), were known as the "Fair Deal." Choice (B), Ronald Reagan's policies, were the "New Federalism," and choice (E), John F. Kennedy's policies, were known as the "New Frontier."

55. The correct answer is (C). Choices (A), (C), and (E) are true, but in the larger context of U.S. history, choice (C) is the most significant. The pictures of the active army demolishing the veterans' Hooverville added to the belief that Hoover was indifferent to those suffering in the Depression, an unfair assessment of the man, but one that contributed to his losing the 1932 election. The RFC, choice (D), did provide additional money for relief, but it was unrelated to the Bonus Army. Choice (B) is incorrect; the U.S. Army destroyed the veterans' makeshift camp.

56. The correct answer is (A). Harrington was a socialist and writer who is credited with making visible the "invisible poverty" in the United States. Carson, choice (B), was a marine biologist and science writer who wrote about the dangers of environmental pollution. Nader, choice (C), is a lawyer and consumer advocate whose work has resulted in investigations and regulations to protect consumers. Helper's book, choice (D), was written in the 1850s and attacked slavery on economic grounds. Galbraith, choice (E), was an economist who urged (1) government spending to fight unemployment and (2) the use of private wealth to help the needy.

57. The correct answer is (B). This question may seem a snap for the right reason and the wrong reason. If you remember that the largest single group of immigrants to the United States in the nineteenth century was German, you might have decided that this is true overall—and you'd be correct. But you might have decided that if the immigration of the twentieth century was added to the nineteenth century total, choice (C) would be correct. That's a good try, but wrong. Mexicans were by far the largest nationality to emigrate to the United States at the end of the twentieth century but still ranked behind German immigration by some 1.5 million people in 1997.

58. **The correct answer is (A).** Barry Goldwater represented very conservative Republicans in 1964 and George McGovern, antiwar members of the Democratic Party in 1972. With the exception of Thomas Dewey, choice (C), who lost against Harry Truman in 1948, all the other Republicans and Democrats were elected president.

59. **The correct answer is (D).** Through the power of the purse, colonial legislatures exercised control over taxes and expenditures, choice (A), which limited the authority of the governors, choice (E). Only Pennsylvania had a unicameral legislature, choice (C). Choice (B) was also true.

60. **The correct answer is (D).** Like the weakening of established churches, choices (A) and (E) were effects of the Great Awakening, choice (D). Choices (B) and (C) are distracters to confuse you and are incorrect.

61. **The correct answer is (E).** Choices (D) and (E) are correct, but the response that describes the larger concept and provides the more inclusive answer is choice (E). Choice (A) is the opposite of the First Continental Congress's activities. The Congress did not establish Committees of Correspondence, choice (B), but did set up "committees of safety and inspection" to act against the British government's restrictive policies. (Committees of Correspondence had grown out of an effort by Sam Adams and fellow colonists in Massachusetts to let the other colonies know about British repression against Massachusetts.) Choice (C) is incorrect because independence had not been declared, so there was no war.

62. **The correct answer is (E).** Southern plantation owners voted for Jackson because they believed that as a plantation owner himself, he would understand their problems and help them. Other segments of voters, choices (B) and (D), as well as urban workers, also felt that Jackson, as a self-made man, would understand their needs.

63. **The correct answer is (B).** All the answer choices figured in the election of 1844, but choice (B) is the most inclusive. Clay made Polk's lack of qualifications an issue, choice (A), but it appealed to only a small segment of the public. Democrats joined the annexation of Texas, choice (D), to demands that the United States take control of all of Oregon, thereby balancing slave and free states, choice (C). Clay agreed to the annexation of Texas only if it could be achieved without a war with Mexico, making choice (E) incorrect. With the exception of choice (A), the issues revolved around manifest destiny.

Test-Taking Strategy

Be sure all parts to an answer are correct. A partially correct answer is a partially incorrect answer— and a quarter-point deduction.

Test-Taking Strategy

Highlight key words in the questions. What is the key word in this question?

Test-Taking Strategy

The key word is primarily.

Test-Taking Strategy

The key word is principal. *Which is the most inclusive answer?*

64. The correct answer is (B). Delaware, Maryland, Missouri, and Kentucky were the so-called border states. Choices (A) and (C) are incorrect. The Emancipation Proclamation, choice (D), effectively freed no one because it was applied only to those states still under Confederate governments on January 1, 1863. Copperheads, choice (E), were Northerners, many of them Democrats, who believed that the Union should make peace with the Confederacy.

65. The correct answer is (E). The Morrill Act established land-grant colleges, dedicated to agriculture and the mechanical arts and paid for by the sale or rental of public lands donated by the federal government. Herefords, choice (A), were hardier cattle; barbed wire, choice (B), enabled cattle ranchers to control the size of their herds and potential problems among themselves and with farmers and sheepherders; and railroads, choice (C), ended the need for long cattle drives. Choice (D) drove up the demand for beef.

66. The correct answer is (E). Hawaii, choice (A), was annexed at this time but not as a result of the war. The United States purchased Alaska, choice (B), in 1867 from Russia. Panama, choice (C), received its independence from Colombia in 1903 with U.S. help and the United States took control of the Panama Canal, but neither event came as a result of the war. The island of Hispaniola, choice (D), is home to Haiti and the Dominican Republic.

67. The correct answer is (A). To be the correct answer, the response needs to include economic incentives. Choice (A) provided $50 billion in money, weapons, and supplies to the Allies; the purpose of Lend-Lease was to strengthen the Allies against Hitler and buy time until the United States would enter the war, the military objective. Choice (B) stated that the United States would not intervene in the affairs of any Latin American nation, the political means; the purpose of the declaration was to foster ties with potential allies in case of a war against fascism and nazism, the military objective. Choice (D), established by Theodore Roosevelt, used military means for political ends—intervention in the affairs of Latin American nations often to aid American businesses. Choices (C) and (E) are illogical. Both were measures of the New Deal; choice (C) provided relief, and choice (D) was part of the reform of the banking system.

68. The correct answer is (C). The summer of 1964 in the South saw the murder of three white voter registration workers from the North, firebombings, and mob violence, but African Americans registered in record numbers. Choice (A) was the goal of the Freedom Rides of 1961. Choice (D) refers to sit-ins at lunch counters. Choices (B) and (E) are incorrect.

69. The correct answer is (C). When William Penn established Pennsylvania, he insisted that Native Americans be paid for their land. This did not continue after Penn returned to England. With the exception of Rhode Island, settlers simply assumed that they could take any land they considered uninhabited.

70. The correct answer is (C). When the Spanish discovered that a group of French traders had crossed Texas from Louisiana to the Rio Grande with the idea of opening a trade route to New Mexico, they decided to build settlements to discourage the French from taking Texas. Choices (A) and (D) would be effects of settlement but not causes. This was 150 years after the expeditions for Cibola, so choice (E) is illogical, as is choice (B). There was a vast French territory between the English colonies and Texas.

71. The correct answer is (D). The opposite of this statement is true. Although single women were generally considered dependent on fathers or brothers, they did have more rights than married women in some states.

Test-Taking Strategy

The key word is primarily.

72. The correct answer is (A). A sound currency, choice (B), was not a primary concern of Jackson's. The Second Bank was the depository of federal money, choice (C), until Jackson had all funds removed and placed in state banks that become known as "pet banks." Choice (E) jumbles these facts and is incorrect. It was Jackson's own policies that put millions of acres of land on the market and sparked land speculation, so choice (D) is incorrect.

73. The correct answer is (C). Douglas reluctantly agreed with the decision in Dred Scott, so choice (A) is incorrect. The basis for the Doctrine was the right of slave owners to the protection of their property, so choice (B) is incorrect. Douglas was a Democrat, so choice (D) is illogical. Douglas built his career on championing popular sovereignty, and the Freeport Doctrine was an effort not to repudiate it, so choice (E) is incorrect.

Test-Taking Strategy

The key words are most significant.

74. The correct answer is (D). Choices (A), (B), (D), and (E) are all true, but the most important in the larger context of U.S. history is choice (D). This was the first time in the history of the United States that civil and political equality was granted to all African American men (women still could not vote), and it would be the last time in the South until the mid-twentieth century. The Civil War, not Reconstruction, ended the plantation economy of the antebellum South, choice (C).

75. The correct answer is (D). Based on the shovels dumping people at the feet of the Statue and the names on the ships, *European Garbage Ship* and *Refuse,* choice (D) seems the best answer. Choices (A), (B), and (E) are not worded strongly enough for the symbolism of garbage shown in the cartoon. Choice (C) is the opposite of what the cartoon suggests.

76. The correct answer is (A). Congress passed the first law restricting immigration in 1882. It set a head tax on each incoming immigrant and barred convicts, the insane, and those liable to become public charges. In the same year, Congress passed the Chinese Exclusion Act that barred immigration by Chinese laborers for ten years. The law was renewed and was still in effect in 1920 when Congress passed a law barring all Chinese immigration. In 1906, Theodore Roosevelt and the Japanese government signed the

Gentlemen's Agreement ending the immigration of Japanese labor-ers into the United States. The first quota system limiting European immigration did not go into effect until 1921. The National Origins Act of 1924 severely limited immigration in general and immigration from Eastern and Southern Europe in particular. Because of the way quotas were set, any Japanese immigration was ended. Choices (B), (C), (D), and (E) are, therefore, all incorrect.

Test-Taking Strategy

This question is asking you to evaluate the consistency among points of view and find the two that match.

77. **The correct answer is (B).** The quotation is from *The Battle with the Slum*, by journalist and social reformer Jacob Riis. According to the "Gospel of Wealth," a term coined to describe Andrew Carnegie's views, those with great wealth had a responsibility to help those among the poor who wanted to help themselves. Choice (A) would have believed that slums were the expected consequence of natural selection applied to humans. Choice (C) was more likely to have been concerned with tariff rates and cheap money than slum reform. Choices (D) and (E) are illogical.

78. **The correct answer is (B).** The National Origins Act of 1924 resulted from a fear of anarchy and the flood of immigrants after World War I. Joseph McCarthy, Republican senator from Wisconsin, gave his name to an era in the early 1950s characterized by red-baiting, scare tactics, and the use of publicly made but unproven charges to smear people and agencies.

Test-Taking Strategy

The key words are best characterized.

79. **The correct answer is (D).** Choices (A), (B), (D), and (E) are all true, but choice (D) is the most inclusive response. Choice (C) is incorrect. Black power, which generated anger and fear in parts of the white community, was a call to action to improve the conditions of African Americans.

Test-Taking Strategy

Be sure both parts of an answer are correct. A partially correct answer is a partially incorrect answer— and a quarter-point deduction.

80. **The correct answer is (C).** Basing its actions on the principle of virtual representation, Parliament believed that it had the right to make all laws, including the levying of taxes for all its subjects—in England and in the colonies. The colonists believed that only their own legislatures had the right to tax them, the theory of direct rep-resentation. Popular sovereignty, part of choices (A) and (E), was the theory that the people in the Western territories should decide for themselves whether they would enter the Union as free or slave states. The conquered provinces theory, part of choices (B) and (D), was the basis of Thaddeus Stevens's views on how the South should be treated after the Civil War; the states were not even to be consid-ered territories. Rebellion of individuals, part of choices (D) and (E), was Lincoln's view of secession; since individuals had rebelled, he could use his pardon power to reinstate Southern states into the Union.

Test-Taking Strategy

The key word is primarily.

81. **The correct answer is (E).** The colonists, especially on the fron-tier, wanted to be allowed to move into the territory that was closed to them by the Proclamation. Choice (A) is incorrect; Native Ameri-cans were free. Choice (B) occurred as a result of four nations of the Iroquois Confederacy joining the British but was not a cause of their supporting the British. Choice (C) is incorrect. Choice (D) is true

but was not a reason for Native Americans' interest in supporting the British against the colonists.

82. **The correct answer is (A).** One of the provisions that Mexico had insisted on in welcoming American settlers was that they obey Mexican law, and slavery was against Mexican law. Until Americans outnumbered Mexicans in Texas by about six to one, Mexico did not enforce the law. Choice (E) occurred as a result of choice (A); the Mexican government included enforcement of customs duties in its new regulations. Choice (D) was probably the ulterior motive for choice (A). Choice (B) is the reverse of what occurred. Choice (C) did not occur until after Texas won its independence.

83. **The correct answer is (A).** Only Andrew Jackson did not add any territory to the United States during his terms in office. McKinley, choice (B), annexed Hawaii, the Philippines, and Guam. Polk, choice (C), oversaw the addition of Texas, California, and New Mexico Territory. Monroe, choice (D), acquired East Florida from the Spanish. Johnson's Secretary of State, William Seward, purchased Alaska, choice (E).

84. **The correct answer is (A).** Choice (B) is the opposite of what occurred. The end of the lobby to expand the currency system meant an end to the lobby for free and unlimited coinage of silver. The Bland-Allison Act, choice (C), had been passed before the economy improved, had done little to expand the money supply, had brought little relief to debtors, and had made little profit for silver miners. Choice (D) had already begun after the election of 1878. The demonetization of silver, choice (E), was known as the "Crime of 1873" and is irrelevant to this period.

85. **The correct answer is (A).** The concept of the Talented Tenth was the idea of W.E.B. Du Bois, choice (C), so that choice is illogical. Choice (B), George Washington Carver, is a distracter. Herbert Spencer was the most prominent advocate of Social Darwinism, making choice (D) incorrect. Choice (E), Horace Mann, is also incorrect.

86. **The correct answer is (D).** Choices (A), (D), and (E) state correct information. Choice (A) refers to the Platt Amendment, choice (D) to the establishment of Panama, and choice (E) to a situation that caused Roosevelt to use the Roosevelt Corollary to the Monroe Doctrine for the first time. Of these three, the most significant effect in the long-term history of the United States and the world was the assigning of the right to build a canal across the isthmus of Panama to the United States, so choice (D) is the best answer. Choice (B) is an action of President Wilson. Choice (C) is only partially correct. Theodore Roosevelt legitimized the "big stick" policy through the Roosevelt Corollary, while Franklin Roosevelt adopted the Good Neighbor Policy to Latin America.

87. **The correct answer is (D).** Mellon believed that the wealthy should pay a smaller proportion of taxes so that they could accumulate wealth that would then be invested back into business, so

Test-Taking Strategy

The key words are stated reason. *Circle or underline the key words in the question, so you can be sure you are looking for the answer to the right question.*

Test-Taking Strategy

The key words are most significant.

choice (D) is incorrect. Choices (A), (B), and (C) fed the stock market crash and the Depression.

88. **The correct answer is (E).** Choice (E) is one of the reasons why the Conference had only short-term effects, choice (C); no such agreements were reached. There were no provisions for enforcing choices (B) or (D), so choice (A) proved true for the nation, but is not the correct answer.

89. **The correct answer is (C).** Federal personal income taxes take a larger share of higher incomes than lower ones. Federal corporate income taxes are also progressive. Choice (A) takes the same percentage of all incomes. State or local sales taxes are regressive, choice (B), in that they take a larger proportion of lower incomes than higher ones. FICA is both proportional, because it takes the same percentage of tax out of everyone's income up to a maximum wage, and regressive, because it takes a larger percentage out of smaller incomes. Choice (E) is incorrect.

90. **The correct answer is (C).** After Spiro Agnew was forced to resign, Nixon nominated Ford as vice president. When Nixon was forced to resign, Ford nominated Rockefeller as vice president. These are the only two times Section 2 of the Twenty-Fifth Amendment has been used. Choices (D) and (E) are instances of the normal succession of the vice president upon the death of the president, as stated in Section 1 of Article II.

PRACTICE TEST 3

While you have taken many standardized tests and know to completely blacken the ovals on the answer sheets and to completely erase any errors, you will need to indicate on the answer key which test you are taking. The instructions on the answer sheet will tell you to fill out the top portion of the answer sheet exactly as shown.

1. Print *U.S. HISTORY* on the line to the right under the words *Subject Test (print)*.

2. In the shaded box labeled *Test Code*, fill in four ovals: —Fill in oval 2 in the row labeled V.
   —Fill in oval 5 in the row labeled W.
   —Fill in oval 5 in the row labeled X.
   —Fill in oval C in the row labeled Y.
   —Leave the ovals in row Q blank.

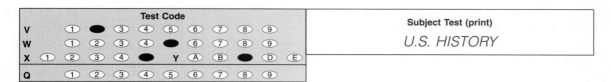

There are two additional questions that you will be asked to answer: How many semesters of U.S. history have you taken? Have you taken courses in government, economics, geography, psychology, sociology, and/or anthropology? The College Board is collecting statistical information. If you choose to answer, you will use the key that is provided and blacken the appropriate ovals in row Q. You may also choose not to answer, and that will not affect your grade.

When everyone has completed filling in this portion of the answer sheet, the supervisor will tell you to turn the page and begin. The answer sheet has 100 numbered ovals on the sheet, but there are only 90 (or 95) multiple-choice questions in the test, so be sure to use only ovals 1 to 90 (or 95) to record your answers.

GO ON TO THE NEXT PAGE ➤

PRACTICE TEST 3—*Continued*

Directions: Each of the questions or incomplete statements below has five suggested answers or completions. Choose the response that is best and then fill in the corresponding oval on the answer sheet.

1. Native Americans in which of the following culture regions used the potlatch ceremony to display their wealth?

   (A) Southwest
   (B) Northeast Woodlands
   (C) Basin and Plateau
   (D) Plains
   (E) Northwest

2. All of the following are true about the Stamp Act EXCEPT

   (A) the act directly affected all colonists
   (B) as a result of colonial resistance to the Stamp Act, all taxes were repealed except a small tax on tea
   (C) the stamp tax was a direct tax
   (D) the act resulted in a boycott of British goods that severely damaged British merchants
   (E) the colonists' theory of "taxation without representation" developed in response to this act

3. Which of the following statements best describes government under the Articles of Confederation?

   (A) The Confederation government established guidelines for settling the Northwest Territory and admitting the new states to the Union.
   (B) Because of the colonists' experience with Great Britain, the Articles of Confederation had been written so that real power remained with the states.
   (C) States could not make treaties without Congress's approval nor could the states pass laws that conflicted with treaties made by the central government.
   (D) The Confederation government was hampered in its ability to levy taxes.
   (E) Because of sectional interests, the central government could not agree on whether or not to set customs duties or how high the tariffs should be.

4. Which of the following amendments was passed as a result of the confusion in the election of 1800?

   (A) Tenth
   (B) Thirteenth
   (C) Twelfth
   (D) Seventeenth
   (E) Nineteenth

PRACTICE TEST 3—*Continued*

5. Which of the following would be LEAST useful in gathering information to write a report about Lewis and Clark's exploration of the Louisiana Purchase?

(A) Journals kept by expedition members

(B) Photos of flora and fauna of the area that the expedition explored

(C) Terrain maps of the area

(D) A historical novel of the life of Sacajawea

(E) Translations of the logs of Spanish or Russian ships that stopped in the area of the Columbia River

6. Speaker I: "Our Federal Union—it must and shall be preserved."

Speaker II: "The Union—next to our liberty, the most dear! May we always remember that it can be preserved only by respecting the rights of the states."

This exchange most probably took place in regard to

(A) the election of Abraham Lincoln in 1860

(B) ratification of the Constitution

(C) ratification of the Articles of Confederation

(D) the nullification crisis that resulted from the Tariff of 1828

(E) Madison's veto of an internal improvements bill

7. All of the following helped Lincoln win a second term in office EXCEPT

(A) Sherman's successes in Georgia

(B) rise in tariffs

(C) Pacific Railway Acts of 1862 and 1864

(D) Democrats' internal party problems

(E) Homestead Act

8. The indirect purpose of the Pendleton Act was to

(A) establish a civil service system for the federal government

(B) make the assassination of the president a federal crime

(C) make the federal government more efficient and less susceptible to corruption

(D) prohibit political parties in power from soliciting campaign contributions from federal officeholders

(E) limit the level of federal officeholders who were appointed rather than elected

9.   I. The war will end soon, and the United States should stay out of it.
   II. Most people supported the Allies, although some people supported the Central Powers.
   III. By selling war matériel to nations at war, the United States was undermining its own neutrality.

Which of the above statements best describes Americans' attitude toward World War I prior to 1915?

(A) I only

(B) II and III only

(C) III only

(D) I and II only

(E) I, II, and III

GO ON TO THE NEXT PAGE

PRACTICE TEST 3—*Continued*

10. Which of the following best describes the 1920s?

(A) Period of surface prosperity with underlying economic problems

(B) Period of international and national prosperity and social progress

(C) Period of prosperity marked by social and labor unrest and underlying economic problems

(D) The Jazz Age

(E) Period of prosperity for the few and poverty for the many

11. The most significant fact about the 1960 presidential election was

(A) that the primaries pitted the Democratic Northeast against the Democratic South

(B) John Kennedy's age

(C) the role that television played in determining the outcome of the election

(D) the fact that Kennedy became the first Roman Catholic to be elected president

(E) that Kennedy chose a Southerner, Lyndon Johnson, as his vice presidential running mate

12. One result of the rapid settlement of Western lands between 1789 and 1803 was

(A) the departure of British soldiers from forts in the Ohio Valley

(B) the extension of suffrage by eliminating property qualifications for voting

(C) the end of the arming of Native Americans on the frontier by French and British allies

(D) the Whiskey Rebellion

(E) the adoption of the Northwest Ordinance

13. The War of 1812 is considered a turning point in U.S. history because

(A) the nation embarked on its policy of manifest destiny

(B) the United States began to militarily intervene in Latin American nations

(C) Great Britain entered a period when it would not cooperate with the United States

(D) the United States no longer allowed events in Europe to shape U.S. foreign and domestic policies

(E) the War Hawks were able to gain enough support to declare war

PRACTICE TEST 3—*Continued*

14. The election of 1824 was decided in the House of Representatives because

(A) of the corrupt bargain

(B) Jackson did not have a majority of the popular vote

(C) each state has only one vote in the electoral college

(D) Jackson did not have a majority of the electoral vote

(E) The Twelfth Amendment had not yet been ratified

15. The border states that remained in the Union were

(A) Ohio, Indiana, and Illinois

(B) Tennessee

(C) Kentucky and Missouri

(D) Delaware, Maryland, Kentucky and Missouri

(E) Kansas and Missouri

16. The Treaty of Fort Laramie stated that

(A) Native Americans would not attack settlers crossing their lands

(B) former Mexican settlers in the newly acquired New Mexico Territory would be guaranteed all the rights of U.S. citizens

(C) the U.S. Army would not build any more forts in the West

(D) the Black Hills would be closed to white settlers

(E) the United States would pay $10 million to the Mexican government for the southern right-of-way for a transcontinental railroad

GO ON TO THE NEXT PAGE

PRACTICE TEST 3—*Continued*

Questions 17 and 18 refer to the following cartoon.

17. King Monopoly would most likely have favored all of the following EXCEPT

(A) labor unions

(B) a high protective tariff

(C) cheap money

(D) U.S. expansionism

(E) unregulated immigration

18. The cartoonist who drew this picture would most likely have been in favor of which of the following laws?

(A) Bland-Allison Act

(B) Interstate Commerce Act

(C) Pendleton Act

(D) Sherman Antitrust Act

(E) Sherman Silver Purchase Act

19. A debate on U.S. imperialism would most likely have included all the following subjects EXCEPT

(A) annexation of Hawaii

(B) the Open Door Policy

(C) the Platt Amendment

(D) support for Panamanian rebels

(E) support for Pan-Americanism

20. Which pair of presidents had opposing views on U.S. policy toward the People's Republic of China?

(A) Dwight Eisenhower and Lyndon Johnson

(B) Richard Nixon and Jimmy Carter

(C) Dwight Eisenhower and John F. Kennedy

(D) Harry Truman and Richard Nixon

(E) Harry Truman and Dwight Eisenhower

PRACTICE TEST 3—*Continued*

21. In the mid-twentieth century, what issue would most likely have resulted in a vote along sectional lines in Congress?

    (A) Gay rights legislation
    (B) Civil rights legislation
    (C) Aid to education
    (D) Equal Rights Amendment
    (E) Social Security increases

22. Which of the following best describes the British response to the colonies?

    (A) Parliament levied a series of taxes that it then had to enforce on belligerent colonists.
    (B) Great Britain continued to use old policies to solve new problems.
    (C) Parliament insisted on the theory of virtual representation in the face of colonial demands for direct representation.
    (D) The position of the British was undermined by the violence that occurred in Boston.
    (E) The British were caught in a cycle of action- reaction-action with no escape.

23. Which of the following writers added to the growing tensions between North and South?

    (A) Phillis Wheatley
    (B) James Fenimore Cooper
    (C) Edith Wharton
    (D) Thomas Paine
    (E) Harriet Beecher Stowe

24. The Irish immigrated to the United States in the 1840s and 1850s and settled mainly in

    (A) the South
    (B) urban areas along the Northeastern seaboard
    (C) the Upper Midwest
    (D) the Far West
    (E) the Great Plains

25. Popular sovereignty was to be used to decide the question of slavery in

    (A) Utah and New Mexico Territories
    (B) Kansas and Nebraska Territories
    (C) California
    (D) Utah, New Mexico, Kansas, and Nebraska Territories
    (E) Texas

26. Great Britain came to the brink of entering the Civil War in support of the Confederacy as a direct result of

    (A) the Union's seizure of two Confederate representatives from the British ship *Trent*
    (B) John Slidell's mission to gain French support for the Confederacy
    (C) the Union's blockade of Southern ports that closed off the supply of cotton to English mills
    (D) the Emancipation Proclamation
    (E) the Union's refusal to lower tariffs

27. All of the following influenced the nature of Congressional Reconstruction EXCEPT

    (A) concern for the rights of African Americans
    (B) political conciliation
    (C) concern that the Republicans would become the minority party when Southerners returned to Congress
    (D) belief that it was Congress's responsibility to direct Reconstruction
    (E) doubt about the loyalty to the Union of ex-Confederate officials

GO ON TO THE NEXT PAGE

28. The "Crime of 1873" refers to

    (A) the rise in the ratio of silver to gold from 16 to 1 to 18 to 1
    (B) the falling price of silver on the open market
    (C) passage of the Bland-Allison Act
    (D) Congress's decision to stop coining silver
    (E) the decline of the Greenback Party

29. All of the following New Deal measures dealt with reform EXCEPT

    (A) Securities and Exchange Commission
    (B) Social Security Act
    (C) Tennessee Valley Authority
    (D) Civilian Conservation Corps
    (E) National Labor Relations Act

30. The so-called secret agreements that were negotiated at the Yalta Conference

    (A) guaranteed that Eastern Europe would be dominated by the Communists
    (B) occurred because Truman did not trust Stalin
    (C) called for Soviet occupation of Japan
    (D) split Korea into two zones
    (E) drafted plans for the United Nations

31. All of the following statements are true about the Korean War EXCEPT

    (A) The American people ultimately decided that they did not want to go to war to support MacArthur's assessment of the need for victory in the Korean War.
    (B) MacArthur did not read the situation in Korea or in the United States accurately.
    (C) The advantage in the Korean War seesawed between the North Koreans and the UN forces.
    (D) MacArthur was correct in believing that the Chinese would not enter the war.
    (E) "Limited warfare" was the guiding principle behind the U.S.'s position and, therefore, the UN's position.

PRACTICE TEST 3—*Continued*

32. All of the following statements are true about the 1960s EXCEPT

(A) The 1960s saw a sexual and cultural revolution, in part because of the Supreme Court decision in *Roe* v. *Wade.*

(B) The 1960s was a time of social unrest and political activism.

(C) The cost of waging the Vietnam War forced cuts in spending for social programs.

(D) The 1960s saw a renewed interest in protecting the environment and the rights of consumers.

(E) The Civil Rights Movement had some of its greatest successes in this period before a white backlash set in.

33. All of the following occurred during the Bush administration EXCEPT

(A) the Persian Gulf War

(B) a cut in taxes

(C) the fall of the Berlin Wall

(D) the bailout of the savings and loan industry

(E) the end of the civil war in Nicaragua that had been supported by the United States

34. *Durante vita* was the term applied to

(A) the offer of land to attract people to Virginia

(B) the contract of indenture

(C) the status of Africans after the 1660s in Maryland

(D) the compromise that the Puritans reached to enable the Plymouth and Massachusetts Bay colonies to join

(E) another name for the Great Awakening

PRACTICE TEST 3—*Continued*

Questions 35 and 36 refer to the following map.

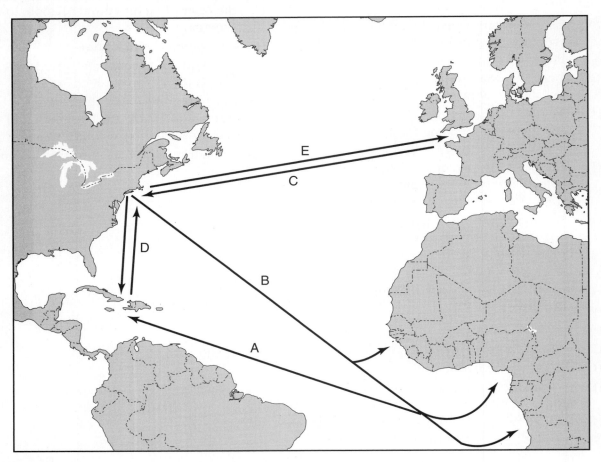

35. The Middle Passage refers to which segment of the colonial trade routes?

(A) A

(B) B

(C) C

(D) D

(E) E

36. The items that would have been traded on the route labeled E were

(A) slaves, molasses, and sugar

(B) rum, cloth, and guns

(C) manufactured goods

(D) dried fish, grains, whale oil, and ships

(E) manufactured goods and rum

PRACTICE TEST 3—*Continued*

37. A forerunner of the Declaration of Independence was

(A) the Proclamation of Rebellion

(B) Lee's Resolution

(C) Suffolk Resolves

(D) Declaration of Rights and Grievances

(E) Olive Branch Petition

38. The Fourth Amendment grew out of the colonists' grievance against the British practice of

(A) quartering troops at the expense of the colonists

(B) writs of assistance

(C) strict libel laws

(D) courts of admiralty

(E) supporting the Church of England as the established church

39. All of the following are true about the Cherokee EXCEPT

(A) the Cherokee adopted farming and converted to Christianity

(B) the Cherokee had a written constitution and a form of government similar to that of the United States

(C) Jackson sided with the Cherokee against Georgia

(D) in *Worcester* v. *Georgia,* the Supreme Court ruled in favor of the Cherokee

(E) the Cherokee supported the Confederacy in the Civil War

40. Reduction of the tariff, restoration of the independent treasury, settlement of the Oregon boundary, and acquisition of California were the four goals of

(A) James K. Polk

(B) William Henry Harrison

(C) Henry Clay

(D) Daniel Webster

(E) Franklin Pierce

41. The Wilmot Proviso supported

(A) popular sovereignty to determine whether a state created from the Louisiana Territory would be free or slave

(B) the argument of Southern senators that Congress had no constitutional power to forbid slavery in the territories

(C) a moratorium on the admission of any new states to the Union until a permanent solution would be found

(D) a ban on slavery in any state created out of land acquired from Mexico

(E) a ban on the slave trade in Washington, D.C.

42. Who wrote the influential muckraking book *History of the Standard Oil Company?*

(A) Ray Stannard Baker

(B) Ida B.Wells

(C) Frank Norris

(D) Upton Sinclair

(E) Ida Tarbell

43. Which of the following was NOT a cause of the U.S.'s declartion of war against Spain in 1898?

(A) The desire on the part of U.S. business interests to protect their $50 million investment in Cuba

(B) Americans' desire to see the Cubans' free of Spanish rule

(C) The influence of yellow journalism

(D) The propaganda campaign waged by Cubans in exile in the United States

(E) The explosion on board the USS *Maine*

GO ON TO THE NEXT PAGE →

PRACTICE TEST 3—*Continued*

44. In 1904, the Supreme Court ruled that which of the following was a "combination in restraint of trade"?

(A) Sherman Antitrust Act

(B) AFL

(C) Grange Movement

(D) Standard Oil Company

(E) Northern Securities Company

45. Which of the following was a U.S. program that was meant to provide aid to poverty-stricken countries anywhere in the world fighting communism?

(A) Marshall Plan

(B) NATO

(C) Square Deal

(D) Point Four

(E) Alliance for Progress

46. By the mid-1700s, the largest city in the colonies was

(A) New York

(B) Boston

(C) Philadelphia

(D) Charleston

(E) Wilmington, Delaware

47. All of the following were obstacles to ratification of the Constitution EXCEPT

(A) lack of a Bill of Rights

(B) the federal structure established by the Constitution placed the national government over state governments

(C) Rhode Island's boycott of the Constitutional Convention

(D) ratification by a special convention in each state rather than by the states' legislatures

(E) lack of leadership among Federalists

48. The defeat of which Native American leader made William Henry Harrison's presidential ambitions possible?

(A) The Prophet

(B) Tecumseh

(C) Cochise

(D) Chief Joseph

(E) Blue Jacket

49. Which of the following recommended that the United States offer Spain $120 million for Cuba and, if rejected, take the island by force?

(A) Hay–Bunau-Varilla Treaty

(B) Ballinger-Pinchot Controversy

(C) Ostend Manifesto

(D) Gadsden Purchase

(E) Seward's Folly

50. Organized labor would have supported which of the following demands in the "Omaha Platform" of the Populist Party in the 1892 election?

(A) An increase in currency resulting from the free and unlimited coinage of silver

(B) Government ownership of railroads

(C) 8-hour workday

(D) Graduated income tax

(E) Direct election of senators

PRACTICE TEST 3—*Continued*

51. "This perennial rebirth, this fluidity of American life, this expansion westward with its new opportunities, its continuous touch with the simplicity of primitive society, furnish the forces dominating American character. The true point of view in the history of this nation is not the Atlantic coast, it is the great West."

    The person who wrote this would most likely NOT have agreed with

    (A) the passage of the Pacific Railway Acts
    (B) the Mexican War
    (C) internal improvements bills
    (D) the Gadsden Purchase
    (E) the establishment of the Indian Territory

52. The major difference between W.E.B. Du Bois and his fellow African Americans Booker T. Washington and Marcus Garvey was Du Bois's

    (A) appeal to the Talented Tenth
    (B) belief that education alone would correct all injustices
    (C) disinterest in all things African
    (D) focus on economic equality
    (E) use of white politicians to gain an audience for African American causes

53. The administration of Warren G. Harding was most notable for

    (A) pressing the Supreme Court to find boycotts organized by labor to be legal
    (B) supporting business interests
    (C) passing the Fordney-McCumber Act, which raised tariffs to an all-time high
    (D) reducing the excess profits tax
    (E) supporting McCarthyism

54. All of the following were accomplishments of the New Deal EXCEPT the

    (A) establishment of Social Security
    (B) right of collective bargaining
    (C) establishment of a program to fund low-cost mortgages
    (D) passage of a civil rights act
    (E) funding of farm mortgages through the Farm Credit Administration

55. During wartime conferences, the Allies agreed to all of the following EXCEPT

    (A) a combined U.S.-British invasion of France
    (B) Japan must agree to unconditional surrender
    (C) a nonbinding vote for permanent members of the Security Council
    (D) the Soviet Union's entrance into the war against Japan
    (E) Stalin's support for the Nationalist Chinese

56. Which of the following third parties participated in the 1948 presidential election?

    (A) Know-Nothing
    (B) Communist
    (C) Populist
    (D) Dixiecrat
    (E) Bull Moose

GO ON TO THE NEXT PAGE ▶

57. Which of the following presidents and foreign policy initiatives are NOT correctly paired?

(A) Lyndon Johnson: "two China" policy

(B) Harry Truman: Point Four Program

(C) Ronald Reagan: "Star Wars" antiballistic missile system

(D) John F. Kennedy: Alliance for Progress

(E) Jimmy Carter: agreement to return the Panama Canal Zone to Panama

58. Which statement best describes Richard Nixon's attitude toward Watergate?

(A) He did not believe that wiretapping the Democratic National Headquarters and trying to cover it up were serious enough to be impeached over.

(B) He felt he was being unjustly prosecuted by political adversaries in both parties.

(C) He did not believe that there was anything wrong with wiretapping the Democratic National Headquarters.

(D) He felt that Vice President Spiro Agnew should have been impeached for his role.

(E) He left office for the good of the country while continuing to maintain his innocence.

59. Over time, colonial Maryland developed an economy very similar to that of

(A) Pennsylvania

(B) Virginia

(C) New Jersey

(D) Georgia

(E) Massachusetts

60. Even while the Revolutionary War was being fought, it was clear that attitudes about a number of things had changed. All of the following are true about this period EXCEPT

(A) interest in extending civil and political rights to women was apparent in New England

(B) the hold of religion on people's lives had declined

(C) titles of nobility were eliminated by state legislatures

(D) interest in abolishing slavery in some areas of the nation was growing

(E) most new state constitutions called for a strong legislative branch and a weak executive

61. According to the Navigation Acts,

(A) goods did not have to be shipped through England so long as customs duties were paid

(B) enumerated goods could be sold only to England

(C) hatmakers in the colonies could sell their beaver hats to England or to the colonies

(D) colonists could export raw wool, yarn, or wool cloth to countries other than England if customs duties were paid

(E) smugglers would be tried in admiralty courts

62. All of the following were provisions of the Constitution as originally ratified EXCEPT

(A) indirect election of senators

(B) the counting of three fifths of slaves for purposes of determining representation in the House

(C) abolition of the internal slave trade

(D) enumerated powers

(E) the elastic clause

PRACTICE TEST 3—*Continued*

63. Which of the following was NOT a cause of the War of 1812?

(A) Macon's Bill No. 2

(B) Westerners' interest in seizing Canada

(C) Impressment of U.S. sailors

(D) U.S. attack on the *Chesapeake*

(E) British repeal of the Orders in Council

64. The underlying cause for the depression that lingered after the Panic of 1837 was

(A) the high tariff

(B) cheap money

(C) overspeculation in Western lands

(D) a corresponding depression in European markets

(E) Van Buren's independent treasury system

65. Which of the following statements best describes the purpose of the Fourteenth Amendment?

(A) The Fourteenth Amendment overrode the provision of Article I, counting African Americans as three fifths of a person for apportioning representatives in the House.

(B) The federal government has used the Civil War amendments to prosecute civil rights cases in the twentieth century.

(C) The Fourteenth Amendment limits the power of the federal government in cases involving a citizen's civil rights within a state.

(D) The Fourteenth Amendment protects citizens from acts of the states.

(E) Together, the Fourteenth and Seventeenth Amendments have extended the franchise to all Americans of voting age.

66. Which of the following issues cost both Hayes and Arthur their party's renomination as president?

(A) Tariff reform

(B) Cheap money

(C) Proposed regulation of big business

(D) Civil service reform

(E) Their use of federal troops to intervene in strikes

GO ON TO THE NEXT PAGE ➡

PRACTICE TEST 3—*Continued*

Question 67 refers to the following photograph.

67. The photograph captures the significance of the election of 1920 because it shows

(A) Harding running his "front porch" campaign

(B) the absence of African Americans in the crowd

(C) Harding running his "Rose Garden" campaign

(D) the presence of women in the crowd

(E) the lack of enthusiasm from both Harding and the crowd

PRACTICE TEST 3—*Continued*

68. Which of the following agreements re-nounced war as a vehicle of national policy?

(A) Five-Power Treaty

(B) Treaty of Versailles

(C) United Nations Charter

(D) Kellogg-Briand Pact

(E) Rush-Bagot Agreement

69. The War Powers Act of 1973 was passed in response to Johnson's use of his power as commander in chief to send troops into Vietnam. Which of the following presidents also used his authority as commander in chief to send troops to fight without asking Congress's approval?

(A) Harry Truman

(B) Franklin Roosevelt

(C) Dwight Eisenhower

(D) Woodrow Wilson

(E) Jimmy Carter

70. Critics of Reagan's economic program

(A) complained that an increase in taxes would damage economic growth

(B) advised "priming the pump"

(C) were supply-siders

(D) believed that he was passing the problem of the huge federal deficit to future generations

(E) urged a tax cut to jump-start the economy

71. All of the following were associated with colonial Pennsylvania EXCEPT

(A) Quakers

(B) theocratic government

(C) varied economy

(D) diverse population

(E) Lower Counties

72. Speaker I: The Constitution provides a framework for what we should do and how we should do it, but we—and future generations—will need that elastic clause to cover ideas we'll never think of in 1794.

Speaker II: We are too weak as a nation and too dependent on trade with Great Britain to join the French—even if they did help us in the Revolution.

Speaker III: We need some way to carry out the financial powers listed in the Constitution, such as collecting taxes, but a national bank is not the way to do it.

Which of the above statements is INCONSISTENT with the Federalists' position?

(A) I only

(B) I and II

(C) I and III

(D) II and III

(E) III only

73. All of the following are characteristics of Transcendentalist thought and writing EXCEPT

(A) the unity and divinity of nature and humankind

(B) the use of nationalist themes and symbols

(C) a belief in the importance of intuition

(D) an interest in mysticism

(E) belief in a Supreme Being

GO ON TO THE NEXT PAGE ➤

PRACTICE TEST 3—*Continued*

74. Which of the following reformers is INCORRECTLY paired with his or her interest?

    (A) Dorothea Dix: women's suffrage

    (B) Horace Mann: education

    (C) Thomas Gallaudet: deaf and hearing impaired

    (D) Frederick Douglass: abolition

    (E) Robert Owen: utopian society

75. The end of the excess profits tax in the 1920s was meant to

    (A) help people continue buying on credit by reducing interest rates

    (B) stimulate investment by the wealthiest members of society

    (C) end the buying of stocks on margin

    (D) "prime the pump"

    (E) provide money for the average person to begin setting aside a retirement fund

76. Which of the following statements is TRUE about Franklin Roosevelt's relations with the Supreme Court?

    (A) Once the so-called "court-packing scheme" went through, Roosevelt named so many justices that it became known as the "Roosevelt Court."

    (B) Roosevelt was concerned that the Supreme Court might overturn the Social Security Act, so he asked Congress to enlarge the number of judges in the Circuit Court and justices on the Supreme Court.

    (C) The Supreme Court did less harm to his programs than Roosevelt claimed.

    (D) Roosevelt made the record of the Supreme Court a campaign issue in 1936.

    (E) The lower courts actually had more impact on the New Deal than the Supreme Court had, but Roosevelt was determined to punish the higher court.

77. Since World War II, the trend in population movement in the United States has been

    (A) from the Rust Belt to the Sunbelt

    (B) from all sections of the country to the Sunbelt

    (C) from the Northeast to the Southeast

    (D) from the Snowbelt to the Sunbelt

    (E) relatively stable

78. "I have always believed that, in order for a movement to be lasting, it must be built on the people. . . . Money by itself will not get the job done. . . . If workers are going to do anything, they need their own power. They need to involve themselves in meaningful ways."

    All of the following would most likely agree with these words EXCEPT

    (A) César Chavez

    (B) Herbert Spencer

    (C) Samuel Gompers

    (D) Eugene V. Debs

    (E) Martin Luther King, Jr.

79. The significance of the Immigration Act of 1965 is that the Act

    (A) abolished the national quota system for immigration

    (B) reinstated the elements of the Gentlemen's Agreement of 1906

    (C) continued the system of preferences for skilled workers and relatives of U.S. citizens

    (D) provided an amnesty under which undocumented aliens could become legal citizens

    (E) made it easier for the INS to deport illegal aliens

PRACTICE TEST 3—*Continued*

80. Which of the following was the major campaign issue in the 1992 election?

(A) the "Contract with America"

(B) health care

(C) the economy

(D) gun control

(E) aid to education

81. The writings of which of the following led to the end of the encomienda system?

(A) King Ferdinand

(B) Fray Junípero Serra

(C) Hernán Cortés

(D) Bartolomé de Las Casas

(E) Fray Eusebio Kino

82. The major reason that slavery did not develop in New England was

(A) the presence of natural resources more suited to industrial development

(B) the presence of a large pool of native-born women as workers

(C) Puritan teachings that opposed slavery

(D) its climate and land features were less adaptable to large-scale farming

(E) that New England merchants did not mind selling slaves but did not want to be reminded by the presence of slaves

83. "Everything that is right or reasonable pleads for separation. The blood of the slain, the weeping voice of nature cries, 'Tis Time to Part!' "

The above statement, which deeply affected the delegates to the Second Continental Congress, is from

(A) *Letters from a Farmer in Pennsylvania* by John Dickinson

(B) *Poor Richard's Almanack* by Ben Franklin

(C) *Letters from an American Farmer* by Hector St. John de Crevécoeur

(D) *Common Sense* by Thomas Paine

(E) A letter from Abigail Adams

84. All of the following are examples of the concept that third parties often develop out of some radical approach to a problem EXCEPT

(A) Populists

(B) Progressives

(C) Know-Nothings

(D) Democrats (Andrew Jackson era)

(E) Republicans (founded in 1854)

GO ON TO THE NEXT PAGE

PRACTICE TEST 3—*Continued*

Question 85 refers to the following pie charts and table.

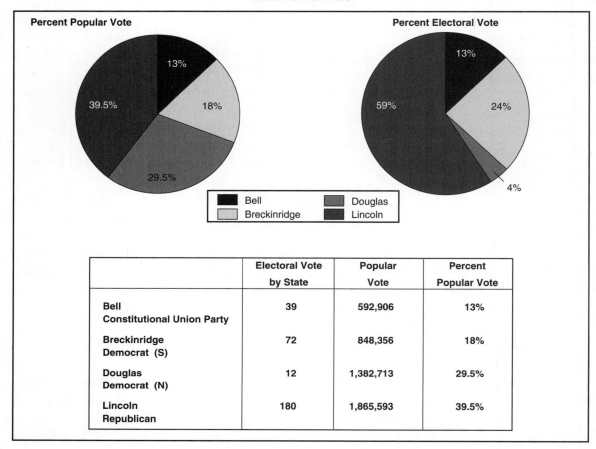

ELECTION OF 1860

Percent Popular Vote

Percent Electoral Vote

	Electoral Vote by State	Popular Vote	Percent Popular Vote
Bell Constitutional Union Party	39	592,906	13%
Breckinridge Democrat (S)	72	848,356	18%
Douglas Democrat (N)	12	1,382,713	29.5%
Lincoln Republican	180	1,865,593	39.5%

85. Which of the following statements best describes the significance of the 1860 election data?

(A) Lincoln was a minority president.

(B) Douglas's electoral percentage does not adequately reflect his popularity.

(C) Voters did not vote by regional interest.

(D) While Douglas won the states with few electoral votes, he won the majority of popular votes.

(E) The two Democratic candidates out- polled Lincoln in electoral votes.

PRACTICE TEST 3—*Continued*

86. All of the following were among the reforms inspired by progressives at the state and local level EXCEPT

    (A) setting the maximum working hours for women at 10 hours a day

    (B) regulation of child labor

    (C) women's suffrage

    (D) establishment of worker's compensation funds

    (E) regulation of railroad rates

87. Roosevelt would have preferred that the Neutrality Acts of 1935, 1936, and 1937

    (A) limited U.S. economic aid to belligerents

    (B) banned loans to warring nations in the Western Hemisphere

    (C) distinguished between aggressor nations and victim nations

    (D) banned the sale of nuclear weapons

    (E) allowed the sale of weapons after a certain period of time

88. All of the following were writers of the "Beat Generation" EXCEPT

    (A) William Burroughs

    (B) Allen Ginsberg

    (C) Laurence Ferlinghetti

    (D) Jack Kerouac

    (E) Jasper Johns

89. "To resist without bitterness; to be cursed and not reply" reflects the philosophy of

    (A) Booker T. Washington in the Atlanta Compromise

    (B) Malcolm X and the Black Muslims

    (C) Stokely Carmichael and Black Power

    (D) Martin Luther King and the Southern Christian Leadership Conference

    (E) W.E.B. Du Bois and the NAACP

90. During Bill Clinton's administrations, which of the following was struck down as unconstitutional by the U.S. Supreme Court?

    (A) Balanced budget amendment

    (B) Family and Medical Leave Act

    (C) "Don't ask, don't tell" policy in the military

    (D) Line item veto

    (E) AAA

S T O P

If you finish before the hour is up, you may review your work on this test only. You may not turn to any other test in this book.

ANSWERS AND EXPLANATIONS

QUICK-SCORE ANSWERS								
1. E	11. C	21. B	31. D	41. D	51. E	61. B	71. B	81. D
2. B	12. B	22. B	32. A	42. E	52. A	62. C	72. E	82. D
3. B	13. D	23. E	33. B	43. A	53. B	63. E	73. B	83. D
4. C	14. D	24. B	34. C	44. E	54. D	64. C	74. A	84. D
5. D	15. D	25. D	35. A	45. D	55. C	65. B	75. B	85. A
6. D	16. A	26. A	36. D	46. C	56. D	66. D	76. B	86. E
7. D	17. A	27. B	37. B	47. E	57. A	67. D	77. B	87. C
8. C	18. D	28. D	38. B	48. A	58. A	68. D	78. B	88. E
9. E	19. E	29. D	39. C	49. C	59. B	69. A	79. A	89. D
10. C	20. D	30. D	40. A	50. C	60. A	70. D	80. C	90. D

EXPLANATION OF ANSWERS

1. **The correct answer is (E).** The abundant fishing grounds of the Pacific coast provided the Native Americans of the Northwest with surplus food. Because they did not need to spend all their time engaged in finding or producing food, these peoples developed a class system as well as arts and crafts. To display their rank in the class system, the wealthy gave away their goods in annual potlatch ceremonies. While peoples in the other culture regions, choices (A), (B), (C), and (D), had some form of hierarchical system and arts and crafts, none had the abundance nor displayed it in the potlatch ritual.

2. **The correct answer is (B).** Choice (B) refers to the 1767 imposition of the Townshend Acts and then their repeal in 1770. The Stamp Act is significant because it was the first direct tax, choice (C), levied on the colonists; that is, the tax on the item was paid directly to the government, rather than included in the price of the item.

3. **The correct answer is (B).** While choices (A), (B), and (C) are all true about government under the Articles of Confederation, choice (B) is the most inclusive answer. Choices (A) and (C) state specific instances of government policy. Choice (D) is incorrect because the central government could not levy taxes at all. Choice (E) is incorrect because the central government had no power to establish customs duties or tariff rates. Only the states had these powers, and they could not agree because of sectional differences.

4. **The correct answer is (C).** The Twelfth Amendment was added in 1804. The Tenth Amendment, choice (A), deals with the powers reserved to the states. The Thirteenth Amendment, one of the Reconstruction Amendments, abolished slavery. The Seventeenth Amendment, choice (D), provided for the direct election of senators. The Nineteenth Amendment, choice (E), gave women the vote.

5. **The correct answer is (D).** A historical novel, although probably based on some general information about the life of Sacajawea, would not be a suitably accurate reference for a research report. Meriwether Lewis kept a journal, choice (A), which has been published as the *Journal of Meriwether Lewis.* Photographs, choice (B), would be useful in describing the animals and plants that the expedition might have seen, especially if cross-referenced with Lewis's journal. Terrain maps, choice (C), would be useful in providing information about the country the expedition moved through. Choice (E) might provide additional information about the mouth of the Columbia River and the coastline to validate the conclusions of the expedition.

6. **The correct answer is (D).** Speaker I is Andrew Jackson, and Speaker II is John C. Calhoun. Jackson is pledging loyalty to the federal union, whereas Calhoun is qualifying that loyalty by interjecting the concept of states' rights. Even if you did not know who the speakers were, you could figure out that choice (D) is the answer by using the key words. Choice (A) is incorrect because secessionists would not have said, "The Union—next to our liberty, the most dear!" Choice (B) is incorrect because there was no Union yet to preserve (Speaker I). Choice (C) is incorrect because the Articles did not establish a federal structure (Speaker I). Although Madison vetoed an internal improvements bill, choice (E), because he believed that it violated states' rights, the choice is irrelevant here.

7. **The correct answer is (D).** It was the Republicans in 1864 that were in disarray, not the Democrats. Angry over Lincoln's veto of the Wade-Davis bill, the Radical Republicans, for a time, threatened to call a second convention to nominate someone other than Lincoln. The passage of choices (B), (C), and (E) had provided help for the Northeast and the West—high tariffs for manufacturing and cheap land and access to cheap land—during Lincoln's first term in office and solidified his support in those sections. Choice (A) gave people hope that the war would soon be over.

8. **The correct answer is (C).** Choices (A), (C), and (D) are all true, but (A) and (D) are specified in the Act. Choice (C) was the underlying reason for passing the Act. Choice (B) is incorrect, as is choice (E). The Pendleton Act set up competitive examinations for hiring employees; it did not deal with elected officeholders.

9. **The correct answer is (E).** All three choices reflect Americans' attitudes toward World War I prior to the U.S.'s declaration of war. Item I was prevalent at the beginning of the war, whereas item III reflected the opinion of some Americans, such as Secretary of State

William Jennings Bryan, later in the period. Counter to item III was the attitude that the United States needed to be more aggressive in demanding that the Central Powers honor the U.S.'s neutrality. Ex-President Theodore Roosevelt advocated this position.

10. **The correct answer is (C).** While choices (A) and (D) are correct, choice (C) is a more complete response. Not only were there underlying economic problems, but the decade was marked by the red scare; restrictions on immigration; an increase in intolerance toward African Americans, Catholics, and Jews; and a number of strikes. Choice (D) refers to only a small aspect of the United States in the 1920s. Choice (B) is incorrect because by the mid-1920s, there was a worldwide depression underway. Choice (E) is correct in that real wealth was limited to the few—the top 5 percent—but incorrect in stating that most people were living in poverty in the 1920s. However, by 1929, the minimum earnings for a decent standard of living was $2,500, and fully two thirds of the nation made less than that. About 20 percent of those people were considered in extreme poverty.

11. **The correct answer is (C).** Television was used for the first time to showcase the candidates. In a series of televised debates between Vice President Richard Nixon, the Republican nominee, and John F. Kennedy, the Democratic nominee, Kennedy showed that he had the experience and ability to handle himself that Nixon claimed he lacked. The television camera was also more flattering to Kennedy, who was more handsome and more at ease than the heavy-jowled and perspiring Nixon. Choices (A), (B), (D), and (E) are all true about the 1960 election, but all are not necessarily significant in the long-term. Lincoln, for example, had also chosen a Southerner, Andrew Johnson, for his vice president. The 1960 election, however, marked the arrival of television as an important medium for communicating—and manipulating—political messages.

12. **The correct answer is (B).** Choices (A), (C), and (E) contributed to choice (B), so they were causes of, rather than the result of, settlement. Choice (D) occurred on the frontier but was a result of Hamilton's excise tax on whiskey.

13. **The correct answer is (D).** Choice (A) is incorrect because the term "manifest destiny" was not coined until 1845 in the midst of the debate over annexation of Texas and the Oregon boundary line. Choice (B) is incorrect; the United States did not begin its interventions until 1898. Choice (C) is incorrect; Great Britain wanted to issue what became known as the Monroe Doctrine jointly. The information in choice (E) is true, but irrelevant.

14. **The correct answer is (D).** Although Jackson did not have a majority of the popular vote, choice (B), that is not the reason that the election was decided in the House. The winning presidential candidate must have a majority of electoral votes, and no candidate in 1824 did, choice (D). Choice (A) is the term Jackson's supporters gave to what they considered the deal that Adams and Clay made. In

return for being named secretary of state, Clay swung his support to Adams for president. Choice (C) is incorrect; each state's electors equals the sum of the number of its senators and representatives. Choice (E) is incorrect; the Twelfth Amendment was ratified in 1804.

15. **The correct answer is (D).** Choice (A) is a distracter, because those states were the seat of Copperhead power, opponents of the Civil War, many of whom were Democrats. Although Andrew Johnson was a senator from Tennessee and remained in the Senate after secession, Tennessee seceded, choice (B). Choice (C) is only partially correct. Kansas did not border the Confederacy and remained in the Union, choice (E).

16. **The correct answer is (A).** The treaty that was signed in 1851 by the representatives of Native American nations and the U.S. government was never ratified by the Senate, although the United States paid $50,000 a year for fifteen of the fifty years for which the treaty called. In exchange, the Native Americans kept their side of the treaty until after the Civil War. Choice (C) is the opposite of a provision in the treaty. The Treaty of Guadalupe Hidalgo covered choice (B). The federal government had set aside the Black Hills, choice (D), as the Sioux reservation, but when gold was found in the mountains in the 1870s, the area was opened to whites. Choice (E) refers to the Gadsden Purchase.

17. **The correct answer is (A).** Choice (B) discourages foreign competition. Choice (C) means people have more money to spend. Choice (D) meant more markets for U.S. goods, and choice (E) would mean a larger pool of cheap labor.

18. **The correct answer is (D).** Choice (A) related to the purchase and coinage of small amounts of silver. Choice (B) related to the regulation of railroads; it set up the Interstate Commerce Commission, the first regulatory body in the nation's history. Choice (C) regulated the federal civil service system. Choice (E) authorized the government to purchase silver; this law was passed almost twenty years after the Bland-Allison Act.

19. **The correct answer is (E).** Choices (A), (B), (C), and (D) all supported U.S. imperialist interests. Choice (E) was an attempt to promote inter-American unity. It grew out of the efforts of James G. Blaine, secretary of state under Benjamin Harrison, to create closer cooperation among the nations of the Western Hemisphere. This contradicted U.S. imperialism, although both Harrison and Blaine supported U.S. interests in the Pacific, including annexation of Hawaii.

20. **The correct answer is (D).** Truman recognized only one government for China, that of Chiang Kai-shek on Taiwan. Nixon initiated the "two China" policy by recognizing the People's Republic of China.

21. **The correct answer is (B).** In the mid-twentieth century, civil rights legislation still caused Southerners to vote as a bloc in Congress. Choice (A) was not an acknowledged political issue at mid-century. Choices (C), (D), and (E) are incorrect

22. **The correct answer is (B).** All five choices are true about British policies in the colonies, but choice (B) is the most inclusive. The old policy in choice (A) is the levying of taxes; the new problem is the strong reaction of the colonists after the French and Indian War. The theory of virtual representation is the way Parliament had always considered its colonies, whereas direct, or actual, representation was the new view of the colonists, choice (C). Choice (D) is undoubtedly true but irrelevant to the question. The British were in a cycle in which they passed a law, the colonists reacted, and the British passed another law, rescinded the first law, issued a proclamation, shut down a legislature, and so on—choice (E). Whether the cycle was inescapable is arguable.

23. **The correct answer is (E).** Stowe, choice (E), was the author of *Uncle Tom's Cabin.* Phillis Wheatley, choice (A), was an African American and former slave who wrote poetry at the time of the American Revolution. James Fenimore Cooper, choice (B), developed an American identity in his novels by using material from the colonial frontier as the basis of his characters and plots. Edith Wharton, choice (C), wrote novels and short stories that dissected New York and European society at the turn of the twentieth century. Thomas Paine, choice (D), was a pamphleteer during the American Revolution; his works urged the colonists to separate from Great Britain.

24. **The correct answer is (B).** Although most Irish immigrants had been farmers, once in the United States, they stayed in cities and became laborers and factory workers. Because there were few factories in the South and farm labor was done by slaves, there was little incentive for the Irish to move to the South, choice (A).

25. **The correct answer is (D).** Choices (A) and (B) are only partially correct. While admitting California as a free state, choice (C), the Compromise of 1850 called for Utah and New Mexico Territories to delay statehood until they had determined for themselves if they would be free or slave. The Kansas-Nebraska Act of 1854 called for popular sovereignty to determine the issue in those two territories as well. The Compromise had no effect on Texas's admission as a slave state, choice (E).

26. **The correct answer is (A).** John Slidell was one of the Confederate representatives who was seized aboard the *Trent,* but it was not the reason the British almost entered the war. He was on his way to seek French support, so choice (B) is incorrect. The British welcomed choice (D) because they had recently abolished slavery themselves. Although choice (C) was a problem, the British decided that it was not worth going to war over. Choice (E) is incorrect.

Test-Taking Strategy

The key word mainly *tells you that the question is looking for a generalization as the answer. While some Irish undoubtedly moved to farming areas and took up farming again, most did not.*

27. **The correct answer is (B).** Many Republicans, including moderate Republicans, were truly concerned about ensuring the political, legal, and economic rights of African Americans. But choice (C) also figured, to an extent, in the thinking of some Republicans. Choice (D) was the major area of contention between Congress and both Lincoln and Johnson. Some Republicans also worried about the loyalty of former Confederates, choice (E).

28. **The correct answer is (D).** The "Crime of 1873" is the term given to Congress's decision not to coin silver by silver miners who were burdened with huge new silver mines and debtors who wanted cheap money with which to repay their debts. Choices (A) and (B) meant that it would have been more profitable for owners of silver mines to sell their silver to the government at the government's old ratio of 16-to-1. This prompted their calling the demonetizaton of silver in 1873 the "Crime of 1873." Choice (C) was a response to the call for cheap money but helped little in enlarging the money supply and reducing the value of the dollar. Choice (E) is irrelevant; the party survived into the 1880s.

29. **The correct answer is (D).** The SEC, choice (A), was set up in 1934 to reform and regulate the stock market. Choice (B), the Social Security Act, passed in 1935, was a reform measure of the New Deal and the first step in establishing what is known as the "welfare state." The TVA, choice (C), was an experiment in flood control, electric power generation, and social engineering in an effort to improve the lives of people living in the economically depressed Tennessee River Valley area. The National Labor Relations Act, choice (E), also known as the Wagner Act, established the right to collective bargaining for labor unions and set up the National Labor Relations Board.

30. **The correct answer is (D).** Choice (A) is incorrect because the Soviets already had troops in the nations of Eastern Europe, so there was little that Roosevelt and Churchill could do. Truman had not yet become president, so choice (B) is incorrect. Choice (C) never occurred. The conference at Dumbarton Oaks in 1944 drafted plans for a United Nations.

31. **The correct answer is (D).** The Chinese entered the Korean War on the side of the North Koreans in 1950. This was a major miscalculation by MacArthur. Choice (B) refers to a second such mistake. He thought that his reputation as a hero in World War II would convince Americans that Truman's idea of limited warfare, choice (E), was wrong, but MacArthur failed to win the nation's support, choice (A). Choice (C) is also correct and a major reason why a resolution to the war was so long in coming.

32. **The correct answer is (A).** *Roe* v. *Wade* was handed down in 1973 during the Nixon administration, so choice (A) is incorrect. Don't be fooled by the word *renewed* in choice (D). Remember the

progressives' interest in the environment and in consumer protection. Theodore Roosevelt, for example, championed conservation of the West and passage of laws such as the Pure Food and Drug Act.

33. **The correct answer is (B).** Bush had campaigned in 1988 on the promise of "no new taxes." When circumstances made that an impossible promise to keep, the voters never forgot it. Choice (A) is also known as "Operation Desert Storm." The collapse of communism in Eastern Europe and the fall of the Berlin Wall, choice (C), which had begun in the mid-1980s, finally occurred. Choice (E) ended clandestine support for the Contras.

34. **The correct answer is (C).** The first Africans had been considered indentured servants, but as tobacco became the major crop and planters looked for a stable and cheap labor force, Maryland passed a law in 1663 to make Africans slaves "for life." Choice (A) describes the practice of headright. Choices (B), (D), and (E) are incorrect.

35. **The correct answer is (A).** The Middle Passage was that part of the triangular trade route that linked the colonies in the Caribbean and on the mainland with Europe and West Africa. The major cargo was Africans who had been captured and were on their way to enforced slavery in the colonies.

36. **The correct answer is (D).** The goods transported on this leg of the triangular trade route were those things that the colonies produced—raw materials for the most part. Choices (A) and (B) were the items that were transported from the Caribbean colonies to the mainland. Manufactured goods, choice (C), were the traded goods from England to the colonies. Choice (E) is an incorrect grouping of items: manufactured goods from England, and rum from the Caribbean islands.

37. **The correct answer is (B).** In June 1776, Richard Henry Lee introduced a resolution that called for independence, and while it was debated, a committee worked on the Declaration of Independence. Lee's Resolution was approved by the Continental Congress on July 2, and the Declaration was adopted two days later. George III issued the Proclamation, choice (A), calling on his loyal subjects to oppose rebellion. Choice (C) was issued in response to the Intolerable Acts. Choice (D) listed the basic rights of British subjects and rejected Parliament's right to tax the colonists. Choice (E) was the colonists' attempt to find a peaceful solution to the increasing conflict with Great Britain.

38. **The correct answer is (B).** The Fourth Amendment prohibits unlawful searches and seizures and was aimed at the British use of writs of assistance to search for smuggled goods. The Third Amendment corrects choice (A). The seeds of responses to choices (D) and (E) can be seen in various provisions of the Constitution, such as the right to a speedy trial by one's peers and separation of church and state, choice (E). The American principle of assessing the truthfulness of statements to determine libel was established in the trial of John Peter Zenger, choice (C).

39. The correct answer is (C). Even though the Supreme Court ruled in favor of the Cherokee in *Cherokee Nation* v. *The State of Georgia* and *Worcester* v. *Georgia,* Jackson, the old "Indian Fighter," sided with Georgia. Because of the Indian Removal Act of 1830 and his refusal to aid the Cherokee, Jackson and then President Martin Van Buren oversaw the transfer of thousands of Native Americans from the Southeast to the Indian Territory.

Test-Taking Strategy

Educated guessing can help you when you don't immediately know the answer.

40. The correct answer is (A). Logic tells you that Webster, choice (D), cannot be the answer, because as a New Englander, he would not have wanted to reduce the tariff. If you knew that Pierce became president in 1852 and that by then the Oregon boundary dispute had been solved and the annexation of California had been accomplished, you could eliminate choice (E). Choices (B) and (C) are incorrect.

41. The correct answer is (D). This was an amendment to a bill that authorized the purchase of land from Mexico. While the House approved the amendment, the Senate did not, but the proviso created bitterness in the South. Choice (A) is incorrect because the question asks about Mexican lands. David Wilmot did not accept the argument stated in choice (B) or he would not have submitted his rider. Choice (C) is incorrect. Choice (E) relates to the Compromise of 1850.

42. The correct answer is (E). Baker, choice (A), wrote *Follow the Color Line,* which was about racial discrimination. Wells, choice (B), was a journalist and antilynching crusader. Norris was a novelist who wrote *The Octopus,* which was about the railroad industry's hold on farmers. Sinclair, choice (D), wrote *The Jungle,* which was about the meat-packing industry.

43. The correct answer is (A). Choices (C) and (D) helped to stir up Americans' sympathy for the Cubans, and choice (E) was the immediate cause of the declaration of war. While you might think that choice (A) would be a cause for war, President McKinley and U.S. business interests feared that war would send the United States back into an economic depression. The nation was just coming out of the severe depression of 1893.

44. The correct answer is (E). The Northern Securities Company had been formed in 1902 when competing combinations had been unable to win control of the Northern Pacific Railroad. J.P. Morgan and James J. Hill joined with E.H. Harriman and the banking house of Kuhn, Loeb to create a holding company with a monopoly over rail transportation from Lake Michigan to the Pacific. This Supreme Court case was the first in a series under Theodore Roosevelt to rein in trusts and combinations. Choice (B) may have given you a moment's pause because strikes and boycotts by labor unions had once been considered against the law, but choice (B) is incorrect in this context. Choice (A) was the federal law under which the Northern Securities case was prosecuted. Choices (C) and (D) are incorrect.

45. The correct answer is (D). Choice (A) provided aid to war-torn Europe after World War II. Choice (B) was established after World War II to provide for the mutual defense of non-Communist nations in Europe. Choice (C) was the name Theodore Roosevelt gave to his domestic program. Choice (E) was Kennedy's program to halt the spread of communism in Latin America.

46. The correct answer is (C). By 1754, Philadelphia was the second-largest city in the British Empire after London. New York, choice (A), was the second-largest city in the North American colonies and Boston, choice (B), the third. Charleston, choice (D), was an important port for the South. Wilmington, choice (E), was an important port in the southern Middle Colonies. Note that all these cities were ports.

47. The correct answer is (E). The Federalists had strong leadership in Alexander Hamilton, John Jay, and James Madison, who co-authored *The Federalist*. Choices (B) and (D) were concerns of the Anti-Federalists. Having a special convention in each state seemed to usurp the power of the states.

48. The correct answer is (A). Do not be confused because The Prophet, choice (A), was the spiritual leader and Tecumseh, choice (B), was the warrior. Tecumseh was not in the village of Tippecanoe when Harrison's troops attacked, so choice (A) is correct. Choice (C) was an Apache chief who was captured in 1871. Choice (D) was a chief of the Nez Perce who surrendered to the U.S. Army in 1877. Choice (E) led the Shawnee and their allies against General Anthony Wayne at the Battle of Fallen Timbers in 1794.

49. The correct answer is (C). Southern slave owners pushed for purchase or annexation of Cuba to add more slaveholding territory to the United States, but nothing came of the offer. Choice (A) ceded to the United States what became the Panama Canal Zone. Choice (B) involved Taft's Secretary of the Interior Richard Ballinger and Gifford Pinchot, Chief Forester, over Ballinger's opening of lands in Montana, Wyoming, and Alaska for private purchase. Choice (D) was the purchase of land from Mexico in order to secure a Southern route for a transcontinental railroad. Choice (E) was the name given to the purchase of Alaska; Secretary of State William Seward arranged for the sale.

50. The correct answer is (C). The other four planks were more representative of the interests of the farmers, miners, and small business owners who also made up the Populist Party.

51. The correct answer is (E). The statement is by historian Frederick Jackson Turner in his book *The Frontier in American History*. The American who agreed with his views most likely would have applauded choices (A), (B), (C), and (D), which opened up the continent to U.S. settlement, and disapproved of closing off any of it as a home for Native Americans, choice (E).

52. **The correct answer is (A).** Both Washington and Garvey addressed their messages to ordinary African Americans. None of the them believed in choice (B). Both Du Bois and Garvey celebrated their African heritage, Garvey with his "back-to-Africa" movement and Du Bois with Pan-Africanism. Choice (D) was Washington's focus. Choice (E) was also true of Washington's approach.

53. **The correct answer is (B).** Choices (B), (C), and (D) are all true of Harding's administration, but choices (C) and (D) are specific actions that support choice (B). Choice (B), then, is the most inclusive answer. Choice (A) is the opposite of what occurred under Harding, and choice (E) is incorrect for the time period.

54. **The correct answer is (D).** Although the New Deal was to a degree sympathetic to the economic problems of African Americans, it did nothing to ensure their civil rights. The first effective civil rights act was passed during Lyndon Johnson's administration in 1964. President Eisenhower had pushed for the passage of civil rights acts in 1957 and 1960, but little came of the acts. Choice (A) was guaranteed by the Social Security Act of 1935. Choice (B) was part of the National Labor Relation Act of 1935, also known as the Wagner Act. Choice (C) refers to the Home Owners Loan Corporation (HOLC) of 1933. The information in choice (E) is correct, but it is the incorrect answer.

55. **The correct answer is (C).** At Dumbarton Oaks in 1944, representatives of the Allies worked out permanent seats on the Security Council and veto power for the United States, Great Britain, the Soviet Union, France, and China, so choice (C) is incorrectly stated. In 1943 at the Moscow Conference of Foreign Ministers, Great Britain, the Soviet Union, and the United States agreed to the invasion of Normandy, choice (A). Choice (B) was one outcome of the Potsdam conference in 1945, the only wartime conference that Truman attended. Choices (D) and (E) were results of the Yalta Conference in early 1945.

56. **The correct answer is (D).** The Southern Democrats broke ranks with the national Democratic Party over a civil rights plank in the party platform and formed their own States' Rights Party, also known as the Dixiecrat Party. Strom Thurmond, then governor of South Carolina, ran as their presidential candidate. A new Progressive Party that formed in 1948 supported Henry Wallace for president. Choice (A) ran a slate of candidates in the 1852 election on an anti-immigration, anti-Catholic platform. The Communist Party, choice (B), is registered and may run candidates for election; however, it did not enter the 1948 presidential election. Choice (E) was the party of Theodore Roosevelt in the 1912 election.

57. **The correct answer is (A).** The "two China" policy was an initiative of Richard Nixon and his Secretary of State, Henry Kissinger. Truman's Point Four Program, choice (B), provided technical, education, and health-care assistance to underdeveloped nations. Choice (C) was an experimental space-based antiballistic

missile system that was shelved in the Clinton administration. Choice (D) was aimed at providing aid to Latin American nations and undermining the appeal of Fidel Castro. Choice (E) was accomplished in 1999.

58. **The correct answer is (A).** Nixon may have privately thought that choice (B) was true, but his public response was choice (A). Choices (C), (D), and (E) are incorrect. Agnew had resigned earlier and pleaded no contest in a plea bargain to a single charge of having failed to report income from money received as a kickback while governor of Maryland.

59. **The correct answer is (B).** The climate and terrain were similar to those of the Virginia colony, where tobacco grew well. Over time, Maryland adopted tobacco agriculture on large plantations that were worked by enslaved African Americans. While you might have thought twice about selecting choices (A), (C), and even (D), you should have immediately rejected choice (E), Massachusetts, because of the difference in climate and terrain.

60. **The correct answer is (A).** Considering that it took from 1776 to 1920—144 years—for women to gain the right to vote, choice (A) would seem to be a good answer to select for this *except* question. The truth of choice (B) was apparent in the separation of church and state built into the Constitution. Choice (D) was apparent in the ending of slavery in the Middle Atlantic and New England states by early in the nineteenth century. The principle behind choice (E) turned out to be the problem with the Articles of Confederation when the states tried to establish a new national government.

61. **The correct answer is (B).** Choice (A) is the opposite of what the Navigation Acts stated. According to the Hat Act, choice (C), beaver hats could be sold only in the colonies. The Woolen Act, choice (D), forbade the export of wool to other colonies or to England to protect English manufacturing. Choice (E) was a later provision under George Grenville.

62. **The correct answer is (C).** The Constitution forbade the importation of slaves after 1808 but said nothing about the internal slave trade, which grew dramatically in the following decades with the spread of cotton agriculture.

63. **The correct answer is (E).** The British repeal of the Orders in Council, which had forbidden neutral ships to trade with European nations unless the ships stopped in British ports first, was meant to avoid hostilities with the United States. However, the United States had already declared war on Great Britain.

64. **The correct answer is (C).** The effects of Jackson's release of several million acres of Western land, the destruction of the Second Bank, and the issuing of credit by unstable state banks were felt for a number of years. Choice (A) had been reduced after the bitter fight in 1833. Choice (B) became an issue in the second half of the 1800s. Choices (D) and (E) are incorrect.

Test-Taking Strategy

Try educated guessing if you don't immediately know the answer. Eliminate those answers that you know are incorrect or don't make sense.

Test-Taking Strategy

Knowing the time frame can help you eliminate choices. Except for choices (A) and (B), the answer choices relate to later English policies.

65. The correct answer is (B). Choices (A), (B), and (D) are correct, but choice (B) best answers the question. Choice (D) describes how the Amendment is used, not what its purpose, or provisions, are. Choice (A) describes one specific provision, but choice (B) states a more significant and long-lasting effect of the law. Choice (C) is incorrect, as is choice (E). Together, the Fourteenth, Nineteenth (women's suffrage), and the Twenty-Sixth (the right to vote to 18-year-old citizens) Amendments have extended the franchise.

66. The correct answer is (D). Hayes appointed people to positions because of their qualifications rather than their party affiliation and insisted that government positions be filled by competitive examination. This alienated both the Halfbreeds and the Stalwarts in the Republican Party. Arthur pushed for civil service reform and supported passage of the Pendleton Act. Arthur supported choice (A). Hayes opposed the issuance of greenbacks and vetoed the Bland-Allison Act, which became law over his veto, choice (B). Choice (C) is incorrect. Hayes set a precedent for choice (E).

67. The correct answer is (D). Harding did run a "front porch" campaign, choice (A), but the significance of the 1920 election was that women could vote for the first time in a national election, choice (D). Incumbent presidents sometimes run what is known as the "Rose Garden" campaign, because they do not venture far from the White House in order to remind voters that they have the experience to run the country and are busy doing just that.

68. The correct answer is (D). Ultimately, sixty-two nations signed the Pact. It had little practical effect since there were no provisions for enforcing it other than popular opinion. Choice (A) was signed as part of the Washington Conference; the signatories agreed to limit production of large warships. Choice (B) included the charter for the League of Nations, which would peacefully settle international disputes and punish errant nations. Choice (C) established a world organization to promote peace and cooperation and to work to improve the welfare of poor countries. Choice (E) was an agreement between the United States and Great Britain for mutual disarmament of the Great Lakes.

69. The correct answer is (A). Harry Truman sent troops into Korea without asking for a declaration of war from Congress. He claimed the power as commander in chief and the UN charter. Both choices (B) and (D) asked Congress for formal declarations of war. Choices (C) and (E) do not apply.

70. The correct answer is (D). Reagan greatly increased defense spending, cut domestic programs, and cut taxes, creating a huge deficit and high interest rates, which gave rise to choice (D). Reagan's policy was known as supply-side economics, so choice (C) is illogical. Choice (B) would only have added to the deficit, so it is also illogical. Reagan cut taxes, so choice (A) is illogical. Choice (E) is what Reagan was doing, so it is incorrect.

71. **The correct answer is (B).** Although William Penn founded Pennsylvania as a haven for Quakers, choice (A), it was not a theocracy, or government by those who claim to rule by divine authority. The economy of the colony, choice (C), was based on agriculture and trade, with the largest port city in the colonies in 1750. One of the Middle Colonies, Pennsylvania's population had come originally from England, Sweden, the Netherlands, Germany, and Ireland. To have an outlet to the sea, the Duke of York gave Penn what was known as the Lower Counties, today the state of Delaware, choice (E).

72. **The correct answer is (E).** A Federalist would typically have supported chartering the First National Bank, so choices (C), (D), and (E) might be the correct answer to this *except* question. However, a Federalist would also have supported the elastic clause and avoiding war with France, so only choice (E) is correct.

73. **The correct answer is (B).** Transcendentalist thought and writing exhibited choices (A), (C), (D), and (E) but not choice (B), the themes and symbols of nationalism. Those were found in the works of James Fenimore Cooper and Nathaniel Hawthorne, not Ralph Waldo Emerson and Henry David Thoreau.

74. **The correct answer is (A).** Dorothea Dix worked to improve the treatment of the mentally ill. Frederick Douglass, choice (D), while better known for his abolitionist work, also championed women's suffrage. After the Civil War, he continued to work for better treatment of former slaves.

75. **The correct answer is (B).** Andrew Mellon, Secretary of the Treasury, believed that the wealthy should not be heavily taxed because they alone had the capital to invest in business and, thus, stimulate economic growth. Choices (A), (C), (D), and (E) are incorrect. Choice (D) was the method that was favored by Franklin Roosevelt to get the economy moving again and to end the Depression. It was a theory that was advocated by economist John Maynard Keynes and one that underlay much of the economic policy of subsequent presidents until Ronald Reagan's supply-side economics.

76. **The correct answer is (B).** In an attempt to disguise his true purpose, Roosevelt claimed that he wanted to make the federal judiciary more efficient by adding judges for those who chose not to retire at age 70 but no more than forty-four judges to the Circuit Court and six justices to the Supreme Court. Choice (A) is partially incorrect because the scheme was never approved by Congress. However, the Supreme Court began to hand down decisions that were more favorable to the New Deal, and as justices retired, Roosevelt was able to name several replacements, making it the "Roosevelt Court." Choice (C) is incorrect because the Court did strike down the AAA and the NIRA, centerpieces of Roosevelt's early New Deal. Choice (D) is incorrect because Roosevelt did not make the Court's record a campaign issue in the election; this was

338

one reason why he failed in his attempt to change the Court. He did not gather public opinion to his cause. Choice (E) is incorrect.

77. **The correct answer is (B).** Although choices (A), (B), (C), and (D) are all true about population movement, choice (B) is the most inclusive and is, therefore, the best answer. The Rust Belt, choice (A), includes the Northeast and the Upper Midwest. The Southeast, choice (C), is part of the Sunbelt. Choice (E) is incorrect.

78. **The correct answer is (B).** These words were written by César Chavez, choice (A). Herbert Spencer, choice (B), was the champion of Social Darwinism and would not have believed that people could help themselves. Samuel Gompers, choice (C), led the American Federation of Labor (AFL) for thirty-two years. Eugene V. Debs, choice (D), was a labor organizer and socialist. Martin Luther King, Jr., choice (E), was a civil rights activist.

Test-Taking Strategy

The key word is significance.

79. **The correct answer is (A).** The quota system had been established by the immigration laws of 1921, 1924, and 1929. Choice (C) is incorrect because the 1965 act established the preference system for relatives. The Immigration Reform and Control Act of 1986 provided an amnesty program, so choice (D) is incorrect. The Illegal Immigration Restriction Act of 1996 made it easier for the Immigration and Naturalization Service (INS) to deport illegal aliens, so choice (E) is incorrect. Choice (B) is incorrect.

Test-Taking Strategy

The key words are major issue.

80. **The correct answer is (C).** The 1992 campaign revolved, to a large extent, around the lackluster performance of the economy under the Bush administration and Bush's promise not to raise taxes—a promise he went back on. Choice (A) was the social and economic program that the Republicans in the House attempted to push through after the 1994 midterm elections. Choice (C) was an important issue in the 1992 election but not the central issue, nor were choices (D) and (E).

81. **The correct answer is (D).** By protesting the ill treatment of Native Americans, de Las Casas unwittingly aided in the enslavement of Africans. A king need simply to decree that the system end, so choice (A) is illogical. Choice (B) established a series of missions in California in the late 1700s. Choice (C) conquered the Aztec empire in Mexico. Choice (E) explored the Spanish borderlands, establishing some twenty-five missions and mapping the territory in the late 1600s and early 1700s.

Test-Taking Strategy

The key words are major reason.

82. **The correct answer is (D).** Poor quality, rocky soil, and a cold climate did not lend themselves to large-scale cotton, tobacco, rice, or indigo agriculture. Choices (A), (B), and (C) were true, but none was the major reason why slavery did not develop in New England. Choice (E) is illogical.

83. **The correct answer is (D).** The clues are the tone and the reference to the Second Continental Congress. Choice (A) was written in 1767 and 1768, so it was too early to be an influence on the delegates. More importantly, although a delegate to the Continental

Congress, Dickinson was against independence. Choice (B) is illogical, given the nature of the *Almanack*. Choice (C) was written in 1782 and is a description of the period, not a political tract. Although Abigail Adams was influential, she wrote private letters, so it is doubtful that the delegates would have read these words, choice (E).

84. **The correct answer is (D).** The purpose of the Jacksonian Democrats was to elect Jackson; there was no particular social, political, or economic problem that they wished to solve. Choice (A), the Populists, were interested in reforms that were aimed at helping farmers, such as coinage of silver. Choice (B) advocated a number of reforms at all levels of society: government, business, social mores, and politics. Choice (C) formed to limit immigration and keep Catholics and naturalized citizens out of government. Choice (E) formed from the Whig and Free Soil Parties and abolitionists.

Test-Taking Strategy

The key words are best describes *and* significance.

85. **The correct answer is (A).** While choice (B) is correct, it is not particularly important in the larger view of U.S. history. Choice (A) is more significant because it shows that Lincoln, as he began his first term, did not have the support of the majority of the people. Choices (C), (D), and (E) are incorrect.

86. **The correct answer is (E).** Choices (A), (B), (C), and (D) were all reforms at the local and state levels before they became national laws. National regulation was needed to regulate railroads because they were interstate.

87. **The correct answer is (C).** Choice (A) is the opposite of the Acts; the United States could provide aid only to nonbelligerents. Choices (B), (D), and (E) are incorrect. Choice (D) is easy to eliminate because there were no nuclear weapons in this time period.

88. **The correct answer is (E).** Johns was a painter of the 1950s. Choices (A) and (D) were novelists, and choices (B) and (C) were poets.

89. **The correct answer is (D).** This quotation reflects the philosophy of nonviolence that Dr. Martin Luther King brought to the SCLC and the civil rights movement. It is the antithesis of the beliefs of Stokely Carmichael, choice (C), who believed in aggressive confrontation, and Malcolm X, choice (B), who advocated revolution. Du Bois, choice (E), also believed in peaceful resistance, but the NAACP waged its campaigns more through lobbying legislators, its publications, and court cases. Washington, choice (A), proposed that African Americans should seek progress through economic efforts and not political protest, so choice (A) would not apply.

Red Alert!

Highlight in some way—by underlining, circling, or bracketing—the key words in the question. Clinton administration and unconstitutional are key here. By misreading the question, you might choose choice (E) and be incorrect.

90. **The correct answer is (D).** Although members of Congress and presidents for several administrations had pressed for a line item veto, the Supreme Court held that it was unconstitutional. According to the ruling, the line item veto, in effect, gave the president the power to rewrite legislation. This contradicted the Constitution, which gives the president only two options in regard to legislation: either to sign a bill or to veto it. Choice (A) was never ratified, but if it had been, this could not be the correct answer, because once an amendment is added to the Constitution, it becomes the law of the land and cannot be held unconstitutional. Choice (B) is incorrect. Choice (C) was the Clinton policy in regard to gays' and lesbians' serving in the armed forces. Choice (E) is a good distracter, because the Agricultural Adjustment Act was overturned—in 1936 as part of the New Deal.

ANSWER SHEETS

Leave any unused
answer spaces blank.

	Test Code											Subject Test (print)					
V	①	②	③	④	⑤	⑥	⑦	⑧	⑨								
W	①	②	③	④	⑤	⑥	⑦	⑧	⑨								
X	①	②	③	④	⑤	Y	Ⓐ	Ⓑ	Ⓒ	Ⓓ	Ⓔ	FOR ETS USE ONLY	R/C	W/S1	FS/S2	CS/S3	WS
Q	①	②	③	④	⑤	⑥	⑦	⑧	⑨								

1 Ⓐ Ⓑ Ⓒ Ⓓ Ⓔ   21 Ⓐ Ⓑ Ⓒ Ⓓ Ⓔ   41 Ⓐ Ⓑ Ⓒ Ⓓ Ⓔ   61 Ⓐ Ⓑ Ⓒ Ⓓ Ⓔ   81 Ⓐ Ⓑ Ⓒ Ⓓ Ⓔ
2 Ⓐ Ⓑ Ⓒ Ⓓ Ⓔ   22 Ⓐ Ⓑ Ⓒ Ⓓ Ⓔ   42 Ⓐ Ⓑ Ⓒ Ⓓ Ⓔ   62 Ⓐ Ⓑ Ⓒ Ⓓ Ⓔ   82 Ⓐ Ⓑ Ⓒ Ⓓ Ⓔ
3 Ⓐ Ⓑ Ⓒ Ⓓ Ⓔ   23 Ⓐ Ⓑ Ⓒ Ⓓ Ⓔ   43 Ⓐ Ⓑ Ⓒ Ⓓ Ⓔ   63 Ⓐ Ⓑ Ⓒ Ⓓ Ⓔ   83 Ⓐ Ⓑ Ⓒ Ⓓ Ⓔ
4 Ⓐ Ⓑ Ⓒ Ⓓ Ⓔ   24 Ⓐ Ⓑ Ⓒ Ⓓ Ⓔ   44 Ⓐ Ⓑ Ⓒ Ⓓ Ⓔ   64 Ⓐ Ⓑ Ⓒ Ⓓ Ⓔ   84 Ⓐ Ⓑ Ⓒ Ⓓ Ⓔ
5 Ⓐ Ⓑ Ⓒ Ⓓ Ⓔ   25 Ⓐ Ⓑ Ⓒ Ⓓ Ⓔ   45 Ⓐ Ⓑ Ⓒ Ⓓ Ⓔ   65 Ⓐ Ⓑ Ⓒ Ⓓ Ⓔ   85 Ⓐ Ⓑ Ⓒ Ⓓ Ⓔ
6 Ⓐ Ⓑ Ⓒ Ⓓ Ⓔ   26 Ⓐ Ⓑ Ⓒ Ⓓ Ⓔ   46 Ⓐ Ⓑ Ⓒ Ⓓ Ⓔ   66 Ⓐ Ⓑ Ⓒ Ⓓ Ⓔ   86 Ⓐ Ⓑ Ⓒ Ⓓ Ⓔ
7 Ⓐ Ⓑ Ⓒ Ⓓ Ⓔ   27 Ⓐ Ⓑ Ⓒ Ⓓ Ⓔ   47 Ⓐ Ⓑ Ⓒ Ⓓ Ⓔ   67 Ⓐ Ⓑ Ⓒ Ⓓ Ⓔ   87 Ⓐ Ⓑ Ⓒ Ⓓ Ⓔ
8 Ⓐ Ⓑ Ⓒ Ⓓ Ⓔ   28 Ⓐ Ⓑ Ⓒ Ⓓ Ⓔ   48 Ⓐ Ⓑ Ⓒ Ⓓ Ⓔ   68 Ⓐ Ⓑ Ⓒ Ⓓ Ⓔ   88 Ⓐ Ⓑ Ⓒ Ⓓ Ⓔ
9 Ⓐ Ⓑ Ⓒ Ⓓ Ⓔ   29 Ⓐ Ⓑ Ⓒ Ⓓ Ⓔ   49 Ⓐ Ⓑ Ⓒ Ⓓ Ⓔ   69 Ⓐ Ⓑ Ⓒ Ⓓ Ⓔ   89 Ⓐ Ⓑ Ⓒ Ⓓ Ⓔ
10 Ⓐ Ⓑ Ⓒ Ⓓ Ⓔ   30 Ⓐ Ⓑ Ⓒ Ⓓ Ⓔ   50 Ⓐ Ⓑ Ⓒ Ⓓ Ⓔ   70 Ⓐ Ⓑ Ⓒ Ⓓ Ⓔ   90 Ⓐ Ⓑ Ⓒ Ⓓ Ⓔ
11 Ⓐ Ⓑ Ⓒ Ⓓ Ⓔ   31 Ⓐ Ⓑ Ⓒ Ⓓ Ⓔ   51 Ⓐ Ⓑ Ⓒ Ⓓ Ⓔ   71 Ⓐ Ⓑ Ⓒ Ⓓ Ⓔ   91 Ⓐ Ⓑ Ⓒ Ⓓ Ⓔ
12 Ⓐ Ⓑ Ⓒ Ⓓ Ⓔ   32 Ⓐ Ⓑ Ⓒ Ⓓ Ⓔ   52 Ⓐ Ⓑ Ⓒ Ⓓ Ⓔ   72 Ⓐ Ⓑ Ⓒ Ⓓ Ⓔ   92 Ⓐ Ⓑ Ⓒ Ⓓ Ⓔ
13 Ⓐ Ⓑ Ⓒ Ⓓ Ⓔ   33 Ⓐ Ⓑ Ⓒ Ⓓ Ⓔ   53 Ⓐ Ⓑ Ⓒ Ⓓ Ⓔ   73 Ⓐ Ⓑ Ⓒ Ⓓ Ⓔ   93 Ⓐ Ⓑ Ⓒ Ⓓ Ⓔ
14 Ⓐ Ⓑ Ⓒ Ⓓ Ⓔ   34 Ⓐ Ⓑ Ⓒ Ⓓ Ⓔ   54 Ⓐ Ⓑ Ⓒ Ⓓ Ⓔ   74 Ⓐ Ⓑ Ⓒ Ⓓ Ⓔ   94 Ⓐ Ⓑ Ⓒ Ⓓ Ⓔ
15 Ⓐ Ⓑ Ⓒ Ⓓ Ⓔ   35 Ⓐ Ⓑ Ⓒ Ⓓ Ⓔ   55 Ⓐ Ⓑ Ⓒ Ⓓ Ⓔ   75 Ⓐ Ⓑ Ⓒ Ⓓ Ⓔ   95 Ⓐ Ⓑ Ⓒ Ⓓ Ⓔ
16 Ⓐ Ⓑ Ⓒ Ⓓ Ⓔ   36 Ⓐ Ⓑ Ⓒ Ⓓ Ⓔ   56 Ⓐ Ⓑ Ⓒ Ⓓ Ⓔ   76 Ⓐ Ⓑ Ⓒ Ⓓ Ⓔ   96 Ⓐ Ⓑ Ⓒ Ⓓ Ⓔ
17 Ⓐ Ⓑ Ⓒ Ⓓ Ⓔ   37 Ⓐ Ⓑ Ⓒ Ⓓ Ⓔ   57 Ⓐ Ⓑ Ⓒ Ⓓ Ⓔ   77 Ⓐ Ⓑ Ⓒ Ⓓ Ⓔ   97 Ⓐ Ⓑ Ⓒ Ⓓ Ⓔ
18 Ⓐ Ⓑ Ⓒ Ⓓ Ⓔ   38 Ⓐ Ⓑ Ⓒ Ⓓ Ⓔ   58 Ⓐ Ⓑ Ⓒ Ⓓ Ⓔ   78 Ⓐ Ⓑ Ⓒ Ⓓ Ⓔ   98 Ⓐ Ⓑ Ⓒ Ⓓ Ⓔ
19 Ⓐ Ⓑ Ⓒ Ⓓ Ⓔ   39 Ⓐ Ⓑ Ⓒ Ⓓ Ⓔ   59 Ⓐ Ⓑ Ⓒ Ⓓ Ⓔ   79 Ⓐ Ⓑ Ⓒ Ⓓ Ⓔ   99 Ⓐ Ⓑ Ⓒ Ⓓ Ⓔ
20 Ⓐ Ⓑ Ⓒ Ⓓ Ⓔ   40 Ⓐ Ⓑ Ⓒ Ⓓ Ⓔ   60 Ⓐ Ⓑ Ⓒ Ⓓ Ⓔ   80 Ⓐ Ⓑ Ⓒ Ⓓ Ⓔ   100 Ⓐ Ⓑ Ⓒ Ⓓ Ⓔ

Test Code

V	①	②	③	④	⑤	⑥	⑦	⑧	⑨	
W	①	②	③	④	⑤	⑥	⑦	⑧	⑨	
X	①	②	③	④	⑤	Y Ⓐ	Ⓑ	Ⓒ	Ⓓ	Ⓔ	
Q		①	②	③	④	⑤	⑥	⑦	⑧	⑨

Subject Test (print)

FOR ETS USE ONLY	R/C	W/S1	FS/S2	CS/S3	WS

1 Ⓐ Ⓑ Ⓒ Ⓓ Ⓔ   21 Ⓐ Ⓑ Ⓒ Ⓓ Ⓔ   41 Ⓐ Ⓑ Ⓒ Ⓓ Ⓔ   61 Ⓐ Ⓑ Ⓒ Ⓓ Ⓔ   81 Ⓐ Ⓑ Ⓒ Ⓓ Ⓔ
2 Ⓐ Ⓑ Ⓒ Ⓓ Ⓔ   22 Ⓐ Ⓑ Ⓒ Ⓓ Ⓔ   42 Ⓐ Ⓑ Ⓒ Ⓓ Ⓔ   62 Ⓐ Ⓑ Ⓒ Ⓓ Ⓔ   82 Ⓐ Ⓑ Ⓒ Ⓓ Ⓔ
3 Ⓐ Ⓑ Ⓒ Ⓓ Ⓔ   23 Ⓐ Ⓑ Ⓒ Ⓓ Ⓔ   43 Ⓐ Ⓑ Ⓒ Ⓓ Ⓔ   63 Ⓐ Ⓑ Ⓒ Ⓓ Ⓔ   83 Ⓐ Ⓑ Ⓒ Ⓓ Ⓔ
4 Ⓐ Ⓑ Ⓒ Ⓓ Ⓔ   24 Ⓐ Ⓑ Ⓒ Ⓓ Ⓔ   44 Ⓐ Ⓑ Ⓒ Ⓓ Ⓔ   64 Ⓐ Ⓑ Ⓒ Ⓓ Ⓔ   84 Ⓐ Ⓑ Ⓒ Ⓓ Ⓔ
5 Ⓐ Ⓑ Ⓒ Ⓓ Ⓔ   25 Ⓐ Ⓑ Ⓒ Ⓓ Ⓔ   45 Ⓐ Ⓑ Ⓒ Ⓓ Ⓔ   65 Ⓐ Ⓑ Ⓒ Ⓓ Ⓔ   85 Ⓐ Ⓑ Ⓒ Ⓓ Ⓔ
6 Ⓐ Ⓑ Ⓒ Ⓓ Ⓔ   26 Ⓐ Ⓑ Ⓒ Ⓓ Ⓔ   46 Ⓐ Ⓑ Ⓒ Ⓓ Ⓔ   66 Ⓐ Ⓑ Ⓒ Ⓓ Ⓔ   86 Ⓐ Ⓑ Ⓒ Ⓓ Ⓔ
7 Ⓐ Ⓑ Ⓒ Ⓓ Ⓔ   27 Ⓐ Ⓑ Ⓒ Ⓓ Ⓔ   47 Ⓐ Ⓑ Ⓒ Ⓓ Ⓔ   67 Ⓐ Ⓑ Ⓒ Ⓓ Ⓔ   87 Ⓐ Ⓑ Ⓒ Ⓓ Ⓔ
8 Ⓐ Ⓑ Ⓒ Ⓓ Ⓔ   28 Ⓐ Ⓑ Ⓒ Ⓓ Ⓔ   48 Ⓐ Ⓑ Ⓒ Ⓓ Ⓔ   68 Ⓐ Ⓑ Ⓒ Ⓓ Ⓔ   88 Ⓐ Ⓑ Ⓒ Ⓓ Ⓔ
9 Ⓐ Ⓑ Ⓒ Ⓓ Ⓔ   29 Ⓐ Ⓑ Ⓒ Ⓓ Ⓔ   49 Ⓐ Ⓑ Ⓒ Ⓓ Ⓔ   69 Ⓐ Ⓑ Ⓒ Ⓓ Ⓔ   89 Ⓐ Ⓑ Ⓒ Ⓓ Ⓔ
10 Ⓐ Ⓑ Ⓒ Ⓓ Ⓔ   30 Ⓐ Ⓑ Ⓒ Ⓓ Ⓔ   50 Ⓐ Ⓑ Ⓒ Ⓓ Ⓔ   70 Ⓐ Ⓑ Ⓒ Ⓓ Ⓔ   90 Ⓐ Ⓑ Ⓒ Ⓓ Ⓔ
11 Ⓐ Ⓑ Ⓒ Ⓓ Ⓔ   31 Ⓐ Ⓑ Ⓒ Ⓓ Ⓔ   51 Ⓐ Ⓑ Ⓒ Ⓓ Ⓔ   71 Ⓐ Ⓑ Ⓒ Ⓓ Ⓔ   91 Ⓐ Ⓑ Ⓒ Ⓓ Ⓔ
12 Ⓐ Ⓑ Ⓒ Ⓓ Ⓔ   32 Ⓐ Ⓑ Ⓒ Ⓓ Ⓔ   52 Ⓐ Ⓑ Ⓒ Ⓓ Ⓔ   72 Ⓐ Ⓑ Ⓒ Ⓓ Ⓔ   92 Ⓐ Ⓑ Ⓒ Ⓓ Ⓔ
13 Ⓐ Ⓑ Ⓒ Ⓓ Ⓔ   33 Ⓐ Ⓑ Ⓒ Ⓓ Ⓔ   53 Ⓐ Ⓑ Ⓒ Ⓓ Ⓔ   73 Ⓐ Ⓑ Ⓒ Ⓓ Ⓔ   93 Ⓐ Ⓑ Ⓒ Ⓓ Ⓔ
14 Ⓐ Ⓑ Ⓒ Ⓓ Ⓔ   34 Ⓐ Ⓑ Ⓒ Ⓓ Ⓔ   54 Ⓐ Ⓑ Ⓒ Ⓓ Ⓔ   74 Ⓐ Ⓑ Ⓒ Ⓓ Ⓔ   94 Ⓐ Ⓑ Ⓒ Ⓓ Ⓔ
15 Ⓐ Ⓑ Ⓒ Ⓓ Ⓔ   35 Ⓐ Ⓑ Ⓒ Ⓓ Ⓔ   55 Ⓐ Ⓑ Ⓒ Ⓓ Ⓔ   75 Ⓐ Ⓑ Ⓒ Ⓓ Ⓔ   95 Ⓐ Ⓑ Ⓒ Ⓓ Ⓔ
16 Ⓐ Ⓑ Ⓒ Ⓓ Ⓔ   36 Ⓐ Ⓑ Ⓒ Ⓓ Ⓔ   56 Ⓐ Ⓑ Ⓒ Ⓓ Ⓔ   76 Ⓐ Ⓑ Ⓒ Ⓓ Ⓔ   96 Ⓐ Ⓑ Ⓒ Ⓓ Ⓔ
17 Ⓐ Ⓑ Ⓒ Ⓓ Ⓔ   37 Ⓐ Ⓑ Ⓒ Ⓓ Ⓔ   57 Ⓐ Ⓑ Ⓒ Ⓓ Ⓔ   77 Ⓐ Ⓑ Ⓒ Ⓓ Ⓔ   97 Ⓐ Ⓑ Ⓒ Ⓓ Ⓔ
18 Ⓐ Ⓑ Ⓒ Ⓓ Ⓔ   38 Ⓐ Ⓑ Ⓒ Ⓓ Ⓔ   58 Ⓐ Ⓑ Ⓒ Ⓓ Ⓔ   78 Ⓐ Ⓑ Ⓒ Ⓓ Ⓔ   98 Ⓐ Ⓑ Ⓒ Ⓓ Ⓔ
19 Ⓐ Ⓑ Ⓒ Ⓓ Ⓔ   39 Ⓐ Ⓑ Ⓒ Ⓓ Ⓔ   59 Ⓐ Ⓑ Ⓒ Ⓓ Ⓔ   79 Ⓐ Ⓑ Ⓒ Ⓓ Ⓔ   99 Ⓐ Ⓑ Ⓒ Ⓓ Ⓔ
20 Ⓐ Ⓑ Ⓒ Ⓓ Ⓔ   40 Ⓐ Ⓑ Ⓒ Ⓓ Ⓔ   60 Ⓐ Ⓑ Ⓒ Ⓓ Ⓔ   80 Ⓐ Ⓑ Ⓒ Ⓓ Ⓔ   100 Ⓐ Ⓑ Ⓒ Ⓓ Ⓔ

Leave any unused
answer spaces blank.

Test Code

V	①	②	③	④	⑤	⑥	⑦	⑧	⑨	
W	①	②	③	④	⑤	⑥	⑦	⑧	⑨	
X	①	②	③	④	⑤	Y Ⓐ	Ⓑ	Ⓒ	Ⓓ	Ⓔ	
Q		①	②	③	④	⑤	⑥	⑦	⑧	⑨

Subject Test (print)

FOR ETS USE ONLY	R/C	W/S1	FS/S2	CS/S3	WS

1 Ⓐ Ⓑ Ⓒ Ⓓ Ⓔ   21 Ⓐ Ⓑ Ⓒ Ⓓ Ⓔ   41 Ⓐ Ⓑ Ⓒ Ⓓ Ⓔ   61 Ⓐ Ⓑ Ⓒ Ⓓ Ⓔ   81 Ⓐ Ⓑ Ⓒ Ⓓ Ⓔ
2 Ⓐ Ⓑ Ⓒ Ⓓ Ⓔ   22 Ⓐ Ⓑ Ⓒ Ⓓ Ⓔ   42 Ⓐ Ⓑ Ⓒ Ⓓ Ⓔ   62 Ⓐ Ⓑ Ⓒ Ⓓ Ⓔ   82 Ⓐ Ⓑ Ⓒ Ⓓ Ⓔ
3 Ⓐ Ⓑ Ⓒ Ⓓ Ⓔ   23 Ⓐ Ⓑ Ⓒ Ⓓ Ⓔ   43 Ⓐ Ⓑ Ⓒ Ⓓ Ⓔ   63 Ⓐ Ⓑ Ⓒ Ⓓ Ⓔ   83 Ⓐ Ⓑ Ⓒ Ⓓ Ⓔ
4 Ⓐ Ⓑ Ⓒ Ⓓ Ⓔ   24 Ⓐ Ⓑ Ⓒ Ⓓ Ⓔ   44 Ⓐ Ⓑ Ⓒ Ⓓ Ⓔ   64 Ⓐ Ⓑ Ⓒ Ⓓ Ⓔ   84 Ⓐ Ⓑ Ⓒ Ⓓ Ⓔ
5 Ⓐ Ⓑ Ⓒ Ⓓ Ⓔ   25 Ⓐ Ⓑ Ⓒ Ⓓ Ⓔ   45 Ⓐ Ⓑ Ⓒ Ⓓ Ⓔ   65 Ⓐ Ⓑ Ⓒ Ⓓ Ⓔ   85 Ⓐ Ⓑ Ⓒ Ⓓ Ⓔ
6 Ⓐ Ⓑ Ⓒ Ⓓ Ⓔ   26 Ⓐ Ⓑ Ⓒ Ⓓ Ⓔ   46 Ⓐ Ⓑ Ⓒ Ⓓ Ⓔ   66 Ⓐ Ⓑ Ⓒ Ⓓ Ⓔ   86 Ⓐ Ⓑ Ⓒ Ⓓ Ⓔ
7 Ⓐ Ⓑ Ⓒ Ⓓ Ⓔ   27 Ⓐ Ⓑ Ⓒ Ⓓ Ⓔ   47 Ⓐ Ⓑ Ⓒ Ⓓ Ⓔ   67 Ⓐ Ⓑ Ⓒ Ⓓ Ⓔ   87 Ⓐ Ⓑ Ⓒ Ⓓ Ⓔ
8 Ⓐ Ⓑ Ⓒ Ⓓ Ⓔ   28 Ⓐ Ⓑ Ⓒ Ⓓ Ⓔ   48 Ⓐ Ⓑ Ⓒ Ⓓ Ⓔ   68 Ⓐ Ⓑ Ⓒ Ⓓ Ⓔ   88 Ⓐ Ⓑ Ⓒ Ⓓ Ⓔ
9 Ⓐ Ⓑ Ⓒ Ⓓ Ⓔ   29 Ⓐ Ⓑ Ⓒ Ⓓ Ⓔ   49 Ⓐ Ⓑ Ⓒ Ⓓ Ⓔ   69 Ⓐ Ⓑ Ⓒ Ⓓ Ⓔ   89 Ⓐ Ⓑ Ⓒ Ⓓ Ⓔ
10 Ⓐ Ⓑ Ⓒ Ⓓ Ⓔ   30 Ⓐ Ⓑ Ⓒ Ⓓ Ⓔ   50 Ⓐ Ⓑ Ⓒ Ⓓ Ⓔ   70 Ⓐ Ⓑ Ⓒ Ⓓ Ⓔ   90 Ⓐ Ⓑ Ⓒ Ⓓ Ⓔ
11 Ⓐ Ⓑ Ⓒ Ⓓ Ⓔ   31 Ⓐ Ⓑ Ⓒ Ⓓ Ⓔ   51 Ⓐ Ⓑ Ⓒ Ⓓ Ⓔ   71 Ⓐ Ⓑ Ⓒ Ⓓ Ⓔ   91 Ⓐ Ⓑ Ⓒ Ⓓ Ⓔ
12 Ⓐ Ⓑ Ⓒ Ⓓ Ⓔ   32 Ⓐ Ⓑ Ⓒ Ⓓ Ⓔ   52 Ⓐ Ⓑ Ⓒ Ⓓ Ⓔ   72 Ⓐ Ⓑ Ⓒ Ⓓ Ⓔ   92 Ⓐ Ⓑ Ⓒ Ⓓ Ⓔ
13 Ⓐ Ⓑ Ⓒ Ⓓ Ⓔ   33 Ⓐ Ⓑ Ⓒ Ⓓ Ⓔ   53 Ⓐ Ⓑ Ⓒ Ⓓ Ⓔ   73 Ⓐ Ⓑ Ⓒ Ⓓ Ⓔ   93 Ⓐ Ⓑ Ⓒ Ⓓ Ⓔ
14 Ⓐ Ⓑ Ⓒ Ⓓ Ⓔ   34 Ⓐ Ⓑ Ⓒ Ⓓ Ⓔ   54 Ⓐ Ⓑ Ⓒ Ⓓ Ⓔ   74 Ⓐ Ⓑ Ⓒ Ⓓ Ⓔ   94 Ⓐ Ⓑ Ⓒ Ⓓ Ⓔ
15 Ⓐ Ⓑ Ⓒ Ⓓ Ⓔ   35 Ⓐ Ⓑ Ⓒ Ⓓ Ⓔ   55 Ⓐ Ⓑ Ⓒ Ⓓ Ⓔ   75 Ⓐ Ⓑ Ⓒ Ⓓ Ⓔ   95 Ⓐ Ⓑ Ⓒ Ⓓ Ⓔ
16 Ⓐ Ⓑ Ⓒ Ⓓ Ⓔ   36 Ⓐ Ⓑ Ⓒ Ⓓ Ⓔ   56 Ⓐ Ⓑ Ⓒ Ⓓ Ⓔ   76 Ⓐ Ⓑ Ⓒ Ⓓ Ⓔ   96 Ⓐ Ⓑ Ⓒ Ⓓ Ⓔ
17 Ⓐ Ⓑ Ⓒ Ⓓ Ⓔ   37 Ⓐ Ⓑ Ⓒ Ⓓ Ⓔ   57 Ⓐ Ⓑ Ⓒ Ⓓ Ⓔ   77 Ⓐ Ⓑ Ⓒ Ⓓ Ⓔ   97 Ⓐ Ⓑ Ⓒ Ⓓ Ⓔ
18 Ⓐ Ⓑ Ⓒ Ⓓ Ⓔ   38 Ⓐ Ⓑ Ⓒ Ⓓ Ⓔ   58 Ⓐ Ⓑ Ⓒ Ⓓ Ⓔ   78 Ⓐ Ⓑ Ⓒ Ⓓ Ⓔ   98 Ⓐ Ⓑ Ⓒ Ⓓ Ⓔ
19 Ⓐ Ⓑ Ⓒ Ⓓ Ⓔ   39 Ⓐ Ⓑ Ⓒ Ⓓ Ⓔ   59 Ⓐ Ⓑ Ⓒ Ⓓ Ⓔ   79 Ⓐ Ⓑ Ⓒ Ⓓ Ⓔ   99 Ⓐ Ⓑ Ⓒ Ⓓ Ⓔ
20 Ⓐ Ⓑ Ⓒ Ⓓ Ⓔ   40 Ⓐ Ⓑ Ⓒ Ⓓ Ⓔ   60 Ⓐ Ⓑ Ⓒ Ⓓ Ⓔ   80 Ⓐ Ⓑ Ⓒ Ⓓ Ⓔ   100 Ⓐ Ⓑ Ⓒ Ⓓ Ⓔ

Leave any unused answer spaces blank.

1 Ⓐ Ⓑ Ⓒ Ⓓ Ⓔ 21 Ⓐ Ⓑ Ⓒ Ⓓ Ⓔ 41 Ⓐ Ⓑ Ⓒ Ⓓ Ⓔ 61 Ⓐ Ⓑ Ⓒ Ⓓ Ⓔ 81 Ⓐ Ⓑ Ⓒ Ⓓ Ⓔ
2 Ⓐ Ⓑ Ⓒ Ⓓ Ⓔ 22 Ⓐ Ⓑ Ⓒ Ⓓ Ⓔ 42 Ⓐ Ⓑ Ⓒ Ⓓ Ⓔ 62 Ⓐ Ⓑ Ⓒ Ⓓ Ⓔ 82 Ⓐ Ⓑ Ⓒ Ⓓ Ⓔ
3 Ⓐ Ⓑ Ⓒ Ⓓ Ⓔ 23 Ⓐ Ⓑ Ⓒ Ⓓ Ⓔ 43 Ⓐ Ⓑ Ⓒ Ⓓ Ⓔ 63 Ⓐ Ⓑ Ⓒ Ⓓ Ⓔ 83 Ⓐ Ⓑ Ⓒ Ⓓ Ⓔ
4 Ⓐ Ⓑ Ⓒ Ⓓ Ⓔ 24 Ⓐ Ⓑ Ⓒ Ⓓ Ⓔ 44 Ⓐ Ⓑ Ⓒ Ⓓ Ⓔ 64 Ⓐ Ⓑ Ⓒ Ⓓ Ⓔ 84 Ⓐ Ⓑ Ⓒ Ⓓ Ⓔ
5 Ⓐ Ⓑ Ⓒ Ⓓ Ⓔ 25 Ⓐ Ⓑ Ⓒ Ⓓ Ⓔ 45 Ⓐ Ⓑ Ⓒ Ⓓ Ⓔ 65 Ⓐ Ⓑ Ⓒ Ⓓ Ⓔ 85 Ⓐ Ⓑ Ⓒ Ⓓ Ⓔ
6 Ⓐ Ⓑ Ⓒ Ⓓ Ⓔ 26 Ⓐ Ⓑ Ⓒ Ⓓ Ⓔ 46 Ⓐ Ⓑ Ⓒ Ⓓ Ⓔ 66 Ⓐ Ⓑ Ⓒ Ⓓ Ⓔ 86 Ⓐ Ⓑ Ⓒ Ⓓ Ⓔ
7 Ⓐ Ⓑ Ⓒ Ⓓ Ⓔ 27 Ⓐ Ⓑ Ⓒ Ⓓ Ⓔ 47 Ⓐ Ⓑ Ⓒ Ⓓ Ⓔ 67 Ⓐ Ⓑ Ⓒ Ⓓ Ⓔ 87 Ⓐ Ⓑ Ⓒ Ⓓ Ⓔ
8 Ⓐ Ⓑ Ⓒ Ⓓ Ⓔ 28 Ⓐ Ⓑ Ⓒ Ⓓ Ⓔ 48 Ⓐ Ⓑ Ⓒ Ⓓ Ⓔ 68 Ⓐ Ⓑ Ⓒ Ⓓ Ⓔ 88 Ⓐ Ⓑ Ⓒ Ⓓ Ⓔ
9 Ⓐ Ⓑ Ⓒ Ⓓ Ⓔ 29 Ⓐ Ⓑ Ⓒ Ⓓ Ⓔ 49 Ⓐ Ⓑ Ⓒ Ⓓ Ⓔ 69 Ⓐ Ⓑ Ⓒ Ⓓ Ⓔ 89 Ⓐ Ⓑ Ⓒ Ⓓ Ⓔ
10 Ⓐ Ⓑ Ⓒ Ⓓ Ⓔ 30 Ⓐ Ⓑ Ⓒ Ⓓ Ⓔ 50 Ⓐ Ⓑ Ⓒ Ⓓ Ⓔ 70 Ⓐ Ⓑ Ⓒ Ⓓ Ⓔ 90 Ⓐ Ⓑ Ⓒ Ⓓ Ⓔ
11 Ⓐ Ⓑ Ⓒ Ⓓ Ⓔ 31 Ⓐ Ⓑ Ⓒ Ⓓ Ⓔ 51 Ⓐ Ⓑ Ⓒ Ⓓ Ⓔ 71 Ⓐ Ⓑ Ⓒ Ⓓ Ⓔ 91 Ⓐ Ⓑ Ⓒ Ⓓ Ⓔ
12 Ⓐ Ⓑ Ⓒ Ⓓ Ⓔ 32 Ⓐ Ⓑ Ⓒ Ⓓ Ⓔ 52 Ⓐ Ⓑ Ⓒ Ⓓ Ⓔ 72 Ⓐ Ⓑ Ⓒ Ⓓ Ⓔ 92 Ⓐ Ⓑ Ⓒ Ⓓ Ⓔ
13 Ⓐ Ⓑ Ⓒ Ⓓ Ⓔ 33 Ⓐ Ⓑ Ⓒ Ⓓ Ⓔ 53 Ⓐ Ⓑ Ⓒ Ⓓ Ⓔ 73 Ⓐ Ⓑ Ⓒ Ⓓ Ⓔ 93 Ⓐ Ⓑ Ⓒ Ⓓ Ⓔ
14 Ⓐ Ⓑ Ⓒ Ⓓ Ⓔ 34 Ⓐ Ⓑ Ⓒ Ⓓ Ⓔ 54 Ⓐ Ⓑ Ⓒ Ⓓ Ⓔ 74 Ⓐ Ⓑ Ⓒ Ⓓ Ⓔ 94 Ⓐ Ⓑ Ⓒ Ⓓ Ⓔ
15 Ⓐ Ⓑ Ⓒ Ⓓ Ⓔ 35 Ⓐ Ⓑ Ⓒ Ⓓ Ⓔ 55 Ⓐ Ⓑ Ⓒ Ⓓ Ⓔ 75 Ⓐ Ⓑ Ⓒ Ⓓ Ⓔ 95 Ⓐ Ⓑ Ⓒ Ⓓ Ⓔ
16 Ⓐ Ⓑ Ⓒ Ⓓ Ⓔ 36 Ⓐ Ⓑ Ⓒ Ⓓ Ⓔ 56 Ⓐ Ⓑ Ⓒ Ⓓ Ⓔ 76 Ⓐ Ⓑ Ⓒ Ⓓ Ⓔ 96 Ⓐ Ⓑ Ⓒ Ⓓ Ⓔ
17 Ⓐ Ⓑ Ⓒ Ⓓ Ⓔ 37 Ⓐ Ⓑ Ⓒ Ⓓ Ⓔ 57 Ⓐ Ⓑ Ⓒ Ⓓ Ⓔ 77 Ⓐ Ⓑ Ⓒ Ⓓ Ⓔ 97 Ⓐ Ⓑ Ⓒ Ⓓ Ⓔ
18 Ⓐ Ⓑ Ⓒ Ⓓ Ⓔ 38 Ⓐ Ⓑ Ⓒ Ⓓ Ⓔ 58 Ⓐ Ⓑ Ⓒ Ⓓ Ⓔ 78 Ⓐ Ⓑ Ⓒ Ⓓ Ⓔ 98 Ⓐ Ⓑ Ⓒ Ⓓ Ⓔ
19 Ⓐ Ⓑ Ⓒ Ⓓ Ⓔ 39 Ⓐ Ⓑ Ⓒ Ⓓ Ⓔ 59 Ⓐ Ⓑ Ⓒ Ⓓ Ⓔ 79 Ⓐ Ⓑ Ⓒ Ⓓ Ⓔ 99 Ⓐ Ⓑ Ⓒ Ⓓ Ⓔ
20 Ⓐ Ⓑ Ⓒ Ⓓ Ⓔ 40 Ⓐ Ⓑ Ⓒ Ⓓ Ⓔ 60 Ⓐ Ⓑ Ⓒ Ⓓ Ⓔ 80 Ⓐ Ⓑ Ⓒ Ⓓ Ⓔ 100 Ⓐ Ⓑ Ⓒ Ⓓ Ⓔ

Leave any unused answer spaces blank.

Test Code

V	①	②	③	④	⑤	⑥	⑦	⑧	⑨
W	①	②	③	④	⑤	⑥	⑦	⑧	⑨
X	①	②	③	④	⑤	Y	Ⓐ	Ⓑ	Ⓒ	Ⓓ	Ⓔ
Q	①	②	③	④	⑤	⑥	⑦	⑧	⑨

Subject Test (print)

FOR ETS USE ONLY	R/C	W/S1	FS/S2	CS/S3	WS

1 Ⓐ Ⓑ Ⓒ Ⓓ Ⓔ 21 Ⓐ Ⓑ Ⓒ Ⓓ Ⓔ 41 Ⓐ Ⓑ Ⓒ Ⓓ Ⓔ 61 Ⓐ Ⓑ Ⓒ Ⓓ Ⓔ 81 Ⓐ Ⓑ Ⓒ Ⓓ Ⓔ
2 Ⓐ Ⓑ Ⓒ Ⓓ Ⓔ 22 Ⓐ Ⓑ Ⓒ Ⓓ Ⓔ 42 Ⓐ Ⓑ Ⓒ Ⓓ Ⓔ 62 Ⓐ Ⓑ Ⓒ Ⓓ Ⓔ 82 Ⓐ Ⓑ Ⓒ Ⓓ Ⓔ
3 Ⓐ Ⓑ Ⓒ Ⓓ Ⓔ 23 Ⓐ Ⓑ Ⓒ Ⓓ Ⓔ 43 Ⓐ Ⓑ Ⓒ Ⓓ Ⓔ 63 Ⓐ Ⓑ Ⓒ Ⓓ Ⓔ 83 Ⓐ Ⓑ Ⓒ Ⓓ Ⓔ
4 Ⓐ Ⓑ Ⓒ Ⓓ Ⓔ 24 Ⓐ Ⓑ Ⓒ Ⓓ Ⓔ 44 Ⓐ Ⓑ Ⓒ Ⓓ Ⓔ 64 Ⓐ Ⓑ Ⓒ Ⓓ Ⓔ 84 Ⓐ Ⓑ Ⓒ Ⓓ Ⓔ
5 Ⓐ Ⓑ Ⓒ Ⓓ Ⓔ 25 Ⓐ Ⓑ Ⓒ Ⓓ Ⓔ 45 Ⓐ Ⓑ Ⓒ Ⓓ Ⓔ 65 Ⓐ Ⓑ Ⓒ Ⓓ Ⓔ 85 Ⓐ Ⓑ Ⓒ Ⓓ Ⓔ
6 Ⓐ Ⓑ Ⓒ Ⓓ Ⓔ 26 Ⓐ Ⓑ Ⓒ Ⓓ Ⓔ 46 Ⓐ Ⓑ Ⓒ Ⓓ Ⓔ 66 Ⓐ Ⓑ Ⓒ Ⓓ Ⓔ 86 Ⓐ Ⓑ Ⓒ Ⓓ Ⓔ
7 Ⓐ Ⓑ Ⓒ Ⓓ Ⓔ 27 Ⓐ Ⓑ Ⓒ Ⓓ Ⓔ 47 Ⓐ Ⓑ Ⓒ Ⓓ Ⓔ 67 Ⓐ Ⓑ Ⓒ Ⓓ Ⓔ 87 Ⓐ Ⓑ Ⓒ Ⓓ Ⓔ
8 Ⓐ Ⓑ Ⓒ Ⓓ Ⓔ 28 Ⓐ Ⓑ Ⓒ Ⓓ Ⓔ 48 Ⓐ Ⓑ Ⓒ Ⓓ Ⓔ 68 Ⓐ Ⓑ Ⓒ Ⓓ Ⓔ 88 Ⓐ Ⓑ Ⓒ Ⓓ Ⓔ
9 Ⓐ Ⓑ Ⓒ Ⓓ Ⓔ 29 Ⓐ Ⓑ Ⓒ Ⓓ Ⓔ 49 Ⓐ Ⓑ Ⓒ Ⓓ Ⓔ 69 Ⓐ Ⓑ Ⓒ Ⓓ Ⓔ 89 Ⓐ Ⓑ Ⓒ Ⓓ Ⓔ
10 Ⓐ Ⓑ Ⓒ Ⓓ Ⓔ 30 Ⓐ Ⓑ Ⓒ Ⓓ Ⓔ 50 Ⓐ Ⓑ Ⓒ Ⓓ Ⓔ 70 Ⓐ Ⓑ Ⓒ Ⓓ Ⓔ 90 Ⓐ Ⓑ Ⓒ Ⓓ Ⓔ
11 Ⓐ Ⓑ Ⓒ Ⓓ Ⓔ 31 Ⓐ Ⓑ Ⓒ Ⓓ Ⓔ 51 Ⓐ Ⓑ Ⓒ Ⓓ Ⓔ 71 Ⓐ Ⓑ Ⓒ Ⓓ Ⓔ 91 Ⓐ Ⓑ Ⓒ Ⓓ Ⓔ
12 Ⓐ Ⓑ Ⓒ Ⓓ Ⓔ 32 Ⓐ Ⓑ Ⓒ Ⓓ Ⓔ 52 Ⓐ Ⓑ Ⓒ Ⓓ Ⓔ 72 Ⓐ Ⓑ Ⓒ Ⓓ Ⓔ 92 Ⓐ Ⓑ Ⓒ Ⓓ Ⓔ
13 Ⓐ Ⓑ Ⓒ Ⓓ Ⓔ 33 Ⓐ Ⓑ Ⓒ Ⓓ Ⓔ 53 Ⓐ Ⓑ Ⓒ Ⓓ Ⓔ 73 Ⓐ Ⓑ Ⓒ Ⓓ Ⓔ 93 Ⓐ Ⓑ Ⓒ Ⓓ Ⓔ
14 Ⓐ Ⓑ Ⓒ Ⓓ Ⓔ 34 Ⓐ Ⓑ Ⓒ Ⓓ Ⓔ 54 Ⓐ Ⓑ Ⓒ Ⓓ Ⓔ 74 Ⓐ Ⓑ Ⓒ Ⓓ Ⓔ 94 Ⓐ Ⓑ Ⓒ Ⓓ Ⓔ
15 Ⓐ Ⓑ Ⓒ Ⓓ Ⓔ 35 Ⓐ Ⓑ Ⓒ Ⓓ Ⓔ 55 Ⓐ Ⓑ Ⓒ Ⓓ Ⓔ 75 Ⓐ Ⓑ Ⓒ Ⓓ Ⓔ 95 Ⓐ Ⓑ Ⓒ Ⓓ Ⓔ
16 Ⓐ Ⓑ Ⓒ Ⓓ Ⓔ 36 Ⓐ Ⓑ Ⓒ Ⓓ Ⓔ 56 Ⓐ Ⓑ Ⓒ Ⓓ Ⓔ 76 Ⓐ Ⓑ Ⓒ Ⓓ Ⓔ 96 Ⓐ Ⓑ Ⓒ Ⓓ Ⓔ
17 Ⓐ Ⓑ Ⓒ Ⓓ Ⓔ 37 Ⓐ Ⓑ Ⓒ Ⓓ Ⓔ 57 Ⓐ Ⓑ Ⓒ Ⓓ Ⓔ 77 Ⓐ Ⓑ Ⓒ Ⓓ Ⓔ 97 Ⓐ Ⓑ Ⓒ Ⓓ Ⓔ
18 Ⓐ Ⓑ Ⓒ Ⓓ Ⓔ 38 Ⓐ Ⓑ Ⓒ Ⓓ Ⓔ 58 Ⓐ Ⓑ Ⓒ Ⓓ Ⓔ 78 Ⓐ Ⓑ Ⓒ Ⓓ Ⓔ 98 Ⓐ Ⓑ Ⓒ Ⓓ Ⓔ
19 Ⓐ Ⓑ Ⓒ Ⓓ Ⓔ 39 Ⓐ Ⓑ Ⓒ Ⓓ Ⓔ 59 Ⓐ Ⓑ Ⓒ Ⓓ Ⓔ 79 Ⓐ Ⓑ Ⓒ Ⓓ Ⓔ 99 Ⓐ Ⓑ Ⓒ Ⓓ Ⓔ
20 Ⓐ Ⓑ Ⓒ Ⓓ Ⓔ 40 Ⓐ Ⓑ Ⓒ Ⓓ Ⓔ 60 Ⓐ Ⓑ Ⓒ Ⓓ Ⓔ 80 Ⓐ Ⓑ Ⓒ Ⓓ Ⓔ 100 Ⓐ Ⓑ Ⓒ Ⓓ Ⓔ

NOTES

NOTES

NOTES

NOTES

NOTES

NOTES

NOTES

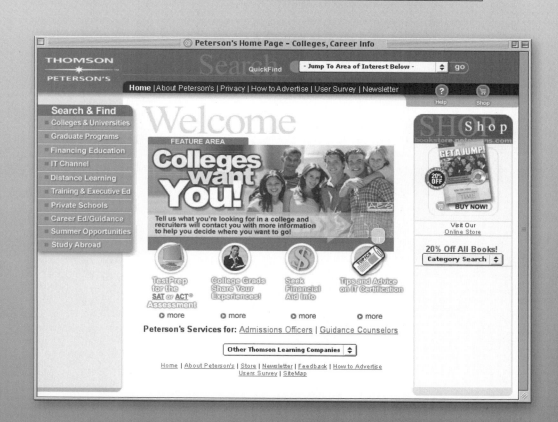